ELIZABETH THE GREAT

Elizabeth Jenkins was educated at St Christopher School, Letchworth, and Newnham College, Cambridge. A distinguished novelist, historian and biographer she was awarded the Femina Vie Heureuse Prize in 1934 for her novel *Harriet*, and she received the OBE in 1981.

Also by Elizabeth Jenkins

The Winters

Lady Caroline Lamb

Harriet

The Phoenix's Nest

Jane Austen

Robert and Helen

Young Enthusiasts

Henry Fielding

Six Criminal Women

The Tortoise and the Hare

Ten Fascinating Women

Elizabeth and Leicester

Brightness

Honey

Dr Gully

The Mystery of King Arthur

The Princes in the Tower

The Shadow and the Light

A Silent Joy

ELIZABETH THE GREAT

Elizabeth Jenkins

PHOENIX
PRESS

5 UPPER SAINT MARTIN'S LANE
LONDON
WC2H 9EA

A PHOENIX PRESS PAPERBACK

First published in Great Britain
by Victor Gollancz in 1958
This paperback edition published in 2000
by Phoenix Press,
a division of The Orion Publishing Group Ltd,
Orion House, 5 Upper St Martin's Lane,
London WC2H 9EA

A CIP catalogue record for this book
is available from the British Library.

Printed in Great Britain by
Butler & Tanner Ltd, Frome and London

ISBN 1 84212 162 6

TO MY FATHER

PREFACE

THE AIM OF this book was to collect interesting personal information about Queen Elizabeth I. As I have tried to focus attention all the time upon the Queen, the shape of the book is very irregular; sometimes events of great importance are briefly mentioned or omitted while minor ones are dwelt on in detail. There is nothing in the book which has not already been published in some form but some of it is, I believe, very little known; historians have not room in their books for such matters and the popular writers have not made use of them.

I would like here to deal with the story that after the age of thirty Elizabeth was bald. It seems to have arisen in 1922 when F. C. Chamberlin, in his useful *Private Character of Queen Elizabeth*, stated that there appeared to be no references after 1564 to the Queen's own hair, only to her wigs, and that "all her portraits after this date indicate that it was soon after this that she became bald" (p. 54). Mr. Chamberlin submitted his data to Sir Arthur Keith, F.R.C.S., and printed the opinion which the latter based on it. Assuming Mr. Chamberlin's data to be correct, Sir Arthur Keith said (op. cit.) "she would appear to have become bald" (p. 98) and by p. 102, this tentative statement was developed into: "women at thirty may suddenly become bald as Elizabeth did". Whereupon Mr. Hilaire Belloc, in his *History of England* (1931), announced: "at thirty she was as bald as an egg."

Both Mr. Chamberlin's statements are incorrect. Contemporary references to the Queen's own hair after 1564 are as follows: the lock of greying red hair preserved at Wilton, she is said to have given to Philip Sidney in 1572 when she was thirty-nine, though Fox Bourne argues that the date should be 1582 when her age would have been forty-nine. In 1596, when she was sixty-three, the Bishop of St. David's offended her by saying in his sermon that "time had sowed meal upon her hair", and the contemporary account of Essex bursting into her bedroom in September 1599, when she was sixty-six, says that he surprised the Queen, "her hair about her ears".

There is a portrait of Elizabeth dated 1569 (Frontispiece to *Christian Prayers*) when she was thirty-six, in which the hair is clearly not a wig; it is strained back from the temples and pushed into a net. The portraits of the last two decades show the Queen with a dark red wig; the authorities of the National Portrait Gallery are unwilling to commit themselves as to whether a portrait of the 1570's showing closely-curled hair of the Queen's own shade of reddish yellow represents a wig or not. If it does, the wearing of a wig does not imply baldness but merely a following of the sixteenth-century fashion for wearing wigs, which is established by numerous contemporary references.

The colour of Elizabeth's eyes has been variously described by modern writers. I have examined nine contemporary paintings, in all of which the eyes are either golden-brown or darker brown. From a distance they sometimes look agate-grey: an effect produced by a large black pupil and a dash of light across the iris.

No one could attempt to write on this period without wishing to record a debt of admiration and gratitude to the works of Sir John Neale, Dr. A. L. Rowse and Mr. Conyers Read. My personal thanks are due to Mrs. Austin Duncan-Jones, who introduced me to the portrait of Elizabeth at Gripsholm, and to Mr. Thurston Dart of Jesus College, Cambridge, who very kindly gave me the words of the two songs set by Byrd, pp. 280–281.

E. J.

I

When henry viii died in January 1547, the most remarkable beings left in the realm were three pale and close-lipped children. One was his daughter Elizabeth by his second wife Ann Boleyn, another was his son Edward by his third wife Jane Seymour, the third was his great-niece Jane, granddaughter of his sister Mary and eldest child of Lord Henry Grey, Marquess of Dorset. Elizabeth was fourteen, Edward nine and Jane eleven.

The children bore considerable resemblance to one another, but the faces of the King's son and daughter were stamped with a look at once repressed and preternaturally vigilant. They were not robust, but their intellects were remarkable, and the greatest scholars had been employed to stimulate them into a state of alarming precocity. Jane Grey had received the same treatment and shared their unchildish passion for books, but she had a capacity for religion rare at any age, and her radiant serenity was almost that of mysticism.

The second generation of the King's family circle was completed by a figure very different in age and outlook. The Princess Mary, only child of his first wife, Catherine of Aragon, was twenty-seven at the time of her father's death. For the past fifteen years her life had been very unhappy. She had most dearly loved her mother, and had seen her divorced so that the King could marry her lady-in-waiting, the disagreeable and dazzling Ann Boleyn. She was an ardent member of the Roman Church, and she had seen the English Government throw off papal authority and her father style himself the Church's Supreme Head. She had vowed passionately she would never call him so, and a fearful dispute was joined in which the King did not contend with her himself but banished her from his presence and left her to the mercy of his ministers. On her mother's death she succumbed to his will, avowing her own birth illegitimate and accepting the King as Supreme Head of the Church. These sufferings had made her old before her time and had given a twist to her unselfish and affectionate nature, the results of which were yet to show themselves.

The King's obsessive desire for the son whom his first twenty years of marriage had not given him was the source of the energy with which he shouldered through the breach with Rome; its immediate inspiration was his passion for Elizabeth's mother. Thin, black-eyed, excitable, tart and witty, Ann Boleyn made gentleness and amiability appear insipid. The French Ambassador Du Bellay said that the King's infatuation for her was such, that only God could abate his madness. For six years she refused to gratify his passion, keeping the lustful and domineering King in a white heat of desire. When the divorce was all but accomplished she yielded to him, and the marriage was performed secretly that the coming child might be the heir to its father's throne.

The marriage was celebrated in the dark of a winter's morning, but the coronation procession was made in brilliant weather on the last day of May. In her ruby wreath and her robes of glittering silver, "a woman clothed with the sun", Ann was borne on her way, the King's wife, to be crowned Queen and five months gone with child. Her long-sustained effort had resulted in an enormous triumph.

Her child proved to be a girl, and from that hour her influence began to wane. Two miscarriages diminished it further. The shrewishness, verging upon hysteria, to which she was driven by the dreadful sense of failure, paved the way for a successor of meek, adoring tenderness. The situation grew rapidly worse and alarm only sharpened her overbearing temper. When she discovered the King making love to her lady-in-waiting, Jane Seymour, she burst into furious denunciation; the rage brought on a premature labour and she was delivered of a dead boy. In Sir John Neale's words, "she had miscarried of her saviour".

Her reckless behaviour had provided ample means to destroy her. She was at Greenwich after the fatal miscarriage, where she was suddenly arrested and brought to the Tower in the month of May. The only description of the Queen with her child Elizabeth belongs to the days immediately before the arrest. A Protestant refugee to whom the Protestant Ann had seemed a being of angelic virtue, writing to congratulate Queen Elizabeth on her accession, exclaimed:

"Alas I shall never forget the sorrow I felt when I saw the sainted Queen your mother, carrying you, still a little baby, in her arms, and entreating the most serene King your father in Greenwich Palace, from the open window of which he was looking into the courtyard where she brought you to him. The faces and gestures of the speakers plainly showed the King was angry, though he concealed his anger wonderfully well."[1]

The Queen was charged with having committed adultery with five

[1] C.S.P. Foreign, 1558.

men, of whom one was her brother, and condemned on a verdict of
high treason to be beheaded or burned alive at the King's pleasure.
The Lieutenant of the Tower reported her as falling into fit after fit,
alternately weeping and laughing. Some mercy was shown to her by
the bringing over from Calais of a notably skilful headsman who used
a sword instead of an axe. The Lieutenant assured her she would feel
no pain, and she accepted his assurance. "I have a little neck," she
said, and putting her hand round it, she shrieked with laughter.

On May 19 she was beheaded on Tower Green, a few minutes
before noon. The guns of the Tower were fired to mark the act and
the King, who was hunting in Richmond Park, paused beneath an oak
tree to catch the sound. That night he was at the Seymours' house in
Wiltshire, whence he married Jane Seymour the next morning.
Meanwhile the head and body of Ann Boleyn had been put into a
chest made for arrows and carried a few paces from the scaffold into
the chapel of St. Peter ad Vincula, where she was buried in a grave
beside her brother's. Her daughter was not three years old.

The child was a lively little creature with reddish golden hair, a very
white skin, and eyes of golden-brown with brows and lashes so fair
as to be almost invisible. Though headstrong, she was remarkably
teachable. Her excellent governess, Lady Bryan, said that she was
spoiling the child at present because she was in pain with cutting her
double teeth, but once this was over, Lady Bryan meant to have her
behaving very differently.

The question of how the King would now regard her was an
anxious one to those in charge of Elizabeth. Lady Bryan wrote with
pathetic eagerness to the great minister Cromwell, saying she was
sure that when the Princess had got over her teething, the King would
be delighted with his little girl. Meanwhile, she was in dire need of
clothes.

Her mother had dressed her beautifully, and in the mercer's
account for the last year of Ann Boleyn's life, included in the lists of
the Queen's dresses, are the kirtles made for "my Lady Princess":
orange velvet, russet velvet, yellow satin, white damask. One of the
last items was green satin for "a little bed". But the account had been
closed in April 1536, over a year previously, and Elizabeth had out-
worn and outgrown almost everything she had; she wanted gowns
kirtles, petticoats, smocks, night-gowns, stays, handkerchiefs, caps.
"I have driven it off as best I can," Lady Bryan wrote, "that by my
troth I can drive it off no longer; beseeching you, my Lord, that ye
will see that her Grace hath that which is needful for her."

That her father had killed her mother was no doubt concealed from her for the time being, but the fact that her governess was very anxious about her and they had not clothes to put on her could not fail to make a deep impression on so young a child, and a year or so later, Elizabeth proved capable of asking a disconcerting question. When Jane Seymour was pregnant, she asked to have the Princesss Mary recalled to court, as a companion.

"She shall come to thee, darling," said the King; and as Mary was now reinstated in her honours it was decided that, *ipso facto*, Elizabeth must no longer be called Princess. The decision was communicated to the governor of her household and he repeated it to Elizabeth. She listened carefully, and then asked: "How haps it, Governor, yesterday my Lady Princess, and to-day but my Lady Elizabeth?"[1]

The third Queen fulfilled the King's hopes and was brought to bed of a son in October 1537; he was christened when he was three days old, and both his sisters played a part in the supreme occasion. The ceremony took place at night in the chapel of Hampton Court Palace. In the great procession which took the baby from his mother's bedchamber to the chapel, Elizabeth carried the chrisom, the cloth in which the child was received after his immersion in the font. As she was so very small, she herself was carried by the Queen's brother, Edward Seymour, the Earl of Hertford. The ceremony was not over till after midnight, and as the procession re-formed itself Princess Mary disregarded the prescribed order and took her little sister by the hand. The return was even more exciting and disturbing, for at the announcement of the Prince's name and titles, the gentlemen had lit their torches, and these were now carried flaming through the chambers and galleries, while trumpeters sounded before them all the way; but the sisters walked hand in hand.

Jane Seymour had been raised to almost supernatural importance by her situation. She had endured agonies in a labour of thirty hours, but this was her moment of supreme triumph. Because they had failed of it, Catherine of Aragon had been divorced and Ann Boleyn beheaded. The trumpeters, having led the procession to the door of the Queen's bedchamber, retired to the courtyard beneath her windows and sent fanfare after fanfare shrilling to the stars. While the King exulted beside her, the invaluable baby was laid in her arms that she might bless him and call him by his baptismal name. Within a week she was dead, and with letters announcing the King's loss and grief were

[1] H.M.C. Rutland.

mingled enquiries about the beauty and other marriageable qualities of French princesses.

Before the little Prince could speak, he showed an affection for his sister Elizabeth. The children formed a natural alliance: each was motherless, with a splendid, ominous father whom they scarcely saw. The value of his sister's companionship to the frail, precocious little boy was recognized by everyone; that her exceedingly important brother loved her and wanted her society, increased Elizabeth's own importance, a fact no child was likely to overlook, but that she felt for him a genuine natural fondness was never in doubt by those who saw them. On New Year's Day in 1539, when Edward was two, the King gave him a superb equipage of silver-gilt plate and his sister Mary a beautiful crimson satin coat and cap, embroidered with gold and pearl. Elizabeth gave him a cambric shirt that she had sewed herself.

The King owned many palaces, and as the lack of sanitation made it necessary for houses with a large number of inmates to be vacated from time to time, to be "aired and sweetened", the King's own establishment and that of each of his children progressed regularly from one abode to another. With no family circle and with only short periods of her brother's society, ended suddenly when the King's Council thought it time that one or another of the households should be conveyed away to its next destination, Elizabeth's existence owed such stability as it had to the governess who was appointed when she was four. This was a young woman called Katherine Champernowne. It turned out later that she was not suited to the post in all respects, but she had one qualification: she not only recognized the child's remarkable abilities, she loved her and thought the world of her. When Katherine Champernowne had been with her eight years she had, besides her love and care, another claim on Elizabeth's affection: she married a Mr. John Ashley, and the Ashleys were related to the Boleyns.

No one knows when, or from whom, Elizabeth found out what had happened to her mother. A dead silence involves the whole matter. Once, when she was twenty, she hinted to the Spanish Ambassador that her sister's hostility to her was due to injuries that Mary and her mother had received from Ann Boleyn, and once she told the Venetian Ambassador that her mother would never have co-habited with the King except by a marriage declared legal by the Primate of England. Apart from these instances there is no record of her having uttered her mother's name. But with this determined silence, there went a marked kindness towards her mother's connections—to Careys, Howards, Knollys, the humble Ashleys, and to that Henry Norris whose father had been put to death as her mother's lover, and had died declaring her mother's innocence. In her kindness to these, she paid a mute tribute where she would not speak.

The King's fourth marriage, his farcical union with the uncouth but sensible Ann of Cleves, was dissolved in June 1540, and left him free to contract his fifth marriage with the girl who inspired the second great passion of his life. Catherine Howard was nineteen, and her effect on the King was only less potent than that exercised by her cousin Ann Boleyn.

The French Ambassador wrote: "The King is so greatly enamoured, he knows not how to show enough affection for her." Her power to charm Henry recalled her cousin Ann, but Catherine would never have refused him for six years, as Ann had done. Free, generous, loving, a sweet-natured wanton, it turned out, indeed, that she had refused nobody. Her lavish kindness was bestowed on all from the King downwards, and she was particularly kind to Elizabeth as her own relation. The first time the new Queen dined in public, in the great hall of Hampton Court, the seven-year-old Elizabeth had a place of honour opposite to her. Above their heads, the superb roof with its hammer-beams and carved pendants painted crimson, blue and gold, bore among its ornaments the King's arms impaled with those of Ann Boleyn, and behind Elizabeth's back at the far end of the hall was the oak screen, on the upper panels of which the carvers had just finished interlacing the initials H and A.

Kindness always made an impression on Elizabeth. Her young, sweet step-mother, who was so powerful with her great father, went out of her way to be good to her, and might, in time, have laid the past; but a hideous repetition called up the spectre from the grave. Within eighteen months the intrigues in which Catherine had indulged since the age of twelve were uncovered, and she was charged with having committed adultery since her marriage with her cousin Culpepper. During the investigations she escaped from her apartment in Hampton Court and rushed down the gallery towards the chapel where she knew the King was at mass. The guards caught her before she could reach him and she was dragged back, shrieking: a scene that impressed itself so vividly on the public mind, that the gallery is said to be haunted still. On the morning of February 3, 1542, she was beheaded on the spot where her cousin had died before her, and her head and body, wrapped together in a cloth, were carried into the chapel of St. Peter ad Vincula and buried near her cousin's grave.

Twenty years later, when England and the courts of Europe were agog with the idea that Queen Elizabeth might marry the Earl of Leicester, Lord Leicester told the French Ambassador that he had known Elizabeth since she was a child of eight, and from that very time she had always said: "I will never marry." Little notice was paid to the words. It did not occur to anyone, it seems, to look back and recall that when Elizabeth was eight years and five months old, Catherine Howard was beheaded.

Had she disliked or despised her father, the impression would have been less dreadful, but she admired him with her whole heart. It was indeed impossible to know the King and remain indifferent to him, for in every aspect of his personality Henry displayed overwhelming force: engrossingly affectionate where his feelings were engaged, severe and cruel when his confidence was betrayed; when his purposes were served, cold-blooded to a degree hard to reconcile with his sanguine nature, his florid golden colouring and large physique—until his eyes were noticed, small, narrow and set in a hard stare. Strype said: "Henry VIII lived and died highly beloved of his subjects," adding doubtfully, "however that might be." But the people as a whole were not affected by his cruelties, his treacheries, his ruthless acts; they saw in the splendid figure of the King, with his power, his energy, his personal authority, a man who identified them with the modern world, and whose firm establishment on the throne was a reassurance against the horror and ruin of the past. Behind Henry VIII was his father Henry VII—but behind Henry VII stretched the thirty years' desolation of the Wars of the Roses.

Elizabeth was only fourteen when her father died, and her admiration for his genius and pride in his relationship were the instinctive emotions of childhood. It would have been impossible for her to range herself against him. The one execution which she had been too young to understand, and the second which had taught her, at the age of eight, everything she had not known about the first: these events could not be judged from any point of view unfavourable to the glorious King, but the effect they made went the deeper for that. To the child of her own age she said what she might not have said to an older person; even to him, she had not explained herself. She had said merely: "I will never marry." It was her comment on her mother and her mother's cousin, who had married her father and were lying headless in their graves.

Though terribly bereaved, Elizabeth was never without affection. Katherine Ashley, whose name the Princess shortened to Kat, supplied the doting fondness that could see no fault, and her sister Mary would always be kind to her as long as she was a good girl. Mary's account books show that she made Elizabeth numerous presents. She bought yellow satin to make her a dress when Elizabeth was seven; there are many entries of money given to her for playing at cards, and notes that necklaces and brooches from the Princess's store were given to her young sister; when the latter was thirteen, Mary gave her a gold ball made to hold scents, with a clock in it.[1]

In 1543 the King contracted his last marriage. This was to have very serious consequences for Elizabeth, but it seemed at first as if the whole Royal family must benefit by the King's choice. Catherine Parr was thirty years old; she had been twice widowed and was very rich. Her disposition was one of radiant kindness, she was intelligent and cheerful, and she possessed mature but still youthful good looks.

The King was now fifty-two, but appeared much older. It was noticed that after the death of Catherine Howard, his deterioration had been rapid. He had an ulcer in his leg which gave him savage pain, and his once handsome body was a pitiable and disgusting ruin. His will, decreeing that in the succession his children by Catherine Parr (or by any future queens, the will added) were to take precedence over Mary and Elizabeth, showed that the marriage was to be no mere companionship. The sufferings entailed by her situation may well have been the harder to bear, since before the King made his proposal she was being courted by the only man for whom she had felt a passion. This was Sir Thomas Seymour, the younger brother of the late Queen Jane; but Seymour was the last man to urge his suit in such circumstances. When the King's wishes were known, Catherine Parr's other suitor disappeared from the court.

The new Queen fulfilled her duties with inspired goodwill. She made the King so comfortable that he liked to sit with his sore leg on her lap. She was allowed to have Edward and Elizabeth in her household, and for the first time in their lives the King's younger children had a home. Their stepmother encouraged them in their lessons and continued her own reading under the guidance of their tutors. Unknown to the King, she also encouraged their interest in the teaching of the Reformed Church.

The seven-year-old Edward appeared to resemble his favourite sister very closely: they had the same reddish-blonde hair, pale face

[1] Madden, *Privy Purse Expenses of Princess Mary.*

and searching eyes, the same slight and upright figure; they were alike in their intense concentration upon books and the consummate elegance of their manners. But Edward's cast of mind was radically different from Elizabeth's. It was not so much she whom he resembled, as Mary. In his mind were the seeds of that fanatical belief that salvation could be found only in a particular system of worship, and he embraced the system presented to him in his impressionable years with the same fervour and exclusiveness as his elder sister embraced Catholicism.

Elizabeth held the unquestioning belief in the Christian faith which was universal in Europe, but her mind was incapable of religious fanaticism. The famous saying of her later years, "There is only one Christ Jesus and one faith: the rest is a dispute about trifles," is an expression, not of experience, but of temperament. She accepted the Roman observances of her father's court and the private teachings of her step-mother, and her name was not associated with either.

Cautious beyond her years and of exemplary behaviour as a rule, at the age of twelve her discretion was not entirely perfect: in this year she offended the King. Nothing is known of the offence, only of its consequence. She was banished from his household, and it was a year before her humble entreaties and the Queen's good offices brought her back to the family circle. One lesson was enough; the attitude of respectful worship was henceforward maintained unblemished, and anything unfavourable to it was thrust out of sight, like corpses buried under a church pavement. Her gratitude to the Queen was ardent. As a New Year's gift for 1545, she wrote out in a small vellum book her own translation of a French poem, called "The Mirror or Glass of the Sinful Soul", and bound it in a cover she had embroidered in blue silk and silver twist, with clusters of heart's-ease in purple and yellow. The dedication said: "To our most noble and vertuous Queen Katerine, Elizabeth her humble daughter wisheth perpetual felicity and everlasting joy."

Considering the length and delicacy of Elizabeth's fingers, her control over them was the more surprising; her needlework and her handwriting showed an exquisite precision. When she made the book of "The Glass of the Sinful Soul", she wrote the clear, regular script of an intelligent child; this was later transformed by her Italian master Castiglioni into the famous hand, so beautiful that the sight of letters written in its prime gives a pang of aesthetic pleasure. Besides the clerkly hand she had a rapid long-hand for private use, whose curved and pointed shapes looked like the print of birds' feet.

Edward and she wrote their letters to each other in Latin, and they could speak the language conversationally. When Edward was staying at Ampthill the antiquary Leland visited the Prince's tutor, Cheke. After Leland had been presented to Edward, Cheke brought him "to the Lady Elizabeth to have a sight of her". Cheke asked her to greet this learned old man and to say something to him in Latin, "the which she did". Leland was charmed and commemorated the occasion in Latin verses.[1]

Elizabeth was Edward's companion and friend, but he was also on good terms with his cousin Jane Grey, who joined his stepmother's household at the age of nine. Jane's mother Frances was the eldest daughter of the King's sister Mary, and had therefore inherited a tincture of the royal blood, which she passed on to her children with consequences to them which were very serious. Her marriage to Lord Henry Grey, Marquess of Dorset, had produced three daughters: Jane, Catherine and Mary. The two younger were unremarkable, except that the youngest had the unfortunate distinction of being a dwarf. All the moral and intellectual endowments and all the graces of the family were concentrated in the eldest daughter. Like her cousins, she had been very carefully taught. A young Cambridge scholar, John Aylmer, had been appointed as the family tutor when Jane was four years old. He had carried her in his arms and taught her to pronounce words.[2] He had given her a thorough education in Greek and Latin, but his chief concern was with her spiritual development, over which he watched with anxious devotion. When she was nine he was obliged to resign her for the time being, but the Queen's household was one in which her education would not be neglected, nor the practice of her religion according to the tenets in which Aylmer had instructed her.

Although she was now under the same roof with her cousin Elizabeth, and though the Queen's relations with both young ladies are recorded, nothing is heard of any intercourse between the two of them. There was perhaps some instinctive lack of sympathy, in spite of cousinship, nearness in years and great fondness for reading. Elizabeth's ability at her lessons was now generally recognized as something unusual; she was learning history, geography, mathematics, the elements of architecture and astronomy and four modern languages: French, Italian, Spanish and Flemish. Her Greek and Latin had been entrusted to a young Cambridge scholar, William Grindal; he was

[1] Strype: *Cheke.*
[2] Strickland, *Lives of Tudor and Stuart Princesses.*

considered to have brought the Princess on very well, the more so as he had had the help and advice of his master, the celebrated Roger Ascham.

Ascham's book, *The Scholemaster*, shows that he was a teacher so enlightened that he would be considered progressive even to-day. He vehemently denounced the brutal flogging by which "children are driven to hate learning before they know what learning means". The amount of work he expected would now be looked at askance, but within the framework of sixteenth-century usage, his sympathy with the childish mind was that of a first-rate teacher.

Through Grindal and through his wife's relationship to John Ashley, Ascham was now brought into contact with his famous pupil. He had at this time no official concern with the Princess's education, but he took the matter upon himself with the authority and self-confidence of the expert. He advised Grindal on books and method; on the question of the Princess's preparation, he addressed himself to Mrs. Ashley. Kat Ashley had some degree of education herself: without it, she would not have been considered for the post she held, and she still supervised the Princess's private study, for Ascham speaks of her "diligent overseeing". He was in two minds as to how to exhort the governess; he wanted energy used, that the pupil's brilliant promise might be fulfilled. "Good mistress," he wrote, "I would have you in any case to labour and not give yourself to ease." But then came the dread of that calamity with which he was but too familiar, of seeing the young mind injured by too much severity, and he begged Mrs. Ashley "to favour somewhat" this rare intelligence; for, he said, "the younger, the more tender, the quicker, the easier to break". The process should be like pouring water into a goblet: too much at once would dash out, but slowly it might be filled to the brim. His active interest covered every detail. "Send the silver pen," he wrote, "and it shall be mended quickly."

While her education in classical and European languages was being carried on by teachers of this distinction, Elizabeth acquired another language from a homelier source. One of her attendants was the Welshwoman, Blanche Parry, who had been with her even longer than Mrs. Ashley, for Blanche Parry said that she had seen the Princess rocked in her cradle. This lady was surprisingly knowledgeable; on Elizabeth's accession, she made Mistress Parry, then fifty years old, Keeper of the Royal Books, and it is assumed that it was she who taught the great-grand-daughter of Owen Tudor to speak Welsh.[1]

[1] Bradford, *Blanche Parry*.

To this period, when she was thirteen, is ascribed the portrait of Elizabeth at Windsor Castle. The smooth red-gold hair is worn hanging straight down her back, she holds a book with hands whose fingers are so long and delicate they look inhuman, and her expression is watchful and disillusioned. The unchildlike wariness on the youthful face shows the effect of what had happened to her from the age of three. But despite the caution that appeared in her countenance, an inherent haughtiness sometimes showed itself to those whom the Princess neither liked nor saw any reason to conciliate. Jane Dormer, a childish companion of Edward, saw a good deal of his younger sister and left it on record that as a girl of twelve or thirteen she was "proud and disdainful" and that her scornful behaviour "much blemished the handsomeness and beauty of her person".[1] The more general view was given by Mr. William Thomas, Clerk of the Closet, who wrote: "The Lady Elizabeth which is at this time of the age of fourteen years or thereabouts, is a very witty and gentyll young lady."

In November of 1546, Edward and Elizabeth were together at Hatfield, the brick palace whose remains still stand in the beautiful wooded park. Their companonship was in its closest phase, and when it was abruptly broken by orders from the Council, directing the Prince to Hertford and the Princess to Enfield, Elizabeth wrote to Edward immediately, consoling him as best she could for their being driven from their favourite place and suggesting an exchange of letters as the next best thing to being with each other. Edward's reply, written in Latin, showed not only his affection, but a pitiable sense of insecurity:

Dec. 5. 1546.

Change of place did not vex me so much, dearest sister, as your going from me. Now there can be nothing pleasanter than a letter from you. . . . It is some comfort in my grief that my chamberlain tells me I may hope to visit you soon, (if nothing happens to either of us in the mean-time). Farewell dearest sister.

The visit was made before they expected it and in impressive circumstances. Henry VIII was sinking fast, and early in the morning of January 28, holding Cranmer's hand, he died. No sooner was the breath out of his body than Lord Hertford, whose ambitions had been cautiously advanced during the ten years since the King had married his sister, broke from cover and out-distanced all competitors.

[1] Clifford, *Life of Jane Dormer.*

Henry's will left the succession, first to Edward, then, in default of heirs, to Mary, then, in default of heirs, to Elizabeth. Should Elizabeth die childless, it was to devolve on the family of his sister Mary: her daughter Frances, and the latter's daughters, Jane, Catherine and Mary. Hertford had been appointed one of sixteen guardians to the young King, but he rapidly assumed a supreme authority. His nephew was instructed to make him Duke of Somerset and Parliament acquiesced in his becoming Lord Protector with powers to act independently of the Council's advice. His first action however was to secure the person of the child who was King. He and Sir Anthony Brown rode to Hatfield, where they told Edward merely that he was to visit his sister at Enfield. When the children were brought face to face, Hertford announced to them their father's death. The shock was succeeded by fits of uncontrolled crying in both of them, which went on so long that the onlookers were filled not only with pity but with awe. Hertford's manoeuvre had had a double purpose: Edward, allowed to cry with his sister to his heart's content, was less of a burden to his guardians than he would have been without her, and by bringing the children together Hertford could thenceforward ensure the safe custody of Elizabeth. From the moment her father's will became known, her doings would take on an importance which, though not enough to put them in the forefront of events, no one could afford to overlook.

Two days later Hertford rode with the King rapidly to London. Delighted by the thunderous salute of cannon, with Hertford riding before him and his retinue behind him, Edward entered the precincts of the Tower, where the Archbishop of Canterbury, the Lord Chancellor and the other Lords of the Council were waiting to do him homage.

Fifteen miles separated Elizabeth from her brother, but there was a distance between them now that miles could not measure; nevertheless she kept their relationship a living one by such means as she had. She wrote continually, the letters Edward liked so much to receive, and she adopted without effort the adoring and respectful attitude which in Henry VIII's daughter was natural towards a King, even though he were a small boy four years younger than herself. She had a strong instinct to keep in touch with Edward because he was the King, but she did so also because he was her brother. Her writing-book shows his presence in her mind. When she tried a new quill, she wrote "Edwardus".[1]

[1] Her writing book in the Bodleian Library.

With the publication of the late King's will, some information became known concerning the Princesses besides their claims to the succession. The claim of either Princess was to be cancelled, should she, during her brother's life-time, marry without the consent of the Council. By inference, any man who attempted to marry either sister without the necessary permission would involve himself and her in a most serious charge. This was an obvious precaution to take with regard to heiresses to the crown. There was indeed only one matter in the will which caused surprise. The late King's elder sister Margaret had married James IV of Scotland, but her conduct had caused scandal, and her family had been entirely left out of the succession. The Stuarts, therefore, though by primogeniture their claim was superior to the Greys', were, it seemed, to have no chance of succeeding to the English throne.

II

When Hertford had himself created Duke of Somerset, Thomas Seymour was made Lord Scymour of Sudeley and Lord High Admiral. Somerset, though arrogant, grasping and unscrupulous, had some enlightened ideas of government. Seymour, on the other hand, had the total selfishness and irresponsibility of a criminal. He bitterly resented the fact that the office of Protector was not shared equally between Somerset and himself; from the time of their nephew's accession, they behaved like a pair of brothers in some classical tragedy of fratricide.

Vain, reckless and unreasonable as Seymour was, he had the charm of a handsome man who is genial and high-spirited. "Fierce in courage," runs the famous description, "courtly in fashion, in person stately, in voice magnificent, but somewhat empty in matter." The latter drawback, as far as women were concerned, did not injure the rest of his qualities.

On the King's death, Seymour proposed to the Council that he should marry Elizabeth, and Mrs. Ashley who thought the King himself had favoured the idea was disappointed that the matter came to nothing. But Seymour received an unequivocal rebuff from the Council, and immediately renewed his old suit. The Queen Dowager, released from the sufferings of her marriage to Henry VIII, behaved like an enamoured girl. She married Seymour secretly, and received his clandestine visits at her house in Chelsea, where her porteress let him in at five in the morning. The situation was full of submerged danger, for by the Council's permission Elizabeth was now living with her stepmother. Seymour, for all his geniality, was a man of ruthless ambition. He was twenty years older than Elizabeth, but as he was in his prime this meant only that he had the maturity a very young girl admires, and his attractions were of the kind to which she was susceptible all her life. He had been put into her head already as a possible husband, and now he was coming and going in romantic secrecy, in the first light of the May mornings, as the husband of her still-youthful stepmother.

Had Seymour left Elizabeth alone, no harm would have come of it; but one of his reasons for marrying the Queen Dowager was that

Elizabeth had been consigned to her care. His brother had control of the King: he himself would have control of the King's enigmatic young sister. It was true that if she were drawn into any entanglement it might be regarded as high treason, and that the penalty for this was, for a woman, beheading or burning alive. Seymour knew these facts, but he preferred to disregard them.

The Queen Dowager's household was a charming one. Beyond it, indeed, matters were stormy. Seymour was perpetually at variance with his brother, refusing to accept his authority or to carry out his own duties as Lord Admiral, while the situation between the brothers was the more embittered by the hostility of their wives. The Duchess of Somerset, eminently strong-minded and disagreeable, had once been obliged to treat Catherine Parr with ceremonious respect; she now took pains to show her that the Queen Dowager was merely the wife of the Protector's younger brother. This occasioned anger abroad, but at home all was pleasure, ease and a delightful freedom from past restraints.

The Princess's household formed a unit within the Queen Dowager's; it included Mrs. Ashley, the tutor, young Mr. Grindal, and several ladies-in-waiting. There was also attached to it a man who would seem to have had more sense than all the rest put together; this was the Princess's distant cousin John Ashley. In the months after the King's death he gave his wife a warning "to take heed for he did fear that the Lady Elizabeth did bear some affection to my Lord Admiral".[1] He had noticed that she looked pleased and sometimes blushed when Seymour was spoken of. His wife was coarser-fibred; either she saw no danger, or in the congenial atmosphere of ease and pleasure with the exciting undercurrent that Seymour's presence brought, she would not recognize it.

Seymour went openly to work. He began romping with the Princess, and his wife did what many women do in such a case: to prove to herself and everybody else that there was no harm in the romp, she joined it herself. There was no doubt as to Elizabeth's state of mind—Ashley had recognized it at once; but with the passion there was considerable fear. Seymour's boisterous approaches were liable to be alarming to a girl of fourteen, and one with, who knows what buried dread of men? Seymour would come into her bed-chamber in the mornings. If she were up "he would strike her familiarly on the back and buttocks". If she were in bed he would open the bed curtain "and make as though he would come at her",

[1] Haynes, *State Papers.*

while she "would go further into the bed". One morning he tried to kiss her in her bed, at which Mrs. Ashley, who slept in the Princess's room "bade him go away for shame". Elizabeth's bedroom, at Chelsea and at Seymour's town house, Seymour Place, was above the Queen Dowager's, and Seymour used to come up "in his night-gown, bare-legged in his slippers". Mrs. Ashley told him "it was a shame to see a man come so, bare-legged, to a maiden's chamber", but her protests were not taken seriously. The Queen Dowager, however, took to coming with her husband on his morning-visits and one morning they both tickled the Princess as she lay in her bed. In the garden one day there was some startling horse-play, in which Seymour indulged in a practice often heard of in police courts; the Queen Dowager held Elizabeth so that she could not run away, while Seymour cut her black cloth gown into a hundred pieces. The cowering under bedclothes, the struggling and running away cul-minated in a scene of classical nightmare, that of helplessness in the power of a smiling ogre. Seymour had possessed himself of a master-key, and early one morning at Chelsea, Elizabeth heard the privy lock undo, and, "knowing he would come in"—Seymour, smiling in his long red beard—"she ran out of her bed to her maidens and then went behind the curtains of the bed, the maidens being there; and my Lord tarried a long time in hopes she would come out". Afterwards, "she was commonly up and at her book", by the time Seymour came, and then he would merely look in at the door and say good morning. But he had overcome her initial resistance; the Queen Dowager, who was undergoing an uncomfortable pregnancy, could not bring herself to make her husband angry by protesting about his conduct, but she began to realize that he and Elizabeth were very often together; then one day in May, she went into a room unexpectedly and found Elizabeth in his arms.

There was no quarrel and no public appearance of her being sent away in disgrace, but it was decided she should remove with her establishment to the house of Sir Anthony Denny at Cheshunt. She and her train arrived there just after Whitsun, and Elizabeth wrote to her stepmother to say that at their parting she had been too much moved to thank her properly for her kindness, so sad was she to go away, leaving her "in doubtful health", and, she said, "albeit I answered little, I weighed it the more, when you said you would warn me of all evils you should hear of me, for if your Grace had not a good opinion of me, you would not have offered friendship to me that way".

The abrupt parting from Seymour, the disgrace and the contrition, and the warring of sexual excitement with deep-buried dread, all this coming upon her at the critical age of fourteen-and-a-half, coincided with, if it did not bring on, an illness. In Mrs. Ashley's words: "She was first sick about mid-summer." At times she was "sick in her bed", and so unwell for the rest of the year that Mrs. Ashley said she herself had never been more than a mile from the house.[1]

For the next few years, the Princess suffered from intermittent ill-health; she developed migraine attacks and pains in the eyes, and by the time she was twenty, it was a matter of common rumour, of particular interest to ambassadors, that her monthly periods were very few or none, a condition often accounted for by shock and emotional strain. In Elizabeth's history, the events of her mother's death, and that of her mother's cousin, and the engaging of her own affections by Seymour's outrageous siege, seem to have done her nervous system and her sexual development an injury from which they never recovered. But her loyalty in her affections remained unshaken. She wrote anxiously of her stepmother's condition, "so big with child and so sickly", and to Seymour she wrote a letter, brief and touching. She waived away an apology he made for not being able to fulfil some small promise:"I shall desire you to think that a greater matter than this could not make me impute any unkindness to you, for I am a friend not won with trifles, nor lost with the like."

In August the Queen Dowager's daughter was born, and in the delirium of fever, Catherine complained that those she had meant well to, and tried to be good to, stood around her bed, laughing at her pain. She died within a week, and was buried in the small chapel of Sudeley Castle. The chief mourner in the scene of sable draperies and attendants hooded in black was Lady Jane Grey, in deepest mourning, with a long mourning train upheld by another young lady.

Her parents now wished Lady Jane to return to them, but the child's body contained an infusion of the precious royal blood and Seymour did not intend to let her go. He held out a dazzling prospect: "If I can get the King at liberty, I dare warrant you he shall marry none other than Jane." The Dorsets were elated, and that Seymour might have complete authority in negotiating their daughter's marriage, Dorset sold him her wardship for £2,000, of which Seymour gave him £500 on account immediately.

While these matters were transacting, it was understood that Seymour was in deep distress over his wife's death. One person

[1] C.S.P. Domestic, Edw: vi, vi. 20. Quoted by Chamberlin.

however did not believe it. When Mrs. Ashley told the Princess that she should write him a letter of condolence, Elizabeth refused the disagreeable suggestion. In her own words: "I said I would not do it for he needed it not." Meanwhile she was very anxious to come to London to see her brother, but a practical difficulty prevented her. Durham House, about the middle of the Strand, had been left to her in her father's will, but Somerset had appropriated it and turned it into a mint. She was now without a town house, and as her household numbered 120 persons, she could not remove without ample accommodation. Seymour heard of her lack, and meeting her treasurer Thomas Parry in London, he sent a message, offering the Princess the loan of Seymour Place with all its "household stuff" for as long as she cared to make use of it. Parry returned to the Princess, who was at Hatfield, and here, on December 11, he had a long conversation with his young mistress. He saw that she was much pleased with the offer of Seymour Place, and he made a bold push. He asked her whether, if the Council liked it, she would be willing to marry his Lordship. The question was a most dangerous one, but it was perhaps not caution only that made Elizabeth reply: "When that time comes, I will do as God shall put in my mind." Parry went on to relate the searching examination Seymour had put him through, as to the details of Elizabeth's property, what she held, and on what terms, and the suggestion Seymour had made that the Princess's lands should be exchanged for others which lay beside his own property in the west. The significance of this was clear, but all her life Elizabeth liked to hear of people who wanted to marry her, and now she insisted on the explanation from Parry's own lips. Parry said he could not tell what the Lord Admiral meant by the suggestion "unless he go about to have you also." Then he told her of Seymour's plan for getting the exchange accomplished; it was none other than that Elizabeth should make herself pleasant to the Duchess of Somerset. An unscrupulous man of the world saw nothing wrong in the proposal; to a high-spirited child it was anathema. Not only had the Duchess shown great insolence to the Queen Dowager; she had interfered when Kat Ashley allowed the Princess to go to a party on the Thames at night. "Not fit to have the governance of a King's daughter," she had said. Make suit to *her* indeed! Elizabeth was first incredulous, then very angry. ' "Well!" quoth she, "I will not do so, and so tell him!"' Then she showed how much superior her discretion was to that of her elders. She told Parry to let Mrs. Ashley know at once what the Lord Admiral had said to him, for, she said, "I will know nothing but she shall know it." Parry went to Mrs. Ashley, who assured him he could tell her nothing she did not know already, and declared: "I would wish her his wife before all men living," adding that "he could bring it to pass at the Council's hands well enough." Parry demurred, saying that the Admiral had used his late wife badly. "Tush, tush," said Mrs. Ashley, "I know him better than you do. . . . I know he will make but too much of her and that she knows well enough." Then she told him, for the first time, the cause of their removal to Cheshunt. He exclaimed in amazement. She sighed and said, "I will tell you more another time."[1]

More—the word covered an unknown quantity of very great importance, but it had not yet come to examination.

Meanwhile Seymour was rapidly spreading the web in which he meant to take all the royal children. He had gained Elizabeth's affections and had the charge of Jane Grey; now he concentrated on the young King. He saw that Somerset kept Edward far too short of money, and he sent him some privately. Edward was pleased with this, but when Seymour tried to tamper seriously with the Protector's authority, in Edward's words, "I desired him to let me alone." The eleven-year-old King was obedient, not from docility, but from unchildlike common sense; he understood what his position required of him. Nevertheless when Seymour said, "Your uncle is not likely to live long," Edward answered: "It were better he should die." The abnormal coldness, like that of a fairy changeling, misled Seymour; he thought it meant hostility to the Protector, and he made his plans to abduct Edward accordingly.

His possession of master-keys seemed to put the royal children at his mercy; he had one that opened all the gates in the palace garden, and at dead of night on January 18, he came with some confederates to the ante-chamber of the King's bedroom. While he was groping at the bedroom door, the King's spaniel barked. Seymour killed the dog instantly but it was too late. An officer of the guard appeared, demanding angrily to know what he did there at that time of night? At daybreak he was arrested and taken to the Tower.

The news of the arrest spread quickly, and when Sir Anthony Denny and his train appeared at the gates of Hatfield Palace, Parry needed no explanation of their arrival. He turned pale as death and said he wished he had never been born. Denny interviewed the Princess and asked for the details of her intercourse with the Lord Admiral. She related some innocuous episodes. Denny did not press

[1] Haynes.

her: he went another way to work. Out of her sight he arrested Parry and Mrs. Ashley and was on the way to London with his prisoners before the Princess knew what had happened to them. Of the two, Parry at least understood the acuteness of the peril. If the Council could prove that the Lord Admiral had proposed marriage to Elizabeth, he was as good as dead already. If they could prove that Elizabeth had accepted his proposal, then she herself was standing in the shadow of the scaffold. The Council sent their commissioner Sir Robert Tyrwhit down to Hatfield to interrogate the Princess and to extract the confession that might prove a death-warrant.

When it was disclosed to her that her governess and the treasurer were in gaol, she burst out crying and wept "for a long time". When she had recovered herself Tyrwhit held his first interrogation, which he began with the extremely ominous reminder that "she was but a subject". He tried to get her to dissociate herself from Mrs. Ashley, saying that if she would confess everything, the Council would exonerate her and lay the blame on her elders; but here he met with implacable resistance. "She will not", he wrote, "confess any practice by Mrs. Ashley or the cofferer . . . and yet I do see it in her face that she is guilty." "I do assure your Grace," he added, "she hath a very good wit and nothing is gotten of her but by great policy." Meanwhile he had been looking at Parry's accounts and was shocked to find that in addition to his other drawbacks the treasurer could not keep his books straight. "So indiscreetly made," they were, "it doth appear that he had little understanding to execute his office."

In the meantime Elizabeth was told of rumours that were spreading about her, that she was herself in the Tower, with child by the Lord Admiral. She wrote to Somerset, "My lord, these are shameful slanders, for which, besides the great desire I have to see the King's Majesty, I shall most heartily desire your Lordship, that I may come to the court . . . that I may show myself there as I am." Her words had the boldness of truth; she was not secretly betrothed to the Lord Admiral, she was not with child by him. But in the first week in February the Council ordered the interrogation of the two prisoners in the Tower. In the garrulity of deathly fright they tumbled out the whole story of Seymour's behaviour with Elizabeth from the time of his coming under her stepmother's roof.

The depositions were sent down to Tyrwhit, who laid them before her. She read them, aghast and half-breathless, and studied the prisoners' signatures at the bottom of each page, although, said Tyrwhit, "she knew them with half a sight". Two days later he had her confession to send to the Council, but he said regretfully that even so, "she will in no way confess that our mistress Ashley or Parry willed her to any practise with my Lord Admiral either by message or writing". The confession indeed added nothing to the depositions of the prisoners, and dreadful as it was to read Kat Ashley's revelations, made for all to see, there was nothing in them that contradicted what Elizabeth had originally said. The disclosures were painful and damaging but they were not what the Council were looking for. It could hardly be expected however that they would take no action. With a governess who lacked elementary discretion and a treasurer who could not balance his books, it was not surprising that the Council should think the Princess's household arrangements in need of some revision. They decided that a responsible lady must replace Mrs. Ashley and they fixed upon the unfortunate Lady Tyrwhit. The latter was most unwilling to undertake the task, and Elizabeth's reception of her justified her fears. The Princess exclaimed that Mrs. Ashley was her mistress, and that she had not so demeaned herself that the Council needed to appoint other mistresses to her.

After a stormy interchange, Elizabeth cried all night, and "lowered" all the next day; but she collected herself to write to Somerset, a letter which showed the unmistakable evidence of a master-passion: the desire that the people should think well of her and take her part. The reason she had objected to Lady Tyrwhit's appointment, she said, was merely that she thought "the people will say that I deserved through my lewd demeanour to have such an one". The Council had offered to punish anyone she could point out who had slandered her. She could name them, she said, but she feared she might seem glad to punish them and so get the ill-will of the people, "which thing I would be loth to have". But she suggested that the Council themselves should issue a proclamation forbidding the detraction of the King's sisters; so practical a suggestion could hardly be refused, and the proclamation was issued according to the Princess's draft.[1]

On March 4 a bill of attainder was passed condemning Seymour to death. The news was known at Hatfield within three days, for on the 7th Elizabeth wrote to Somerset again. A plea for Seymour would have been useless and worse, but there was someone for whom she must intercede at once, for Seymour's condemnation meant that the situation of his associates was now critical. Mrs. Ashley was enduring great hardship in a prison cell, lamenting "my great folly that would either talk or speak of marriage to such as her". The cell was bitterly

[1] Mumby, *Girlhood of Queen Elizabeth.*

cold, and dark even in the daytime, as there was no glass and she had to stuff the window up with straw.[1] Elizabeth implored the Protector's mercy for Mrs. Ashley, because she had been with her so long and brought her up in learning and honesty; and then the ruling instinct showed itself: "and because it doth make men think I am not clear of the deed myself, but that it is pardoned to me because of my youth, because she I loved so well is in such a place".

The Council released Mrs. Ashley but forbade her to return to the Princess; and now Elizabeth had thirteen days to wait for the news of Seymour's death. When the word came, she made the comment which she had doubtless prepared: "This day died a man of much wit and very little judgment." Or if the words are apocryphal their tenor shows the effect of her bearing. No one who saw her doubted the intensity of her emotion: they merely admired the fortitude with which she restrained it. But she had now made the greatest effort of which she was capable. The results of nervous strain began to show themselves almost immediately, not in sudden collapse, but in increasing weakness. For days at a time she could not leave her bed. By midsummer she was a helpless invalid.

Lady Tyrwhit had at first seemed odious because she was not Kat Ashley, but in her state of exhaustion, and receptive as she always was to kindness, Elizabeth now found that Lady Tyrwhit was not unacceptable. One memento of their present intercourse Elizabeth was to retain for the rest of her life. Lady Tyrwhit had a collection of mottoes,[2] many of which were commonplace enough, but one took strong hold of Elizabeth's mind. "Be always one", it said. Turned into Latin it became her own motto, identified with her like some favourite jewel. Camden says: "She took this device unto herself: SEMPER EADEM."

She was now looked on more favourably by the Council; she had not been discovered in any intrigue against them, she had been the victim of a scoundrel, and her state of health was alarming. Somerset sent Dr. Bill to prescribe for her, and Elizabeth, in a grateful letter, said that she owed her recovery to him. He may have been responsible for the most effective prescription of allowing Mrs. Ashley to return to her. This had been brought about by August, for on August 2, 1549, Mrs. Ashley wrote a letter for the Princess to which Elizabeth added one line of postscript. The letter was written to the Protector's secretary, William Cecil, a lawyer, grave, quiet,

[1] Howe, *Galaxy of Governesses.*
[2] Bentley, *Monument of Matrons.*

immensely able and thirty years old. He was distantly related to Thomas Parry, and he had already made an unobtrusive alliance with Parry's mistress, while she was yet a wan, sick girl whose future could not be foreseen. Mrs. Ashley said the Princess had asked her to write to him "because she is so much assured of your willingness to set forth her causes to my Lord Protector's grace". This cause concerned the exchange of a poor man, the father of several children, who was lying a prisoner with the Scots, for a Scotsman imprisoned in Colchester. The postscript in Elizabeth's own hand is the earliest known of her writings to her future great minister: "I pray you, further this poor man's suit. Your friend Elizabeth."[1]

In September, Parry himself had been allowed to return to her. Elizabeth had both her friends again, but the recent commotion had taught her one thing among many. Her household account books for the years after 1549 show that she audited them herself, signing her name at the bottom of every page.

A principal step in her rehabilitation was the appointment of Ascham as her tutor. Grindal had died of the plague the previous year, and Ascham, who for long had hovered over the process of the Princess's education, at last had his professional ambition realized. He had had experience of many learned young ladies, whom he admired very much, but the Princess Elizabeth was unique; to teach her was the supreme experience of his career. His view of her inspires a strange excitement, for it is the first one gained at close quarters by a trained observer. Her mind, he said, seemed to be free from female weakness, and her power of application was like a man's. He had never seen a quicker apprehension or a more retentive memory. She had a grasp already of several languages, speaking French, Italian and Spanish as fluently as English, Latin easily and Greek moderately well; and under his guidance she quickly developed a critical appreciation of the use of words. They began the day by reading the New Testament in Greek, and then passages from Sophocles, which Ascham had chosen not only for their beauty but because they contained ideas which he thought would strengthen her mind against misfortune. She spent hours translating works from one foreign language into another and conversing with Ascham on intellectual topics in all the languages in turn; her favourite study, however, was history. She liked to spend three hours a day reading it, and would study the same period in all the different books she could get hold of. Her handwriting was now of exquisite beauty. Her manners, too,

[1] Conyers Read, *Mr. Secretary Cecil and Queen Elizabeth*.

charmed him, they were so gracious and so modest. Another trait that aroused his admiration was the plainness of her dress and hair. "She greatly prefers a simple elegance to show and splendour," he wrote, "despising the outward adorning of plaiting the hair and wearing of gold."[1]

Ascham's régime soothed her mind and was invaluable to her reputation, but it was not calculated to relieve a tendency to eye-strain and headaches. These were sometimes so severe that she could not write or even dictate anything, and she asked Edward to put down her neglect of letter-writing, "not to my slothful hand but to my aching head". But when a long spell of migraine attacks had abated, she wrote to him, in Latin, that he might be sure she never altered in her love and her respect, "I, who from your tender infancy have ever been your fondest sister."

Edward well remembered that she had, and his enforced separation from her did not mitigate his dislike of Somerset. The King was now thirteen; with admirable sense he made no attempt at an independent use of his power, but he coldly resented Somerset's domination. The latter was on treacherous ground and within sight of an evil end. John Dudley, Earl of Warwick, a worse man than himself but a capable soldier, had succeeded in a campaign against the Scots and put down Kett's rebellion at home. Somerset had discontented the Council and Parliament by a combination of arrogance and failure, and in January 1550 he was deprived of his office, although re-admitted to a place on the Council in April. Edward's official manners to his uncle were ceremonious and cordial, but to a boy of thirteen, calm and clever though he was, the state of affairs was disturbing, and it was natural his mind should turn to his favourite sister with her sympathy, her sharp wits and her unfailing admiration for himself. In May he wrote asking her to send him her portrait.

Elizabeth was delighted with the request. "The face I grant I might well blush to present but the mind I shall never be ashamed to offer." The mind, she said, wished that the body were oftener in his presence, but she would not urge a visit. "I see as yet not the time agreeing thereto." She kept the objective in mind, however. In August Dudley had himself created Duke of Northumberland, and he took over his rival's secretary, Mr. Cecil. This was very convenient for the Princess when she wanted to approach the new Protector. She was ill again in September, and wrote to Northumberland with a shaky hand to ask if she might come to court to see her

[1] Giles, *Letters and Works of Roger Ascham.*

brother. This letter Parry sent to Cecil for delivery and enclosed a note with a message from the Princess. "Write my commendations in your letter to Mr. Cecil," she had said, "that I am well assured that though I send not daily to him, that he doth not, for all that, daily forget me; say indeed that I assure myself thereof."

The opportunity for coming to court presented itself a few months later. The King, with his precocity and intensity, his starry eyes and air of supernatural brightness, was not then diagnosed as a tuberculous subject, but some observers had gained the idea that his life might not be a long one. Northumberland's conduct showed that he himself recognized this possibility. If Edward died without children, his successor by Henry VIII's will would be Mary, and Mary, harassed but indomitable, had shown that she would be no pawn in the Council's hands. Under her, the restoration of Catholicism was certain. They had not been able to coerce her while she was a subject; what could they hope to do if she were Queen? Their fortunes, so far as these were bound up with the maintenance of Protestantism, would founder altogether. But the heir after Mary was Elizabeth, a Protestant by education and still very young, seventeen-and-a-half this March. It would be useful to gain a closer view of her and estimate her qualities.

On March 17, the Princess Elizabeth entered London and rode with a retinue of 200 persons to St. James' Palace. The opportunity had come at last. The personal magnetism that Henry VIII had never lost, even when corpulent and old, was present in the pale, erect young woman, and it was emphasized by a plainness of dress that was dramatic in contrast to the rich and elaborate costumes of the court. Curling and double-curling was the fashion, but the Princess's red-blonde hair was smooth. Aylmer, who saw her with rapture, described her unadorned head and "her pure hands".[1]

There were no mistakes now, no indiscretions. Edward was enthusiastic in his welcome; he called her "his dearest, sweetest sister", "his sweet sister Temperance". The events of eighteen months ago seemed to have vanished without a stain; yet there was one conversation that recalled the past. Between March and October, when Somerset was finally committed to the Tower, he spoke, if not privately to Elizabeth, at least in her presence, of Thomas Seymour. He said that had his brother been able to speak to him, he would have been spared. The Council feared this and saw to it that the Lord Admiral was not allowed access to the Protector, and that the latter

[1] Aylmer, *Harbour for a Faithful Subject*.

had understood this only when it was too late. Such words could not be spoken or listened to without emotion, but their importance lay in the lesson they conveyed. Elizabeth did not forget it.

In October, the Scottish Queen Regent, Mary of Guise, on her way back to Scotland from France, was entertained with her ladies at the English court. The French ladies, fresh from Paris, electrified the English ladies by their elegance and fashion, and the latter could think of nothing but new dresses and new methods of hair-dressing: all of them except one. "The Princess Elizabeth," said Aylmer, "altered nothing but kept her old maiden shame-fastness." So lovely did she seem to him in manners and appearance, he was astonished that other women, with their frizzled hair and gaudy clothes, could not see how much they would be improved by following her example.

Quietness, simple clothes and the interest of a very clever mind in the theology of the Reformation were captivating to a scholar and reformer, but Northumberland was looking for something else. During the months of her stay at St. James' he decided that the younger Princess, though a Protestant, carried about her something as dangerous to his plans as the militant Catholicism of the elder sister. She was sent back to the country before the end of the year, but she did not go empty-handed. Edward conveyed Hatfield Palace to her; it was a gracious as well as a valuable gift, for the late gothic, red-brick pile in the lovely fields and woods of Hertfordshire had been, after Greenwich, her earliest home, and in it she and her brother had spent some of their happiest times. It was an expression of his love, and the last.

Somerset was beheaded in January without Edward's lifting a finger to save him. His nephew recorded the execution in his journal: "The Duke of Somerset had his head cut off upon Tower Hill between eight and nine in the morning." Henry VIII had taken the death of those once intimately connected with him with a similar matter-of-factness.

Northumberland was now in complete control of the King, but the spring showed that his ascendancy might be shortlived. In April Edward fell ill with an eruptive disease that was diagnosed as small-pox followed by an attack of measles. He made a surprising recovery and wrote to tell Elizabeth he was better; but towards Christmas he developed a cough, whose paroxysms were frightful. Elizabeth determined to see him; but Northumberland had no intention of allowing the brother and sister to meet. He had seen all too plainly how Edward delighted in her society, and the Princess's visit was prevented. Northumberland's animosity towards her was now well-known, but not known, unhappily, to her brother. For the next six months, all that remained of Edward's life, Northumberland bent every effort to destroy Edward's affection and confidence in her. As the King's illness increased he was possessed by two ideas: one was the sacred duty of protecting the realm against a return to Catholicism, the other was a conviction of the absolute nature of his kingly power.

Northumberland's only unmarried son was the nineteen-year-old Guildford Dudley, and he had arranged with Lord Henry Grey, who had now inherited the Dukedom of Suffolk, that Jane Grey should be married to Guildford, and should claim the crown on Edward's death. When matters had been brought to this point, it was not to be supposed the mere unwillingness of Jane Grey to be married to Guild-ford Dudley could be allowed to interfere. Her mother assailed her with furious reproaches and her father with blows; between them she was reduced to acquiescence and the marriage was celebrated on Whit Sunday of 1553.

Meanwhile Edward, shut off from all influence except Northumber-land's, and in the throes of a galloping consumption whose effect upon his mind was to increase its passion and fanaticism to a fearful pitch, had prepared what he called "My device for the Succession", in which he struck out the claims of his sisters and settled the crown upon Lady Jane and her heirs male. It was now absolutely essential to Northum-berland's success to make certain that Elizabeth and her brother did not see each other. Elizabeth would have answered Edward's purpose better than Jane Grey. She was a Protestant, and she was, if Mary were excluded, the heir nominated by Henry VIII; all his life her brother had recognized her abilities and loved her dearly. Northum-berland had done his work well, but he knew that at the eleventh hour Elizabeth might undo it at her brother's bedside. When she set out on a journey to London Northumberland had her stopped half way, and given a message, supposedly from the King, telling her she had better go home. On her return to Hatfield she wrote to Edward at once, of her fears for his health, her longing to see him. Nothing but a message from himself, she said, would have prevented her from finishing her journey. But Northumberland's grip was not to be loosened; not only had the King been deprived of her visit: her letter was not allowed to reach him either.

Edward was now very near death. He could scarcely eat and could get no sleep without a powerful sleeping-draught. On July 6 a fearful storm blew up and the summer afternoon was as black as night.

Edward, lying in his bed, thought no one was within ear-shot and spoke aloud the prayer he had composed for himself: "Lord, thou knowest how happy I shall be may I live with thee for ever, yet would I might live and be well for thine elect's sake," and he implored God's protection for the realm and the Protestant religion. He opened his eyes and saw Dr. Owen sitting by him. "I had not thought you had been so near," he said.[1] Three hours later, at six in the evening, he died.

The tempest continued in fury, with darkness, wind and thunder.[2] It was said afterwards that these terrors were supernatural, and that in the extremity of the storm, the grave itself had opened, and Henry VIII had risen at this crossing of his will.

[1] Strickland, *Edward VI*.
[2] Zurich Letters.

III

NORTHUMBERLAND KNEW THAT his success largely depended on his getting hold of both Princesses and shutting them up while he proclaimed Jane Grey Queen. He sent messages to them in their brother's name calling them to London. Mary was warned in mid-journey and made off to Framlingham Castle, where she raised her standard and proclaimed her accession. Elizabeth too was prevented from running into the snare. Someone, deep in Northumberland's counsels, had a lively interest in her safety. It is assumed that the warning, to stay where she was, came from William Cecil.

Ten days were enough to rally public support to Mary, and Northumberland was brought back to the Tower in abject defeat. Jane Grey, who had been lodged in the White Tower to await her coronation, was now taken to the Yeoman Gaoler's house, a timbered dwelling-house fronting Tower Green. Beside it stood the stone-built Beauchamp Tower, and here her husband was shut up with his brothers John, Ambrose, Henry and Robert.

Elizabeth was told to meet Mary at Wanstead on July 30, that they might enter London together. She received the kindest welcome. Mary kissed her and held her by the hand as she spoke. At seven in the evening, they entered Aldgate riding side by side. Streamers decked the gateway from the summit down to the ground, and over the heads of the wildly shouting crowds, far and near, the church bells were ringing.

The first public appearance of Elizabeth in her sister's reign was watched by Simon Rénaud, ambassador from the Queen's cousin, the Emperor Charles V. His business was to secure the alliance with England for the Emperor, by the marriage of Mary with his son Philip, the Prince of Spain. From the first, Rénaud regarded Elizabeth as his master's enemy. Her heretical taint was of course obnoxious to him, but her chief and indelible offence was her extraordinary popularity with the people. Rénaud was observant, and this first sight of Elizabeth, riding through the streets on a summer evening, told him almost everything he needed to know about her. Happiness had given Mary an appearance almost of beauty, but it was the momentary transfiguration of a sickly woman of thirty-seven. Riding beside her, it was Elizabeth who drew the eye. An extremely good horsewoman, she was always seen to advantage on horseback, while the way she looked and bore herself, no less than her aquiline nose and the tint of her hair, were immediately recognized by anyone who had seen Henry VIII. It was said at once how much more like him the younger daughter was than the elder, and as she passed, white and smiling, the vital current of personal popularity magnetized the shouting crowds. Rénaud noted it.

The procession made its way to the Tower, where the Queen was greeted by a group of released prisoners on their knees. Among them were the Marchioness of Exeter and her son Edward Courtenay, who had been imprisoned by Henry VIII because of the fatal nobility of his birth. His father had been the grandson of the Princess Katherine Plantagenet, and Courtenay was therefore the great-great-grandson of Edward IV. He had the height and the fair, bright colouring of the Plantagenets, but his beautiful face lacked countenance. The confinement of half his lifetime within the citadel of the Tower had not bowed him, but it had left him looking a good deal younger than his twenty-seven years. This sinister fact was not however immediately noticed. The Queen cordially welcomed him and his mother and withdrew with them into the White Tower. As her retinue crossed Tower Green in the evening light, they turned their backs on the windows behind which were Lady Jane and the young Dudleys.

In every direction except that of religious fanaticism, Mary was unusually merciful. To Rénaud's alarm she declared that Jane Grey, a girl of sixteen, was not to blame for the affairs of the past month, and though not formally pardoning her and Guildford Dudley, she allowed them to remain in easy conditions of imprisonment; Northumberland's execution even she could not avoid, though she would have spared him if she could. But the restoring of Catholicism as the national religion, and the re-establishing of Papal authority—these ends were to be pushed on with eager and fierce determination.

In the first flush of happiness the Queen looked at her sister with warmth and tolerance; provided her reconciliation to the Church could be brought about, Mary was ready, not entirely to trust her, but to treat her with sisterly kindness.

Rénaud strongly disapproved of this attitude; he pointed out that Elizabeth's almost magical popularity was a threat on account of French support. The Emperor wanted the English resources to use in the Hapsburgs' struggle with France; Henri II wanted the same thing. The Emperor meant to acquire the control of England through the marriage of Mary with his son; but Henri II had in his court, be-trothed to the Dauphin, the eleven-year-old Mary Stuart, Queen of Scotland, who, though omitted from the will of Henry VIII, was one of the lineal heiresses to the English crown. Through her, if Mary Tudor were disposed of, France might acquire a controlling interest in the combined realms of England and Scotland. What, in that case, was to happen to Elizabeth, the French King had not entirely made up his mind: a marriage possibly, with some ally of France—or there were other, simpler methods. Meanwhile, Elizabeth was to be en-couraged as the readiest means of injuring Mary, and the French Ambassador, Antoine de Noailles, relentlessly inquisitive but con-summately agreeable and discreet, was soon on confidential terms with the Princess.

Elizabeth wore at her waist a gold replica of a book, two inches square,[1] in which was transcribed "The Prayer of King Edward VI which he made the 6th day of July 1553, and the 6th year of his reign, 3 hours before his death, to himself, his eyes being closed, and think-ing none heard him, the 16th year of his age", but she declined to go to the requiem mass held for her brother, or to any mass whatsoever, and by the time the court removed to Whitehall, Mary refused to grant her an interview when she asked for one. At last an audience was granted her, in which Elizabeth wept and asked if it were her fault that she could not believe? Mary spoke kindly, and told her that if she went to mass, belief would come. Elizabeth went to mass in the Chapel Royal, but on the way she complained of a bad pain and made one of the Queen's ladies rub her stomach for her. It was thus seen by many and reported to more that the Princess had not gone to mass in any cheerful spirit. Mary, however, was pathetically pleased by her obedience, and gave her a diamond-and-ruby brooch and a rosary of white coral.[2] On a second interview, when the Queen had questioned her about her state of mind, Rénaud heard that she had trembled and looked pale, but he did not believe it. "We maintain that she appears quite composed and proud." He did not allow that both impressions might be correct, and that a haughty composure could sometimes give way to the trembling and tears of nervous strain.

The first Parliament of the reign, in which Gardiner as Lord Chancellor was the leading spirit, revoked the divorce of Mary's parents, thereby stating Elizabeth to be illegitimate; but so far from

[1] Clifford Smith, *Jewellery*.
[2] Madden.

diminishing her importance, the work of the session brought her into perilous prominence. Mary's announcement of her intended marriage with Philip of Spain was greeted with widespread, furious dismay. The reformers were alarmed at the idea of a powerful Catholic alliance, but the nation as a whole was united in a thorough detestation of foreigners. The Queen had rejected a suggestion that she herself should marry Courtenay, and now there was a clamourous demand that he should be married to Elizabeth. The direct Plantagenet descent of the one, the claim to the succession through Henry VIII's will of the other, made the suggestion a menacing one. There was no evidence of treason against Elizabeth, but Gardiner and Rénaud openly and shamelessly assured the Queen that her sister would be better dead: both as a heretic whose accession would defeat the Catholic revival, and as an object of the people's love, who might provoke a rebellion against the betrothed wife of the Prince of Spain.

It was not only the Queen, Gardiner and Rénaud who objected to the scheme for marrying Courtenay to Elizabeth: Courtenay himself was terrified at the prospect. If he were to marry, he besought the Queen it might be "to some simple girl", not to Elizabeth, who was a heretic and "too proud".[1] It was not surprising. In these years of her early twenties Elizabeth showed something indescribably strange, a cold, eerie brightness like a fairy changeling's. Her brother Edward had had something of it, and though it faded from her face when other aspects developed, it looks out in the portrait of her in coronation robes at Warwick Castle, in the plate engraved by Geminus in the first year of her reign, and a last gleam of it touches the miniature in the statutes of Corpus Christi College, painted in 1572. Rénaud described it in a sentence of unusual felicity: "The Princess Elizabeth is greatly to be feared; she has a spirit full of incantation."

The kindness of the older sister to the younger, persevered in for so long a time, was disappearing before the evidence of Elizabeth's two fatal attributes: her heretical taint and her popularity. The first, if incurable, would make the Queen fear that her sister were not fit to live; the second showed a temper in the nation that wounded and angered her. She now admitted to Rénaud that she would do her best to prevent Elizabeth from ever succeeding her, even should she herself prove childless.

The act annulling Henry VIII's divorce had not injured Elizabeth's claim to the throne, which depended on Henry's Act of Succession, but it had drastically altered her social position. She was now required

[1] C.S.P. Spanish 1553.

to give place to two of her cousins; one was the Duchess of Suffolk, and this in spite of the fact that Lady Jane Grey was in the Tower on a charge of high treason in which the mother was at least as much implicated as the daughter. The other was the Countess of Lennox, the daughter of Margaret Tudor Queen of Scotland, by her second marriage. Elizabeth had ridden beside the Queen when she entered London and, dressed in white and silver, she had followed in an open carriage immediately after her at her coronation; on both these occasions, the crowds by their enthusiastic recognition had showed that they felt the Princess to be in her proper place. She did not now find it amusing to walk out of rooms after these female relatives, one discredited, the other outlandish. At the beginning of December she asked permission to go down to her house at Ashridge. Rénaud thought it a good thing she should go—properly spied upon. Away from the court she might be tempted into some incriminating step and then . . . they would profit by their opportunity. But, he said, the Queen must say goodbye to her sister affectionately, so that she should suspect nothing. Mary acquiesced. Elizabeth begged her passionately that whatever she might hear about her, the Queen would not condemn her without giving her a chance to speak for herself. This Mary promised. Perhaps some of the old kindness remained; at all events, the old custom was kept of giving her younger sister presents. She now gave Elizabeth some pearls and a beautiful sable hood, and the Princess rode away into Hertfordshire.

She left behind her an air murmuring with conspiracy. De Noailles believed that if she and Courtenay were married and appeared in the south-west, they would provoke such a rising that the Queen and the Spanish influence would be overthrown. He was all for the thing's being attempted, at whatever risk to the protagonists. He saw only one obstacle to the plan, and that was Courtenay's faint-heartedness: that there might be objection on Elizabeth's side does not seem to have occurred to him. Elizabeth had in fact a powerful reason for refraining from any conspiracy; in the event of failure, it meant a charge of high treason. This implied almost certain death, but it carried another consequence: a verdict of high treason was the only thing understood to cancel a claim to the succession. No one who thoroughly knew Elizabeth now, could believe that she would take this enormous risk, still less that she would unite her fortunes with those of so vapid a being.

But to those who saw them only from a distance it seemed that the marriage of these fair young creatures of the blood royal would be a heaven-sent alternative to the Queen who persisted in her odious match. In the middle of January the rebellion of which Rénaud had always been talking burst out with alarming force. Its avowed object was to break off the Spanish match and put Elizabeth and Courtenay on the throne. The leader, Sir Thomas Wyatt, was to advance on London from Kent, Courtenay was expected to join a contingent from the west, and the Duke of Suffolk to bring forces from the midlands. Courtenay lost heart and stayed at home, Suffolk was ignominiously rounded up, and Wyatt, after a series of mishaps, was cut off in the London streets and taken to the Tower. A rising that with a run of luck might have been very serious was quickly extinguished.

When the news of the rebellion reached her, the Queen had written to Elizabeth to come to London at once; but Elizabeth could see as well as Rénaud that a rebellion which announced as its object the setting of herself and Courtenay on the throne was an excuse for putting her into prison that could scarcely be improved on. If she returned to London while Wyatt was advancing on it, she would go to the Tower and never leave it alive. She sent back the answer that she was too ill to travel and could not obey the Queen's command.

Wyatt's confession at first implicated Elizabeth and Courtenay, and although he afterwards withdrew it, Gardiner felt that Elizabeth might be beheaded out of hand. First, however, there was something else to do.

The rebellion had made the execution of Lady Jane and her husband inevitable, and it was carried out on February 12. Guildford Dudley was beheaded outside the Tower, and his wife, who had refused a farewell interview with him lest it should uselessly agitate their minds, was standing at the window of the Yeoman Gaoler's house when the cart crossed the green beneath bearing the corpse to the chapel; she looked down into it and saw the head by itself and the body wrapped in a bloody sheet.[1] Her supernatural tranquillity was unshaken, and though she had firmly resisted all the efforts of Dr. Feckenham, the Abbot of Westminster, to persuade her to renounce her faith, the old man's goodness, his intense compassion and concern, had been gratefully felt. On the scaffold she turned to him and said with child-like simplicity, "Shall I say this psalm?" It was the Miserere. When she had repeated it she kissed him. Her head was cut off with one blow, and de Noailles heard that the torrent of blood was extraordinary.

Meanwhile the Queen had turned her attention to her sister. If

[1] Holinshed.

Elizabeth were indeed ill, Mary had no wish to act inhumanly. She sent a commission to Ashridge headed by Lord William Howard the Lord Admiral, who was Elizabeth's great-uncle. Two of the Queen's physicians, Dr. Owen and Dr. Wendy, had been sent on before, taking with them the Queen's own litter as the most comfortable means of transporting an invalid; but the commission had orders to bring the Princess to London immediately if the doctors said she might be moved.

It was, perhaps, Dr. Owen who had given her the copy of Edward's prayer. He and Dr. Wendy found that the Princess was undoubtedly ill: "replenished with watery humours", suffering from what is now supposed to have been nephritis; but they said she could make the journey. Elizabeth exclaimed that she was willing, she only feared her weakness was too great.

Throughout her life she had moments of collapse, in which some man took charge of her and told her what she must do. Lord William Howard did so now. Supported by her servants, he told her that since the doctors said she could travel she must come at once: to do anything else would be acutely dangerous. Preparations were made, therefore, and on February 12 the journey began that was to bring the Princess to London.

It was the morning of Jane Grey's execution.

Elizabeth was brought towards the litter in a half-fainting condition; in the litter she was sick;[1] but even so, Lord William Howard dared not let her linger; everything might now depend on a show of prompt obedience to the Queen's commands. All he could do was to send word to the Council that the party would be unable to travel more than six or seven miles a day. In five days' time they reached Highgate, where they halted. Below them London was lying, in whose streets the passers-by were terrified and sickened by the sight of corpses hanging upon gibbets. The corpses had been men whose leader had told the King of France that he would put Elizabeth and Courtenay on the throne of England.

On February 23 the last stage of the journey was begun. The cortege descended from Highgate, and as it entered the London streets, Elizabeth's spirit rose to the occasion. She had the curtains of the litter pulled back that everyone in the streets might see her, and Rénaud heard that she had appeared dressed all in white and deathly pale, "her look proud, lofty, superbly disdainful". She was taken to Whitehall, and her fears were confirmed when all but a handful of

[1] Holinshed.

her servants were parted from her and she learned that the Queen would not see her.

For three weeks Elizabeth remained under the same roof with her sister and barred from her presence. Her fate would now be decided by whether it could be proved that she had known of Wyatt's plans; if the Council could show that she had had any communication with him, then her assent to the plot would be regarded as certain.

Gardiner examined the Princess and threatened her with the severest punishment if she did not throw herself on the Queen's mercy. Elizabeth denied all communication with Wyatt and said that she could not ask mercy for a fault she had not committed. While matters remained at this impasse, the Queen expected to leave London to hold a Parliament at Oxford. It was necessary that Elizabeth should be in absolutely safe keeping during the absence of Queen and Council, and it was decided, though some of the Council had considerable misgiving on the subject, to put her into the Tower.

On March 18, the Marquess of Winchester and the Earl of Sussex, two of the Queen's staunchest supporters, came to the Princess and told her where she was to go. The news turned Elizabeth almost frantic. The blood of Jane Grey had soaked the straw in its fearful torrent only four weeks ago; but perhaps even this execution did not invest the Tower with such terror as the one of which all trace had vanished seventeen years before. She exclaimed that the Queen did not know what was being done—it was Gardiner's doing, and she implored to be allowed to write a letter to her sister.

Winchester replied harshly that she neither could nor ought to have permission, but Sussex paused: something in the look of the desperate young woman made a strange impression on him. He went down on his knee and declared that she should write her mind and he himself would deliver the letter.[1]

Elizabeth there and then wrote in her exquisite hand a letter of passionate entreaty. She was panic-stricken that once inside the Tower she would perish for lack of the personal interview that would save her; but even in this extremity, she showed her concern at what the people would think if they saw her put into "a place more wonted for a false traitor than a true subject, which, though I know I deserve it not, yet in face of all this realm appears that it is proved". She reminded her sister of her promise not to condemn her unheard, and she gave the terrible example that only desperation would have prompted: "In late days I heard my Lord of Somerset say that if his

¹ Foxe, *Imprisonment of the Princess Elizabeth.*

brother had been suffered to speak with him, he had never suffered."
The use twice over of the latter word shows the mind too rapt to
notice repetition, and the writing of this passage is larger and less even
than the rest. The closing words are written with the greatest beauty.
Indeed, it was an object to write them as slowly as possible, for all the
time the tide was going down, and at low water, the river, racing
through the piers, was not navigable under London Bridge. Sussex
carried the letter to the Queen but Mary angrily refused to read it,
and demanded to know why her orders had not been immediately
carried out. She wished her father were alive again and among them
but for a month! she said. This tide was lost and the one at midnight
must go by, for the Council were afraid that someone might attempt
a rescue of the Princess under darkness, while the fear of public
indignation made it too risky to take her through the streets. It was
decided that she should go by water at nine o'clock next morning,
which was Palm Sunday; and at that hour Sussex and other members
of the Council led the Princess from her apartments across the garden
to the river-stairs. It was raining.

In the covered cabin of the barge, Elizabeth sat with six ladies, a
gentleman and a gentleman usher. When the barge stayed, she came
out of the cabin and saw she had landed at the Traitor's Gate.[1] The
sight of the archway with its overhanging grating aroused her
vehement indignation. She cried that such a gate was not fit for her
to enter, that she would not use it. One of the nobles told her she
could not choose. As it was still raining he offered her his cloak, but
she dashed it impatiently aside. Stepping out over the shoes in water
she exclaimed: "Here lands as true a subject as ever landed at these
stairs. Before Thee, O God, do I speak it, having no other friend than
Thee alone!" She mounted the stairs, and the arch yawned above her
head. Like an animal that smells the blood of the slaughter-house, she
made a last, demented effort at resistance; she sat down on a damp
stone and declared that she would go no farther.

Left to himself, the Lieutenant of the Tower might have ordered
the use of force, but in the presence of the Earl of Sussex, this straightforward method was not open to him; nor were the results certain
even if he tried it: there was a posse of yeomen warders drawn up
inside the gate and at the sight of the Princess some of them had
broken rank and knelt down, shouting: "God preserve your Grace!"

The Lieutenant tried persuasion. "You had best come in, Madam,"
he said, "for here you sit unwholesomely." "Better sit here than in a

[1] Foxe.

worse place," she said; and then the gentleman usher broke down and sobbed aloud.

The response was unfailing. Elizabeth stood up. She rated the man for giving way when he should be supporting her by his firmness. Her truth, she said, was such, she thanked God her friends had no cause to weep for her. She entered the gateway and was led to the left, where the Bell Tower rose on an angle of the curtain wall. On the first floor of the tower was a large, vaulted, stone-walled chamber with a great fireplace, opposite to which were three pointed windows with stone hoods and deep stone window-seats. The rest of the floor consisted of a small passage and three latrines in tall and narrow niches. Into this chamber the Princess and her ladies were shut and the door was bolted behind them. When she had disappeared from view, Sussex said uneasily to the rest: "Let us take heed, my Lords, that we go not beyond our commission, for she was our King's daughter."

Gardiner had achieved part of his aim in that the Princess was now under lock and key; the next object was to extract a confession from her that she had been in Wyatt's confidence. He had failed of this when he attempted it in Whitehall; in these more propitious surroundings he hoped to do better.

He and nine Lords of the Council repaired to the Tower and conducted a vigorous examination of the prisoner. How, she was asked, did she explain the coincidence that Wyatt had written her a letter, advising her to remove to Donnington Castle, and that she had actually made preparations to move there? In a moment of blinding panic, she made a futile pretence of knowing nothing even of the existence of Donnington, one of her own properties. The moment passed, and she recollected herself. She replied haughtily that she had received no letter from Wyatt, as the Council knew, for they had intercepted it, and as to her meaning to go to Donnington, she said: "Might I not, my Lords, go to mine own houses at all times?"

And now occurred another strange capitulation. Henry Fitzalan, twelfth Earl of Arundel, a Catholic of long descent, not only supported the Queen but had been one of those who urged her to put Elizabeth to death; but the sight of the Princess with her back to the wall affected him as it had affected Sussex. He went down on his knee and said: "Her Grace spoke the truth, and for his part he was sorry to see her troubled about such vain matters." Gardiner was obliged to end the interview without having achieved anything. He told Rénaud bitterly that if everyone worked as hard as he, Gardiner, did, matters would show a striking improvement.

On April 11, Wyatt was executed; it was both claimed and denied that on the scaffold he had exonerated Courtenay and Elizabeth. If he had, his words carried no weight. Courtenay indeed was released and went abroad, but Elizabeth remained in the Bell Tower; and here, so near to the last scenes of her mother's life, her mind was filled with all she had heard of her mother's death. Years afterwards, she told the French Ambassador de Castelnau that at this time she was in such despair, she thought only of sending to her sister to ask that she might be beheaded with a sword instead of the axe.

She grew so weak and exhausted from confinement that in the middle of April she was allowed to walk on the leads. This walk, about three feet wide, extends some seventy feet from a door in the Bell Tower to one in the Beauchamp Tower, and lies in a trough between the battlements on one hand, and the gables of the King's House and the Yeoman Gaoler's House on the other. Even in this strait path she was not allowed to walk without two persons in front of her and two behind,[1] but it gave movement, light and air, and presently she was allowed to walk in the Tower garden. This liberty took off the worst edge of her imprisonment, for it brought her into touch again with some of the common people, a contact that renewed her like air and light. The son of one of the gaolers, a child of three years old, was attracted by the lady who walked in the garden. He used to watch for her coming, and, it being April, bring her little bunches of flowers. As soon as this was noticed, it was suspected that the boy was being used to convey messages and his father was sternly ordered to keep him away from the Princess. The child came to the locked garden-gate and called through it: "Mistress, I can bring you no more flowers now."[2]

Gardiner had got his heresy bill through the Houses of Parliament. The church lands were to remain in the hands of their present owners, but the bishops were to have the power of examination of religious opinions, and putting to death for heresy. Few people who heard the bill passed foresaw its dire consequences. Meanwhile, preparations were made for the Prince of Spain's arrival and it was thought wise to convey Elizabeth out of the capital. Gardiner's proposal to send her to Pomfret Castle in Yorkshire, remote as to situation and with the added attraction of having been the scene of Richard II's murder, was regretfully given up. Lord William Howard had command of the fleet, and he might take it over to the French if

[1] Oral tradition of the Tower.
[2] Foxe.

his great-niece were too severely treated. It was decided that the Princess should be removed as a prisoner to the palace of Woodstock in Oxfordshire, and Sir Henry Bedingfield was appointed as her gaoler.

When Elizabeth heard that Bedingfield had invested the Tower with one hundred men she could think at first of but one errand that might have brought him. She asked if the Lady Jane's scaffold were still standing? Her destination, however, was explained to her by the Marquess of Winchester, and with her recollections of close confinement still fresh, she demanded of him whether she would be allowed to walk in Woodstock Park? Yes, said Winchester; she might take it, that would be allowed her. On the next day, May 20, she was led out of the Tower and taken by water as far as Richmond.

Bedingfield had been given a charge extremely onerous to his conscientious mind. He was to keep the Princess in strict custody, and to manage her removal with as little stir as possible. The first was within his power; the second was like trying to catch and cover up the reflections of light. His difficulties began with the first moments of embarkation. Seeing the Princess's barge on its way upstream, the gunners in the steel-yards fired a thunderous salute, to the indignation of the Queen, the Chancellor and the Spanish Ambassador, when the matter was reported. The difficulty of transporting her secretly increased as they proceeded; by some means the identity of the closely guarded lady was known in the villages through which they passed, and as the retinue appeared, the church bells were set ringing. Bedingfield had the ringers put in the stocks. At Ricote, a severer trail awaited him. It had been planned that the party should bait at the house of Lord Williams of Tame, but instead of the discreet arrangements Bedingfield expected, he found that Lord Williams had convened the neighbouring gentry to a banquet in the Princess's honour.[1] It was with difficulty that he got the party under weigh again after this delightful respite.

Inside the domain of Woodstock, however, Elizabeth's imprisonment began once more. The palace was solitary in its great park, and though the town was not far distant, bad weather made the roads impassable. She was not lodged in the royal apartments but in four rooms in the gate-house, two upstairs and two down, of which the larger one had a groined roof painted blue and sprinkled with gold stars.[2]

[1] Mumby.
[2] Nichols, *Progresses*.

Bedingfield, deliberate and tenacious as a bull-dog, was both admiring and apprehensive of his prisoner, of whom he spoke in his reports to the Council as "that great Lady". She was perpetually demanding something, and he told them: "I am marvellously perplexed to grant her desire or to say her nay." He allowed the Princess to walk in the upper and lower orchard, and though she complained to her gentlewomen that the promise had not been kept of allowing her to walk in the park, he was thankful to say she had not so far raised the matter with himself. Her ladies were now all the Queen's choice, but one of them, Elizabeth Sands, had become greatly attached to her. Bedingfield made a note to keep this young person under special observation, and in June she was dismissed, "with great mourning by her and my Lady's grace".

Elizabeth's mental disquiet grew as the summer came on; she feared that out of sight was out of mind in the green retreats of Woodstock, and that she might be left to languish there indefinitely. She demanded that Bedingfield should send a message from her to the Council and was fretted beyond bearing when he replied merely: "I shall do for your Grace what I am able to do."[1]

The preparations for the Queen's marriage were going forward, and the Emperor was turning over in his mind the desirability, since he could not have her put to death, of removing the heiress to the throne from her country before his son's arrival. He thought of sending her to the Netherlands, to the court of his sister, the Regent; but a doubt assailed him—his sister might not find the Princess a congenial guest.

The Regent reassured him. "As to the Lady Elizabeth," she wrote, "it is quite possible our characters may be different, but if your Majesty's interests would be served by sending her to me, I should be quite satisfied and would never refuse to do anything that might improve the general state of affairs."[2] This display of self-abnegation was not, after all, required. The Council discussed the project of deporting the Princess, but they abandoned it; the formidable shadow of Lord William Howard once again fell across their path.

Elizabeth at last gained permission to write to the Queen. She could not write without it, for Bedingfield doled out ink, pens, rough paper for a draft and smaller sheets of writing-paper for a fair copy, and when the writing was finished, took away again the material that had not been used.

[1] Mumby.
[2] C.S.P. Spanish 1554.

But the letter, protesting loyalty, had no effect. The Queen replied to Bedingfield that the traitors would not have made Elizabeth the object of their conspiracy "unless they had more certain knowledge of her favour . . . than is yet confessed by her", and ended by saying she wanted no more such letters. Elizabeth was appalled; recovering herself, she begged him to let her send a reply to the Council. This he refused to do. The next morning, the 3rd of July, at ten o'clock, she called him up to her as she was walking in the little garden and told him that if he would not allow her to appeal to the Council, she was worse off than the worst prisoners in Newgate, "for they are never gainsaid, in the time of their imprisonment, by one friend or another, to have their cause opened and sued for". The refusal meant that she "must continue this life without all worldly hope". She could only leave her cause to God, determining that whatever should happen to her, she would remain, as she had been all her life, the Queen's true subject. As she spoke, the summer rain came on. " 'It waxes wet,' " she said, " 'and therefore I will depart to my lodging again.' And so she did."

On July 25, the marriage of Philip and Mary took place in Winchester Cathedral. This great event was celebrated without any word to the Queen's sister, who remained in imprisonment, wearing herself down by agitation and restless repining. She wrote with a diamond on a window-pane:

"Much suspected, by me
Nothing proved can be,
Quoth Elizabeth, prisoner."

She heard a milk-maid singing in the park, and in her desperation she exclaimed that "the girl's lot was better than her's, and her life merrier".

In the silence of the heavy-leaved month of August, her sense of abandonment and despair was reflected in what she wrote on the fly-leaf of St. Paul's Epistles: "August. I walk many times into the pleasant fields of the holy scriptures where I pluck up the goodlisome herbs of sentences . . . that having tasted their sweetness, I may the less perceive the bitterness of this miserable life."

The long strain was telling on her nerves. One day in the garden, the sight of Bedingfield, unlocking and locking six pairs of gates after her, was too much. She burst out into vehement reproaches, calling him her gaoler. Like Sussex and Arundel before him, Bedingfield was deeply moved by her passion. He knelt and begged her not to call him by that harsh name; he was her officer, appointed to take care of her and protect her from any injury.

In October the Princess said that she wanted to be bled, and the Council were asked to send Dr. Owen, Dr. Wendy and Dr. Huick to her; to these doctors, she said, she would commit all the privacies of her body, but not to any others, unless the Queen so ordered it, which she hoped Her Majesty would not do. Dr. Owen and Dr. Wendy came, bringing a surgeon to perform the bleeding, and Bedingfield was present while they bled Elizabeth in the arm in the morning and from the foot in the afternoon. "Since which time," he said, "she does reasonably well."

A danger now loomed, beyond the Emperor's desire to deport her and Gardiner's to cut off her head. The Queen's marriage and her supposed pregnancy had given her confidence, and the extirpation of heresy by burning alive, which had been determined by Gardiner and herself and was abetted by Cardinal Pole, who arrived in England in November, was to be put in hand forthwith. The punishment of death by fire had been used against heresy for centuries, and it was not the burning itself, but the choice and number of the victims that made the persecution appear abominable to its own time. The stubborn determination of the Queen, so merciful in every other matter, showed not only the strength of her feelings but the outrage they had suffered in the treatment of her mother and herself. The force of her nature had hitherto shown itself in courage and patience; now it was seen in another aspect.

The burnings began in February 1555, but the coming storm had been forecast. Someone, by some means, it would seem, had conveyed a warning to Elizabeth, for in the previous September she took communion according to the Roman Catholic rites. The capitulation was of extreme urgency, because, as the case of Cranmer and the humbler one of Bembridge were to show, once the Queen's morbid ferocity was aroused, recantation did not mean a reprieve from the fire. The notes made by William Cecil on the numbers burned show an ominous suggestion:

1556. In the compass of the year were burned 80 persons, whereof many were maidens.

1557. In this year were burnt about London above 64, whereof 20 were women.[1]

Hooper, Latimer, Ridley and Cranmer were the famous victims;

[1] Peck, *Desiderata Curiosa*

the rest were in humble life; some were infirm, some blind, and one was a pregnant woman. The popular anguish and fury is heard in the crude rhymes and uneven verses of the "Compendious Register, containing the names and patient sufferings of the tormented and cruelly burned", in which each verse is a collection of names ending with the refrain:

When these with violence were burned to death
We wished for our Elizabeth.

The release from Woodstock came about unexpectedly.

Mary, who had mistaken the symptoms of ovarian dropsy for those of pregnancy, expected to be confined early in May. Parliament had refused Philip the Crown Matrimonial and had scouted Mary's attempt to put him into the succession. If the Queen were now to die, his hold on the kingdom would depend on his either marrying Elizabeth or controlling her as his protégée. Rénaud had told him that he must on no account leave the country without seeing the Princess and giving her a severe and threatening lecture. This interview was now to take place.

On April 30 Elizabeth arrived at Hampton Court, still as a prisoner. She was not allowed to see the Queen, but Mary sent a message to say the King would see her, adding the ingenuous and touching command that Elizabeth was to put on her richest clothes for the occasion.[1] A time was appointed and the two beings who for forty years were to represent the struggles of opposing worlds met face to face: one was a short, fair, phlegmatic man of twenty-eight, the other a pale young woman of twenty-two, with a weird brightness like sea-fire, and hands of miraculous delicacy. Nothing transpired of their conversation, but it was said years afterwards that Philip was heard to reproach himself because he had allowed himself to entertain a passion for his sister-in-law, while on her part, it amused Queen Elizabeth to say that her brother-in-law had been in love with her.

The imprisonment continued none the less; Gardiner and some of the Lords of the Council now came to examine her once more with a view to forcing a confession, and Elizabeth greeted them by saying, "My Lords, I am glad to see you, for methinks I have been kept a great while from you, desolately alone," but when Gardiner said that if she wanted her liberty she must confess her guilt and beg the Queen's mercy, the words were scarcely out of his mouth, before she exclaimed that rather than confess a fault she had not committed, she

[1] Wiesener, *Jeunesse d'Elizabeth.*

was prepared to stay in prison for the rest of her life. This outburst was reported to the Queen, who sent word back again by Gardiner that she was astonished at such brazen defiance and that Elizabeth "must tell another tale ere she were set at liberty".

By the third week in May, there were still no signs that Mary's confinement was to take place; she feared that she had offended Heaven because she had not sufficiently persecuted the heretics, and issued a circular to the bishops, commanding them to increase their efforts to detect and punish the offenders, but the disappointment inspired Philip to more practical measures. If the Queen died without a child, he himself might not only lose control of the country, he might lose it to the King of France; for many people believed that succession could not be settled by will, even the will of Henry VIII, but only by descent, and since all Catholics believed Elizabeth to be illegitimate, on the death of Henry's daughter Mary, the legitimate heir was, despite Henry's having excluded the line, the descendant of his elder sister Margaret—and this heir was none other than the future Queen of France. To a Spaniard such a prospect was intolerable. No matter what other Catholics might think, Philip was determined to support Elizabeth's claims against those of Mary Stuart.

At the end of May, at ten o'clock at night, Elizabeth was sent for by the Queen. She was led across the garden and brought up the privy stair to the Queen's bedroom. She had not seen Mary for over a year. She knelt, and in a burst of tears declared that she was and always had been her sister's loyal subject. Mary turned away and said aloud, in Spanish, "God knoweth." She did not speak to empty air. Behind some hangings, with his eye to a hole, Philip had watched the scene. He had an unpleasant fondness for looking at ladies through spy-holes. He spied into the dressing-room of one of his wife's ladies, the Lady Magdalene Dacre, and stretching his arm into it, received a smart blow with a staff which the girl found handy.[1] But the Queen no doubt felt it reasonable that Elizabeth should be subjected to the close scrutiny of a being so wise and virtuous as her husband.

When even the Queen was convinced that she was not carrying a child, Philip's impatience could no longer be restrained. In August he left his wretched, despairing wife, impressing on her that her policy towards Elizabeth must be one of conciliation. Mary did not find the command wholly uncongenial. With an ambivalence not unusual in sisters, she was kind to Elizabeth, while the Venetian Ambassador, Michele, thought he could see that she hated her.

[1] Smith, *Lady Magdalene Dacre.*

Bedingfield had been discharged, exclaiming at his dismissal that God Almighty knew this was the joyfullest news he had ever heard, and the Queen now appointed Sir Thomas Pope, a rich and amiable gentleman, to be the Princess's governor. Pope, who was not required to keep her as a state prisoner, cordially accepted the charge. He had founded Trinity College, Oxford, the previous year, and was charmed to hold long conversations about his darling project with a listener who combined so much learning and intelligence in the person of an attractive young woman. The Princess withdrew to Hatfield in October, and as she and her retinue passed through the streets, the crowds made such an uproar of enthusiasm that she detached some gentlemen from her train and sent them among the people to keep order. The route out of London from Fleet Street to the north led through the parish of Shoreditch, and the parishioners were among those who had the habit of welcoming the Princess's approach with a peal of bells. She loved to hear the loud, sweet ringing that spoke affection for her, and as she came and went on the Hatfield road, "she would pause and listen attentively and commend the bells".[1]

At Hatfield, old friends were gathered: Kat Ashley and Parry were in residence, and Ascham, now Latin Reader to the Queen, had permission to visit Hatfield and resume his reading with the Princess. His previous admiration was confirmed and deepened; the relationship was now complementary rather than that merely of master and pupil. He said in a letter to Aylmer that he learned more from her day by day than she from him. "I teach her words and she me, things."

The unhappy Queen, deprived, as de Noailles said, both of her husband and of her subjects' love, now received a fresh proof of her unpopularity. Sir Henry Dudley with a band of refugees, malcontents and pirates, was in France, planning, with the unconcealed help of the French government, an invasion once again to set Elizabeth and Courtenay on the throne. The Queen sent a message assuring Elizabeth that no suspicion attached to her, and when a young man who bore a remarkable likeness to the Plantagenet family appeared in Essex and announced that he was Courtenay, and his followers proclaimed in Yaxley Church, "The Lady Elizabeth Queen and her beloved bed-fellow Lord Courtenay, King," this also the Queen accepted as having nothing to do with her sister. It seemed that the boat had weathered the storm, but the strain of endurance

[1] Nichols, *Progresses.*

had gone on for a very long time. Elizabeth was in weak health again; she had an attack of jaundice, and spasms of breathlessness, which were said to have oppressed her "ever since the time when her sister began to maltreat her".[1] Illogical as it might seem, some point of temporary exhaustion had been reached, at which she was prepared to give up the struggle. De Noailles had never ceased assuring her that if she would confide herself to the King of France she would find eager and chivalrous support; she was now prepared to avail herself of the promise. She sent Lady Sussex, incognito, to the French Ambassador.

Another occasion now arose on which, in a state of collapse, she was saved by the decision and guidance of a man. Had the Ambassador been de Noailles himself, there would have been but one outcome of Lady Sussex's mission—before Elizabeth had come to herself she would have been half way across the Channel; but by inestimable good fortune, de Noailles had been recalled and his place taken by his brother, the Bishop of Acqs. The Bishop stood her friend in the most unexpected manner. He told Lady Sussex that such a flight would be disastrous, and that if Elizabeth meant to be Queen she must in no circumstances leave the country; if she did, she would never come back. Twice Lady Sussex visited him and each time she was given the same advice. Afterwards the Bishop used to say he had saved Queen Elizabeth's throne for her.

The Princess settled again to an existence which appeared to be pleasant and reassuring but in a house where, said Michele, "no one comes or goes and nothing is spoken or done without the Queen's knowledge".

Mary's wretchedness was temporarily relieved by the return of Philip in February 1557. His objects were two: to bring about what he had for a long time wanted to arrange, the marriage of Elizabeth to his cousin Philibert of Savoy, and to bring the English into his war against the French. Elizabeth was summoned to court to meet Philip but she refused the proposed marriage with calm resolution. She had overcome the wild temptation to leave the country as the French King's protégée; it was not likely that she would consent to leave it as the wife of a minor connection of the Hapsburgs. Philip blamed Mary for her sister's intransigence; it was his wife's duty to him to command that the marriage he wished should take place. In vain the unfortunate Queen assured him that anything she could do for him, should be done; it was not in her power to force her sister into a

[1] Bishop of Acqs to King of France: Quoted by Chamberlin.

marriage against Elizabeth's own wishes and those of the realm. Philip, like his father but with less excuse since he himself had actually lived in the country, was under a misapprehension as to what an English parliament would allow him to do with a daughter of Henry VIII.

In his second object, Philip was unhappily successful. An attempt at invasion by Sir Thomas Stafford, sponsored by the French, irritated the government into promising aid to the Spanish forces. Having gained this end, Philip left the country. The misery of his wife at his departure was extreme, but the summer months were marked by an intercourse of the sisters that appeared to have almost the cordiality of the early years when the elder sister had been good to the little one. At midsummer Elizabeth was invited to Richmond, and a barge was sent to convey her and her ladies which had an awning of green silk embroidered with gold, and was garlanded with fresh flowers. The Queen returned the visit at Hatfield, where Elizabeth's preparations to entertain her ran the gamut from the savage to the exquisite: in the morning there was an exhibition of bear-baiting; in the evening the children of St. Paul's acted a play, and afterwards one of the choir-boys, with a voice of enchanting sweetness, sang, while the Princess accompanied him on the virginals.[1]

A relic of the sisters' sympathy remains, of peculiar interest. Mary again imagined herself pregnant, and Elizabeth made baby-linen for her. Needlework is favourable to reflection, and the head bent over these exquisite pieces can seldom have known more disturbing and complicated thoughts.[2]

For herself, Elizabeth it seemed had already determined that no such preparations were ever to be needed. Gustavus of Sweden sent a letter to her, asking if she would consider a proposal from his son, Prince Eric; if so, the Swedish King would open negotiations with the Queen of England. Elizabeth replied, much to the satisfaction of the Queen, that she could consider no proposal that did not come to her through her sister. She stated, further, that she had always wished, and wished still, to live unmarried. Sir Thomas Pope, incredulous and gallant, suggested that she would scarcely persevere in this attitude if some suitable wooer approached her with the Queen's consent.

Elizabeth's reply was impressive: "What I shall do hereafter I know not, but I assure you . . . I am not at this time otherwise minded than I have declared unto you." Words could scarcely speak plainer, but

[1] Strickland, *Queen Elizabeth.*
[2] Exhibition of the Royal House of Tudor: Catalogue, 1895.

however plainly and however often she was to make this declaration, she could not get men to believe it. On this occasion Sir Thomas put it down to "maiden shamefastness".

It was clear now that Mary had once again been disappointed and that she was very ill. The miseries of the last months of her life were of a concentrated bitterness. The English intervention in France had drawn the French attack on the crumbling stronghold of Calais. Though the English had never had a shadow of right to it in the first place, the loss of the last remains of the conquests of Edward III and Henry V was bitterly resented by the nation, whose anger redounded on the Queen and caused her famous exclamation of despair. The desertion by her husband and the loss of her hope of a child had produced a keenness of suffering that had driven her almost beside herself. All that remained was to attempt to propitiate Heaven by continued burning of heretics. Cecil noted: "In June now burning in Smithfield seven at one fire." The last martyrs were burned on November 11, and after their names, the Register exclaims:

> Six days after these were burned to death
> God sent us our Elizabeth.

At Hatfield, in the excruciating excitement of the hour, Elizabeth had not let go of caution. She had told Sir Nicholas Throckmorton that he was to bring her the black-and-gold betrothal ring that would never leave Mary's hand till she was dead. Meanwhile Cecil came and went, with drafted proclamations and plans to take over the government in the new Queen's name. While Elizabeth waited, among so many cares and preoccupations one thing forced itself on her attention that she was never to forget: it was the sight of the road from London, thronged with horses and their riders, all streaming away from the capital of the dying Queen, agog to establish themselves with her successor. The grim moral it conveyed remained with her for the rest of her life.

At daybreak on November 17 Mary died, and Throckmorton set out for Hatfield with the ring, but he was outdistanced on the road by the Lords of the Council. When they arrived Elizabeth was walking in the park and they came up with her as she stood beneath a leafless oak. At their words she knelt on the grass and exclaimed: "A domino factum est et mirabile in oculis nostris!"

Why she was ready with words from the hundred-and-eighteenth psalm is plain to see; verse after verse of it reads like a pæan of thanksgiving for her own particular case:

I called upon the Lord in distress and He answered me and set
me in a large place . . .

I shall not die but live and declare the works of the Lord . . .

The stone that the builders refused has become the headstone of
the corner.

The passion of joy for the new reign, and of love for the young
Queen who had captured the imagination before she had been seen,
echoes still in nameless popular verse:

> *Then God sent us your noble Grace*
> *As indeed it was high time . . .*
> *For whom we are all bound to pray, Lady, Lady,*
> *Long life to reign! Both night and day, most dear Lady!*[1]

[1] Harleian Miscellany.

IV

THE NEW QUEEN was just twenty-five, "indifferent tall, slender and straight". On public occasions her slow, stately movement was much admired, but it was noticed that "she walked apace for her pleasure, or to catch her a heat in the cold mornings". She loved to ride fast, to dance, and to watch other people dancing.

Her appearance, which was to change a good deal in the next few years, was still very young and fragile, with an unself-conscious intensity. Her skin, more than white, was "candidus", of a glowing paleness;[1] her hair was variously described as "redder than yellow" and "tawny inclining to gold". Her eyes, golden and large-pupilled from short sight, had eyebrows arched but faint. Her face was a long oval like her mother's, but her mother had been sallow and dark. Elizabeth's colouring was her father's and though in the grossness of the King's later years it was lost sight of, her likeness to him in the aquiline nose and the shape of the brow is shown in the miniatures on the early documents of Henry VIII.[2] Her father's ability and his physical magnetism, infused with something of her mother's fascination, had distilled themselves into a personal magic that was admitted even by those who distrusted and disliked her. She had also inherited from her mother a strain of hysteria, and while her mental power and nervous energy were equal to excessive demands, brain-storms, fainting fits and moments of paralysing dread for which no cause was seen, showed a nervous system that was overstrung.

The immediate impression she made was one of remarkable intelligence. Machiavelli said: "It is an unerring rule and one of universal application, that a Prince who is not wise himself cannot be well advised by others." Elizabeth's claim to wisdom was formally made three days after her accession; at her first council meeting, held in the great hall of Hatfield Palace, she announced the appointment of William Cecil as her chief Secretary of State, "to take pains" for her and her realm. She told him that she knew him to be faithful and incorruptible, and that he would advise her, regardless of her private wishes, and she herself made a promise: "If you shall know anything

[1] Johnston, *Historia Britannicarum.*
[2] Auerbach, *Tudor Portraits.*

necessary to be declared to me of secrecy, you shall show it to myself only, and assure yourself I will not fail to keep taciturnity therein." Her words told Cecil nothing he did not know already, but they were the seal on a bond of life-long partnership.

Cecil was now thirty-eight, quiet, formidable, with a spare frame and clear, pale eyes in a forehead oppressed by care. His talents were extraordinary not so much in kind as in degree; he had the abilities of the professional man, raised to a pitch far beyond mere ability. Camden said: "Of all men of genius he was the most a drudge; of all men of business, the most a genius." Though he had conformed under Mary, he had a personal devotion to the Protestant creed, and in his private life he much resembled the present-day Quakers.

In many ways Elizabeth was his opposite. Though formidable, she was not quiet; she had a keen instinct for the dramatic and a capacity for passion. A natural elegance of mind led her to prefer the ritual of the Catholic Church, and she would have found no difficulty in adopting its tenets, if every consideration connected with the great end of her existence had not pointed in the contrary direction. But she and her Secretary had an absolute community of aim. They wanted, beyond anything, to make a success of governing the country, and on three major points they were agreed as to how this was to be done. They saw the nation's future as bound up with the Reformation, and they abhorred the ruinous waste of war. Cecil's maxim was: "A realm gains more in one year's peace than by ten years of war," and "No war, my Lords!" in the Queen's vehement and ringing tones was to cut across many an argument at the council table. Thirdly, they agreed that a re-establishment of the national credit was a step without which nothing else could be done, and that this itself could not be achieved without vigilant economy. There was a further point of similarity between them: in their life's business, the art of government, they recognized no distinction between work and pleasure.

Of the appointments announced beneath the arched wooden roof at Hatfield, Cecil's was the one of supreme importance, but others were interesting. Kat Ashley was made First Lady of the Bed Chamber, and her husband, Keeper of the Queen's Jewels. Parry was knighted and made Treasurer of the Household, an office in which the arithmetical drudgery could be performed by clerks, and Blanche Parry, elderly, learned and wise, was made Keeper of the Royal Books in the library of Windsor Castle. The Earl of Arundel and Lord William Howard were created Privy Councillors, but even before the council meeting on November 20, a friend had arrived post-haste from London to tender his allegiance. "Immediately after Queen Mary's death, this young nobleman mounted a snow-white steed and went to the Princess Elizabeth at Hatfield, being well-skilled in riding a managed horse."[1]

Lord Robert Dudley's emergence in the new reign was altogether in character: a splendid appearance and a promptness and energy of devotion. He had known Elizabeth since they were both eight years old, at a time when his father Northumberland was Master of the Horse to Ann of Cleves. In 1550, when he and Elizabeth were seventeen, he had married an heiress, Amy Robsart. The marriage, though sanctioned by Northumberland, had not been an arranged one; it was the result of a violent if short-lived passion between the bride and bridegroom. At the wedding of the enamoured pair, one of the guests had been the Princess Elizabeth. However long his passion for his wife lasted, it did not prevent Dudley from showing considerable friendship for Elizabeth during her sister's reign. The Venetian Ambassador had noted that in spite of her talent for economy, the Princess was in debt, and according to Elizabeth herself, Dudley at some time between 1553 and 1558 sold part of his property and gave her the proceeds. The transaction was a secret one at the time, and Elizabeth, who was much moved by personal kindness to herself, spoke of it afterwards when saying that Dudley had a claim on her affections.

When she was allowed, during her imprisonment in the Tower, to walk on the leads, her promenade behind the battlements had led directly towards the narrow door of the Beauchamp Tower, behind which was the great stone-walled chamber in which Robert Dudley was shut up with his surviving brothers. Guarded as she had been, with two persons before her and two behind, the nearness of the door had availed nothing; but the situation, romantic and desperate, was of a kind to make the two prisoners even more interesting to each other. Camden said they were born on the same day at the same hour and that this "synastria" or sympathy in their stars was the cause of their being, throughout their lives, so congenial to each other. Their compatibility was obvious. Dudley, like all Northumberland's sons, was tall; his portrait at full-length shows the striking beauty of his legs, long, slender and elegantly turned. "Of a tall personage and manly countenance," said the Venetian Ambassador, adding that he was "somewhat brown of visage", and Sussex, who hated and dis-

[1] Nichols, *Progresses*.

trusted him, called him "the gipsy". His face, with its round, hard eyes and short, beak-like nose, was that of a handsome and not un-amiable bird of prey. His strong qualities were physical: he rode, jousted and danced with the perfection that makes spectators idolize the man they watch, and he had an inborn knack of managing horses. The post Elizabeth gave him fitted him to a hair. As Master of the Horse, he was responsible not only for the Queen's riding-horses and hunters, but for all the horses used in the royal transport, for riders, coaches and baggage waggons, for buying them, maintaining them and making them available. He could do the practical work of the office efficiently, and he was eminently suited to its decorative function, which required him to make a splendid public appearance in close attendance on the Queen.

"A man eminent for his person, deficient in wit and integrity",[1] —in contemporary opinion, the antithesis is always there. As Elizabeth's fondness for him was the source of wealth and influence which he could never have gained without it, any just assessment of him by his peers was next door to impossible. The charge brought against him was, and has always been, that his show of devotion to her was an odious sham. No doubt he would have betrayed her had it ever been to his interest to do so, but his interest was served by attaching himself as closely to her as possible; it was not his fault that he was not her husband, and the advantages his attachment brought him were so great that he could not escape the accusation of self-interest and hypocrisy. But Elizabeth was not a woman who gave anything for nothing. If Dudley had felt no passion for her in their youth, and if the affection he afterwards professed had been nothing but a fraud, he would not have gained his unique ascendancy over her and kept it without a serious rival for thirty years.

Dudley's motives were naturally mixed, but his devotion, from whatever cause, was unequivocal. In the dawn of the reign he was at her feet. Everyone knew he was a married man, but his wife, at whose wedding Elizabeth had stood by as an onlooker, remained in the country.

Six days after her accession, the Queen and her retinue, followed by a great crowd of ladies and gentlemen on horseback, took the road from Hatfield to London. Her destination was Lord North's town house at the end of the Barbican. Here she stayed a fortnight and here, at a large assembly, the Spanish Ambassador had his first sight of her as Queen. Since the late Queen's death, de Feria had

[1] Naunton, *Fragmenta Regalia*.

found himself kept at arm's length, and what he could see of affairs he did not like.

"What can be expected of a country governed by a Queen, and she a young lass, who, although sharp, is without prudence?" he lamented.

He had sent the Queen, in Philip's name, two precious rings that Philip had originally given to her sister, and had taken it on himself to tell her that the King would be glad for her to take a box of Spanish jewels left in Whitehall, and anything else of his she fancied, "as a good brother should". This was a successful move, he reported, for "she is very fond of having things given to her". At the party the Queen treated him most graciously; as soon as she saw him making his way towards her, she began taking off her glove that he might kiss her hand. Amidst expressions of friendship and encouragement, Feria said his master hoped that she would be extremely careful in her handling of religious matters. The Queen answered that it would be very bad of her to forget God, who had been so good to her: "which," said Feria, "seemed to me rather an equivocal reply."

Equivocal and sparkling, she presented to the Spaniard's penetrating eye an appearance that was far from reassuring, but to the English themselves she had already shown an earnestness of singular force. The daily council meetings were continued at Lord North's house, and at one of these she spoke to a deputation of judges. Cecil was a lawyer: he cared deeply for the efficiency and good name of the legal profession, and he got the Queen to raise the salaries of the Queen's Bench judges. It was clear that he had told her his view of the state to which the administration of the courts had fallen. Bishop Jewel heard the Queen say to the judges, with the repetition that marked her speech when she was deeply moved: "Have a care over my people . . . they are *my* people. Every man oppresseth them and spoileth them without mercy. They cannot revenge their quarrel nor help themselves. See unto them, see unto them, for they are my charge."

On Monday, November 28, the Queen took possession of the Tower. She went in a chariot to Cripplegate, but there she mounted, and began the first of her great processions. First rode the Lord Mayor carrying her sceptre, with Garter-King-at-Arms beside him; next came Lord Pembroke, bearing the sword of state in a gold scabbard loaded with pearls. Then came the serjeants-at-arms, surrounding the Queen. Her incandescent paleness appeared above a riding-habit of purple velvet. In the words even of a hostile critic, she was "a gallant and a gracious lady." Behind her, this time on a black horse, came Lord Robert Dudley.[1]

At fixed stages along the route, bursts of music greeted her; choirs of children poured their sweet, shrill notes, schoolboys stood forward to make orations. The Queen "accepted and noticed everything so gratefully", the people felt that not half enough had been done to welcome her; they threw themselves into a great personal demonstration, and then, as the procession reached Mark Lane, the Tower guns began to sound. The roar of cannon continuously discharging filled the narrow streets. It ceased as the Queen drew rein on Tower Hill.[2]

Below them, girdled by its curtain wall, the great fortress lay on the river strand, the pinnacles of the White Tower rising into the wintry air. Those in earshot around her heard her say that some had fallen from being princes of the land to being prisoners in that place. The ghosts of the Plantagenets rose thronging at her words. She herself, she said, had risen from being a prisoner there, to be a prince of the land. She ended: "Let me show myself to God thankful and to men merciful."

Inside the walls she gave herself a thrilling indulgence. She entered the Bell Tower, and mounting to the three-windowed room, she stood looking about her where she had last stood as a prisoner.

She remained a week in the State Apartments of the White Tower, holding councils daily. Before the court left Hatfield, the pressing problems confronting the government had been analysed and the work of resolving them had begun. A peace-treaty between France and Spain with her English ally was being discussed at Câteau-Cambrésis; a religious settlement had to be devised which would satisfy the Protestants without being more offensive to the Catholics than could be helped; three bad harvests had spread poverty and labour unrest; the coinage, which had been debased by Henry VIII, again under Edward VI and yet again by Mary, was now so worthless that trade was very seriously affected; above all there was a threat, distant as yet but already visible, more ominous than all the other troubles put together: on the death of Mary Tudor, Henri II of France had quartered the arms of England on the bearings of his son and his daughter-in-law, Mary, Queen of Scots.

[1] Nichols, *Progresses.*
[2] Hayward, *Annals of Elizabeth.*

These matters of extreme weight and urgency, as well as the minutiae of administration, meant that the Privy Council were sitting, day in, day out, and the Queen with them. From the first hours of the reign, and to Cecil's private knowledge, long before, she had shown herself to have the memory and penetration that goes with a mind of uncommon ability, and an inexhaustible interest in the theory and practice of government. The element she lacked was experience. Cecil had had practical experience in three reigns. Like a man riding some high-spirited horse whom he guides but without whom he cannot cover the ground, he was now advising and instructing the remarkable being, without whose signature he and his colleagues could, in the last resort, do nothing. The collaboration was the closest sort of professional relationship, the intense concentration on the common end made it at times even impersonal; but there was, about to be revealed, one serious discrepancy in which the personal factors were brought into spectacular prominence. Everyone assumed that the Queen's coronation would be followed speedily by the announcement of her marriage; and everyone regarded the potential alliance as of the greatest importance in the European balance of power. Feria said: "Everything depends on the husband this woman takes." But to Cecil, the marriage and the children of it were more than a matter of European importance; they were a guarantee of personal safety. He had trimmed successfully in Mary Tudor's reign; he would not be able to do so again. He had now committed himself. If this frail-looking young woman were to die without a child, a Catholic revival under Mary Stuart would mean not only his political eclipse but his execution.

It was taken for granted that this urgency, felt by the government, by all upholders of the Reformation and by everyone who shrank from the prospect of civil war, was felt no less acutely by the Queen. If the threat represented by Mary Stuart became a fact, the first victim would be Elizabeth herself. Her strongest defences would be a powerful husband and a male infant. It was fully believed that she would take steps to gain them as soon as possible.

Nor was it unreasonable for Philip to assume that Elizabeth would eagerly accept his hand and his great alliance if he offered it. His only doubt was whether he could make up his mind to the step. He was not personally averse from the match and it entailed some very useful advantages, but it was necessary to approach the matter with extreme circumspection. He told Feria to make it clear among other stipulations that if the marriage took place, Elizabeth must become a

Catholic, so that it would be seen that he was sacrificing himself for the sake of religion; and that it must be understood that he could spend very little time with her, "whether he left her pregnant or not".

Elizabeth received the Spanish approaches in a manner both sharp-tongued and evasive. On one occasion she seemed to be forestalling the comments Feria was about to make. She said she had been told that the King would marry her and go off to Spain immediately. Then she gave a peal of laughter. Feria's memorandum of the interview says: "It looks as if she had seen His Majesty's letter. This should be taken good note of." The suspicion was disconcerting; and her conduct in concealing her intentions in sparkling ambiguities, instead of snatching at the proposal, seemed to the Ambassador reckless, improper and extraordinary.

There was, in fact, something mysterious about her altogether. Her intellectual qualities were apparent to anyone who talked to her, her magnetism could be seen by anyone who watched a crowd that was watching her, and there was no mistaking, at close range, various regal characteristics. "She gives her orders and has her own way as absolutely as her father did," said Feria. But there were qualities, too, which were not immediately recognized. A belief in astrology and clairvoyance, though widely held at the time, was an unexpected trait in that clear and practical intelligence. Her Celtic ancestry had perhaps disposed her to it; at all events her Welsh associates had introduced her to it. Blanche Parry had a cousin, Dr. John Dee, of great cultivation. He had been a university lecturer in mathematics, he had tried to persuade Mary Tudor to found a Historical Manu-scripts Commission, he was a geographer, an astronomer and the promoter of an early system of shorthand. Though he had not qualified as a physician, he was greatly interested in medicine, and had noted in his travels that the medicinal herbs planted by the Romans were still growing along Hadrian's wall.[1] Dee was also an astrologer. He had drawn Elizabeth's horoscope during her sister's reign, and the result was, not surprisingly, a sentence of imprisonment from the Court of Star Chamber. The importance attached, by the Queen at least, to astrology, as well as to astronomy, is shown by her two astrolabes: the navigational astrolabe made for her by Geminus in 1559, a piece of exquisite craftsmanship with a gilt star-map showing 29 stars, and the beautiful astrological astrolabe,

[1] Transactions of the Radnor Society.

undated, but assumed to have been made for her from Dee's instructions.[1]

Elizabeth sent Lord Robert Dudley to Dee privately, to ask him to cast a date that would be fortunate for her Coronation. Dee chose Sunday, January 15, 1559, and the achievements of the reign appeared to justify the doctor's advice.

[1] *Archeologia*, 1937.

V

THE SATURDAY BEFORE the Coronation was the day of the recognition-procession through London, of very great importance when those who did not see the Queen with their own eyes could gain no idea of what she looked like. She had returned to the Tower the previous Thursday, and at two in the afternoon she set out from Tower Hill to make the journey through the streets to Westminster. Her retinue went before and behind her, and she herself was seated in a chariot draped with crimson velvet, over which four knights, walking beside it, held a canopy.

The English are fond of their sovereign and fond of a spectacle, and the miseries of the immediate past and the present hopes would have ensured considerable success for the occasion; to this was added the magical quality of the central figure. The crowds lining the streets broke into exclamations at the sight of her, "with prayers, welcoming cries and tender words".[1] Those within ear-shot heard her reply to them "in most tender language", those who could see her saw her gesture with her hands towards them. As she was borne along, some sixth sense told her when to halt. "How often stayed she her chariot when she saw some simple body approach to speak to her!" What they saw when they pressed up to the chariot was a straight and narrow figure in a cloth-of-gold dress, under a cloth-of-gold mantle with an ermine cape. From a gold circlet, limp strands of red-gold hair fell down, framing the delicacy and strangeness of an oval, pale face, a face with faint brows spanned like Norman arches, and heavy-lidded golden eyes, smiling at them.

The route was studded with pageants and demonstrations, of which children recited the meaning in verse. In Gracechurch Street, the shouts and cheers of the crowd drowned the child's voice: the Queen, halting her chariot, begged for silence and then sat listening attentively. In Cheapside her brilliant smile was remarked when a voice shouted: "Remember old King Harry the Eighth!" The governors and boys of Christ's Hospital met her, and one of the boys was put forward with a Latin speech, hailing the Queen as the saviour of the Reformation. While she listened she sat all the time with hands raised

[1] Holinshed.

and eyes looking up. The onlookers could watch the gold figure in its pose of edification like some image in a stained-glass window. At the Little Conduit there were the figures of an old man and a girl. The Queen asked who these were, and was told that they were Time and his daughter Truth. "Time!" she exclaimed, looking round on the sea of faces. "And Time hath brought me here!"

In the early dusk she arrived at Whitehall and was at last shut up from sight. The achievement of sustained responsiveness was over, the looking and listening and answering, going at a foot-pace along three crowded, tumultuous miles. The people had been prepared to welcome her: now they were wild about her. In all the action and excitement of the spectacle, two details had particularly struck the public imagination: the Queen's smile at her father's name, and the fact that a branch of rosemary a poor woman had put into her hand was still in her chariot when she came to Westminster Bridge.

The populace of London were wild with enthusiasm, but not so the Marian bishops. The reign was barely two months old, and a religious policy had not yet been announced, but the Privy Council had forbidden public preaching for the time being and sanctioned the reading of the Gospels and the Litany in English. This was enough; and though preparations for the Coronation had been made with services of gold and silver plate and the tapestries from Raphael's cartoons that had been bought by Henry VIII, there still lacked a bishop willing to put the crown on the Queen's head. At last Oglethorpe of Carlisle consented to do so; he never forgave himself and died shortly afterwards of a broken heart, but his co-operation was secured for the time.

A long carpet of purple cloth had been spread for the Queen to walk on into the Abbey. She came wearing a crimson velvet robe high to the throat with a small ermine cape and a crimson velvet cap on her head. The Earls of Shrewsbury and Pembroke walked each side of her, supporting her arms, and the Duchess of Norfolk carried the long train of her crimson mantle. As she entered the Abbey, prepared for the great ceremony with its constellations of wax lights, its incense, its pipers and drummers who were to augment the organ music, the crowd outside fell upon the purple carpet she had trodden and cut pieces from it.

When she had been anointed the Queen withdrew to a side-chapel and changed her crimson robes for the gold ones she had worn the day before. Her nose was always sensitive and she complained to the ladies who were re-robing her "that the oil was grease and smelt ill".[1]

In her gold robes the Queen was crowned with the Crown of St. Edward, the State Crown, and lastly with the beautiful little crown that had been made for her brother at nine years old: a wreath of pearls and diamonds with a large sapphire in front, and pearl hoops at whose intersection was mounted the great crimson gem, the Black Prince's ruby.[2] She was then presented to the people, with trumpets sounding, pipes and drums playing, the organ pealing, and in the towers above, bells ringing, "as if," said the Venetian Ambassador, "the world were coming to an end". When she had been dressed in a robe of purple velvet, she was led to the state banquet in Westminster Hall, and by three o'clock she had washed her hands and was sitting at table on the daïs under the vast window. Below her, four tables seated 200 persons each and a crowd of servitors attended, all dressed in red. The Earls of Arundel and Norfolk were in charge of the banquet and they rode about the hall on horseback. Lord William Howard and the Earl of Sussex stood one each side of the Queen and served her with everything she ate and drank. It was observed that she spoke very little; but at one point she thanked the Lords for their trouble about her Coronation and drank to them. As she raised the cup to her lips, the peers took off their coronets and the trumpets sounded.

The banquet was not over till after one in the morning. A joust had been arranged for the coming day but this was put off, for the Queen was exhausted. The fatigues of the Saturday and Sunday ended in a bad cold, and the opening of Parliament was postponed from January 23rd to the 25th.

The Queen came to the opening soon after 10 a.m., in her crimson robes with the small ermine cape, "a most marvellous pendant" round her neck and a small cap of gold and pearls on her head. In the streets, people cried: "God save and maintain thee!" and she smiled, saying, "god'a' mercy, good people!"[3] As she had been crowned according to Catholic rites, the government's policy was still in doubt, but one of the Queen's unrehearsed symbolic gestures gave a strong indication. The Abbot of Westminster met her with his monks holding lighted torches, and she exclaimed in carrying tones: "Away with those torches! We see very well."

Cecil's brother-in-law, Sir Nicholas Bacon, had been appointed

---

[1] Goodman, *Court of James I.*   [2] *Archeologia*, 1937.
[3] C.S.P. Venetian, 1559.

Lord Keeper of the Great Seal. In his opening speech he said how fortunate they were in "a princess to whom nothing—what, nothing? no, no worldly thing—was so dear as the hearty love and goodwill of her subjects".[1] The words were no oratorical flourish: they were literally true, and uttered as they were in the first Parliament, they expressed the one fact about a complex, paradoxical and mysterious character which, throughout a long reign, was never once in doubt.

The session's outstanding work, the evolving of the Religious Settlement in the Acts of Supremacy and Uniformity, was a feat of distinguished statecraft, the work of the Privy Council and both Houses of Parliament, but not only was its spirit of tolerance and moderation in key with the Queen's own attitude (she said she wished to open no window into men's consciences), but the Act of Uniformity contained a sign of her own handiwork. The Act of Supremacy defined the Queen's title as Supreme Governor, not Supreme Head of the Church, and was for the time unusually lenient in its provisions. It was to be administered only to those holding spiritual or temporal office under the Crown, and though to attack it was made treason the penalty was incurred only for the third offence. The Act of Uniformity restored the First Prayer-Book of Edward VI, but with two alterations meant to conciliate the Catholics: one was the putting together of two lines from the First and Second of Edward VI's Prayer-Books, so that the Communion service could be used both by those who believed in the Real Presence and those who regarded the rite as a commemoration; the other was the Queen's own handiwork. The Litany of the First Prayer Book had prayed: "From the Bishop of Rome and his detestable enormities, Good Lord, deliver us." The Queen removed this aspiration. She also crossed out "Roman Catholics" from the clause praying for the conversion of Jews and infidels.

The question next in importance with which the session dealt was the Queen's marriage and child-bearing. The urgency of this was underlined by a note in Cecil's diary:

"On January 16, 1559, the Dauphin of France and the Queen of Scots his wife did, by the style and title of King & Queen of England and Ireland, grant to Lord Fleming certain things."

From the hour of Mary Tudor's death, Mary Stuart and her supporters considered, not that she ought to be Queen of England, but

[1] Neale, *Elizabeth and her Parliaments*, I.

that she was. The English Catholics who could not admit that Elizabeth's birth was legitimate or that succession could be settled by law, must always think that Mary Stuart's claim was superior to Elizabeth's; but large numbers of them were willing to be loyal to Elizabeth, provided that some concessions were made to them and, above all, provided that her government was a success. The Catholics were as English as the Protestants and they, no less than the Protestants, wanted to see the ruinous incompetence and neglect of the last two reigns repaired as quickly as they might.

The Queen wanted leniency and toleration used: "Let it not be said that *our* reformation tendeth to cruelty," she said, and of the large proportion of the nation who were Catholics (estimated at something near half), the majority were prepared to be loyal, but she and they were the victims of an enormous European combination which was waiting to overpower England as a bastion of the Reformation. In the struggle the political and economic factors were to prove inseparable from the religious. Philip was determined to reduce the wealthy Netherlands, in the name of Catholicism. France was determined to gain control first of Scotland, then of England, in the name of Catholicism. In Mary Stuart's cause, the French might pour into Scotland and thence over the Border, where in the northern shires, the great Catholic families had still their almost feudal powers; they might gain control of half England in a week—and then Spain would rouse. Scotland and England in French hands would be intolerable to the Hapsburgs. Spanish forces from the Netherlands would land on the south coast, and the miseries which the English had endured in the Wars of the Roses would be as nothing to their fate while French and Spanish soldiers fought a savage war for the possession of English soil. It is no wonder that among the prayers for mercy on travellers by land and water, women labouring of child, sick persons and young children, and prisoners and captives everywhere, the Litany also prays:

"From sedition, privy conspiracy and rebellion . . . good Lord, deliver us."

The sum of these possibilities was that the Queen and her government had no margin for error. They must start to consolidate their position immediately, and the Queen's marriage, as a means of defensive alliance and the establishment of the succession, was in everybody's mouth.

As a Princess, Elizabeth had shown invariable resistance to the idea of marriage, and she maintained the attitude now. To a parliamentary deputation who waited on her in the Great Gallery at Whitehall on February 6, and begged her to set about marrying, she replied that she would act as God directed her. If God directed her not to marry, no doubt He would provide for the succession in other ways. From a long, delicate finger, she withdrew the Coronation ring, and holding it up to them, she said: "I am already bound unto a husband, which is the Kingdom of England." As for her own wishes, it would be enough "if a marble stone should hereafter declare that a Queen, having reigned such a time, lived and died a virgin". The words, so early spoken, have a strange air of prophecy.

Her objections to marriage were varied and enclosed one within another like a Chinese puzzle, the innermost of all containing the secret mystery; but the outer circles were legible enough. To marry and establish the succession would take away at once her immense importance as a matrimonial catch for the crowned heads of Europe, and though a strong alliance would bring great advantages it would deprive her of an invaluable diplomatic weapon. It would also alter the character of that intense loyalty and solicitude that was centred upon her by men who knew that her single life stood between them and disaster.

Then, too, in the first delicious exhilaration of freedom and power, many could see that she repudiated the idea of a yoke. Marriage up till now had always been spoken of as a means of curtailing her. Northumberland had looked out for suitors whose obscurity might extinguish her. The Emperor had been advised that "to marry her to some poor German prince would be the safest way to dispose of her", while Rénaud had said that it would be dangerous to recognize her as Mary's heir "without providing her with a husband who could control her". Young, slight, pale and also aquiline, spirited and haughty, she struck those who saw her at close quarters, giving her orders "as absolutely as her father", as a woman with a genius for authority who thoroughly enjoyed the exercise of power. Sir James Melville put the impression in a nutshell. The Queen had been telling him that she did not intend to marry unless she were driven to it— "I know the truth of that, Madam," exclaimed the Scotsman, "you need not tell me. Your Majesty thinks that if you were married you would be but Queen of England, and now you are both King and Queen. I know your spirit cannot endure a commander."

Melville thought that he knew something else. He had been asked to deliver a proposal to the Queen of England from the Duke

Casimir, the son of the Elector Palatine, but he had declined the commission. "I had ground to conjecture that she would never marry," he said, "because of that story one of the gentlemen of her chamber told me." Melville supposed that, "knowing herself incapable of children, she would never render herself subject to any man". This gossip was rife between 1559 and 1561. Feria wrote to Philip II, "for a reason they have given me, I understand she will not bear children", and his successor de Quadra reported: "It is the common opinion, confirmed by certain physicians, that this woman is unhealthy and it is believed that she will not bear children." However discreet the ladies in attendance on the Queen, the fact that she had very few monthly periods could not but be known to laundresses, and it was beyond possibility to keep it secret in a large household. It was stated widely, if cautiously, that the frequent bleedings to which the Queen was subjected were meant to repair this deficiency. In June 1559, the Venetian Ambassador said, "Before leaving London, Her Majesty was blooded from one foot and from one arm, but what her indisposition is, is not known. Many persons say things I should not dare to write, but they say that on arriving at Greenwich she was as cheerful as ever she was."

The doctors as a body had not made up their minds as to whether this symptom meant infertility. On two later occasions the official medical opinion was given that the Queen might be expected to bear children; and indeed, another consideration altogether caused great apprehension to the men whose personal safety depended on the life of this young woman. The prayers printed in *The Monument of Matrons*, "in long and dangerous travail of child, to be used by the woman herself or the women about her", with the despairing entreaty: "Wilt Thou not bring forth that which Thou hast formed?", are a grim reminder of how little even the skilful doctor and midwife could then do. Grave anxiety was felt for any first confinement: for the Queen's, the apprehension would be fearful. Yet the mere fact that mothers did survive this ordeal, required rational recognition, and Sir Thomas Smith threw the pros and cons into a dialogue, in which Wedspite declared: "Her Grace should never enter into that danger and battle, wherein she herself, hand to hand without aid, must fight with Death himself a more perilous fight than any set battle"; while his opponent argued: "So many fair ladies, so goodly gentlewomen, so fine and trim maids, pass these pikes so well . . . so easily, so merrily, so quietly in their fine beds of down . . . and after it look so fair and ruddy and so beautiful that it would make any man in the world enamoured of them", to say nothing of "what haste they make to go to the battle again".[1]

Cecil, despite his ceaseless anxiety and care, always took the view that Elizabeth could and should bear a child. In drawing up a memorandum of arguments for and against a marriage, against the peril of childbirth he wrote merely: "In God's hands." But his attitude on other matters was one of clinical precaution. He prepared a memorandum of "Certain cautions for the Queen's apparel and diet". This urged her to eat nothing that had not been prepared in the royal kitchens without its being vouched for, to use no scent given by a stranger, either in the shape of perfume or of scented gloves; while to avoid the danger of irritant poisons on the skin, "we think it very convenient that all manner of things that shall touch any part of your Majesty's body bare, be circumspectly looked unto", and doors should not stand open to all comers where the Queen's laundresses and wardrobe-women did their work.[2]

In the personal sphere Cecil and his colleagues had another anxiety. In March the King of Spain's proposals were transferred to Catherine de Medici's beautiful daughter Elizabeth of Valois, and Philip's nephew the Archduke Charles was put forward as a match for the Queen, but by April it was a matter of public comment that she and Lord Robert Dudley were inseparable. Feria wrote on April 18: "During the last few days Lord Robert has come so much into favour that he does whatever he likes with affairs and it is even said that Her Majesty visits him in his chamber day and night." Feria had heard say that Lady Dudley had a growth in one of her breasts and that her husband was only waiting for her death to marry the Queen.

At the end of May an embassy arrived from France to receive the Queen's ratification of the treaty of Câteau-Cambrésis, and at this, the first great social occasion of the reign after the Coronation, the young Queen appeared in gaiety and exultation. On an evening at the end of May, the ambassadors were entertained at supper in the garden of Whitehall, in a brief interlude of lyrical beauty. The piazza under the Long Gallery was draped with gold and silver brocade, and the side open to the air hung with wreaths and garlands of fresh flowers diffusing an exquisite scent. At six o'clock the guests were received by the Queen, "dressed entirely in purple velvet, with so much gold and so many pearls and jewels, it added very much to her beauty". She gave a hand each to Monsieur de Vielleville and

[1] Strype, *Sir Thomas Smith*.   [2] Haynes.

Monsieur de Montmorenci, and walked up and down with them in the private orchard for an hour while supper was preparing. It was her evening: speaking to them in French, she told her courteous and gallant listeners of her troubles in her sister's reign, and how she would have been put to death but for the love the people bore her. Her carrying tones reached those standing at a distance. When the trumpets sounded to announce supper-time, the Queen entered the piazza by a door made entirely of roses and their leaves. Her own small table where the ambassadors sat with her was set at right angles to the rest, and flanked by two gleaming displays of drinking cups, all of gold or rock crystal.

The farthingales of the ladies took up so much space that some ladies of the Privy Chamber sat on the rushes of the floor, while various gentlemen waited on them with great good will. After the meal the tables were removed and the company danced till eleven o'clock. At the departure of the ambassadors, splendid presents were made to them, of horses and hounds and gold and silver-gilt plate; while to the young brother of Monsieur de Montmorenci, the Queen gave some of the rich clothes that had belonged to Edward VI.[1]

[1] C.S.P. Venetian, 1559.

VI

THE QUEEN'S SUITORS now included Prince Charles of Sweden, the Duke of Saxony and the Archduke Charles; but the talk was all of Lord Robert Dudley. It was widely supposed that the Queen was his mistress. Bishop Quadra, who had replaced Feria at the Spanish Embassy, wrote to the latter: "I have heard great things of a sort that cannot be written about and you will understand what they must be by that." Sir Thomas Challoner was dismayed by reports that reached him at the Imperial Court. He considered them mere slander, but, he said, "so young a Princess cannot be too wary what countenance or familiar demonstration she makes more to one than another". Above all, what distressed him was this "delay of ripe time for marriage"; he saw no safety for the realm without heirs of the Queen's body.

This anxiety that was alternately to glow and dwindle for the next twenty years was now fanned by the march of affairs in Scotland. The Catholic Mary of Guise, Queen Regent for her daughter the Queen of Scots, was almost overborne by the Reforming Party, who called themselves Lords of the Congregation. The latter were determined to secure the Protestant religion and to oust the French. On the brink of open rebellion, they asked Elizabeth to help them. The chance to clear the French out of Scotland was extremely tempting; but open hostilities might result in a French invasion of England. Elizabeth sent money to pay the rebel army, but when, in October, the Scots Lords deposed the Queen Regent, and the Privy Council with Cecil at their head urged open intervention, Elizabeth hung back. Her native caution, which had been increased by two near escapes from death, had come to the pass at which it had sometimes the effect of paralysis. She had begun to reign so straitened for men, ships, money, that to her mind almost anything was to be preferred to the risk of loss. There was not a soldier or a shilling to spare: the idea of being forced to expend either was an agony. To wait and see how things fell out, how others would commit themselves, and then to intervene at the last possible moment, was her method all her life, and it was fully developed in the first year of her reign.

Cecil was cautious, but his caution had not the neurotic quality of

Elizabeth's. He knew that poor as the kingdom was, the risk of financial loss must be balanced against the perils of inaction. The Queen's refusal to unclose her hand drove him to the last resort. In December he addressed a minute to her, saying that if she would not permit open intervention in Scotland, he must retire from the government. He could not, he said, "serve Your Majesty in anything that myself cannot allow". He would occupy himself cheerfully in her kitchen, or her garden, and there do her commandments to his life's end, but as a minister he could go no farther. The upshot was that at the end of the month the Queen allowed Admiral Winter to take fourteen ships up to the Firth of Forth with orders to destroy any French shipping that was bringing reinforcements to Leith. On January 23, Winter entered the Firth and destroyed ships of munition and supplies, and this naval success was followed by a great disaster to the French fleet from stormy weather. Encouraged by this Elizabeth allowed an English army to cross the Border in March. It was severely defeated by the French outside Leith, and Elizabeth, while ordering reinforcements with furious energy, at the same time rounded on Cecil for having urged intervention in the first place. He wrote to Sir Thomas Throckmorton: "I have had such a torment herein with the Queen's Majesty, as an ague hath not in five fits so much abated."[1]

But fortune favoured the English. The Queen Regent was dying and the French had their hands full with conspiracy at home. In June they sent to treat and in July Cecil went north to arrange the Treaty of Edinburgh. Throckmorton, who had already had more experience of the Queen's method than he cared for, saw his colleague depart with misgiving: "Who can as well stand fast against the Queen's doubtful devices? Who shall make despatch of anything?" Cecil, however, was obliged to leave them to get on as best they could. His work on the treaty was a masterpiece, and while it secured favourable terms for the Scots Reformers, it gained three points of major importance for the English: Francis and Mary were to relinquish the Royal Arms of England, Elizabeth's title was to be recognized, and the French forces were to be withdrawn from Scotland. It was assumed that the next step would be the ratification of the treaty made on her behalf by Mary Queen of Scots; but Mary refused to ratify a treaty which renounced her own title as Queen of England and recognized that of Elizabeth. She had not ratified it when, twenty-seven years later, she went to the block.

[1] Conyers Read, *Mr. Secretary Cecil and Queen Elizabeth*.

The French government, however, accepted it, and the prestige of England soared. Sir Thomas Gresham, the financier, was in the Netherlands on transactions to repair the credit of the English Crown, and he saw the effects of the victory on the money-market. Gresham had a keen professional admiration for the Queen's financial sense, and his loyalty and affection were transfused with it. Giving her the credit for the Treaty of Edinburgh, he exclaimed that she had made the proudest Prince in all Christendom to stoop to that noble carcase of hers! The work had been Cecil's and she had, if anything, obstructed it; but it was inevitable that she was now hailed as the brilliant symbol of the nation's success.

Cecil wanted to secure the allegiance of certain Scots Lords by cash payments. He guaranteed "with £1,000 now, to save £20,000 in five years". The soundness of his judgment was not questioned, but saving money in the teeth of great expenses is only done by relentless, fanatical determination. There were many excellent reasons for spending money and this was one, but to Elizabeth none was as important as saving it. She had more than a merely feminine talent for economy. Henry VII had not transmitted his financial genius to Henry VIII, nor to his grandchildren, Mary and Edward; but this one grand-daughter had inherited it. Elizabeth knew that solvency was power. She was surrounded by able men who believed the maxim, but none of them, except Gresham, held it with her burning conviction. The financial situation of the Crown was one on which the sovereign could exert a direct influence. All the expenses of the government and the court had to be met from the sovereign's personal revenues. Subsidies were granted by Parliament only for extraordinary expenses. Elizabeth's personal management of her finances, down to the very details of the household bills, had an immediate bearing upon the independence, and therefore the power, of the Crown. In the last half-year before her death, Mary Tudor had spent £267,000; Elizabeth's expenses for the first half-year of her reign had been reduced to £108,000.[1] Besides using rigid economy in her own spending, she encouraged the giving of presents and of hospitality to herself. The lavish gifts of clothes and jewellery given to her on New Year's Day, the maintenance of herself and her retinue by the noblemen in whose houses she stayed: they were demonstrations of loyalty, of affection, they were bids for Royal favour, they were benefits the Queen relished with a keen acquisitive delight; but they were also part of a financial policy that was the basis

[1] Pollard.

of her success. The lengths to which she pursued financial caution had indeed sometimes an epic character. She told Cecil on his return that considering the amount of money she had been obliged to spend on the Scots campaign, she ought to have had some recompense by the treaty. Why had he not got Calais back from the French? As it was, he would have to pay his own expenses for the Scottish journey; that the Crown should do it was out of the question. Cecil, with the resignation of despair, told his friends that he would be ruined. It seemed a plausible complaint, but the great houses of Theobalds and Stamford Burleigh did not finally bear it out.

An enterprise in which the Queen ardently participated was the reform of the currency, in this year, as Camden says, "brought happily to a pass in a few months without making any stay". Perhaps nothing did more to gain the public confidence. The system adopted had been worked out by Sir Thomas Stanley, but many methods had been proposed, among them one of Elizabeth's own, which Cecil endorsed: "Opinion of her Majesty for reducing the state of the coin." Nor did she stop at theoretical considerations. A minute remains from the Marquess of Winchester and Sir Thomas Sackville, thanking Cecil and Parry "for removing from the Queen's mind that they had deceived her in the coinage".[1]

The Queen had made an excellent beginning but those nearest to her who wished to gaze upon her with approval found their vision blocked by Lord Robert Dudley.

Protective and adoring, the Master of the Horse fulfilled his office thoroughly to the Queen's satisfaction. He wrote to the Earl of Sussex in Ireland that the Queen would like some Irish horses sent over, thinking that they might go faster than hers, "which," he said, "she spareth not to try as fast as they can go. And I fear them much, yet she will prove them."[2] But to the anxious councillors the satisfaction he gave to the Queen was far too great. In their view it accounted for her disinclination to marry, and her marriage was an object they desired with increasing fervour. During the negotiations in Scotland Cecil had written to her, praying that "God would direct your Highness to procure a father for your children . . . neither peace nor war without this will profit us long", and all the answer the Queen had made was to reject the Scots' offer of the hand of the Earl of Arran. The Queen's youth and her glamorous appearance, and the fact that Dudley's young wife was living apart from her

[1] C.S.P. Domestic, Elizabeth XIV, 13.
[2] British Museum, Cotton MSS. Titus B xiii, f. 15.

husband, gave their intimacy a scandalous air. Amy Dudley had no children and no proper establishment of her own; she and her servants occupied part of a house at Cumnor, near Oxford, belonging to a man called Forster, who had been Lord Robert's steward. The house, isolated among fields and orchards, had originally been part of a monastery. Horse-transport and bad roads made every rural district secluded and remote, but a surprising number of people knew about Lady Dudley in her lonely situation. Then they heard that on September 8, a Sunday, she had been found at the bottom of a staircase with her neck broken.

The scandal was appalling. In France, Mary Stuart said with a ringing laugh: "The Queen of England is going to marry her horse-keeper, who has killed his wife to make room for her." Throckmorton, the Ambassador at Paris, wrote to Cecil: "I know not where to turn me, or what countenance to make."

Elizabeth sent Lord Robert away from Windsor at once, and he himself wrote begging his cousin Blount to go to Cumnor to take charge of everything: "The greatness, and suddenness of this misfortune doth so perplex me, until I do hear from you how the matter stands or how this evil doth light upon me, considering what the malicious world will bruit, as I can take no rest."[1] He urged Blount to make sure that the coroner's jury were "discreet and substantial persons", who would sift the matter to the bottom.

The verdict at the inquest was accidental death, but in the general opinion it should have been murder, either at Dudley's instigation, or without his connivance but in his interest. The question, all-important though hardly to be framed, was whether the Queen had been accessory before the fact.

De Quadra told Philip that the Queen had said to him as she came in from hunting that Lady Dudley had fallen down a staircase and broken her neck, and asked him to say nothing about it. He made out that the Queen had said this before the news of the death was brought to Windsor on the 9th. Had Elizabeth connived at the murder, it may be safely asserted that she would not have been so grossly stupid as to tell de Quadra the death had occurred, before she was supposed to know that it had. The explanation, suggested by Maitland and also by Pollard, is that de Quadra here employed "a deft economy of dates". Nor can it be taken for granted that Elizabeth wanted Amy Dudley out of the way. She wanted an engrossing romantic relationship with Robert Dudley; there is no proof that she wanted a mar-

[1] Mumby, *Elizabeth and Mary Stuart.*

riage with him, only that other people supposed she wanted it. If she did not want the marriage, the death was for her an untoward event; now that it could be expected to end in a marriage, her delicious amusement was brought into the realm of state affairs.

When the news was known, Elizabeth had dismissed Lord Robert from the court with orders not to show himself there again till his wife was buried. A few weeks after the funeral, however, he returned; and Elizabeth had now to face the position that if she went on with the liaison she would be expected to marry her lover. The fear that she might, as Throckmorton put it, "so foully forget herself", made the Ambassador say that if that day came, he himself would not wish to live. Indeed, the prospect of her wedding to Robert Dudley aroused general abhorrence. He was the son of a traitor, he was suspected of wife-murder, it was believed that he had dishonoured the Queen already; all those sound reasons reinforced the inevitable ones of envy and jealousy. Yet there was one voice prepared to speak in his favour, that of Sussex, whose chivalry towards Elizabeth was pure, tender and constant. He disliked Dudley to such an extent that their relationship was almost a standing quarrel, but he wrote to Cecil in October, saying that they were all agreed that a child of the Queen's body was their greatest necessity. Therefore, said Sussex, let her choose after her own affection, let her take the man at sight of whom all her being was aroused in desire; for that was the way to bring them a blessed Prince, and, he affirmed, "whomsoever she will choose, him will I love and honour and serve to the uttermost".

Whatever feelings were aroused at the idea of Robert Dudley's wearing the Crown Matrimonial, it was taken for granted that the Queen must want him for her husband. The only question seemed to be, how far she would let I dare not wait upon I would. It was not yet realized how keenly, how exquisitely Elizabeth enjoyed conducting courtships and marriage negotiations which she never intended to complete. The series of brilliant diplomatic manoeuvres involving marriage-alliances with the princes of the House of Valois, which were to be so invaluable for the next twenty years, carried conviction while they lasted because it was plain that the Queen enjoyed every moment of them. To be the object of public and magnificent courtship, with ambassadors, letters and presents, to be intensely desired in marriage, for whatever reason, was to her a fascinating, an absorbing diversion. To talk of love, to talk of marriage, above all, to listen while someone talked, or was talked of, as wanting to marry her, gave her an exhilaration that was the keener because such feelings had to do duty for others that had been put to death. But when she came to the edge of the precipice, and it looked as if she might have to endure a hard struggle to avoid being pushed over it, then nervous strain began to show itself. Sir Nicholas Throckmorton at Paris had sent his secretary Jones to the Queen, to tell her, among other things, what the French view was of the rumours about Dudley. Jones reported on November 30: "The Queen's Majesty looketh not so hearty and well as she did by a great deal, and surely the matter of my Lord Robert doth much perplex her and is never like to take place."

The strange state of mind was the harder to recognize in connection with Robert Dudley because his presence, his love-making, his mere name mentioned in conversation, gave her such obvious delight. Therefore when, early in 1561, Sir Henry Sidney approached de Quadra with a secret proposal that the King of Spain should give his support to the marriage of the Queen with Lord Robert Dudley, in return for Elizabeth's restoring Catholicism as the national religion, it seemed, even to de Quadra's intelligent mind, a plausible proposition. Sir Henry Sidney was the husband of Dudley's sister Mary; there was no doubt that he and Dudley were eager for the scheme, and there seemed on the face of it no reason to doubt that the Queen's wishes were the same as theirs. The Ambassador sent Philip a detailed account of a conversation with the Queen, in which Elizabeth had said that she had indeed some affection for Lord Robert, but had never decided to marry him, or anybody else. Nevertheless, de Quadra believed, from her avid enjoyment in talking of the matter, that she was prepared to make the match, and on the conditions proposed. To all of which Philip merely replied: "Get it in writing, with her signature."

On Midsummer Day, Lord Robert gave a water-party on the Thames. As he, the Queen and de Quadra were all together on deck, Lord Robert, who was talking amorous nonsense to the Queen, exclaimed that the Bishop might as well marry them then and there. Elizabeth said she doubted if he knew enough English to perform the ceremony. De Quadra interposed gravely. He said, let the Queen first free herself of Cecil and his gang of heretics; she could then do as she pleased, and he himself would gladly be the priest to marry her and Lord Robert. This brilliant scene on the midsummer Thames, with Lord Robert as the eager, almost assured lover of the Queen, appeared decisive from the political standpoint. That it was, in itself, intensely enjoyable, and that since a marriage negotiation with Philip was no longer possible, one with his protégé was, diplomatically, of almost equal value, appeared to strike nobody. The general view was that the Queen was being carried away by her feelings to a marriage that would be catastrophic.

The urgent wish that Elizabeth should not make a ruinous marriage was paralleled by the anxiety that she should make a good one and as soon as possible. The pressure upon her to do this now received a sudden and painful impetus.

If Elizabeth died without heirs, her successor by Henry VIII's will was Catherine, the elder of the two surviving sisters of Jane Grey. This young woman was nineteen years old. Though gentle and feminine she had a strong sense of her own importance; she was easily influenced by anyone who paid her attention and easily offended by the appearance of a slight. Emotional and lacking in common sense, she was fated, in her dangerous situation, to be both a nuisance and a victim.

Elizabeth's experience of how the heir is courted at the expense of the reigning monarch had made her determine never to recognize a successor. The lesson had been seared into her memory and it was acted upon with all the force of her intellect. But Catherine Grey cared nothing for this; she resented the fact that Elizabeth had not at once accorded her the position of heiress-presumptive to the Crown. Feria had found that she was "discontented and offended" because she had not been given this official status. The mere fact that she claimed it should have taught Catherine Grey to behave with the utmost discretion. It was generally understood that royal blood con-ferred a condition like that of hæmophilia, in which one reckless contact might result in death. In Catherine's own family the truth had been driven home with shocking force. Her sister Jane at four-teen had been one of the most renowned young ladies in Protestant Europe; at sixteen she was a headless corpse. But Catherine under-stood her situation only in terms of how other people should behave to her; she had no idea of what it demanded of herself. To her, Elizabeth was merely her disagreeable cousin who had once been obliged to walk out of the room after Catherine's mother. She was heard to speak "very arrogant and unseemly words in the presence of the Queen". Feria saw that, married to the Archduke, or to Don Carlos, this sprig of the English Royal stem would be a valuable Spanish asset. He cultivated her closely, but no move was made, and when de Quadra replaced him, the latter reported that "the Queen was making much of Lady Catherine to keep her quiet".

The Duchess of Suffolk was in her last illness, and with disastrous irresponsibility she encouraged a clandestine courtship between Catherine and the young Earl of Hertford, son of the late Protector Somerset. Hertford's sister, Lady Jane Seymour, a charming but delicate girl, was one of Elizabeth's favourite Maids of Honour; she was also Catherine Grey's best friend, and as Lord Hertford's dilatory and languid courtship caused Catherine much jealous misery, he was brought up to scratch by his frail but energetic sister. The wedding took place secretly in the winter of 1560, in Hertford's lodging. The clergyman whom Lady Jane had fetched in was unknown by name to the bride or bridegroom, and she herself was the sole witness.

In the following March this resolute girl died suddenly, and the Queen, much distressed, ordered her a state funeral in Westminster Abbey. Soon afterwards Hertford was appointed to go to France. He made no move to avoid the mission, but before he disappeared, he gave his wife a deed of jointure, settling on her £1,000 a year. This document was not only her sole claim to her husband's support; as the clergyman was unknown and the single witness dead, it was the one and only proof that the marriage had taken place. It is hardly necessary to say what happened: Lady Catherine lost the deed, so completely that she never afterwards "knew where it was become".[1] This was the lady who was eager to take over the cares of government from Queen Elizabeth.

It was August and the Queen was going on a progress through Suffolk and Norfolk. She had the look of someone greatly oppressed; so pale was she, it was said, "she looked like one lately come out of childbed".[2] The question of marriage, pressing heavily on her, sharpened her irritation at the sights which met her at Ipswich and Norwich, of the squalid and disordered state to which wives and children had reduced the Cathedral and college precincts. On progress as she was, the Queen at once wrote out an ordinance and sent copies of it for publication to the Archbishops of Canterbury and York, forbidding the presence of women in cathedral or college lodgings; it was an interruption of studies, she said, and contrary to the intentions of the founders.

Matthew Parker, Archbishop of Canterbury, had once been chaplain to Ann Boleyn. Scholarly, grave, gentle and courageous, he had hoped to spend the rest of his life in a university. To be the Primate of England was the last thing he himself would have chosen. Elizabeth, with her remarkable insight in making appointments, offered

[1] Haynes.   [2] C.S.P. Domestic Addenda, 1601-3.

him the See of Canterbury, and when he declined it, she positively refused to take no for an answer. When Dr. Parker at last submitted, he told Cecil that one of the considerations which influenced him was that he could never forget what Ann Boleyn had said to him about her child, six weeks before her own death.[1] He did not say what the words had been, but his tenderness for Elizabeth was obvious, in spite of the disapproval of some of her doings which, as he saw occasion, he courageously expressed. Elizabeth treated him with the bad behaviour of a spoilt and irritable girl who knows she may say what she likes to an old friend of the family. She told him this summer that she disapproved of married bishops and wished she had not appointed any. Dr. Parker, a married man, did not say that he wished she had thought of this before she insisted on appointing him, but he gently reminded her that the idea of a celibate clergy was a Catholic, not a Protestant one; whereupon the Queen's self-control gave way. "She took occasion to speak in that bitterness of the holy estate of matrimony . . ." that the Archbishop in his own words to Cecil, "was in a horror to hear her".[2] In this frame of mind, Elizabeth was visiting the great houses of Suffolk, with Lord Robert Dudley in attendance and Lady Catherine Grey among the ladies-in-waiting.

The latter was now in miserable plight; she was pregnant, her mother was dead and she could get no word from her husband in France, though other ladies had received presents from him. While the Court was at Ipswich, she decided to make her case known to Lady Saintlow, a brisk matron who after several profitable marriages became known as the redoubtable Bess of Hardwick. Lady Saint-low's response was to call down curses on the wretched girl for making her party to such a secret. Lady Catherine's next bestowal of her confidence was even more unwelcome. At dead of night she glided to the bed-chamber of her dead sister's brother-in-law, Lord Robert Dudley, and poured out at his bedside the story of her deplorable mishaps. The possibility of the Queen's hearing of a woman in his bedroom electrified Lord Robert; he obliged Lady Catherine to remove herself, and the next morning he told Elizabeth the facts.

The mere unfounded suspicion of a secret marriage had once brought Elizabeth herself into extreme peril, so gravely was such an act regarded in anyone who claimed to be in succession to the throne. That Lady Catherine should be removed that afternoon from Ipswich to the Tower, and Lord Hertford sent for, was a matter of course.

[1] Strype: *Parker*.   [2] *ibid.*

But Elizabeth's fury had another source beside the uncovering of potential treason. She had been urged by the Privy Council and by Parliament to marry and become a mother, and this was the thing she could neither face nor bring herself to say she could not do. It remained to be seen whether her brilliance, her dedication, her hold on the public imagination would outweigh the lack of the one, primitive, essential service of bearing a child. Meanwhile, the heiress-presumptive was bearing one.

That August another submerged peril rose into sight in alarming proximity. The husband of Mary Queen of Scots was dead, and there was no future for the young widow in France, where her hostile step-mother Catherine de Medici was now Regent for the boy Charles IX. Mary determined to return to Scotland, and her request for a passport to come through England had been refused because she herself had refused to ratify the Treaty of Edinburgh. "You see," said the English Ambassador, "such as be noted usurpers of other folks' states, cannot patiently be borne withal for such doings."[1] Mary had replied innocently that all this was not her fault; the treaty had been made by other people. She could not be expected to ratify it until she got back to Scotland and consulted her nobles—those nobles who, on her behalf, had agreed to the treaty in the first place. This, her first appearance on the English political scene, was entirely in character: soft, bright, bewitching, full of sweetness, with gracious manners polished by an exquisite education, deceitful but convinced that whatever she did was right, and that in all calamities she was the only sufferer. To disaffected Catholics, she was the hope of a Catholic revival; to loyal Catholics, she was, in theory at least, the Queen of England. On August 19 she arrived at Leith. Before, the Channel had lain between Elizabeth and her. Now she was on the other side of Hadrian's wall.

The situation was full of menace: its potentialities were understood, but no one could foretell which of them would develop. Yet, intricate and perilous as the game was, Elizabeth knew, in the last resort, that she had the ability to play it; that in spite of fears and miseries and the threats of nervous collapse, she was equal to the task, the task that was her passion. The Venetian envoy Surian said of her in this same year: "Queen Elizabeth, who has succeeded to the throne owing to her courage and to her great power of mind . . . declines to rely on anyone save herself, though she is most gracious to all."

[1] *Cabala*, III.

Mary Queen of Scots had been escorted to her kingdom by her uncle the Grand Prior and by the Constable of France, and that the refusal of a passport to the Queen of Scotland should not be construed as an affront to the French, these nobles were entertained at Greenwich with high ceremony and cordiality on their return journey in September. One of the great chambers in the Palace was hung with a famous set of tapestries depicting the wise and foolish virgins, and here there was danced, for the guests' entertainment, a ballet which the Queen had devised for her Maids of Honour, whom she had dressed after the fashion of the virgins in the tapestry. The girls carried silver lamps, some lit and others empty. Brantôme, who was in the Grand Prior's train, recalled the scene in his old age. Elizabeth, who was then, he said, both beautiful and elegant, herself danced with the guests, with a graceful dignity he never forgot,[1] but neither he nor anyone else appeared to notice the significance of the scene, as the Queen, who had been born in September under the zodiacal sign of Virgo, and on the eve of the Feast of the Nativity of the Virgin, danced gracefully among her virgins in the Chamber of the Virgins.

[1] Brantôme, *Lives of Famous Women.*

VII

THE ABILITY ELIZABETH showed in choosing men was uncommon, as uncommon as Mary's lack of it. Not only did the latter choose as favourites, confidantes, husbands, men who contributed largely to her ruin; when a man was before her who could have saved her, she fell out with him. Her base-born brother Lord James Stuart, Earl of Murray, was a strong Protestant but ready to help his sister, and he would have made an invaluable link between her and the Reformed Party whose hair was on end lest the Queen should succeed in destroying them. That she should have antagonized and at last completely alienated Murray illustrates Von Raumer's comment that Mary combined a lust for power with the utmost incapacity for ruling. She had always a certain body of Catholic supporters in Scotland, and those who saw her, of whatever party, were apt to be melted by her loveliness and charm; but she made no appeal to the Scots nation as a whole, and this was not due merely to the fact that they were Protestants who feared a Catholic tyranny, or that many Presbyterians were neurotic savages who were afraid of gaiety and fine clothes. The difference between Mary and Elizabeth was summed up in their attitude to their own kingdoms. Mary never troubled to conceal the fact that her ambition was to gain the throne of England; and to compass this, she was ready to submit Scotland to invasion by French or Spanish soldiers and to destroy the Scottish Reformation. When Sir Thomas Randolph, the English Ambassador at Holyrood, explained to her that Elizabeth would not name Mary as her successor until Elizabeth herself were married or had finally decided not to marry, Mary said bitterly that for the present she would content herself with her small portion, by which she meant her kingdom of Scotland and the Isles, and when better should come, by which she meant England, then she would give God thanks for it but nobody else. Elizabeth would never have spoken of a kingdom of hers in such slighting and contemptuous terms. Had she been Queen of Scotland, the Scots would have known that they had a Queen who was as proud of them as they were proud of themselves.

Mary had two schemes in consideration, one open, one secret, to get the English Crown. One was by ceaseless demands, entreaties and bargainings, to make Elizabeth and the English Parliament give her official recognition as Elizabeth's heir; with this the Scots were naturally in sympathy. The one secretly pursued was to make a marriage alliance with a Catholic power; this, with the presumed assistance of the English Catholics, would lead to a revolution in England on her behalf and get the Crown for her by force. This method would inevitably mean the murder of Elizabeth, and it would also mean that the Scots would be forced either to accept the mass for which the Reformers had developed a maniacal hatred, or else to undergo such hideous sufferings as the Spaniards were now inflicting on the Protestant Netherlanders. It was not surprising that Mary's marriage negotiations should be scanned with extreme distrust on both sides of the Border. The relations of the two Queens were, however, those of ceremonious cordiality: they exchanged affectionate letters and tokens made of diamonds.

Since Mary regarded her marriage as a step towards forcible acquisition of the English Crown, the match she desired most was Philip's son Don Carlos, a criminal lunatic whom his father afterwards had put to death like a mad dog; but though Philip entertained the negotiations, he was not eager for the marriage. He regarded it, as did Mary, as tantamount to a declaration of war on England, and he doubted whether the English Catholics were able, or even willing, to assist very much in dethroning Elizabeth. Mary herself rejected an offer from the Archduke Charles; she said he was too weak and poor to be able to help her to the English throne. Philip's cautious view of the way the English Catholics were likely to behave was quite unshared by her. With the natural self-confidence of a beautiful and extraordinarily attractive woman, Mary felt that she had only to show herself on English soil, and the Catholics, estimated at nearly half the population, would rise to acclaim her. In her own view, she was the rightful Queen and Elizabeth a bastard usurper, and she had another source of superiority. She had more beauty than Elizabeth and much more sexual magnetism; these qualities she had found of such advantage to her in her dealings with the world up till this time, she overlooked the fact that though, generally speaking, they are the most valuable gifts a woman can possess, in the exceptional case of personal sovereignty there are others that men will value even more; of these, she herself was destitute.

Mary's contention that Elizabeth was not Queen of England was countered by that popular feeling among the English themselves that the Queen of Scots was never able to arouse in either Elizabeth's kingdom or her own. The ballad-makers exulted in the Queen's likeness to Henry VIII—

> His daughter doth him so revive
> As if the father were alive

—and one trait of the great king which his daughter faithfully reproduced was a close and practical interest in the Royal Navy. The revolutionary development in English ship-building was of course the work of master-mariners and shipwrights, but the Queen's personal interest in naval matters caused her to be given the credit for it. As early as 1562, Camden said that her ship-building programme and the fact that she increased sailors' wages produced the best-furnished fleet for navigation and war the nation had ever seen. For this, he said, "strangers named her, the Queen of the Sea, the North Star". Camden, who used memoranda given him by Cecil in the writing of his history, gives a picture of affairs seen through the eyes of a Protestant, a whole-hearted enthusiast for the Queen; but at least what he had to say was very largely true, and he noted for this year the double impression of the Queen's popularity and a growing national prosperity: "This good correspondence between the Queen and her people, the commonwealth seeming to take life and strength, to the common joy of all."

Not by temperament only, but in physical mould, Elizabeth was fitted to be a visible symbol, an idea incarnate, to be stared and wondered at. Her slender, upright figure, her pale, aquiline face, the amazing delicacy of the long, transparent, jewelled hand that she held out to be kissed, formed a magnet to the public gaze. Every phase of her self-presentation had been carried to dramatic extremes. The plainness of her dress and hair had once astonished and made an unforgettable impression; now, she both gratified her own love of jewels and made herself a brilliant spectacle to beholders. The outlines of female dress became deplorably exaggerated in the last fifteen years of her reign, but for the first thirty years they were based on a fitted bodice with long sleeves, a full skirt and a small head. On this elegant and shapely mode were displayed those great rubies, emeralds and diamonds she had inherited from her father, the jewelled brooches, necklaces, bracelets and rings she constantly received as presents, and the pearls she wore in her hair, at her ears, round her neck and wrists and sometimes in clasps like a pattern all over bodice and skirt. It is suggested that pearls were given to her as an appropriate present to the Queen of the Sea.[1] They were also a symbol of virginity.

[1] Younghusband. *The Jewel House.*

The Queen was described by Bohun as "a true lover of pearls and jewels", and it was a passion shared by the vigorous age, whose lust for splendour attained the burning heat of poetry. Hilliard, the court painter and jeweller who designed Elizabeth's Great Seal, described in his *Art of Limning* his method of painting jewels to give the effect of sparkling and translucence. He spoke of the ruby, "that flickereth and affecteth the eye like to burning fire, especially by candle-light", the spinell that is like "a delicate, old, paled wine", the sapphire, "the most excellent perfect blue that anything in nature yields", "that excelleth in hardness and therefor in brightness of water", and the amethyst, "delighting the eye exceedingly to behold, being a perfect colour", that "hath his water more bright and lucid than any soft stone can have". Hilliard said that in his first interview with Elizabeth, she told him she admired most the Italian school of painting that gave the face without any shadows; so he took his first likeness of her, out of doors, placing her in an open alley away from the shade of trees. An effect as of bright light on her clear, pale face and aureate hair is characteristic of his miniatures.

The pleasures of magnificence had not displaced the intellectual ones. In December 1563 Ascham wrote to Sturmius from Windsor telling him how he had gone upstairs after dinner to read Greek with the Queen. He said that when she was reading Demosthenes or Aeschines, he was always struck by her grasp of the political scene: by her understanding of "the feeling of the speaker, the struggle of the debate, the inclination of the people". He still dwelt fondly on his pupil's talent for languages. He had one day heard her speak to three Ambassadors together, in Italian, French and Latin, without stopping for a word. He enclosed a scrap of paper bearing in the Queen's hand the word *Quemadmodum*, the first word of the 42nd psalm, that Sturmius might see how exquisitely she wrote.

Among the suitors who were entertained and rejected, one still kept the field. Lord Robert Dudley intended to marry the Queen and was pursuing his quarry with steady determination. Once, at least, it was said that he had succeeded. In June 1562, de Quadra had told the Queen point-blank that he heard everywhere she had been secretly married to Lord Robert. The Queen admitted that the rumour had somehow got about, and that when she had come back that afternoon from the Earl of Pembroke's house, and entered her Presence-Chamber with Lord Robert, her ladies had asked if they were to kiss his hand as well as hers. She had told them no, and that they must not believe everything they heard. In other walks of life, the matter was given a ruder turn. Drunken Burleigh of Totnes was before the magistrates for saying, "Lord Robert did swive the Queen," and Mother Dove, coming in at eight one morning to a tailor's shop, began by saying that there was things nowadays that she might say nothing of—then disproved her words by adding that Lord Robert had given the Queen a child. "Why!" cried the indignant tailor, "she hath no child yet!" Mother Dove replied: "He hath put one to the making."[1] The Earl of Arundel's servants quarrelled with Lord Robert's servants because the latter boasted that when the Queen had supped at Lord Robert's house and was being carried home by torchlight, she had told the torch-bearers she would make their master the greatest of his name. The talk, it was true, went on everywhere; only Lord Robert's ambition halted.

An English candidate now appeared for the hand of Mary Queen of Scots. Lady Lennox, to whom Elizabeth had once been obliged to give place, had two sons, of whom the elder, her darling, she had taught to regard himself as the heir to the English throne. The Lennox Stuarts, like Mary herself, had both been excluded by the terms of Henry VIII's will, since their claim derived from Margaret of Scotland; but as Catholics, they all disregarded Henry's Act of Succession. Lady Lennox had naturally disliked and resented Elizabeth, whom she viewed as an illegal supplanter of her boy's claims, and in Mary Tudor's reign she had taken no pains to disguise her ill-will. When Elizabeth, after Wyatt's rebellion, had been brought to London, miserably ill, she had been lodged on the ground-floor of Whitehall Palace, immediately under Lady Lennox's apartments. In spite of remonstrance, Lady Lennox had allowed her servants to use the room over the Princess's head as a kitchen, with continual "casting down of logs, pots and vessels". No one likes noises overhead, and to Elizabeth's irritable nerves they were particularly trying. The notes made for the steward of one of the houses she was to visit on a progress say that there must be no noise of any household office near Her Majesty's lodging, and that her bed-chamber must be absolutely quiet.[2] Her sufferings while Lady Lennox was overhead were not forgotten. The latter was placed under house-arrest for treasonable activities at her husband's castle in Yorkshire, where, it was said, the family fool was encouraged to deride the Queen as Dudley's mistress, and Lady Lennox had announced that she was looking forward to the day when her son and Mary Stuart should rule both kingdoms

[1] C.S.P. Domestic, XIII, 21.
[2] Hotson, *Queen Elizabeth's Entertainment at Mitcham.*

together. In the list of more serious charges against Lady Lennox, her malign treatment of the invalid Princess was also noted.[1]

The doings of Lady Lennox did not however injure the surface of the cordial relations between Elizabeth and Mary Stuart, and Elizabeth was obliged to justify herself to the latter for an expedition of English troops on French soil. The long religious civil war in France between the Catholics and the Huguenot party had been closely watched by the English Privy Council, who dreaded a great accession of power to the party of Guise, the supporters of Mary Stuart and her English ambitions. The closely woven international considerations of each country's domestic politics were shown by Cecil's comment on the decision of England to give the Huguenots some support in defending Havre. When it had seemed that the French might invade England from Scotland, Cardinal Granvella had exclaimed: "Madrid must defend London as if it were Brussels." Cecil now wrote that the Queen's forces were to be sent, not to invade or make war but merely to aid a defensive action, "to stay the Duke of Guise our sworn enemy", and also, if a chance offered, to regain possession of Calais. Elizabeth's own letter of explanation to Mary Stuart based the English interference on the need "to guard our houses from spoil when our neighbour's are burning", to keep the ports on the Channel open to English trading vessels, and to check the violent cruelties practised against the Huguenot victims. She ended her letter by saying: "My hot fever prevents my writing more." This was on October 15.

The Queen, who was at Hampton Court, had found herself somewhat unwell five days before, and had thought a bath would make her feel better. Washing of the body was done in basins, and the Queen's own expenses for linen towels, as well as the scale of the manufacture and the import of soap, suggest that the well-to-do washed themselves with considerable thoroughness; but total immersion in a bath was regarded as a treatment for health or mere pleasure. Elizabeth was fond of it. The remains of a marble bath-house she used at Ashridge were standing within living memory, and a small stone building over an oval bath, called Queen Elizabeth's Bath, once stood on the site of Trafalgar Square. On October 10, she took a bath and went out afterwards. She shortly developed a temperature and a German doctor, who had successfully treated Lord Hunsdon, was called in to see her. Dr. Burcot's skill in diagnosis was unusual; no sign was present on the skin, but at sight of the feverish Queen, he said: "My liege, thou shalt have the pox." The dreadful sentence was too much

[1] Domestic MSS., Elizabeth XXII, quoted by Froude.

for the patient's equanimity. "Have the knave away out of my sight!" she cried. Five days later there were still no spots, but the Queen's illness had increased, and a raging temperature would not let her finish her letter to the Queen of Scots. That night the doctors sent for Cecil and told him they did not expect Elizabeth to live. The ghastly moment he, above others, had dreaded, was upon them; the Queen was about to die, leaving no successor. The Privy Council gathered at Hampton Court and discussed whether they should back Lord Huntingdon, who claimed Plantagenet descent, or Lady Catherine Grey; no one suggested the Queen of Scots; but it was agreed that a decision must be made before the King of Spain had time to interfere.

Meanwhile the Queen, who had lain in a stupor, recovered consciousness. She saw the Council standing round her bed, and thinking herself at the point of death, she uttered some disconcerting words: she begged them to appoint Lord Robert Dudley Protector of the Realm with a salary of £20,000 a year, and to give his body-servant Tamworth, who slept in his room, £500 a year. In a few words she asked the Lords to be good to her cousin Lord Hunsdon and her household servants; and she called upon God to witness that though she loved and had always loved Lord Robert dearly, nothing improper had ever passed between them. The Council soothed her by promising everything that she asked.

In the meantime two mounted messengers with a third horse between them had sought out Dr. Burcot; but the doctor had been professionally insulted, and when told that he must come to the Queen at once, he replied with the independence of a foreigner: "By God's pestilence! If she be sick, let her die! Call me a knave for my good will!" An old servant of the Carew family saved the hour. He brought Burcot's cloak and boots, then drew his dagger, and said that if the doctor did not dress and go immediately, he should be killed where he stood. In a furious passion, the doctor tore downstairs and without a word, mounted and thundered away to Hampton, the messengers galloping in his wake.

As he was brought to the Queen's bed-side, he said: "Almost too late, my liege." But he ordered a mattress to be put down in front of the fire, and sending for a length of scarlet cloth, he wrapped her up in it, leaving one hand out, and then had her carried to the mattress. He put a bottle to her lips as she lay, and told her to drink as much as she liked, all of it if she were inclined. Elizabeth drank eagerly and said "it was very comfortable". Presently she saw red spots coming out on her hand and said fearfully: "What is this, Master Doctor?" "'Tis the pox," he answered. The Queen began to moan and lament but the irascible doctor stood no nonsense. "God's pestilence!" he cried, "which is better, to have the pox in the hands, in the face, or in the heart and kill the whole body?"

The bringing out of the eruptions saved the patient's life and the scabs left her face without permanent blemishes.[1] She had been nursed by Robert Dudley's sister, Lady Mary Sidney, who took the disease and suffered the horrible disfigurement Elizabeth had so much dreaded. Sir Henry Sidney wrote after seeing his wife for the first time since her recovery: "I left her a full fair lady, in mine eyes at least, the fairest, and when I returned I found her as foul a lady as the smallpox could make her, which she did take by continued attendance on her Majesty's most precious person."

The Queen was soon out of bed and only keeping to her room, de Quadra said, till the marks on her face should be healed. She gave Dr. Burcot a grant of land and a pair of gold spurs that had belonged to Henry VII. The next month she was out and about again. On the afternoon of November 26, Lord Robert Dudley and Lord Windsor were having a shooting match in Windsor Park, and "the Queen's Majesty stole out upon them". Her young cousin Kate Carey, Lord Hunsdon's daughter, and two other ladies went first, and the Queen followed them "as a maid". When they came up to the archers, the Queen said to Lord Robert, "that he was beholden to her, for she had passed the pikes for his sake".[2]

The phrase meant overcoming danger, but in French, at least, it had a secondary meaning. In this sense, Elizabeth had not passed the pikes for him, nor would. When she swore on what she thought was her death-bed, "that nothing improper had passed between Lord Robert and her", and at the same time asked for a lavish pension to be given to the servant who slept in his bed-chamber, she indicated the nature of their relationship, that it was a sexual one which stopped short only of the sexual act. No one who saw her among men doubted her extreme susceptibility to male attraction; it was in fact more than ordinary; but it would seem that the harm which had been done to Elizabeth as a small child had resulted in an irremediable condition of nervous shock. Saint Ignatius said: "Give me the child till he is seven, and afterwards anyone may have him"; and the discoveries of the present age have only confirmed the strength of the influence

[1] Halliday: "History To-day," Aug. 1955.
[2] Conway MS., quoted by Froude.

of early impressions. In a creature of such intensity and power, the emotions connected with a vital instinct were, inevitably, of tremendous force. Held up in the arms of her imploring mother to her terrible father as he frowned down upon them: hearing that a sword had cut off her mother's head: that her young step-mother had been dragged shrieking down the gallery when she tried to reach the King to entreat his mercy—these experiences, it would appear, had built up a resistance that nothing, no passion, no entreaty, no tenderness could conquer. In the fatally vulnerable years she had learned to connect the idea of sexual intercourse with terror and death; in the dark and low-lying region of the mind where reason cannot penetrate, she knew that if you give yourself to men, they cut your head off with a sword, an axe. The blood-stained key that frightens the girl in "Blue-Beard" is a symbol merely of the sexual act; in Elizabeth's case, the symbol had a frightful actuality of its own. It was the executioner's steel blade, running with blood.

Even the ostensible fears, the loss of liberty and submission of will, were so strong that they made the prospect of marriage seem an alienation of herself. She told the French Ambassador de Foix that whenever she thought about marriage, she felt as if someone were tearing the heart out of her bosom. Up to the point of capitulation, however, she enjoyed being made love to with an abnormal avidity that was the penalty of a deranged instinct; and as she never passed the point at which nature transforms the adoring suitor into the complacent lover, the element of worship that was incense to her vanity was perpetually prolonged.

The tribute which she wished others to accord to her charms, she gave to them herself. Her hair, her white skin, her arms, her hands, her feet, were all recognized as the objects of her own admiration by the observant, astute ambassadors who surrounded her, and her vanity was roused and vigilant at the fame of Mary Stuart's beauty and seductiveness; but vanity was a minor issue in the deadly situation that was taking shape, looming and extending like a landscape in a nightmare.

VIII

THE PARLIAMENT THAT met in January of 1563 were still aghast at the alarm of last October; to avoid another risk of civil war they determined the Queen must be urged, forced even, to marry, and pending the birth of her own children, some candidates for the succession at least must be legally recognized, in order of importance. A deputation from the Commons waited on her in the Great Gallery at Whitehall, and made clear their dread of a Catholic revival under Mary Queen of Scots. "The Papists," they said, "not only hope the woeful day of your death but also lie in wait to advance some title under which they may renew their late unspeakable cruelty."

The Queen assured them that she viewed the outlook as seriously as they did. There was no need to tell her, she said, after her recent experience, that human life hangs by a thread. "Death possessed every joint of me, so as I wished the feeble thread of life . . . might have been quietly cut off . . . I know now, as well as I did then, that I am mortal." As to marriage and the succession, how could they suppose that when she was so careful of other aspects of the common weal, she would neglect this one? She concluded: "I mean upon further advice to answer."

Then the Lords took up the tale. Their deputation told her that the fearful state into which they had been thrown by her illness emboldened them now to say that the succession *must* be defined; they added with pathetic persuasion that the Queen would not delay to marry, "if your Highness would conceive or imagine the comfort, surety and delight that should happen to yourself by beholding an imp of your own".[1]

While Elizabeth was harried by both Houses, an event increased the calamity of her position. Lord Hertford, imprisoned in the Tower at a distance from Lady Catherine, persuaded a sympathetic gaoler to let him into his wife's apartments, where he went to bed with her. After this, the Lieutenant of the Tower thought sequestration was useless and allowed the prisoners to remain together, and on February 10, Lady Catherine was delivered of a second son.

The implied comment on the Queen's obdurate virginity was

[1] Neale, *Elizabeth and her Parliaments*, I.

damaging in the extreme; there were many people who sympathized strongly with the heiress presumptive who was already a mother of two boys. It began to look as if ultimately the struggle might be between Mary Stuart and Catherine Grey. The Queen and the Privy Council did what they could to neutralize the danger. A commission under Archbishop Parker examined Lord Hertford; since he could produce neither clergyman, witness nor marriage settlement, the commission declared that, in absence of proof, it must be assumed that there had been no legal marriage. Lord Hertford was sentenced to a heavy fine for seducing a virgin of royal blood, and his children were pronounced illegitimate.

Whether legitimate or not, the birth of Catherine Grey's second son could but increase the disapproval with which many people regarded the Queen's disastrous liaison with Lord Robert Dudley; but very shortly, Elizabeth caused the gossip about this relationship to take an altogether different turn.

The extreme danger to England inherent in a marriage of Mary Stuart's was a matter of dread not only to the English themselves. Philip had dealt tepidly in her negotiations for Don Carlos because such a match involved a war with England, for which he was not ready. Now he heard that Catherine de Medici was suggesting that Mary should marry her late husband's brother, the young King Charles IX. This, Philip told de Quadra, must be stopped at all costs. Such a marriage would end in a French invasion of England, which for his own sake he would be obliged to repel. "To be at war on account of other people's affairs is not at all to my liking," he wrote, "but in this case, seeing *whom* I should be obliging, it would be doubly disagreeable to me." So acute, so imminent and so widely recognized was the potential danger of Mary's matrimonial choice. While the English government were in a state of apprehension and strained vigilance, Maitland of Lethington, the cleverest of the Scots nobility, for whom Randolph had frankly declared himself to be no match, presented himself in London, and to him Elizabeth made a suggestion so original and unexpected that even Lethington was taken aback. She repeated to him her previous warning that any "mighty marriage" Mary made would cause England to regard her as an enemy. An English nobleman of sufficient distinction would, the Queen felt, provide the solution. She suggested Lord Robert Dudley.[1]

On the face of it, it seemed as if Elizabeth could not be sincere in

[1] Mumby, *Elizabeth and Mary Stuart.*

making the proposal, but the hard-headed men at work on the negotiation thought that she was. Cecil, it was true, warned Randolph, "Of my knowledge of these fickle matters, I can affirm nothing that I can assure will continue," but Randolph was heart and soul in the affair; he was charmed by Mary, he thought well of Lord Robert, and the object of his life was to bring about a peaceful relationship between the two kingdoms. He welcomed the proposal as the readiest way, and urged Lord Robert's suit with all his might; while Mary's envoy Melville explained in his Memoirs that Queen Elizabeth had thought by this plan she would secure herself for ever against action from Scotland.

It will always be doubted whether, if the affair had prospered, she would have had the resolution to go through with it; but what other women would do, or not do, was in the last resort no guide to her actions. The writing on the leaden casket said: "*Who chooseth me, must give and hazard all he hath*", and the chooser's reward was love. Giving and hazarding were both painful ideas to Elizabeth, and for love she would not do either; but for the great aim of her existence, she would give and hazard everything; in a mortal storm, she would throw overboard everything except her crown.

At first it looked as if the offer ran no risk of acceptance. Mary, who on Amy Dudley's death had made the remark about the Queen of England's horse-keeper, was affronted by the suggestion; but she, who had been eager to marry Don Carlos, would have found no objection to Lord Robert's morals had he been a crowned head. Since he was a commoner, she was astonished at the presumption of anyone who offered him to her as a husband. But, said Randolph, the offer might bring certain advantages with it; if Queen Elizabeth were assured that Queen Mary were going to safeguard the interests of England by her marriage, then Elizabeth might consent to the official recognition of Mary as heiress presumptive to the English Crown. Mary's tone began to alter; she could not understand, she said, who could have said that she had spoken ungraciously of Lord Robert Dudley; and Murray and Lethington both told Randolph that if suitable conditions were offered with the match, they would recommend Mary to accept it.

But one person at least was determined the marriage should not take place. Mary Stuart was not the only one intriguing for the English Crown. Lord Robert Dudley meant to have it, and in his view the quickest way to it was not by posting off to Scotland after Mary and her debated claim, but by staying where he was and marrying Elizabeth. He took no active part in the proposal, and some months later, when Randolph imagined that he had gained Mary's consent to the marriage, he was irritated and bewildered at the backwardness of the suitor. But here Dudley was on safe ground. He had allowed his name to be used in the negotiations; he could only gain, in Elizabeth's eyes, from his refusal to show eagerness in the match.

The tortuous, hollow and inconstant manner of Elizabeth's proceeding in politics was hidden from the comprehension of the people; when they saw her act, it was as someone bold, firm and alight with enthusiasm for themselves. The attempt to stiffen Huguenot resistance to the Guises had resulted in the opposing French factions uniting to throw out the foreigners, and after a heroic defence Lord Warwick was obliged to relinquish Havre and withdraw his plague-stricken troops. Elizabeth's official letter, ordering the withdrawal, said that much as the Crown had wanted to hold Havre, "yet . . . we make no small accompt, that by the straight defence thereof against the whole force of France, this our nation shall recover the ancient fame which heretofore it had", and she told Warwick to let his men hear that she had said so.

The returning garrison brought the plague with them and it raged through London. The Privy Council had had such a fright over the Queen's small-pox that they were now running no risks that could be avoided. Elizabeth removed to Windsor, and they not only forbade the entrance to the town of people from the infected area: they set up a gallows in Windsor market-place to hang anyone who disobeyed the order.

It was not thought proper to leave Catherine Grey in the plague-stricken capital. Lord Hertford and the elder child were sent to Hertford's mother, the once-formidable Duchess of Somerset, and Lady Catherine and her baby were sent to the custody of her uncle Lord John Grey in Essex. From here she wrote letters full of penitence and misery to Elizabeth, but it was out of her power to conciliate the Queen. No apologies, however heartfelt, could alter the fact that she had clandestinely married and borne two sons.

One of the plague's victims was de Quadra, and he was succeeded by the most charming and best liked of all the Spanish ambassadors to Elizabeth's Court, Don Guzman de Silva. The latter began his embassy with a series of brilliant despatches to Philip, depicting the Queen as gay, courteous, talkative in the midst of her courtiers. In the first week in July she received de Silva in the London house of one of the nobles who was entertaining her. In the early evening she walked in the garden with her ladies, and after supper she came out into the great hall which had been festally lit with torches. Here she insisted on de Silva's staying to watch a comedy which she translated for him. After the comedy a masque was performed by gentlemen all dressed in black and white. The Queen said to de Silva: "Those are my colours." The Ambassador merely set down the remark without comment and went on to describe a buffet loaded with preserves and candied fruits, and how at two in the morning the Queen had gone back by water to Westminster through a summer dawn that was very windy. The remark about her colours had not seemed to him of any significance; and coming after a conversation in which the Queen had affected an appearance of pique because Don Carlos had been spoken of as a possible husband for Mary Stuart but not for her, de Silva was not on the look-out for any such secret implication; but in some of the works on heraldry of the period, black and white were described as the colours of perpetual virginity.

Philip in his own despatches sent his Ambassador some guidance. "I avail myself of the occasion," he wrote, "to tell you my opinion of that Cecil. I am in the highest degree dissatisfied with him. He is a confirmed heretic and if with Lord Robert's assistance you can so inflame matters as to crush him down and deprive him of all further share in the administration, I shall be delighted to have it done." De Silva was shrewd enough to see at the very outset that it could not be done. His estimation of Cecil showed his own perception and integrity. "He is . . . lucid, modest and just, and although he is zealous in serving his queen, which is one of his best traits, yet he is amenable to reason. He knows the French, and like an Englishman he is their enemy. . . . With regard to his religion I say nothing except that I wish he were a Catholic."

Lucid, modest, just: the qualities, admirable in themselves, do not suggest fire, and yet burning energy there was, maintaining Cecil's super-normal tale of work. His labours as a minister would have been too much for most men, but they were not the whole of his undertakings. In August the Queen was to visit Cambridge, and Cecil as Chancellor of the University took all arrangements for the visit upon himself. He began by drawing up exhaustive notes for the guidance of the Vice-Chancellor and the Masters. He planned where everyone was to sleep: the Queen at King's in the Master's Lodge, her ladies and physicians in the Fellows' Lodgings; Lord Warwick and Lord Robert Dudley in Trinity, he himself in St. John's. There followed a consideration of what learned entertainments were to be devised for the Queen, who, he reminded the University authorities, was extremely well educated. Stringent precautions were to be observed against the plague, but two points above all he desired the University to exhibit: namely, learning and *order*. The excitement of the undergraduates was to be held sternly in check; after they had welcomed the Queen they were to go quietly back to their lodgings; they were not to come crowding in to the disputations and the Latin plays on any account. Everything being now as perfect as his immense competence could make it, Cecil trundled off in his coach that he might be there to receive the Queen. He was only forty-four, but he suffered from an excruciating form of gout, and he took his old nurse with him to look after his comfort.

The Queen and her entourage arrived in the afternoon; a short stop had been thoughtfully arranged for her at Newnham Mill, and she now came riding into the court of Queen's College, where everyone dismounted except herself.[1] She remained on horseback listening to the long and stately welcome. She was wearing black velvet; her hair was drawn back into a gold net sewn with pearls and precious stones, and over this she wore a black hat spangled with gold, with a bush of feathers at the side. All her powers were engaged in listening, noticing and responding, and she never perhaps appeared more strikingly as a product of the Renaissance than on this visit, with her intelligent participation in a long programme of speeches, debates and plays in Latin, while at the same time she was entrancing the onlookers by her state and elegance, her cordial charm and her agility of mind.

King's College became the Court, and its Chapel was the centrepiece of the whole occasion. The lofty walls and exquisite fan-vaulted roof of dove-coloured stone seem as if they existed to frame the astonishing height and range of the jewelled windows, whose lower lights glow with the green and amber, the violet and ruby of scenes and crowds, and whose upper lights are skies of pale, translucent sapphire. On the pavement below these enormous fields of coloured light, the Queen stood, "marvellously revising at the beauty of the chapel", gazing and gazing again, "and praising it above all the others within her realm". Begun by Henry VI and carried on by Henry VII, the divinely beautiful structure had been completed by her father, and he had left his mark upon his work. In one of the bays of the dark rood-screen were carved the twined initials, H and A, and along

[1] Nichols, *Progresses*.

the stone walls the bosses of the Tudor rose were supported by the heraldic bearings of the Boleyns.

On Sunday evening a stage was erected over the whole width of the nave, to take both actors and spectators of the Latin play. At nine o'clock Cecil and the Vice-Chancellor came in and with them the Queen's guard bearing lighted torches. The guard stood below the stage to give illumination, while high up above the windows dimmed and scattered blots only of ruby, of emerald, glowed with the evening sky. "At last Her Highness came with lords, ladies and gentlewomen, and so took her seat." The play lasted till midnight.

The next day the Queen attended a disputation in St. Mary's church, and so far from allowing her mind to wander, she was irritated by not being able to hear the speakers properly. Several times she called to them to speak up, and when this had no effect, she came to the edge of the stage and stood immediately over their heads.

Two days were passed, in processions made in state through the streets, in receptions and banquets at colleges, in listening and replying to speeches, and attending Latin plays at night. Elizabeth was always pleased by intelligent children, and at Peter House she was delighted with Sir William Mildmay's son, "who, being a child, made a very neat and trim oration, and pronounced it very aptly and distinctly", a refreshing change after the muttering disputants in St. Mary's church.

On the last evening, the students of King's were to have performed Sophocles' *Ajax*; but the Queen could not face another play, in which she had all the sympathy of the contemporary journalists.[1] "Her Highness, as it were, tired with going about to the colleges, and with hearing disputations, and over-watched with former plays (for it was very late nightly before she came to them, as also departed from them) . . . could not, as otherwise no doubt she would (with like patience and cheerfulness as she was present at the others), hear the said tragedy."

When the Court returned to London in September, the Earl of Lennox asked the Queen's leave to go to Scotland to see about his Scottish estates. The Scots Parliament had sequestrated them because he had supported Henry VIII; now the Queen of Scots, his wife's niece, was going to restore them. The request seemed harmless, but anything in which Lady Lennox was concerned would bear looking into. However, Lennox's English property was so much greater than

[1] Nichols, *Progresses*.

his Scottish, it was assumed that his English estates would be a pledge for his loyalty.

In the same month that Lennox went up to Scotland, Sir James Melville was sent down from Holyrood to discuss the negotiations for the marriage of the Queen of Scots and Lord Robert Dudley. Such at least was his ostensible commission, but he had another; it concerned Lady Lennox and her elder son. Henry Stuart, Lord Darnley, was nineteen years old, very tall, and though slight, most beautifully proportioned. His face was round, with round and prominent blue eyes and the complexion of a girl. The best of him was seen. He was graceful and athletic, he could play the lute, and his mother had sedulously taught him everything in the way of good manners that he was capable of learning. His interest for his cousin Mary at present was that in Catholic eyes he had a claim to the English Crown nearly as good as her own, for while she was descended from Margaret Tudor by the latter's first husband, Lady Lennox was the child of Margaret's second marriage to the Earl of Angus. Indeed, as Henry Darnley had been born in England, some people would argue that his claim was better than Mary's. Melville was instructed to see Lady Lennox secretly and tell her to use all her efforts to get leave for Darnley to join his father in Scotland.

The public part of Melville's mission resulted in despatches describing the Queen's behaviour at first hand, with unforgettable and disconcerting brilliance. Elizabeth's apprehensive curiosity about her rival caused her to question Melville minutely about Mary and also to challenge his admiration by a display of her own accomplishments. His description suggests less a woman than some exotic bird that stalks with slender body and voracious beak, dragging a sheaf of jewelled plumage and expanding it suddenly in startling display. In reply to her pertinacious questions about Mary's appearance, Melville said: "I said that she was whiter, but that my Queen was very lovely." When he told her about the different fashions in women's dress he had seen on his travels, Elizabeth said she had dresses in the fashions of all those countries, and she wore them for him to see, one after the other. He said he liked her best in the Italian dress, and this pleased her, because in that one she had worn her hair loose over her shoulders. Her hair, Melville said, was a reddish-yellow and looked as if it curled naturally. When he was asked if Mary was a good musician, he said she played "reasonably well, for a Queen". That day after dinner Lord Hunsdon told him he should hear some music and took him to the door of a gallery. Inside, someone was playing the virginals remarkably well. Melville pulled aside the portière and went quietly in; the Queen was playing, with her back towards him. He stood listening while she played, he was obliged to say, "excellently". She was indeed a most accomplished performer. When Dr. Burney examined the manuscript of her Virginal Book, he was surprised at the difficulty of the pieces by Byrd, Tallis, Farnaby and Bull; no master in Europe, he said, would undertake to play those under a month's practice. The complicated procession of twangling notes was broken off; the Queen came forward, pretending to aim a blow at Melville, saying she never played before men but only to enliven herself when she was alone. Melville had to tell her that she played better than the Queen of Scots. His visit was, he believed, prolonged by two days that he might have an opportunity to see Elizabeth dancing. In the comparison that was inevitably demanded, he said that the Queen of Scots' dancing was less stately and elaborate than hers.

In private conversation the thirst for admiration defeated its own ends, but, like every other trait of Elizabeth's, it was turned to advantage in her public life. She was occasionally too much exhausted for her part in the exchange of seeing and being seen, the rite celebrated between the people and herself. She had been almost speechless at her Coronation banquet, she could not sit through the last of the Latin plays at Cambridge; but as a rule, when she was on show, she was indefatigable: immune from weather, discomfort, impatience and nervous strain. The inspiration of such energy and endurance was her ardent wish that the people should see her. With Sir James Melville, the instinct was at fault: it was not at fault coming and going through the London streets, among the crowding boats on the Thames, in the market-places of country towns and on village greens.

But Melville's business was not with set-pieces of exhibition but with what the Queen might inadvertently show, and his shrewd, attentive observation was trained on her behaviour to Lord Robert Dudley. He suggested that the Earl of Bedford and Lord Robert should be sent to the Border to confer with Murray and Lethington, and Elizabeth instantly exclaimed that he made small account of Lord Robert, naming the Earl of Bedford before him; but before Melville went home he should see Lord Robert made the greater Earl of the two.

Elizabeth had already thought of making Dudley a peer, but she had decided against it. He was her lover—but he was also the son of that Northumberland who had kept her from her dying brother and tried to deprive her of her crown. When the letters patent for the peerage were brought for her to sign, she paused: the past rose again and overcast the smiling present. Instead of her qulll, she took up the pen-knife and slit the document to pieces.

But now that it would make him more useful in the political game, Dudley was to receive the Earldom of Leicester with the Barony of Denbigh and a train of attendant advantages. The ceremony was performed at Westminster Palace in great state, and at the Queen's entry the sword of state in its pearl-studded scabbard was carried before her by the fair, extravagantly tall young Darnley.

Kneeling at Elizabeth's feet, Dudley received the title which was to be the most famous, most envied and best-hated in the length and breadth of England. The Queen herself fastened the mantle on the Earl's shoulders, and as she did so, Melville said, "she could not refrain from putting her hand in his neck, tickling him, the French Ambassador and I standing by". She then asked Melville how he liked her new creation. Melville made a courteous reply: then, as a flash of lightning reveals an unfamiliar landscape, the Queen showed that Lady Lennox's intrigues were not entirely secret from her. She pointed to Darnley: "And yet," she said, "you like better of yonder long lad!" The Ambassador collected his wits; he said at once that any woman must prefer so proper a man as the Earl of Leicester to a lady-faced boy.

On a subsequent evening, by candle-light, the Queen took Melville into her bed-chamber to show him some of her treasures. Cecil and Leicester stood talking together at one end of the great apartment; at the other the Queen opened a little cabinet and showed Melville some miniatures, each wrapped up in paper with her handwriting on it. She took out one labelled "My Lord's picture". Melville caught up a candle and begged to see it; it was Leicester's portrait and he asked to be allowed to take it to Queen Mary. Elizabeth replied she could not spare it, she had no other. "Your Majesty has the original," said Melville. The Queen then took out a picture of the Queen of Scots and kissed it, whereupon Melville seized her hand and pressed it to his lips. Then he spied an enormous ruby. Supposing she were to send Queen Mary that, or else Lord Leicester's picture, he suggested. The Queen put her treasures away. She said that if the Queen of Scots followed her counsel, Mary would in time get all she had.

In spite of Elizabeth's public caress, and of her saying that she could not part even with Leicester's picture, Melville did not report that the Queen was insincere in the matter of the marriage proposal. He seemed to have formed the opposite view, that she was willing that the marriage should take place, since "it would best remove out of her mind all fear and suspicion of being supplanted before her death".

But he knew that the Queen of Scots was not interested in the match. It was true that, cleverly handled, it might bring with it the recognition by Parliament of her claim to succeed Elizabeth in default of the latter's heirs, but a marriage with Darnley might mean that they could together claim the English Crown immediately.

As Melville was leaving Hampton Court by water, Leicester came with him in the barge. The Earl made a sort of apology for his presumption in appearing to seek the hand of the Queen of Scots. He said it was all the fault of Cecil, who was trying to ruin him in the eyes of both Queens at once. The ostensible aim of Melville's mission had hung fire; the other one was a different story.

In December the Queen was ill at Westminster with what seemed to be gastric influenza. She complained of pains in the stomach and aches in her limbs, and Cecil informed Sir Thomas Smith: "It came to that which they call diarrhoea . . . for the time she made us sore afraid." The first week in January the Thames froze so thick that people walked on it as if it were a street. De Silva wrote that the weather was very trying to the weak. "It has found out the Queen whose constitution cannot be very strong." The Ambassador had not seen her since she took to her bed. She was now up and had come out as far as the Privy Chamber, but Leicester had told him that she was very thin. "It is true," de Silva wrote, "that young people can get over anything, but your Majesty should note that she is not likely to have a long life." De Silva had been reading books that traced the claims of the various pretenders to the English throne; he enclosed the gist of his researches for the King's attention.

Mary Stuart, to conceal her interest in Darnley, whom she had not yet laid eyes on, was making Randolph believe that she was seriously considering the match with Leicester, and Randolph conveyed his eager, hopeful impression to the English court. Cecil, to give what help he might, wrote to Lethington a testimonial to Leicester's virtues and claims. In the draft of the letter, he wrote that Leicester was a man "most dearly beloved of her Majesty"; then he crossed out "beloved" and wrote "esteemed" instead.[1] But what perplexed and dismayed Randolph was to see, all too clearly, that Leicester himself

[1] Conyers Read: *Mr. Secretary Cecil and Queen Elizabeth.*

was going to refuse the jump. "Now I have got this Queen's goodwill to marry where I would have her, I cannot get the man to take her for whom I was a suitor." Leicester's tepid behaviour astonished him; the Queen of Scots had been lovely at her first coming, but her beauty had brightened until now, he wrote, she excelled any since the framing of mankind. Prudence came to his elbow and he added in brackets "(our own most worthy Queen alone excepted)"; and now that Leicester might have this ravishing creature "in his naked arms" and a kingdom as well, he hung back. But Randolph was hoodwinked in believing that Mary was ready to accept Leicester; under cover of the feint, Lennox got permission for Darnley to come to Scotland, that Lennox might entail his Scots estates on him. In February, Darnley went up to Edinburgh.

IX

In the english court, Leicester continued to glisten with the Queen's favour; he rode with her and he was her partner in her other favourite pastime: one of the most popular dances of the day was called, after him, the Leicester Dance.[1] But de Silva's view of the affair was not quite the ordinary one. He had already told Philip: "I understand that she bears herself towards him in a way that, together with other things that can be better imagined than described, makes me doubt sometimes whether Robert's position is irregular as many think." In the course of an interesting conversation with him, the Queen had said: "The world thinks a woman cannot live un-married, and if she refrains from men that she does so for some bad reason, as they said of me that I avoided doing so because I was fond of the Earl of Leicester, whom I could not marry because he had a wife living. His wife is now dead and yet I do not marry him, al-though I have been pressed to do so even by your King." But in this same month of March, Randolph was horrified to hear it repeated in the Scots Court that while Leicester and the Duke of Norfolk were playing tennis with the Queen looking on, "Lord Robert being very hot and sweating, took the Queen's napkin out of her hand and wiped his face". Norfolk in fury threatened to smash his racket over Leicester's head, and Randolph feared that the fatally revealing familiarity had ruined the negotiations he had in hand; but these had never had a genuine basis and their appearance, even, was about to be thrown aside.

Mary was now promised the support for her darling project that she had been trying for ever since she came to Scotland. Lady Lennox had already assured her of the allegiance of both the English and the Scottish Catholics if she and Darnley would join their claims in marriage and come forward as the King and Queen of Great Britain; but more important still was the encouragement of the King of Spain. Philip had no ambassador in Scotland, but he told de Silva to tell Mary and Darnley: "If they will govern themselves by our advice and not be precipitate, but will patiently await a favourable juncture, when any attempt to frustrate their plans would

[1] Fuller, *Worthies of England*.

be fruitless, I will assist and aid them with the end they have in view."

Mary had been prepared to marry Darnley as she had been prepared to marry Don Carlos, but when the young man appeared, with height, grace, boyish charm and on his best behaviour, her policy chimed with an immediate infatuation; she announced that she would marry him and that he should be made King of Scotland. The contents of Philip's message to her were not known word for word to the English government, but the significance of the marriage was clear to every politician. The French Ambassador de Foix felt obliged to sound the Queen of England on this crucial matter, and having gained an audience he found her playing chess. She did not leave off immediately, and looking down at the board de Foix said: "This game is an image of the works and deeds of men. If we lose a pawn it seems a small matter; but the loss often brings with it that of the whole game." The Queen paused: "I understand you," she said. "Darnley is only a pawn but he may checkmate me if he is promoted." Then she stopped playing.[1]

The matter was now treated with the utmost seriousness. Sir Nicholas Throckmorton was sent post-haste to Holyrood to say that if Mary would marry either the Duke of Norfolk, the Earl of Arundel or the Earl of Leicester, Parliament would recognize her as presumptive heiress to the English Crown. It was clear that at this juncture at least, Elizabeth and Cecil were prepared to see Leicester make the match if Mary would have him, and in this extremity Leicester felt obliged to safeguard himself. According to Mary, he sent her a private word, assuring her that as far as he himself was concerned, the offer was a sham. But had he in fact desired the match, it would have been of no interest to Mary, nor was the promise that she should become Queen of England on Elizabeth's death without children. An armed invasion of England with Spanish help was a far quicker method of realizing her wishes. Throckmorton, a much sharper man than Randolph, picked up in a few days more information than the latter had gained in months. He saw that the forthcoming marriage was part of an international Catholic movement against the heretic Queen. He warned Cecil to keep a vigilant watch on the Catholic families in the north of England, and told him at all costs to prevent Lady Lennox from any further communication with the Spanish Ambassador. Lady Lennox was at once removed to the Tower, and peremptory orders were sent to Lennox and Darnley on

[1] Von Raumer, *Elizabeth and Mary Stuart.*

their allegiance as English subjects to return immediately. Darnley replied with crude impertinence. The English Queen was so envious of his good fortune, no doubt she would like to get him back again, but, he added, "I find myself very well where I am, and so purpose to keep."

The Protestant Lords with Murray at their head declared that to impose a Catholic King upon Scotland without consent of Parliament was illegal. Mary cared nothing for that. On July 27 Darnley was proclaimed King in Edinburgh. The next day she married him.

Mary's blood was up. This was her hour of success; with the long-coveted alliance with Spain behind her, and the young husband with whom she was still infatuated at her side, she summoned Murray and his colleagues to meet her at Edinburgh, and when they did not comply, she had them declared outlaws, and herself riding with her troops with pistols at her belt, she fought the action called the Chase-About-Raid and finally drove Murray across the border into England. In the rapturous excitement of successful action, she exclaimed that she would lead her troops to the walls of London. Such a vision, indeed, was never far from her mind. Bedford, the Governor of Berwick, reported a conversation that had taken place in a merchant's house in Edinburgh, where Mary was a guest. The company were examining the print of a portrait of the Queen of England and discussing whether it were like her? "Nay," said Mary, "it is not like her, for I am Queen of England."[1]

With the state of affairs in Scotland and with private troubles, Elizabeth passed a summer of much disquiet. In the middle of June, Kat Ashley died, and de Silva saw that the Queen was in deep grief at her loss. Capricious, irritable and ungrateful as Elizabeth often proved, she was faithful to old friendships, and all her life she cried bitterly over losses by death. The court was at Windsor in August and the Queen, perhaps to leave care behind, rode so hard that she tired out her ladies. Leicester undertook to show de Silva the extent of Windsor Park and they rode round it early one morning. They returned, said de Silva, "by the footpath leading to the riverside through the wood, to where the Queen lodges". Underneath the Queen's windows, looking on to this secluded place, Leicester's fool shouted so loudly, that the Queen came to the window in her négligée. An hour and a half afterwards, she came downstairs dressed.[2] In this summer retreat, however, the Queen quarrelled with her lover. Cecil told Sir Thomas Smith, "The Queen's Majesty is

[1] Mumby, *The Fall of Mary Stuart*.   [2] C.S.P. Spanish, 1565.

fallen into some misliking with my Lord of Leicester and therewith
he is much dismayed." Cecil added that he himself would act as an
honest man and refrain from making "a flame of this sparkel",
though his enemy had before now attempted to injure him.[1] Negotiations for the Queen's marriage with the Archduke Charles had been
revived, and this project was particularly dear to Cecil and to Sussex:
both as a means of getting Elizabeth with child and, although the
Archduke himself was a Catholic, of making alliance with the
German Protestants. The matter seemed progressing, and Cecil told
Smith: "My Lord of Leicester hath behaved himself very wisely to
allow of it." The words explain the abuse afterwards heaped upon
Leicester for having, it was said, prevented the Queen from marrying,
not only by engrossing her affections but actually interfering with
negotiations. On the same day Cecil wrote in his diary: "The Queen
seemed to be much offended with the Earl of Leicester and so she
wrote an obscure sentence in a book at Windsor."

The Keeper of the Queen's Books at Windsor, old Blanche Parry,
perhaps saw the writing. Her influence with Elizabeth, whom she
had seen rocked in her cradle, was likely to be of a sort directly
opposite to Kat Ashley's. The latter had been but too eager to
promote Elizabeth's marrying; Blanche Parry was an obdurate
virgin, and caused to be inscribed on her tombstone: *With maiden
queen, a maid did end my life.*" Her sympathy with her darling
would extend not only to a lovers' quarrel, but to the resistance to
any lover who might become a master. Although Elizabeth's intellect was extremely subtle, her emotions were not; they were vivid
and, it would have been supposed, easily predictable by someone
who had known her well since she was eight; but Leicester, though
he had great influence over her and, as Camden says, saw farther into
her mind than anyone else, occasionally made blunders so crass in
dealing with her, as any other man would have avoided who had been
in her company only half-an-hour. These extraordinary lapses were
all of the same character: they showed a bumptious self-assertion,
almost inexplicable until the overbearing arrogance of his father is
remembered. With the fire-new honours of his earldom upon him,
he attempted to overpower Bowyer, the official whose business it
was to deny entrance to everyone who had not the entrée to the
Privy Chamber, the apartment beyond the Presence Chamber, which
was the Queen's private retreat. Bowyer having refused entrance to a
protégée of Leicester's, the latter exclaimed that Bowyer was a knave

[1] Murdin.

and threatened him with loss of his place. Bowyer showed that know-ledge of Elizabeth's character which Leicester had momentarily for-gotten. Kneeling at the Queen's feet he stated his case, and begged to know "whether my Lord of Leicester were King, or her Majesty Queen". The violence, the suddenness of the response was like a thunderclap. "God's death, my Lord!" she exclaimed. "I have wished you well, but my favour is not so locked up in you that others shall not participate thereof. . . . If you think to rule here, I will take a course to see you forthcoming. I will have here but one mistress and no master."[1] Yet, so differently did she behave at other times, that even with a scene like this in his memory, Leicester still thought he was going to be able to marry her.

While the Queen was in constant apprehension over Scottish affairs and quarrelling with Leicester in private, an exasperating event revealed itself. The diminutive Lady Mary Grey was found to have repeated her sister Catherine's offence of a clandestine marriage, but almost in caricature. Her husband, a good-natured, foolish giant, was Thomas Keys, a distant connection of the Knollys family who had the office of Sergeant Porter at the water-gate of Westminster Palace. "An unhappy chance and a monstrous," was Cecil's description of the match. The touch of ludicrousness did not make it less offensive to the Crown; the folly of Jane Grey's sisters was almost past belief. The wretched Keys was imprisoned in the Fleet and Lady Mary, after some casting about, was forcibly imposed on her step-grandmother, the Duchess of Suffolk. The poor little atomy had next to no house-hold effects, to the severe annoyance of the Duchess, who was obliged to borrow for her, but she brought with her an armful of books, including *Mr. Knox his Answer to the Adversary of God's Pre-destination*, *The Ship of Assumed Safety*, *The Hunter of the Romish Fox*, *Godly Mr. Whitgift's Answer* and *The Duty of Perseverance*.

Elizabeth disliked her Grey cousins, but she had some true and valued female friends, with relatives among them. There were the daughters of her first cousin Lord Hunsdon, Kate and Philadelphia Carey, and Hunsdon's sister, who had married Sir Francis Knollys; Lady Cobham, her Mistress of the Robes, and her Maid of Honour Ann Russell, who in 1565 married Leicester's brother Ambrose and became Lady Warwick, were her intimate friends till death; so was Leicester's sister Catherine the Countess of Huntingdon. His sister Mary Sidney did not like to show her spoiled face at Court, but as an invalid she came and occupied a bedroom at Hampton Court where

[1] Naunton, *Fragmenta Regalia*.

Elizabeth visited her every day.[1] Visiting the sick was a duty the Queen did not shun. Her friend the Marchioness of Northampton, whose husband had been Catherine Parr's brother, was dying in 1564 of a cancer in the breast, though it was not recognized that the illness was in a fatal stage. De Silva asked to call on the Marchioness because he knew the Queen was fond of her. He received a cordial reply, and when that afternoon he was shown into the Marchioness's bedroom he found the Queen already there and both ladies smiling at his surprise. She had come from St. James', almost alone, to dine and spend the day with the invalid. He remained with the ladies till nightfall, the Marchioness lying on a couch and the Queen sitting near her. When she left, a carriage was waiting to take the Queen back to St. James', but she chose instead to walk through the park.

The summer's cloud between Elizabeth and Leicester had not removed by the autumn, and it may have been darkened by the Queen's discovery of his private cancelling of his proposal to Mary Stuart. At all events, their relationship was disturbed, and Elizabeth set up a strong flirtation with Sir Thomas Heneage, an able young courtier who became eventually Vice-Chamberlain and Treasurer of her household. Heneage was one of the men who thought her personally attractive and was fond of her for her own sake. Thirty years later he left in his will a jewel to the Queen "who, above all other earthly creatures, I have thought most worthy of all my heart's love and reverence". Elizabeth's preoccupation with Heneage caused Leicester to try, for the first time, the strength of her affection for him. He set up a counter-flirtation that was to have very far-reaching consequences. Its object was the Queen's cousin Lettice, the daughter of Sir Francis Knollys; she was at present Lady Hereford, her husband afterwards being created Earl of Essex. Elizabeth was inclined to like all her relations on her mother's side; they were high-spirited and clever and the blank in her existence left by the absence of any family life made her ready to welcome, within bounds of discretion, attractive, affectionate cousins who understood what her position demanded. One of her favourite cousins had been Lettice Knollys, whose youthful good-humour, combined with intelligence, had made her very pleasant, but ebbed to reveal the outlines of a character sensual, scheming and arrogant. Leicester's advances to the Countess aroused a passion that bore fruit twelve years later in a secret marriage; for the present his interest in her was subsidiary to his main

[1] Fox Bourne, *Philip Sidney*.

purpose and his ruse produced the desired result. The estrangement reached its climax in mutual reproaches of faithlessness and neglect. De Silva had heard that in the course of the scene, "both the Queen and Robert shed tears", but afterwards, as he could see for himself, Leicester "returned to his former favour".

The reconciliation left the Queen cool and mercurial and ready as ever to talk about getting married. In October de Silva was in a coach with the Queen and Lady Cobham, all coming back from visiting the Princess Cecilia of Sweden. The Queen said: "There are three of us in this coach and some people would make us out to be four." The remark might have been applied to Lady Cobham, who was pregnant, but de Silva answered as if it referred to rumours like Mother Dove's. He said that, after all, the Queen's people were right in wishing it might be so. "And you," demanded the Queen, "whom do you wish it was by?" The Ambassador replied that he could not venture to choose for her.

Meanwhile Murray, who had received promises of support from Elizabeth to defend the Scottish Reformation against Mary's enmity, now travelled rapidly to London to require their fulfilment. But the case was altered. Elizabeth had meant to give a little help to Murray's party, to keep it in the field. Mary's unexpected and complete victory meant that any assistance given to Murray now would be a declaration by England of war against the Queen of Scots, upon which the French would come to her aid almost before they were asked. Any such action on the English part was out of the question. It was odious treatment of Murray, but Elizabeth's success was the reward that comes to undeviating single-mindedness. Lying, treacherous, hypocritical as she was, the veerings and shiftings and deceits were only the method by which she pursued an end that was hard and unchanging as the rock beneath the infinite flowings and ebbings of the sea. It was not only impossible to fulfil the promises to Murray—it would be highly damaging to be even reminded of them. Murray had got as far towards London as Royston, when the Queen's messengers headed him off. He was brought in to London very quietly at dusk the next evening, and in a secret interview with the Queen and Cecil, the form was explained to him.

Next day, in the presence of the French Ambassador, who had been specially sent for that he might report to the French court how severely Elizabeth dealt with the Scots rebels, Murray, all in black, submitted to a severe scolding from the Queen on the enormity of his behaviour in taking arms against his sovereign; after which he left London and retired to Newcastle.

Cecil bore a vast burden, and of his great gifts one was an extraordinary patience. Leicester, after his reconciliation with the Queen, had come out again, re-gilded with her favour, and as the year drew to an end, he felt that the catch was very nearly in his net. He approached Cecil, and said that as he thought the Queen was making up her mind to marry him, he must ask Cecil to give up any other plans for her marriage; but, he added, he would always befriend Cecil and see to it that he received the promotion and encouragement which his usefulness deserved. Cecil thanked the Earl for his good opinion,[1] and drew up another of his tables, for and against Leicester as King-Consort; the latter considerations outweighed the former, but the desire to see Elizabeth the mother of an heir consumed him. In December he wrote to Sir Thomas Smith, wishing that "it might please Almighty God to lead some person to come and lay hands on her to her contentation"; otherwise, he said, "as things now hang in desperation, I have no comfort to live".

So the year ended. On Christmas Day the Queen came to chapel in purple velvet embroidered all over with silver, very richly set with stones. New Year's Day was occupied by the giving her a treasury of clothes, jewels and precious things, and the Spanish Ambassador was told by the French Ambassador that Lord Leicester slept with her on New Year's Night.

[1] Von Raumer, *Elizabeth and Mary Stuart.*

X

THE YEAR 1566 was the one above all others when it seemed that the Crown Matrimonial was within Leicester's grasp. On April 12 a plan of the lovers went awry and passers-by in the London streets could see strange doings to which they had not the clue. Lord Leicester came into London followed by 700 footmen, his own and the Queen's, and went to the young Earl of Oxford's house, opposite St. Swithin's churchyard, where London Stone stands, but when he reached the rendezvous no one was there. Meantime the Queen came up secretly from Greenwich, attended by two ladies only, with but one pair of oars, and was landed at the Three Cranes. Visscher's Panorama of London shows, as in a magic mirror, exactly where she stood. The three cranes for unlading stood in a row upon the wharf; behind them, several tiers of close-packed houses rose with the slope of the shore; above their roofs loomed the vast cliff of Old Saint Paul's, and behind this all was open fields, reaching to the sky. On the spot to which the cranes had given their name, the Queen entered a coach covered all in blue, and drove to St. Swithin's churchyard; but she found no one, either. Lord Leicester had gone off in a huff. However, he halted his retinue at a spot he knew the Queen must pass on her return to Greenwich. When she saw him there, "she came out of her coach in the highway and she embraced the Earl and kissed him three times". Then he climbed into the coach with her and they drove back to Greenwich.[1] The following August, Leicester repeated to de la Forêt, who had succeeded de Foix, that poignant, little-heeded remark Elizabeth had made as a child of eight. Leicester said: "I have known her since she was eight years of age, better than any man in the world. From that time she has always, invariably, declared that she would remain unmarried." He added, however, that the Queen had done him the honour to tell him, in private, several times, that if she did marry an Englishman, it should be he. He both smiled and sighed as he spoke.[2]

Sussex's enmity towards Leicester was all the sharper for his being at the court of the Emperor Maximilian, in charge of the negotiations for Elizabeth's marriage to the Archduke Charles. These were

[1] Stowe, *Historical Memoranda.*   [2] Von Raumer, *op. cit.*

understood to halt because the Emperor was demanding more in the way of religious concession than the English would grant. Sussex, hoping and believing all things, thought that the Queen would accept the Archduke if her affections were not engaged at home. He looked upon Leicester as the arch-enemy of the negotiations, and of the realm itself; and when he was again in London in the summer, neither his own chivalry nor Leicester's *savoir-vivre* could restrain them from a fierce quarrel in the Queen's very presence; she could barely bring them into some show of decent calmness.

Cecil for his part was exceedingly anxious to allay rumours; he admitted they were natural enough, but he wrote to Smith at Paris: "Briefly I affirm that the Queen's Majesty may be by malicious tongues not well reported, but in truth she herself is blameless and hath no spot of evil intent." The fear, and the assertion, was that Elizabeth had entirely given herself to her lover. The opinion of a man singularly acute who saw her every day and frequently in the lover's company, was that she had not.

It was extremely important to make this opinion carry weight at the French Court. The Queen of Scot's marriage with Darnley had removed the fear of her marrying a foreign prince, but her understanding with Spain, that was to culminate in the invasion of England, meant that an alliance between France and England was urgently desired by both countries. Catherine de Medici hankered to see the Crown of England fall to one or other of her goblin brood; she tried to get it for three of her sons in turn and she began by proposing Charles IX as a husband for the English Queen. The boy was seventeen and Elizabeth was now thirty-two, but the latter was still within the span of physical youth and charm, and the French King, his mother said, was already a man. Brisk, resourceful and a thorough realist, Catherine de Medici was prepared to make every effort for so splendid a *mariage de convenance*. The childish King, easily excited by romantic and ambitious ideas, declared himself eager for the match. Sir Thomas Smith could hardly take the proposal seriously. If the King were a few years older, or if he had actually seen Queen Elizabeth, then it would be understandable enough, he began. The King interrupted him. "But indeed I do love her!" Smith answered with fatherly kindness: "Your Majesty does not yet know what love is." The French court, however, pushed the proposal with every show of earnestness, and though Elizabeth had assured de Silva that "she would not make the world laugh by seeing at the church door an old woman and a child," her replies to the French Ambassador were more encouraging. The latter therefore thought it necessary to find out as far as he was able whether it were thought likely that Elizabeth would bear children.

One of the Queen's physicians, whom he did not name, gave a member of the French embassy an unequivocal reply:[1] "Your King," said the doctor, "is seventeen, and the Queen is only thirty-two. Take no notice of what she says in that respect: it is only her passing fancy. If the King marries her, I will answer for her having ten children, and no one knows her temperament better than I do." Cecil had always assumed that Elizabeth could bear children, and a professional opinion of such weight appeared to justify him. But another of the Queen's physicians, Dr. Huick, though he did not contradict his colleague, gave his own advice on the opposite side; he told her that marriage and child-bearing had better not be attempted.

The news of the consultation and Huick's opinion got out, and Council and Parliament were infuriated. "Dr. Huick," said Camden, "dissuaded her to marry for I know not what womanish infirmity." It was considered unpardonable in Huick to have encouraged her in any such nonsense; and Parliament "besought her to be joined by the sacred bond of marriage with whom she would, in what place she liked and as soon as she pleased, to the end to have children for help to the kingdom", for if she died childless, "England that breathed by her spirit, would expire with her".

Mary Queen of Scots, married and pregnant, seemed to be in a position immeasurably stronger than Elizabeth's; but her misfortunes were gathering over her. Marriage with a Queen and one of the most beautiful of women had been too much for Darnley's weak head. His brainless arrogance had been so much increased that he did not treat even his wife with courtesy. Mary's passion was soon extinct, and her coldness and dislike roused him to the fatuous self-assertion that had been fostered by his mother. Mary's confidence was given to the Italian secretary Rizzio; this base-born man's swaggering manners and his familiarity with the Queen offended the nobles, but he was the object of much more serious disapproval, for he managed the whole of the Queen's correspondence which carried on her negotiations with the Pope and the King of Spain. A group of the Protestant lords headed by Morton, Lethington and Ruthven planned Rizzio's murder for political ends, and by playing on Darnley's jealousy they made him the prime mover in the outrage; the hideous act was deliberately committed in the presence of the Queen,

[1] De la Ferrière, *Projets du Mariage de la Reine Elisabeth.*

who was seven months gone with child. Mary's calibre showed itself when instead of being prostrated by shock and a threatened miscarriage, she collected herself and in twenty-four hours had seduced her husband to her side again and escaped with him at midnight from Holyrood out of a part of the cellarage that was unguarded and open to the air. One instant only she gave way to her real feelings. It was brilliant moonlight and as she, Darnley and a servant made their way across a waste place used as a burial-ground, they came upon a new-made grave. Pausing beside the mound under which Rizzio was lying, in the light of the moon she called down curses on the House of Lennox.[1] Horses were waiting for them and they rode wildly to Dunbar. By her heroic energy and courage, Mary had regained command of the situation. Darnley denounced all the planners of the murder except himself, and they were banished; and in June the Queen was safely delivered of a son.

Sir James Melville brought the news to London and gave it to Cecil, whom he found in his house in Cannon Row, and Cecil at once took boat down the river to Greenwich. He arrived at the palace after supper and found the Queen dancing with some courtiers. At a pause, the news was quietly repeated to her, and her ladies were alarmed to see her sit down suddenly in a chair, leaning her head upon her hand. They gathered round her and before she could prevent herself, the words had escaped her: "The Queen of Scots is lighter of a fair son, and I am but a barren stock."

When Melville was received by her the following morning, she had recovered herself. She bounded forward, congratulating him on his news; she accepted Mary's invitation to stand god-mother; as regards a proxy, she could not, she said, send an English lady northwards at that time of year, but the Duchess of Argyll must stand for her and she gave orders for a splendid silver-gilt font to be sent for her god-son's christening.

Melville told her with unkind relish that Mary had been "so sair-handled" in her labour, she wished she had never married. He did this, he said, to give the English Queen "a little scare of marrying". This was a strange statement from Melville, who, ten years before, had made up his mind that Elizabeth was incapable of bearing children. For twenty years her vitality, high spirits and feminine elegance seemed to give the lie to rumours of malformation, disease or incapacity. Such rumours, never altogether silenced, were never entirely believed; information resolved itself into contradiction and

[1] Lang, *The Mystery of Mary Stuart*.

paradox, as the prismatic rays from a crystal of innumerable facets give light that reveals nothing.

The scare of marrying needed no encouragement. This issue between the Queen and Parliament was about to take a formidable shape; but August and September were given to a particularly enjoyable progress. Its central event was the Queen's visit to Oxford, of which Leicester was Chancellor; the visit was a counterpart to the one paid to Cambridge two years before and was equally brilliant and zestful, but as Cecil was not in charge it suffered from the mishaps which his vigilance and foresight had avoided.[1] The undergraduates being here allowed to crowd in to a performance of *Palamon and Arcite*, a staircase and part of a wall gave way beneath them, and three were fatally injured. The Queen, "much concerned", sent her own doctor, who was in her train, to see what he could do. The next night the play was resumed, and undergraduates were standing round the walls. The stage-manager had arranged a cry of hounds for Theseus in the quadrangle below, and the artless lads who were new to plays thought it a real hunt and started halloo-ing from the windows. The Queen laughed delightedly; she exclaimed: "Those boys are in very troth ready to leap out of the window to follow the hounds!" Their youth, ingenuousness and high spirits charmed her. Among the engaging crew was one whom she was to see again in a different scene. A young Fellow of St. John's, remarkable for his lively intelligence, his gracefulness and his elegant scholarship, read for her amusement a dissertation on the influence of the moon upon the tides: an early instance of the cult of Elizabeth as Diana, the Virgin Goddess. His name was Edmund Campion.

Parliament re-opened at the end of September, and its most urgent concern was to force the Queen to agree to marry, and meanwhile to appoint her successor. At a Council meeting early in October, the Duke of Norfolk, speaking on behalf of the whole nobility, reminded her that in the last session of Parliament she had promised an answer to the petition as to marriage and succession. He begged that she would now sanction the discussion by the Houses of these matters, of such crucial importance to her well-being and the realm's.

That the Queen had not expected this speech, or not expected it at that moment, was clear from the way she received it.[2] She replied with no statesman-like calm or politic evasion. She marshalled her resources with the terrified and desperate energy of a quarry that

[1] Nichols, *Progresses*.   [2] Neale, *Elizabeth and her Parliaments*, I.

hears the hounds. She exclaimed that she had governed the country well up to now, and these matters she would keep in her own hands without submitting to interference. As to appointing a successor, she said passionately she had no desire to be buried alive like her sister! The last days of Mary rushed upon her mind: and the appearance that the London to Hatfield road had presented. She cried that she wanted no such journeyings in *her* reign! The Privy Council could do nothing with her. But Parliament had a weapon. A subsidy was absolutely necessary if the business of government were to be carried on. Among other expenses, the Queen was daily spending large sums not only to maintain ships but to build new ones; it was moved therefore to revive the suit for the succession and make it clear that the granting of the subsidy depended on it. The debate in the Commons developed into unprecedented uproar. Some Members said it was too late in the day to go on, whereupon others rushed to the doors and shut them. Blows were exchanged and when patience was urged, there were cries of: "No! No! We have express charges to grant nothing before the Queen gives a firm answer to our demands!" The House of Lords agreed with the Commons and the steady pressure on the Queen to grant something that she could not grant was driving her almost beside herself. She was brought face to face with the two ungovernable fears of her existence. One was the prospect of living in the shadow of an heir, surrounded by suspicion, misgiving and dread, and this was bad enough. The other was the thing of which she never spoke, the unnameable horror, the nightmare of blood and darkness. The Lords determined that the matter should not drop.[1] Norfolk, Pembroke, Northampton and Leicester sought an audience, and at the sight of them entering the Presence Chamber all together and relentlessly approaching her, Elizabeth behaved like a frantic animal at bay. She poured out a stream of reproaches in which she almost called Norfolk a traitor. The others told her gravely that though Norfolk's words might displease her, he had done only his duty in speaking as he did. The Queen fought off each one in turn. She told Pembroke that he talked like a swaggering soldier, and as for Northampton, whose matrimonial entanglements had been such that his present marriage had required an Act of Parliament to bring it about, if he wanted to talk about marriage, the Queen said, let him talk about his own, instead of mincing words with her.

Leicester, who had no doubt believed that if the Queen gave

[1] C.S.P. Spanish, 156

way to the insistence on marriage, it would be in his favour, found himself as fiercely resisted as the rest. Elizabeth rounded on him, exclaiming she had thought if all the world abandoned her, he would not. Aghast, he swore that he would die at her feet. In passionate irritation she answered, that had nothing to do with the matter.

Cecil made a note: "Because it seemeth very uncomfortable to the Queen's Majesty to hear of this, at this time, and that it is hoped God will direct her heart to think more comfortable hereafter"—it would be as well, he thought, to prorogue Parliament, arrange the marriage meanwhile, and convene the members again when this was a *fait accompli*. But the temper of the Houses was dangerous, and the Crown's need of money was pressing. The Queen, whose alarm was now reined in, prepared to do battle.[1] A deputation of thirty members from each House waited on her, and she addressed them with a vehement, personal eloquence, using indeed the idiom she had used to Parry at fourteen: " 'Well,' she said, 'I will not, and so tell him.' " "Well, there hath been error," she told the deputies: "Well, I wish not the death of any man, but only this I desire, that they which have been the practisers herein, may before their deaths repent the same." The whole speech was a repetition and a justification of her refusal to grant their demands. The passion of resistance and self-defence she had been thrown into in the Presence Chamber was still there, but it was now formed into a collected argument and put into words that flew like a pelting of flints. "So to aggravate the cause against me!" cried the ringing voice. "Was I not born in this realm? Were my parents born in any foreign country? . . . Is not my kingdom here? Whom have I oppressed? Whom have I enriched to other's harm? . . . How have I governed since my reign? I will be tried by enmity itself. I need not to use many words for my deeds do try me."

As for the marriage: "I say again, I will marry as soon as I can conveniently, if God take not away him whom I mind to marry, or myself, or else some other great (hindrance) happen. . . . And I hope to have children, otherwise I would never marry."

For the succession: she rehearsed the danger of appointing one successor among so many who thought they had a claim. It was the sure way to civil disorder. "If you have liberty to treat of it, there be so many competitors . . . some would speed for their master, some for their mistress and every man for his friend."

[1] Neale, *op. cit.*

For any peril to herself, without a husband, or, childless, when her single life would tempt the assassin, she cared not. "Though I be a woman, yet I have as good a courage, answerable to my place, as ever my father had . . . I will never be by violence constrained to do anything. I thank God I am endued with such qualities, that if I were turned out of the realm in my petticoat, I were able to live in any place in Christendom."

Were it not for the danger to the realm, she would allow them to discuss the succession, notwithstanding the danger to her. "As soon as there may be a convenient time, and that it may be done with the least peril to you, although never without great danger to me, I will deal therein for your safety."

"This," she said in conclusion, "is my will and answer, which I would have to be showed to the two Houses." It was not the Queen's habit to leave anything in which she was interested to the discretion of the officers of state. She proceeded to detailed instruction. "And for the doing thereof," she said, "you, my Lord Chief Justice, are meetest to do it in the Upper House, and you, Cecil, in the Nether House." She remembered that the Lower House had had some inappropriate idea that the Speaker should have accompanied the deputation. She could not let this foolish notion pass. "They did not consider that he was not there to speak; *she* was a speaker, indeed. And," said the report, "there ended."

This uncompromising rebuff however was not the whole; it was accompanied by a very bold and able stroke. The subsidy under review was to be paid in three parts. She told the Houses she would relinquish the third part, saying that the money was as good as in her exchequer if it were in her subjects' pockets. It was a gesture of the utmost value in her relations with Parliament, and she could not have made it but for the unsleeping carefulness and economy of her spending.

The concession was received with great enthusiasm but there was still one more attempt to coerce the Queen. Bills that were made Acts were published, and it was suggested that her promise to marry should be incorporated in the prologue to the published version of the Subsidy Bill, as a means of forcing the Queen's hand by letting the nation read what she had actually said. When the draft was brought to Elizabeth for her signature and she saw what had been done, her indignation blazed up again. She wrote at the foot of the draft in her private scrawl: "I know no reason why any of my private answers to the realm should serve as a prologue to a subsidy book, neither yet do

I understand why such audacity should be used to make without my licence an Act of my words."

The prologue was re-worded and in its published form contained merely a polite statement as to "the great hope and comfort" the Members had felt, on hearing a gracious promise from the Queen to marry when it should be convenient.

XI

Affairs in Scotland, though still alarming to the English, were taking an unexpected turn. The situation between Mary and Darnley had gone from bad to worse; Lethington told her ambassador in France that it was "a heart-break" to her to be tied to such a husband, with no prospect of an "outgait". By 1567 the Protestant Lords had decided that some outgait must and should be found to release Mary and themselves. The matter was discussed at Craigmillar Castle between the Queen and a representative body of nobles, including Lethington, Morton, Mar and Mary's evil genius, the Earl of Bothwell. Murray was not present. Mary refused to consider divorce in case it threw doubts on the legitimacy of her son, and the Lords told her to leave the matter to them; she agreed to do so, with the elegant stipulation that nothing must be done that would stain her honour.

The terrific explosion that roused Edinburgh in the early hours of February 11 did more than blow up the house in which the invalid Darnley was lying: it brought down Mary's ambition in ruins. The charges of promiscuous immorality brought against her derived merely from the Presbyterian terror of gaiety, music and fine clothes; but once she had conceived a passion, her determination to gratify it was uncontrollable. Her first husband was a sickly child, her second was Darnley. Her infatuation with Bothwell was but too natural, but it was disastrous. Had she merely accepted the help of the Lords in freeing herself of Darnley, she could have begun afresh, secure in the tolerance of mutual blackmail; but the Lords had not given their support to Bothwell in these compromising measures, to have him, rapacious, arrogant and detested, put over their heads and made, at last, their King. When Mary insisted upon doing this, they turned on her. They had discussed the murder, they knew who was to do it; but the wife's guilt was greater than the councillors', and to Mary's endless anger, this was the aspect placed before the world.

The famous collection of letters was found in a silver-gilt casket under Bothwell's bed; it was characteristic that the casket itself, with its chasing of F's crowned, had belonged to Mary's first husband. Of the letters apparently written by Mary, only two show a foreknowledge of the murder, and much effort has been spent in making out that these are forgeries; but the presumptive evidence against her is so strong, that if all the letters were forgeries, it would make no difference to the appearance of Mary's guilt. By a sudden reconciliation with her sick husband, she took him out of his father's protection at Glasgow and established him in the remote, half-ruinous dwelling, Kirk o' Field. Here she had been sleeping in a room under his own, but on the night of the murder she left for Holyrood two hours before the explosion took place, sending back a servant to bring away a rich counterpane that had been used on her bed.

Suspicious as this was, her behaviour after the murder was damning. That Bothwell had procured it was universally accepted; Mary took no steps to have the crime investigated, and when urged to do so by the wretched father, she replied that Parliament would meet in the spring and they would look into the matter. Meanwhile she gave Darnley's rich clothes to Bothwell. The tailor who altered them was heard to say, this was right enough: the victim's garments were always the hangman's perquisite.

The news of the murder reached London on February 17. Elizabeth sent Lady Howard and Lady Cecil to the Tower to break the news to Lady Lennox. The poor woman fell into such paroxysms of grief that the two ladies were alarmed; on their report, the Queen sent Dr. Huick to her. The news of conspiracy and murder against so near a neighbour at first caused a general panic; Elizabeth had the locks changed on the doors of her Privy Chamber and bedchamber.

The next reports said that after one week's retirement for mourning the Queen of Scots had announced that her health was suffering from confinement, and she had gone to a house-party at Lord Seton's castle, where the guests included Bothwell. When Elizabeth heard this, she was momentarily startled out of herself: she could not credit such idiocy; she declared it could not be true! But it was true.[1]

The whole course of Mary's doings caused Elizabeth a painful agitation of mingled feelings. Jealous, frightened as she was of Mary's power, she was not prepared to see it thrown away by actions which discredited monarchy and seemed likely, by plunging Scotland into civil war, either to encourage rebellion or to bring in the French. Elizabeth was Mary's enemy, but she was by no means incapable of sympathy with her. When she heard how Rizzio was murdered, she exclaimed before she could stop herself, that had she been in Mary's place, she would have stabbed Darnley with his own dagger. Then

[1] MSS. Simancas, quoted by Froude.

she had turned with a laugh to the Spanish Ambassador and said he must not think she would stab the Archduke Charles if he came to woo her. Now she wrote with urgency, exhorting Mary to show some sense. Seven years ago she herself had had to reckon with slander after the death of Amy Dudley. Mary was in a position infinitely worse, and Elizabeth implored her to realize what people were saying, and not to "look through her fingers" at the murder but to have proper enquiries set on foot at once. "I should not do the office of a faithful cousin and friend if I did not urge you to preserve your honour," she wrote. "I counsel you so to take this matter to heart that you may show the world what a noble Princess and loyal wife you are."

The advice was totally ignored. The farcical trial of Bothwell took place on April 12, at which, instead of his being prosecuted by the Crown, the prosecution was left to Lennox, who was forbidden to bring more than six retainers with him, while Bothwell's men, estimated at 4,000, thronged the streets surrounding the court-house. Bothwell, mounted on Darnley's charger, rode out of the gates of Holyrood to stand his trial, and the Queen waved to him from her window as he went. Lennox was too frightened to appear, and the verdict of "not guilty" was the prelude to Bothwell's staged abduction of the Queen, a device which deceived nobody, and to the marriage which the abduction was supposed to render necessary. The marriage was performed with Protestant rites, Bothwell's divorce from his wife, Lady Jane, having been in some manner brought about in time for the ceremony.

Mary's reputation was so completely lost that, for the time being, her political importance in Europe had gone with it and she was now faced with stark ruin at home. The Lords' fury against Bothwell reached its climax when Mary placed in his hands the fortresses of Edinburgh, Leith, Dumbarton and Dunbar. She herself was wild with misery at his open preference for his first wife, but she refused to separate from him. The risings against them began in June; Elizabeth, though she expressed herself freely on Mary's hasty marriage with a subject who, besides what the Queen described as "other notorious lacks", was publicly said to be the murderer of Mary's late husband, promised none the less to do what she could, in face of this insurrection, for Mary's comfort, her child's safety and the tranquillity of her realm.

But nothing could be done. At Carberry Hill Mary's forces disbanded without fighting, and at the end of the day Bothwell rode away leaving her on the field, proving once more how incapable Mary was of choosing men. She was brought back to Edinburgh, where the mob was kept off her with difficulty. Their Queen swore that she would hang and crucify them, and her subjects shouted: "Burn the whore!" After a night of raving hysteria she was taken to Lochleven Castle, a beautiful solitude in the middle of a lake.

Elizabeth had wanted to see Mary's power curtailed by a Protestant Council so that she would not be able to launch a Catholic invasion of England; she did not want to see a neighbouring sovereign a prisoner in her subjects' hands. The spectacle was one damaging to every sovereign. The English Queen felt Mary's imprisonment as a personal affront. Her Privy Council, Cecil in particular, maintained that the Scots had a right to depose a sovereign who had disgraced her calling. This attitude increased Elizabeth's agitation, and the struggle of opposing impulses of such strength produced a state of nervous tension in her that approached distraction.

Each party in Scotland now claimed her help, and Throckmorton was sent to keep communications open. Elizabeth had said of the Lords: "Though she were guilty of all they charge her with, I cannot assist them while their Queen is imprisoned." To Mary she sent a message promising to help her to regain her rights, but saying that it was essential that the truth of the matter with which Mary was charged should be discovered and proclaimed, so that those responsible might be punished. But Mary from the very first was determined never to submit to any enquiry, and she had already made up her mind that England should be the scene of her next activities. Throckmorton wrote: "Queen Mary desires above all places to come to England." It was the last place where Elizabeth wished to see her, and her going to France to bring French armies into Scotland would be nearly as bad. Elizabeth replied: "We find her removal into this realm or into France not without great discomfort to us." But what was to be done with her? Her refusal to give up Bothwell, with all that such a refusal implied, had closed any prospect of her return to the throne. As Throckmorton had shrewdly said: "Queen Mary will never have any more power in Scotland." "The Lords," he said, "considering her former misbehaviour as well in the government of the realm as in her own person . . . could not permit her any longer to put the realm in peril by her disorders." There was a strong party among the Scots themselves who wanted her put to death, and Elizabeth fiercely threatened an invasion to revenge the crime if it were perpetrated. She was savagely answered that any more such threats would lead to Mary's instant execution.

Murray now returned to Scotland, and going to Lochleven saw his sister for the first time since the murder. He told her that her life could be saved only by her giving up Bothwell, making no attempt at escape and no effort to bring foreign soldiers into Scotland. He got the nearest of any living being to making her admit some of her actions. "Sometimes the Queen wept bitterly, sometimes she admitted her misadvisedness and misgovernment, some things she did confess plainly, some she did extenuate." She told Murray she wanted him to act as Regent and to take charge of her jewels. While she was still in bed after miscarrying of twin children, a deed of abdication was forced on her as the alternative to death, and in her weeping she exclaimed: "I am but twenty-five years old!" This was the age at which Elizabeth had assumed the crown of England.

Though Mary afterwards repudiated it, she wrote the signature by which James became King of Scotland at thirteen months old; but it had been prophesied that it would prove easier to catch her than to keep her, and her extraordinary charm, which left a nation unmoved but was irresistible to people at close quarters, got her the assistance she needed to escape out of Lochleven. Her supporters made a stand against the Regent's forces at Langside and were heavily defeated, and Mary made a long, unresting flight to Dundrennan on the shores of Solway. On the other side of a narrow inlet rose the coast of Cumberland; the danger Elizabeth had so long dreaded was now very close. The English Queen had sent Mary a letter congratulating her upon her escape and promising assistance provided she did not appeal to France; but the letter never reached its destination. On Sunday, May 17, Mary, accompanied by Lord Herries and Lord Fleming with eighteen followers, boarded a fishing-boat and crossed the Firth. They touched the English shore at Workington.

Mary had always meant to come to England. She had frequently demanded a meeting with Elizabeth, and when one had been arranged at York, and cancelled by the Privy Council because of the posture of French affairs, she had cried with anger and disappointment. She believed that her mere presence would arouse unlimited enthusiasm and she thought herself to have solid grounds for this optimism. Four years before, Cecil had been told by a spy, Christopher Rokesby, that the Scottish Queen had a list of the families all over England from whom she could expect support. She had no intention of going to France; the French court had shown their opinion of her doings when they sent no embassage to condole with her on Darnley's death; as to remaining in Scotland, and waiting to see if the tide would turn—the last time she had appeared in the streets of her capital, the people were shouting: "Burn the whore!" But England offered a fresh opportunity and a near prospect of a glorious future which would overpay the losses and humiliations of the past. The deputy governor, pending instructions from London, escorted her to Carlisle, and here the neighbouring gentry streamed in to pay their respects and to be charmed by the beautiful, stately, emotional and gracious young woman who might some day, and even shortly, be their queen. Meanwhile Mary wrote to Elizabeth telling her that she had no clothes except those she stood up in and adding: "Pray send for me as soon as you can."

Elizabeth was about to do this, when Cecil, with the energy of a drowning man, managed to deflect the impulse. Mary, he said, considering "her appetite to the Crown", must be handled with extreme caution. To receive her would be tantamount to acknowledging her as Elizabeth's heir; and from every point of view, she could not be admitted to Elizabeth's presence until a full enquiry had been held into the murder of Elizabeth's cousin. The instincts of statecraft and of mere self-preservation were quickly revived, and Elizabeth heard that her deadly enemy was holding court among Elizabeth's subjects; then she had to consider Mary's letter. The Queen of Scots had come to take the kingdom; she began by demanding Elizabeth's clothes.

The demand's symbolic meaning was out of all proportion to the practical one. In her infancy Elizabeth had been deprived of her mother and declared a bastard by her father, and the medium through which she had understood her misfortunes was that her servants had not clothes to put on her. The importance she now attached to clothes and jewels sprang from the ruling passion of her existence: they were part of the apparatus of sovereignty, but they had an additional meaning for her, beyond even this. Giving did not come easy to her, but in face of this request, she felt something more than the reluctance of a vain and greedy woman to part with her things; for her to send a present of clothes and jewels suitable to the Queen of Scots, would have required an effort of which she was incapable.

Sir Francis Knollys, Vice-Chamberlain of the Queen's Household, was sent up to Carlisle to take charge of Mary and her establishment, and before he left Elizabeth told him to tell one of her waiting women to make up a parcel of clothes for the Queen of Scots. The maid, having no personal orders from the Queen as to dresses and ornaments, collected some under-linen. The Spanish Ambassador "heard" that the parcel contained two worn-out chemises, a length of black velvet and a pair of shoes. This was what he was bound to hear. Mary's own version in a letter to France was :"The Queen of England has sent me a little linen." But though not of the grotesque description developed by rumour, the parcel was not suitable to the occasion, and Mary, who would herself have met such a request with lavish attention to comfort and elegance, preserved a well-bred silence when the contents were displayed. Knollys was embarrassed and said the maid must have misunderstood his order, and collected things for a maid such as herself. Mary had, by this time, been provided with "two or three suits of black velvet", bought in Carlisle, but she had wanted and expected from Elizabeth such things as Carlisle could not supply.[1]

Murray, meanwhile, who had taken possession of his sister's jewels, knew, it seemed, of Elizabeth's fondness for pearls. Of the great treasury now in his hands he chose out six ropes of extremely fine pearls strung on knotted thread and twenty-five separate pearls of enormous size whose tinge was "like that of black muscat grapes", and sent them by an agent to London. Catherine de Medici, who had given some of them to Mary, wanted to buy them back, but the French Ambassador told her there was no hope of this. Elizabeth, with Leicester and Pembroke beside her, had examined the pearls and all three had been astonished at their beauty; and Murray had directed that, to gratify the Queen of England, she was to be allowed to buy them at a price one third less than their value.

That Mary had been meanly treated in matters where she would have behaved very well herself, made her pitiable, but it did not alter the facts of how she had behaved in Scotland and how she meant to behave in England if she got the chance. Her impregnable confidence in her rights and merits prevented her from understanding what the majority of the Scots really thought of her or what the majority of the English were likely to think. She knew that she was a potential threat to the English Queen and she flaunted the fact with wild indiscretion. When told that, against her wish, she was to be removed from Carlisle to Bolton Castle, she exclaimed: "I have made great wars in Scotland—I pray God I make no trouble in other realms also!"

[1] Andersen, *Collections*, relating to the history of Mary, Queen of Scotland.

Lord Herries was her Ambassador to Elizabeth and dealt in peremptory language. He demanded either that an armed force should be sent to Scotland to restore his mistress to the throne, or that she should be allowed to go to France to ask the help that was refused in England. To the English government the requests were equally impossible, but Mary followed them with a letter asking for a passport for Lord Fleming to go to France that he might negotiate for her with Catherine de Medici. Fleming had come to England with Mary, but he was the governor of Dumbarton Castle, the great fortress commanding the Firth of Clyde. The mere idea of a man in such a post going on such an errand was enough to freeze English blood. When no answer was received Mary despatched another letter equally forcible. To this Elizabeth was driven to reply: "Madame, I am greatly astonished that you press me so for Lord Fleming's going to France. . . . You surely doubt my wisdom, in asking me to let the keeper of such a place go there. . . . Begging you to have some consideration for me, instead of thinking always of yourself."[1]

Mary's indignation was extreme, and as Murray was putting down the party of her adherents, she regarded delay in meeting her wishes as the worst of injuries. In August Herries declared with a lack of caution and respect worthy of his mistress herself: "If Queen Elizabeth is displeased with a report that the French are coming to Scotland, she has only herself to thank, because she has not despatched my mistress's affairs."[2]

The despatch of Mary's affairs seemed to herself to be a straightforward matter. It was her firm conviction that she ought, with the armed help of friendly princes, to be replaced on her throne immediately; that nothing she had done deserved blame; the murder of Darnley had been the work of a conspiracy in which she herself had had no share; and she went further than this: Bothwell had forced some of the Lords to sign a bond agreeing to his marriage with the Queen, and Mary by a master-stroke re-phrased the matter by saying that they "had presented her in marriage to their wicked confederate the Earl of Bothwell". In any case the question of her guilt did not arise; the sin of her subjects in rebelling against her was so heinous, it cancelled any trivial indiscretions of her own. Her attitude to Elizabeth was uncompromising: she demanded and expected to be received officially by the English Queen, who was to chastise her rebels for her and to restore her crown, paying no heed to the causes for which Mary had been dethroned, other than merely listening to what

[1] Harrison, *Letters of Queen Elizabeth.*   [2] Mignet, *Mary Queen of Scots.*

Mary chose to say about them. At the same time she had never ratified the Treaty of Edinburgh, she continued to demand the recognition by the English Parliament of her right to succeed Elizabeth on
the latter's death and, as her words were soon to show, was secretly
prepared to replace her without waiting for that event.

Elizabeth, at the time of Mary's imprisonment in Lochleven, had
made the natural but fatal mistake of promising to help her to regain
her throne. This Mary never allowed anyone to forget, and the
Queen of England was for ever branded as a treacherous hypocrite.
Mary never acknowledged that Elizabeth had done her best to save
her life. Whatever the Scots' answer to Elizabeth's threat had been,
the fact remained that Elizabeth had threatened reprisals if they took
Mary's life, and that Mary's life had, in fact, been spared. But the
promise of help had been given; and everything that Mary now
demanded on the strength of it was impossible. The English government would never allow an English army to cross the border to
destroy Protestant Scots for the sake of their Catholic Queen; and if
they had allowed it—everyone knew what the consequences would
be. When Throckmorton had spoken to the Lords with veiled
threats of intervention on Mary's behalf, he had received the sinister
reply: "Do not drive us to France faster than we wish to run." If the
French saw a good opportunity to get back into Scotland, it would be
all one to them which side called them in.

Cecil and the Council as a whole had no quarrel with the Scots'
refusal to reinstate their Queen; only Elizabeth stood out. She feared
Mary, she wanted to see her in eclipse, but she had the instinct, half
rational, half superstitious, but amounting to divination, that once the
principle of the subject's obedience to the sovereign was over-ridden,
no sovereign was safe. In vigilance and hard work, the qualities that
were the basis of successful kingship, she and Cecil were in complete
accord; but in the last resort something was needed beyond these: it
was the magic that resided in herself, not in virtue of her own genius,
but of the blood of her crowned ancestors. The spell was in her keeping and anything that might weaken its potency must be put away.
When the magic worked in favour of what Cecil wished his course
was irradiated by it; when it worked against his wishes he found the
Queen almost unmanageable.

"I fear our good Queen has the wolf by the ears!" had been Arch-
bishop Parker's exclamation when he heard of Mary's landing in
England. The position could hardly have been better described.
Every decision Elizabeth now took would be disapproved of by some

influential party, and every course of action open to her would be fraught with some danger to herself. Since neither Mary's side nor Murray's could prevail without English help the latter agreed to let the quarrel be judged by English commissioners.

Mary was at first highly indignant at the idea of submitting to any enquiry but she at last agreed, instructing her agents, Lord Herries and the Bishop of Ross, that they were to treat Murray and his party as defendants only, who were there to answer the charge of rebellion against her; she herself would admit nothing. Her letter to Elizabeth said as much: "I will never plead my cause against theirs unless they stand before you in manacles. Madame, I am no equal of theirs and would sooner die than by any act of mine behave as if I were."

The enquiry opened in October at York, before the Duke of Norfolk, the Earl of Sussex and Sir Ralph Sadler, and Mary told Ross that she hoped and expected they would be in her favour, Norfolk as the representative of the old nobility, Sussex as his friend, and Sadler as a man of inferior station who would not care to oppose them.[1]

Murray asked the commissioners whether, if he proved the charge of complicity in Darnley's murder against Mary, the English government would undertake to keep her a prisoner in England. He was told that question must be referred to the Privy Council in London. He therefore opened his case with the charge of Mary's having handed over the power of the realm to Bothwell; but privately, he showed the commissioners copies of the Casket Letters. The ambivalent Lethington had already shown copies to Mary and Mary had not said that the letters were forgeries; she had only told Lethington to do his best to suppress them. Now the commissioners had seen them, and Norfolk urged Murray most strongly not to put them in as evidence. He spoke of Mary as "our future queen", and he wanted the letters suppressed, not because he thought she had not written them, but because he thought she had.

Norfolk's sister, Lady Scrope, had acted as hostess to Mary in her triumphant weeks at Carlisle, and here it is supposed that Norfolk must have seen, for the first and only time, the woman who was to prove his ruin. He had been discerned by Mary to be favourable to her cause. Though nominally a Protestant his connections were those of the ancient Catholic nobility; he had been married three times and at thirty-two was once again a widower. The urgent need to settle

[1] Mignet.

the succession, and Elizabeth's steady refusal to make an immediate marriage, were leading some people to say that whatever the rights or wrongs of the Scots, the English would be best served by recognizing, under suitable safeguards to the Protestant religion, Mary's claim as heiress presumptive, and marrying her to a distinguished Englishman. Norfolk, the premier Duke of England and head of the great family of Howard, who called himself a Protestant and at the same time was acceptable to the Catholics, might answer the wishes of a very numerous party, to whom the idea of such a marriage and of Mary's recognition seemed the likeliest way of laying the spectre of civil war. Norfolk himself was strongly drawn to the scheme, which gave a romantic and splendid turn to his own fortunes and had the exalted character of a high enterprise undertaken for the public good. He sounded Sussex, who did not altogether reject the plan but made it clear that if he were to have anything to do with it, it must be laid before the Queen, and no steps in the matter must be taken without her knowledge and concurrence. Other peers gave him a more discreet encouragement, among whom was Leicester.

Norfolk had interesting and sympathetic qualities but ability of any sort was not among them. He first incurred the enmity of Leicester and then trusted and tried to make use of him. He had once threatened to strike Leicester in the face for his familiar behaviour to the Queen, and when de la Mothe Fénélon was accredited to St. James', early in the year, he found a dangerous situation existing between Leicester on the one hand and Norfolk and his father-in-law Arundel on the other. The two nobles, speaking on behalf of the old aristocracy, one day addressed Leicester with great severity. They told him that he was a traitor to the realm, since it was his influence that prevented the Queen from making a suitable marriage. They went on to say that an injury to the Queen's reputation was an injury to themselves, and then gave a detailed explanation of what they found fault with in his behaviour.

The Sovereign's bed-chamber was, by usage, a state apartment to which the chief officers of the realm had the entrée on occasion, but their access was through the ranks of Gentlemen Pensioners outside the Presence Chamber, and the Ladies of the Privy Chamber into which the bed-chamber opened, so that there was no danger of the Queen's privacy being disturbed. Leicester as Master of the Horse had the entrée with other officers of state, but Arundel and Norfolk told him that he used it most improperly. They had heard that he was there in the morning before the Queen was out of bed, and that he was in the habit of handing her the shift she was to put on. They expressed their views on this matter in no uncertain terms; and while they were about it, they said, they would tell him that they thoroughly objected to his practice of "kissing the Queen's Majesty without being invited thereto". At the same time, if he could now tell them that the Queen meant to marry him, then, so important did they think it that she should marry somebody, they would support his suit.

Leicester could be amazingly arrogant: he could also be un-expectedly supple and quiet. He was quiet now. He was not able to say that he expected the Queen to marry him, but he made a cour-teous reply and thanked the peers for their advice, by which he promised to be guided. It seemed that he had taken it in excellent part; but soon afterwards it was noticed that there was violent hostility between his servants and Norfolk's, and that they were wearing violet sashes and yellow sashes respectively, as the badge of their vendetta.[1]

When affairs had been in this state less than a year ago, a sensible man would have been very cautious in laying himself open to injury from Leicester; but on the face of it, it appeared natural that Leicester should join any movement to gain the favour of the Queen of Scots. He was of course in favour of Elizabeth's remaining Queen of England, since no other arrangement was likely to suit him so well. He would not promote a rebellion to take away her life, but if some-one else should, or if she were to die in the course of nature, he owed it to himself to stand well with whoever was to succeed her.

Elizabeth had at no time given the impression of being robust. "God send her as good health as she hath a heart!" had been Cecil's exclamation in the beginning of the reign. Her blazing nervous energy was not a quality that suggested sound health. Her very activity, in riding, walking, dancing, coupled as it was with a small appetite and light sleep, was apt to seem like morbid restlessness rather than healthy physical vigour. Her frequent indispositions pulled her down alarmingly: "very thin", "the colour of a corpse", "her bones could be counted", were characteristic descriptions of her appearance after her spells of sickness that figured in ambassadors' despatches as fever, gastric attacks, neuralgia and aching limbs. The anxiety caused by even a minor ailment whose true nature could not be diagnosed was wearing in the extreme. "Her Majesty . . . sud-

[1] Gonzalez, *Documents from Simancas.*

denly sick in her stomach and as suddenly relieved by a vomit. You must think such a matter would drive men to the end of their wits, but God is the stay of all that put their trust in Him," ejaculated Cecil fervently in a letter to the English Ambassador at Paris. Cecil's own alarms were the keener because he could not accept the prospect of recognizing Mary as Elizabeth's successor. Should Mary succeed, Cecil would be ruined, but Leicester did not intend to be.

The details of a projected marriage between Mary and Norfolk were not immediately known to Elizabeth, but the unsatisfactory and inconclusive progress of the enquiry at York made her decide to have the seat of the conference moved to Westminster. Here, Cecil and Bacon, Leicester and his brother Warwick were added to the commissioners, and a summons was sent to the Earls of Northumberland and Westmorland to attend. These nobles were Catholic, and they were, after Norfolk, the most important of the ancient northern families. That they were sent for to attend an enquiry at which the evidence of adultery and murder was to be brought against Mary Queen of Scots, showed that someone in the government had an idea of which way the wind was blowing.

When the conference re-opened at Westminster, a much stronger tone against Mary was obvious. Someone had given Murray confidence, for he now made the charge against her of complicity in Darnley's murder and supported it with a great deal of evidence.

Mary's commissioners had been instructed by her that they were to leave the court if Murray's party moved from defence to accusation, and the Bishop of Ross therefore announced that the proceedings of the commission were null and void and that he and his colleagues would give no further attendance at it. In their absence, Murray produced the confessions of Bothwell's accomplices and at last, with a show of unwillingness, the Casket Letters.

Elizabeth had fallen out with her own advisers as to the immunity which crowned heads should enjoy, but in the face of evidence now produced by Murray, she wrote to Mary to say that if Mary had any reply to these charges, let her make it in God's name, and not do herself the irreparable damage of declining to answer from any considerations of dignity. "We cannot but as one Prince and near cousin regarding another, as earnestly as we may, require and charge you not to forbear answering." But since no answer was in Mary's power she fell back on the effective method of haughty silence. Knollys reported that she would say nothing "unless your Council would take a short answer for a sufficient answer; that is to say, that the accusations of her adversaries are false because that she, on the word of a prince, will say that they are false". As Mary maintained this silence for the rest of her life, the body of her sympathizers, particularly those who were children at the time of the event, forgot what had been proved against her; the stain wore out as Cecil foretold it would; there remained in men's minds only the lovely, tragic figure shut up in a castle, who, in Catholic eyes, was the Queen of England.

Since Mary refused to answer Murray's accusations, Elizabeth was able to terminate the conference by saying that nothing had been brought forward to impair the honour of Murray, but that, on the other hand, the charges against the Queen of Scots were "not sufficiently proven". Murray, his regency for the infant James recognized, went back to Scotland, where he was urgently needed, and the Accounts of the Queen's Purse covering the years from 1559 to 1569 show an interesting entry. Among such items as "Linen cloth bought and made into towels, by Mrs. Ludwell, £26.2.7; To Peter Trinder Goldsmith, for repairing and mending the Queen's Jewels, £32.15.10; Binding of four books for the Queen's Majesty, £1.6.8; Perfumes of sundry kinds occupied to Her Majesty's use, £68.7.1", occurs for February of this year, the entry: "£5,000, drawn by Cecil and given by him to Tamworth to take to the Earl of Murray", to be repaid on November 1.

Since neither party had been declared guilty by the tribunal it was difficult to justify keeping Mary in captivity while Murray was allowed to return to Scotland, but this difficulty was academic, while the difficulty of releasing her was of the most serious practical kind. The prospect of letting her loose to collect Spanish or French troops to bring into Scotland could not be faced, strict equity might demand that it should be faced, but as a matter of practical politics it was not worth discussing. She might have been allowed to return to Scotland for the Scots themselves to decide her fate, but since at the Congress of Perth the following year, the Scots flatly refused to have her back in Scotland either as Queen, co-Regent or private person, it is tolerably certain what that fate would have been, and Elizabeth scarcely injured her when, instead of sending her to Scotland, she had Mary established at Tutbury Castle in Staffordshire under the guardianship of the admiring Earl of Shrewsbury, waited upon by her own ladies and gentlemen, secretaries and servants, allowed to hunt and hawk, the expenses of her miniature court defrayed by the English government while her dowry as Queen Dowager of France was paid into her own hands.

Had Mary acquiesced in this situation, her position with all the English parties would have strengthened, and had her ambition been, as she said it was, merely to be recognized as Elizabeth's heir, she must, with patience, have gained it at last. But it was idle to hope that Mary would submit to any such arrangement.

XII

To the english Court's regret, the charming de Silva was replaced by Don Gerau de Spes, a man so little fitted for ambassadorial duties, it was surprising he should have attained an ambassador's rank. De Spes landed in England in the spirit of a crusader. He thought that the reclamation of England for Catholicism and the Spanish interest could and should be put in hand immediately. He established a *rapport* with the Queen of Scots at Tutbury, and he soon had his hands on a plot of which the aims were to restore Catholicism as the state religion, to remove Cecil and restore to the old nobility the powers and influence Cecil had assumed, and to seal the whole by the marriage of Mary to the Duke of Norfolk. The Earls of Northumberland and Westmorland were more positive in their views than Norfolk himself, and their Countesses, particularly Lady Northumberland, were more positive even than the Earls. De Spes equalled the ladies in sanguine enthusiasm. He thought it would be a simple matter for the Duke of Alva to release a force of picked Spanish veterans from the Netherlands and throw them across the Channel to aid that host of English Catholics who were only waiting for an opportunity to rise and overthrow Queen Elizabeth.

Mary's aptitude for *grande passion* was such that she had already erected the weak, uncertain Norfolk, who was barely known to her, as the master of her affections and her fate. She was writing to him as "My own Lord", and promising to obey his lightest word. Had Norfolk been capable of playing the part Mary assigned to him, the situation would have been very dangerous, but the Duke's doublet should have been made of changeable taffeta, his mind was a very opal. In his position as head of the nobility he had spoken severely to Leicester and even to the Queen, when their conduct seemed to him to require it, but now that he himself was considering a marriage with the heiress presumptive of the realm he had not the resolution to say so. He approached the Queen in the garden of Richmond Palace, that garden where a brick wall with fruit trees trained upon it enclosed a lawn, with four flower-beds and a yew tree in the centre.[1] Elizabeth asked him if he had any news to give her of a marriage? He

[1] Singleton, *The Shakespeare Garden.*

said no. Then she told him straight out she had heard he would marry the Queen of Scots.

Norfolk's nerve failed him; he exclaimed that his loyalty would not allow him to take such a step and added that he preferred to sleep on a safe pillow. A lady came up with some flowers and the Queen dropped the topic. It was perhaps too much to say that Elizabeth's suspicion, once aroused, was ever entirely laid asleep, but this pointed allusion to Darnley's fate seemed for the time being to convince her.

Meanwhile de Spes, in close touch with Mary, nursed his schemes, and the events of the next few months justified their optimism.

The English Channel was swarming with pirates whom Elizabeth tacitly encouraged by taking no steps against them. Cecil was against this toleration; it was Elizabeth's personal favour which supported them—this was the reverse side of her policy as Queen of the Sea. The honest hearts maintained a fleet at their own expense which would augment the Royal Navy if called upon, their crews gained seamanship and the loot was of great value. The pirates also served another turn. The fearful onslaught of Spain on the religious and economic freedom of the Netherlands was entering its fiercest phase under the Duke of Alva, whose aim was to reduce the Provinces completely and to make them a seat of government from which Spain would dominate the rest of Europe. The nearness to England of this great hostile force was a continual menace, and that English pirates whose actions could be disclaimed by the Crown should obstruct Spanish communications through the Channel was a welcome situation, about which least said was soonest mended.

In December 1568 four Spanish ships took refuge from pirates in Plymouth and Southampton. They were carrying between them £85,000 packed in chests, which were being sent to Alva to pay his troops. The contents of the chests and their destination became known to the Privy Council, and another fact also: that the money, which had been advanced by Genoese bankers, was the bankers' property until Alva had received it. The bankers' London agent, when sounded, said warmly that the English Queen's credit was much better than that of the King of Spain, whereupon Elizabeth announced that she herself was borrowing the gold; the chests were disembarked and brought up to the Tower.

Alva was *in extremis* for the money; the act, within the law or not, was deliberately injurious, and with de Spes' strong approval, though Alva was capable of acting without this, he imprisoned the English merchants then in the Netherlands and impounded their goods. The

English government retaliated on the Spanish traders in England, whose property was much greater than that held by Alva, and they put de Spes under house-arrest and opened his correspondence. De Spes, who from the first had gravely underestimated the power of the present government, adopted an airy and mocking manner in writing about it. "Do not be surprised to hear that I am imprisoned," said one of his despatches. "In this island there are all the enchantments of Amadis and I am a prisoner of Queen Oriana." A reference to Oriana, daughter of the King of Britain, whom Amadis, in the Spanish romance, won to wife, was gallant enough, but it was facetious; Cecil did not object to the joke, and endorsed his copy of the despatch: "Against the Queen's Majesty, Oriana", but Elizabeth was becoming alarmed and therefore highly irritable, and de Spes was told that "such vain fancies, taken from Amadis of Gaul, were unworthy of a person holding his office". The coup of the Genoese ryalls had been brilliant, but it might have been bought too dear. Alva had closed the port of Antwerp to English vessels, and a threat of further Spanish reprisals had made the Queen a prey to doubts and fears. It was a hard condition of working with her, which Cecil accepted but which occasionally goaded him to complaint, that when Elizabeth had endorsed a policy that succeeded, she took the credit to herself, and when she had endorsed a failure or what threatened failure, she laid the blame entirely on other shoulders. Now she was reported as saying she wished the devil might fly away with those who had advised her to appropriate the money.[1]

To Mary, the situation looked bright with imminent success, and she wrote a letter to de Spes which, though not known to them at the time, entirely explains the fear, the hatred, the severity, which the House of Commons showed in all its language about her and the anger that Elizabeth drew upon herself by her refusal, throughout seventeen years, to allow the Queen of Scots to be executed for high treason. In this letter Mary revealed not only "her appetite to the Crown" but that she was eager to do the one thing the English never forgive anybody: to bring in a foreign army to coerce them. "Tell your master," she wrote to the Spanish Ambassador, "that if he will help me, I shall be Queen of England in three months and mass shall be said all over the kingdom."[2] But Alva saw that his own actions were causing such economic damage in the Netherlands, he must not keep up his reprisals; and at the same time the English merchants proved themselves largely independent of Antwerp. Two years

[1] C.S.P. Spanish, 1568.　　　　　　　　[2] ibid.

before, Hamburg had been considered as an alternative trading centre, and in May an English fleet, convoyed by the Royal Navy, made a highly successful voyage there. Norfolk, Arundel and de Spes had exhorted Alva to stop this fleet, a step which would inflict enormous damage on the City of London and, by creating panic, would make conditions favourable for rebellion.[1] It is possible to believe that Norfolk genuinely thought himself to be acting for the best, but the bulk of the English nation could not be expected to agree with him.

Cecil, who, with Sussex, had once been Norfolk's friend, knew something of what was going on. He advised Norfolk, if he had anything on his mind, to tell the Queen about it. Norfolk said afterwards how bitterly he regretted having disregarded the advice that would have saved him. Cecil knew also that there was a coalition against himself, whose objectives were to put down the new men, restore the national alliance with Spain and ultimately to restore Catholicism: and that the figurehead of this group was the ambivalent Norfolk. He undermined the latter's stability still further by offering his help, as Master of the Court of Awards, to shepherd Norfolk through a law-suit. The court decided in Norfolk's favour, and his fellow-conspirators, Northumberland and Westmorland, who had come down to London to see Cecil arrested at the council-table and ordered to the Tower, were left in mid-air. Cecil had told Elizabeth what he knew of the enmity against him and had assured himself of her entire support. He wrote to his friend White in Ireland: "I find the Queen's Majesty my good gracious Lady without change of any of her old good meaning towards me."

Norfolk meanwhile thought Leicester was waiting for a favourable opportunity to speak to the Queen in favour of his marriage with the Queen of Scots. The Court was on its summer progress, and he came upon the Queen and Leicester in the Queen's lodging at Guildford. For coolness the cushions had been placed in an open doorway and here the Queen sat, listening with one ear to a little child who was playing the lute and singing to her, and with the other to Lord Leicester who knelt beside her. Norfolk was about to withdraw but Leicester came up to him, leaving the Queen listening to the child, and told Norfolk he had that moment been speaking to the Queen about the marriage-project. How had the Queen received it? asked Norfolk eagerly. "Indifferent well," had been the answer.[2] Norfolk's confidence cannot have been great, for when the Court came to

[1] MSS. Simancas, quoted by Froude.
[2] Norfolk's Deposition, quoted by Strickland.

Thornham, the Queen told him to sit down to dinner at her table, and after the meal, in his words, she gave him a nip, bidding him beware of his pillow. His delusion as to Leicester's support was soon dispelled. The Queen had reached Hampshire in her progress and was entertained by the Marquess of Winchester at Basing House, while Leicester stayed with Lord Pembroke at Titchfield. Here, Leicester, slightly ill from some genuine ailment or, as Camden suggests, "counterfeiting the sick", took to his bed, and sent, imploring the Queen to come to him. Elizabeth hurried to his bedside, and Leicester, with groans and bitter sighs, poured out all that he knew of Norfolk's project for marrying the Queen of Scots, the details of which his sensitive conscience would no longer allow him to keep to himself. A confession so managed could do him nothing but good, but Norfolk was unhinged by the exposure. Elizabeth summoned him and, asking him fiercely how he dared go about such a marriage behind her back, ordered him to give over the scheme at once. Norfolk had drifted beyond the point where frankness could have saved him. He vowed to obey the Queen, saying proudly that so far from wishing to aggrandize himself, "when he was in his own tennis court at Norwich he thought himself as great as a king".

Suspicious and agitated, Elizabeth returned to Windsor in September. Vague but disturbing reports came of doings in the North, and the truth was worse than the rumour. Northumberland and Westmorland were ready to lead a force southwards. Hartlepool was to be invested so that Alva should have a landing-place for his troops, and the Queen of Scots was to be released. These movements were to be supported by Norfolk's activity in the south; between them the two forces were to gain control of the government and Spanish soldiers were to put down all resistance. What then was to be Elizabeth's fate? "Tell your master that if he will help me, I shall be Queen of England in three months," Mary had said. There was only one way to make sure of that. Stone dead hath no fellow.

Norfolk had retired to his London house, and Elizabeth summoned him to Windsor. The Duke replied that he did not feel well, but would come, God willing, in four days' time, "which manner of answer we have not been accustomed to receive from any person", ran the draft of the Queen's reply. Norfolk, who had tried to send to Alva for immediate assistance but found the ports closed, had gone to Kenninghall, his seat in Norfolk, when the letter reached him, rephrased by Cecil in more conciliating terms but demanding his presence with equal plainness. His servants entreated him to stay where he was but Norfolk could not make up his mind to this either. He sent to tell the northern Earls that the rising must be postponed, and he himself mounted and set off for Windsor, while his despairing followers clung to his stirrups in a last attempt to save him. As he came towards Windsor he was arrested and taken to London, where he was committed to the Tower.

XIII

WHEN ELIZABETH ADDRESSED a deputation from the Houses of Parliament she spoke with a pointed decision; on public occasions she was completely in command of herself and of the situation, but to the men who worked in close association with her she seemed at times on the verge of nervous breakdown. Sir Francis Knollys, who had formed his opinion of Mary Stuart at close quarters, was shocked and astounded that Elizabeth should have allowed the Conference at Westminster to break up without drastic action against her. Elizabeth's inconsistent and irresolute tactics had made him conclude that she was in a state of nervous ailment that ought to preclude her from active government. With the freedom of a cousin and of one accustomed to speak his mind, he had written to her the previous January: "It is not possible for your Majesty's faithful councillors to govern your estate unless you shall resolutely follow their opinion in weighty affairs," and to Cecil on the same day he had written even more emphatically: "If her Majesty will needs be the ruler or half-ruler of these weighty affairs herself, then my hope of any good success is clean overthrown."[1] In the second week of October, Fénélon reported that the Queen had not been well for five or six days. While she was in this ailing state, Cecil, on October 6, wrote a minute headed: "My advice to the Queen's Majesty in the Duke of Norfolk's Case." The paper is another instance of the tenderness and chivalry of men's conduct towards her, at the same time that they gave her sound and uncompromising advice. Cecil wrote that he wanted for various reasons to give her his opinion privately in writing rather than in council. He began by saying, "No true councillor to your Majesty can be without inward grief to behold this unfortunate case of the Queen of Scots to become so troublesome to your Majesty. But it is fit that now, any that shall love and counsel your Majesty shall seek either to diminish your grief, without peril, or else to manifest to your Majesty that, in the conception of your grief, the causes appear to be greater than they are. . . . I am bold to show my opinion that your Majesty need not to hinder your health . . . for this case be not so terrible as Your Majesty would have it." "The Queen of

[1] MSS. Queen of Scots, quoted by Froude.

Scots," he went on, "is and indeed always shall be, a dangerous person to your estate," but then he drew up a set of conditions which would reduce the danger: if Elizabeth were married, if Mary were kept in prison, if her divorce from Bothwell were not allowed, if she were publicly declared guilty of murder. To reduce Norfolk's power of injury, he should be encouraged to marry someone else, and he should not be charged with treason. If the charge were made but could not be proved, Norfolk would be more dangerous than before. Cecil did not think it capable of proof; the mere intention of the marriage, which was all that so far was known of Norfolk's activities, could not be described as treason. He said: "If your Majesty yourself would consider the words of the statute concerning treason, I think you would so consider of it." Here he copied out the words of the statute of Edward III.[1]

Two days later Norfolk entered the Tower, and he was examined before Bacon, Cecil, Northampton, Sadler and Bedford, all of whom confirmed the opinion Cecil had already given, that the facts, so far as they were known, did not bear out a charge of treason. Elizabeth heard this verdict with passionate repudiation. She felt more danger than she could see. Several people, even including Sussex, had thought the marriage worth considering in the interests of the state, but she had always been against it, not from jealousy of Mary only, but from a very strong instinct which overrode intellectual arguments: de Spes heard that she had said that if she consented to the match, she herself would be in the Tower before four months were over. Norfolk had twice denied the intention and reaffirmed his fidelity to her, and now it turned out he had kept up his negotiations with the Queen of Scots all the time. After eleven years of very hard-won success in giving the country stable government, the shock and affront of finding the head of the nobility in league against her with Mary Stuart had been dismaying; and to hear that the Privy Council did not regard his act as treasonable threw her into a hysterical passion. She exclaimed that she would have Norfolk's head off by her own authority. Then she fainted.[2]

Norfolk had tried to postpone the movement in the north, but it was too late. Sussex, who was in York as Lord President of the Council of the North, knew that disaffection was working but he did not know to what extent. He was averse from taking any aggressive step that might precipitate an outbreak; left alone, matters might settle themselves, he thought: winter was coming on and no one

[1] Von Raumer.					[2] Fénélon, *Correspondance Diplomatique.*

wanted to march in the bad weather. But Elizabeth had received several warnings from other sources, and to her alarmed imagination Sussex's inactivity seemed to have a sinister implication. Sussex wrote a full declaration of his position to Cecil. Norfolk, he said, had told him that Arundel, Leicester and Pembroke had "earnestly moved him" to marry the Scottish Queen, and he, Norfolk, had asked Sussex's advice. "I answered I would give no advice till I heard how the Queen Majesty liked of it." Any implication that he had dealt otherwise was entirely untrue. "I have written plainly, I do write plainly and I will write plainly to you . . . and truly I will not vary from my writing." He could not bring himself to believe Norfolk a traitor. "I have always loved him above all others, her Majesty excepted." Nevertheless if Norfolk were found to be false, "which God forbid", Sussex would act the part of a true man, "and thereof her Majesty may be most assured".[1]

Putting aside his own view of what the situation required, he summoned Northumberland and Westmorland to York. The news of Norfolk's arrest had made them desperate and they refused to come. Sussex sent a second summons saying: "If you have slipped, your friends will, with all the dutiful means they may, deal honourably as suitors for you to her Majesty, who never showed herself extreme to any." This letter was despatched on November 13, but the very next day the Earls, with their retainers at their backs, entered Durham. Here their men poured into the Cathedral and tore up and trampled on the English translation of the Bible and the Reformation Prayer Book. From Durham they began a march to the south-east.

Lord Hunsdon, who had been sent north with a body of troops, said of the Earl and Countess of Northumberland: "His wife, being the stouter of the two, doth harden and encourage him to persevere, and rideth up and down with the army, so as the gray mare is the better horse." Alva had told the rebels that before he sent them any help, they must first release the Queen of Scots. The Earls made this their first object and they brought their forces south through Staffordshire, making for Tutbury; but the Privy Council had sent Lord Huntingdon and Sir Ralph Sadler to the castle, and they had removed Mary into Warwickshire, holding her at Coventry. Northumberland and Westmorland were disconcerted by this coup: but a more serious sign of failure was forced on their attention. In spite of de Spes' confident predictions, they had marched the length of four counties without attracting popular support. Those throngs

[1] Sharpe, *Memorials of the Rebellion.*

of Catholics waiting only for a word to rise and overthrow the government, whom Mary and de Spes had expected to appear, were inactive and silent. In towns and villages and the countryside, the Earls and their army found themselves in the midst of an ominous vacancy. At Tadcaster they halted, turned and began a rapid retreat.

Three bodies of the Queen's forces were now on foot. The Lord Admiral, Clinton, led one from Lincolnshire, while Lord Warwick brought one from his own county and took a third contingent up to Hull, whence he and Hunsdon went over to join Sussex at York. By the beginning of January the two Earls and their wives had been driven over the Scottish border and the rebellion was extinct.

It was now a question of reprisals, and Sussex's opinion was contradicted on a major point of policy. He had written to the Privy Council on January 1 that he proposed to "execute some for example, imprison principal offenders who might have great lands or wealth and extend her Majesty's mercy to the serving men of meaner sort". Elizabeth however was wound up to a pitch of anger that spurned this suggestion. The harshness with which, on her personal authority, she treated the rebels, showed the fear as well as the fury into which they had thrown her, and on her own reiterated orders to Sussex, 800 of the Earls' humble followers were hanged. What made her policy odious was that the well-to-do were spared that they might either buy their pardons or forfeit their lands. Sussex's order to Bowyer, telling him to get on with the executions, up to 200, adds: "You may not execute any that hath freeholds or noted wealthy, for so is the Queen's Majesty's pleasure. By her special commandment, January 10, 1570."

Elizabeth had many causes for anger. The solid achievements of her twelve years' reign were so identified with her personal policy, that her success was a personal success; therefore the dissatisfaction disclosed by the rebels was felt by her as a personal insult. In the same way her father had felt himself bitterly insulted by the Pilgrimage of Grace. But she had another ground of dire offence. The rebels had cost her a great deal of money. For eleven arduous years she had calculated and contrived, she had withstood Cecil, she had forborne what it would have been advantageous to do, she had acquired a name for close-fistedness and avarice, all, all that she might remain solvent. With all the effort of which she was capable, she had kept the Crown's finances on an even keel. She could have left the task to ministers, but, with the help of first-rate advice, she had done it herself. Fulke Greville described her method from personal knowledge: "She watched over the nimble self-seeking or large-handed-ness of her ordinary secretaries, examining their intelligence, money, packets, bills of transportation, properties of state."[1] Her sacrifices and her sleepless vigilance in the service of this unpopular virtue had attained their end, but only just attained it. Heavy unforeseen calls on the exchequer would imperil it, and loss of credit meant loss of inde-pendence, of power. Her father had used the accumulated wealth of her grandfather—and he had exhausted it. Since the death of Henry VII no ruler in England had cared about solvency, except her; but she cared about it with a fierce, shameless, protective passion. The insolence, treachery and ingratitude of the rebels, as she saw it, was the more intolerable to her because she had been obliged to pay the expenses of three separate bodies of troops sent after them. So maddened was she by the enforced drain on her resources, so anxious not to incur the cost of one unnecessary day, that she insisted on Sussex's disbanding the greater part of his forces in January, while he and the other generals still thought it most unsafe.

That it had a shocking appearance to allow the rich, the leaders, to compound for their lives, while the poor, who had followed them, were hanged, was a matter for which, in this extremity, she was past caring. The plain fact was that if the landowners were executed under martial law, their estates would not fall to the Crown; the Crown would get them only if the owners stood their trial and were con-victed of treason. But though the lives of the well-to-do must be spared, that the Crown might gain their property, harsh reprisals were demanded, that domestic rebellion might once for all be put down, and the death penalty was exacted from a representative number of those who had nothing but life to forfeit.

Infuriated by having to pour out money—and in such a cause—the Queen was also deeply angered and mortified that her religious policy, which in itself and in comparison with that pursued by any other sovereign was exceptionally lenient and tolerant, should have been spurned by the northern Catholics. In the height of her indigna-tion she declared to the Bishop of Ross that Lady Northumberland's guilt was so great, she deserved to be burnt.[2] Her most telling pro-nouncement, however, was reserved for the person whom she knew to be the head and front of the disaffection. Elizabeth was not poetical, but she shared that extraordinary gift of expression that was general among the English of the time, and once or twice she wrote some remarkable verse. On this occasion she composed sixteen lines,

[1] Fulke Greville, *Life of Sidney.*   [2] Von Raumer.

describing her own distraught state of mind and the confidence which, nevertheless, she had in the people's satisfaction with what her reign had accomplished, and prophesying that the Queen of Scots would not be able to overthrow it. In the course of them, she bestowed on Mary Stuart an imperishable soubriquet:

The Daughter of Debate that eke discord doth sow
Shall reap no gain where former rule hath taught still peace to grow.

Peace was the great achievement: however precariously kept, it meant developing trade, low taxes and energy used for prosperity instead of destruction. Across the Channel, the state of France, suffering from repeated outbursts of the religious wars, and the martyrdom of the Low Countries at the hands of Spain, pointed the moral to Catholics as well as Protestants. In the south, at least, Catholics wanted civil security, good markets, reasonable prices and freedom from crushing taxation as much as the Protestants wanted them. If by a moderate monthly fine they could contract out of going to the parish church, and celebrate mass in secret at home, numbers of them were prepared to do that, in the absence of positive instructions from Rome. Penalties for saying mass were upon the statute book and from time to time they were enforced if it appeared that a centre was being made for Catholic disaffection; but of the ordinary householder, outward conformity only was demanded. The Queen's famous saying, that she wanted to open no windows into men's consciences, was echoed in the proclamation that was sent round to parishes after the putting-down of the rebellion. In it she denied the claim the rebels had made that Catholics had been forced to take arms against her to preserve the practice of their religion. They had asserted, said the proclamation, "some general severity intended by us or our ministers against them, only in respect of religion, when no such thing did appear or was any wise by us meant or thought of". The Queen declared that she intended no interference with anyone of the Christian faith "as long as they shall in their outward conversation show themselves quiet and not manifestly repugnant and obstinate to the laws of the realm which are established for frequenting of divine service in the ordinary churches of the realm".

The system was, in fact, working only too well. In the absence of direction from Rome, the English Catholics as a whole would continue to tolerate it indefinitely. Therefore, in February 1570, Pope Pius V issued his Bull of Excommunication against Elizabeth, the wording of which explains why it was impossible for the government to separate the religious from the political aspect of the Catholic faith.

"The Sentence Declaratory of the Holy Father against Elizabeth the Pretended Queen of England and those heretics adhering to her," stated that "Peers, subjects and people of the said kingdom, and all others upon what terms soever bound unto her, are freed from their oath and all manner of duty, fidelity and obedience". This was dangerous enough, but it was nothing to the clause that followed: "commanding moreover and enjoining all and every, the nobles, subjects, people and others whatsoever *that they shall not once dare to obey her or any of her laws, directions or commands, binding under the same curse those who do anything to the contrary*".

A copy of this document was found pinned to the door of the Bishop of London's house in St. Paul's Churchyard on the morning of May 1. Henceforward, English Catholics were disobedient to the Pope if they were loyal to the Queen, and traitors to the Queen if they obeyed the Pope. The putting up of the paper was traced to a rich Catholic gentleman named Felton who lived in Southwark. Since he denied having any accomplices he was racked in an attempt to make him disclose some, but without his uttering a name. The painful entanglement of loyalties was epitomized in Felton's case. The Earl of Sussex was overseeing the execution, and on the scaffold Felton told him that he wished no injury to the Queen and gave Sussex, to give to her, his diamond ring worth £400; while Elizabeth gave his widow a dispensation to have mass said in her own house for the rest of her life.[1]

England was not the only country in which the Pope's Bull caused dismay. Philip and the Emperor Maximilian were, by its implication, made violent enemies of Elizabeth, a position for which they were by no means ready; both they and Charles IX refused to have it published in their dominions. In England, its publication was mistimed, since it was too late to hearten the northern rebels, and while it drove some Catholics who could not face the appalling alternative into the ranks of Anglicans, it made the lot of fervent Catholics incomparably harder than before. But it did the one thing which presumably the Pope intended it to do: it abruptly shattered the compromise which had made the majority of Catholics find Elizabeth's system tolerable. It forced the issue in many Catholic households, and the government persecution, with all the horrors of sixteenth-century state-punishments inflicted on Catholics who were suspected as

[1] Lingard.

traitors, had a parallel effect to the burning of the Protestants under Mary Tudor: it inspired their fellow-religionists and glorified the faith that produced such martyrs.

The Protestant response to the Bull was instantaneous, and sermons, pamphlets and broadsheets poured out on a wave of enthusiasm and affection for the Queen. Bishop Jewel's *Answer to the Pope's Bull* said much against the Pope, but its most pregnant sentence was a simple one in praise of Elizabeth, that showed the rock on which the nation's love for her was based: "God gave us Queen Elizabeth, and with her, gave us peace, and so long a peace as England hath seldom seen before." Beyond these, however, in emotional interest was an anonymous popular expression of feeling, registered as a broadsheet at Stationers' Hall in 1571; it was headed: "*A Song between the Queen's Majesty and England*", and was in the form of alternate verses between England and the Queen.

> *I am thy lover fair*
> *Hath chosen thee to mine heir,*
> *And my name is Merrie England.*
> *Therefore come away,*
> *And make no more delay,*
> *Sweet Bessie, give me thy hand!*

Elizabeth's passion for her kingdom has been celebrated gloriously, but never better than in the simple lines the ballad-writer here put into her mouth:

> *Here is my hand*
> *My dear lover England,*
> *I am thine both with mind and heart.*
> *For ever to endure,*
> *Thou mayst be sure,*
> *Until death we two do part.*[1]

[1] Harleian Miscellany.

XIV

THE FIRST TWELVE years of the reign were passed; Elizabeth was now thirty-seven. *Christian Prayers*, published in 1570, has for frontispiece an illumination of her kneeling, elbows raised and long hands joined. The *élancé* figure with slender arms, the small head whose limp hair is dragged back under a jewelled net, appear on a ground of apple-green. Anyone who described Elizabeth always said that her skin was pure white, and Puttenham, who in his *Art of Poesie* scattered not only anecdotes of the Queen but scraps of admiring verses he had composed upon her appearance, said in one of these:

> *Her bosom, sleek as Paris plaster*
> *Held up two balls of alabaster.*

To preserve this paleness, "white as Albion rocks", she used a cosmetic lotion made of white of egg, powdered eggshell, alum, borax and white poppy-seeds. These ingredients were mixed "with water that runs from under the wheel of a mill", and the milky fluid was beaten until a froth stood on it three fingers deep. This blanching lotion was said to be very effective, but was not to be used more than three times a week.[1] The usual method of washing hair was with lye, a compound of wood-ash and water. While the Queen was at Cambridge, thieves broke into her lodging and stole her looking-glass and comb, a gold bodkin used for braiding her hair and her lye-pot.[2] Teeth were cleaned by rubbing them with a cloth inside and out, and using a tooth-pick, and the Queen's New Year Gifts included holland tooth-cloths, edged with black and silver, and gold tooth-picks. There were many favourite recipes for mouth-washes, whose ingredients included rosemary, myrrh, mastic and cinnamon. Rose-water for the Queen was imported from Antwerp, but some at least of her scent was made in England. "Queen Elizabeth's Perfume" was made from marjoram; it was said to be "very sweet and good for the time", but fugitive.[3] It seems however that she preferred a light scent. When she was to visit Cambridge again in 1578 it was proposed to present her with a book specially bound. Cecil, discussing

[1] Platt, *Delights for Ladies*.   [2] Stowe, *Historical Memoranda*.
[3] Platt.

arrangements with the Vice-Chancellor, warned him that the book-binders must not use the fashionable trick of treating the leather with oil of lavender, for "Her Majesty could not abide such a strong scent".[1]

The clothes in which Elizabeth's portraits were taken were usually variations of black, white and gold, and the dresses in which ambassadors described her, as a rule black, violet, crimson or white. These colours, of striking visibility, were the obvious choice for ceremonial occasions, but, as Bohun said, though she was splendid in public, "she loved a prudent and moderate habit in her own apartments", and the lists of clothes given to her as New Year's gifts, preserved at intervals throughout the reign, suggest a much softer fashion than the stiff, gemmed *"toilette d'apparat"*. They also show, in every period for which they survive, a charming choice of colour for a pale woman with red hair. There were gowns of ash-coloured satin embroidered in silver and black, straw-coloured satin embroidered in silver and gold, dove-colour worked in gold and orange. The same colours are constantly repeated: yellow, ginger, tawny, orange, russet. Pink appears, though less often: a peach-coloured satin doublet covered with white cut-work, and lined with orange sarcenet, a mantle of pink-coloured cobweb lawn striped with silver, "a loose-bodied gown"—the negligée found in every period of tight corseting—of ladies' blush satin. The presents descended to the minutely personal, handkerchiefs, night-smocks and night-coifs, and hair-nets knitted of gold and silver thread. In 1560, Mrs. Montagu, the Queen's silk-woman, gave Elizabeth her first pair of knitted silk stockings. She was enchanted with them and asked Mrs. Montagu to set about making more at once. "I like silk stockings well," she exclaimed; "they are pleasant, fine and delicate. Henceforth I will wear no more cloth stockings."[2] The hose cut out of taffeta or cloth were of course inelastic and fitted only like gaiters. The clinging quality of the knitted stockings made the leg so elegant by contrast that the fashion for them, which spread rapidly, was abused by moralists as worldly and improper. When the Queen saw her own legs in them she at once declared that she would wear nothing else; but it was said in praise of the Lady Magdalene Dacre, that she never wore knit stockings, either of silk, worsted or wool.

Among the splendid presents of the wealthy courtiers, Leicester's make an interesting contrast with those of Cecil. The former's were almost always jewellery, of a personal kind; one was a ruby-and-diamond bracelet "with a clock in the clasp", one a diamond chain with "a round clock set with diamonds and a diamond pendant hanging from it"; another was a gold purse garnished with diamonds, rubies and opals with a blue sapphire in the clasp; once he gave her an amber scent-bottle with his arms, a little gold bear and ragged staff, on the stopper. These were lover's gifts. Cecil's presents were eminently suitable. One was a stand-dish of silver-gilt and mother-of-pearl with a crystal and silver-gilt ink-bottle, and sand-boxes and a penknife of silver-gilt, a beautiful gift from Mr. Secretary. Another time he chose a rock-crystal ewer mounted in silver-gilt, and again, a set of gold plates enamelled with birds.[1]

The Queen loved flowers as well as jewels. Their loveliness was not their only charm for her: her passion for her realm extended to its natural beauty, and on her summer progresses she would "amuse herself", Bohun said, with noticing and exclaiming at the variety of fruit England produced, and at the goodness of God in creating the variety of field, meadow, pasture and wood. In several portraits her dress is embroidered with groups of English wild flowers. In the first summer of de la Mothe Fénélon's embassy, the Queen filled one of her little work-baskets with beautiful apricots and had it carried to him that he might see the fairness of English fruit. She was fond of cherries. Sir Francis Carew, in his garden two miles out of Croydon, managed by an ingenious system of covering up his trees to make them fruit much later than usual, so that when the Queen visited him after the cherry season, he was able to give her a charming surprise.[2] In a portrait in Jesus College, Oxford, the Queen is wearing a double cherry as an ear-ring; a stawberry and its flower are pinned to her breast and a fern is fastened like a plume in her hair.

The winter season meant extreme cold for everyone outside the orbit of a blazing fire, no fresh meat except birds, no green vegetables and no fruit except store apples and imported oranges. The latter were used plentifully by those who could get them, and the inventory taken in 1574 of the Queen's jewels and plate notes numerous gold "orange strainers" with a "writhen steel" spike.[3] The Queen did not suffer much from cold, though she dressed for it. One of her winter garments was a cloak of black-silver tinsel lined with white plush; to put over her knees she had a "lap mantle" of white taffeta lined with orange plush, and one of her presents was "a warming-ball of gold".

[1] Nichols, *Progresses*.   [2] Lysons, *Environs of London*.
[3] Collins, *Jewels and Plate of Elizabeth I.*

While Sir Amyas Paulet was Ambassador in Paris, he was instructed to find the Queen a French muff. He sent one with anxious explanation, "the best I can find at this time, thinking it is better to send this as it is when there is some cold stirring than to wait for a better till the cold be clean gone. I have caused it to be furred . . . but have not perfumed it because I do not know what perfume will be agreeable to her Majesty".[1] Cecil felt the cold much more than the Queen did, and often mentioned it in letters: he wrote to the English Ambassador at Paris in 1568, "From Greenwich the 1st of May which is become a very cold day." The rigours of the winter months made the coming of spring and summer an ecstasy. The accounts of the Revels Office for the 1570's show this in the lavish use of flowers. There were the expenses of "flowers of all sorts taken up by commission, and gathered in the fields", as: "roses, 10 bushels, honeysuckle 6 bushels, pink and privett flowers and strewing herbs", and the wages paid to 214 work folk "that gathered, bound and sorted the flowers". For the festivities of winter, artificial flowers were used, and the cost was noted down of single roses, roses in branch, and "rose-headed nails". The breath of vanished summer was supplied by scent and spice. In the Masque of January, the hailstones were musk comfits, clove comfits, cinnamon and ginger comfits, and the snowballs presented to the Queen were scented with rose water.[2]

The singing for these entertainments was furnished by the Children of the Revels, who were recruited from the four choirs of singing boys paid by the Royal Household: those of St. Paul's, Westminster, St. George's, Windsor, and the Children of the Chapel Royal. Their exquisite notes, accompanied by strings and flutes, added their other-worldly beauty to a scene of congested richness and brilliance, in which the highest point of dramatic interest was not the presentation upon the stage, but the place where, in a half-circle of famous faces, the pale and aquiline lady was sitting, with jewels winking on her long fingers.

The upsurge of national energy was expressed in an increasing appetite for the elaborate and brilliant, and in the rapid development of prosperity which peace had made possible, there was a demand for glass. This fragile and glittering substance had a precious estimation, approaching that of jewels. Its transparency and colour were exciting to people who had seen little of it, and before its present vulgarization, the idea of glass possessed an aesthetic value, like that of the sea of glass in the Revelation of St. John. In 1575 the Venetian glass-

[1] C.S.P. Foreign, 1578.   [2] Cunningham, *Extracts from the Revels Accounts*.

worker Verzelini was given a monopoly of glass-making, provided he taught his craft to the Queen's "natural subjects", and fifteen glass-houses were set up under his supervision near his own in Crutched Friars.

The sparkle of the wares affronted the unaccustomed eye of both the moralist and the economist; it betokened worldly extravagance and a mis-direction of the national resources. *A brief Examination of certain Ordinary Complaints* says: "These eleven years there were not one of haberdashers, not a dozen in all London, and now, from the Tower to Westminster, all along, every street is full of them, and their shops glitter and shine of glass, as well drinking as looking-glass, yea all manner of vessel of the same stuff." The exciting use of glass in the open air was explored in great gardens. Bacon wanted a bathing-pool with sides and bottom "embellished with coloured glass and such things of lustre", but the fashionable enlargement of windows in the façade of great houses which caused the saying: "Hardwick Hall, more glass than wall", seemed to him, at the end of the century, to have been overdone. He said: "You shall have some-times fair houses so full of glass, that one cannot tell where to become to be out of the sun or cold." But to eyes as yet unaccustomed to its use, glass gave the sense of magical luxury, of great riches at hand in a brave new world.

In February 1571 the Queen made Cecil a peer with the title Baron Burleigh of Stamford Burleigh in Northamptonshire. The creation marked the end of the severe crisis which his government had weathered. He had had a great deal to put up with; the Queen, though an indefatigable, an inspiring colleague, was not an easy one; but his life's work was his life's passion, as he said himself some years later: "My service hath been but a piece of my duty, and my vocation hath been too great a reward."

In spite of his enormous industry and a sober temperament, he was capable of enjoyment in private life. He found energy for ambitious building. Of his two great country houses, Stamford Baron and Theobalds, the latter is the more famous, because Hertfordshire is more accessible from London than Northamptonshire. Theobalds was originally a small house called Tongs, and the Queen, who had spent much time in Hertfordshire as a child, continued to call it by the name she had first known. Cecil had bought it in 1560, and he spent years enlarging it into a characteristic red-brick erection, built round successive courtyards. It was approached by a mile-long avenue of cedar trees and the road from London ran to it so straight that the London end of the road became known as Theobald's Road.[1]

Burleigh's relaxations were entirely domestic. His blue-stocking wife appeared somewhat forbidding to the world, but she was her husband's dearest companion. On her death he spoke of her to his son Robert as "thy matchless mother". He was profoundly anxious for the Queen to marry someone who would give her children, but his view of marriage was a serious one. When he drew up a table of pros and cons for her possible marriages with Leicester and the Archduke Charles, he included among the considerations of each man: "In likelihood to love his wife." On this head there was nothing against the Archduke, but Leicester's record, a marriage of passion ending in disaster, was reckoned unpromising. Not every statesman would have troubled to include this point, but to Burleigh marriage with a woman meant consorting with her as well as sleeping with her.

Burleigh's character being such, and so long known to her, Elizabeth never attempted to engage him in her favourite pastime of amorous amusement, nor did he ever adopt what became in time a recognized idiom for those who wanted to gain a near approach to the Queen: a manner in which respect was coloured by an appearance of romantic admiration.

Since it was known that this manner of approach was very successful, it was inevitable that Elizabeth's detractors, then and now, should say that any expression of sexual feeling towards her was gross flattery merely. She was not, it was true, a woman whom men would die to possess, as Chastelard had died for the chance of possessing Mary Stuart; she was self-willed and dictatorial, and she had none of that capacity for sexual passion which, if it is strong enough, will, in a man's view, carry off these or any other failings. Yet she had qualities that aroused the admiration and emotion of men. She was brilliantly responsive; she met with comprehension and sympathy a wide range of interests; anything, indeed, that interested the men about her, interested her. Pale and frail, glittering with jewels, in long, narrow bodice and inordinate skirts that looked fit only for a garden lawn, she rode so fast that it alarmed the Master of the Horse responsible for her safety, and danced and walked as if she could never get enough of rapid motion. But, active and domineering though she was, one of her strongest claims on men was her dependence on them. She excited those whose ambitions and hopes were the same as her own, and she made them understand she could not do without

[1] Gotch, *Homes of the Cecils.*

them. Her ministers groaned at the amount of work she exacted and at having to spend their own money in the public service; they exclaimed that they must retire, or at least take a holiday; but the Queen could not spare them, and they were with her till they died or until she did. Ailing she might be, but her *ambiance* was alight with vitality; she might provoke anger, distrust or even hatred, but in-difference never. In such an atmosphere, the different hues of emotion merge like the colours of a rainbow.

Leicester's passion, whatever its degree, had a smack of common-place reality about it; he sometimes behaved like an offended lover; he had made up to Lady Hereford to try the Queen's feelings, and been reconciled to Elizabeth while they both cried with rage. He would not wait for her at St. Swithin's, though she had come as quickly as she could, and more than once he went off in a huff to his house at Wanstead and waited there till the Queen asked him to come back. But no one else behaved like this, and the only possible rival to himself was of very different calibre.

Christopher Hatton gave signs of an undoubted passion for her. Like Burleigh, he was of Northamptonshire origin, and had entered the legal profession. He was seven years younger than the Queen, tall, large-framed, solid but graceful; he had caught Elizabeth's eye while dancing in a masque at Gray's Inn in 1564. He was made one of the Gentlemen Pensioners, the fifty picked men who were chosen, among other attributes, for height and appearance, and formed the Queen's ceremonial bodyguard. The fact that his looks had first brought him into the Queen's liking gave him a reputation for incompetence that was undeserved. Sir John Neale has shown that Hatton, like every other man Elizabeth employed, was of sound capacity. He may have been no cleverer than Leicester, but his faculties were developed by a steady professional career, while Leicester was merely a man of good general intelligence who had picked up a considerable fund of experience and inside information. Hatton had the gentleness that sometimes goes with large physique; Camden described it as "a modest sweetness of manner", and it may have been partly the attraction of opposites which caused him to develop a passion for the Queen. When Hatton as a young man had written verses, his pseudonym had been "Felix Infortunatus"; this described his plight as a lover of Elizabeth's.

In 1571, when Hatton was M.P. for Higham Ferrers, he was thirty-one and Elizabeth thirty-eight. He had not displaced Leicester as confidential favourite, but he had overhauled him, and while every year showed gifts of leases, wardships, lands, buildings, offices to Leicester and Hatton, during the years 1568 to 1571 the Queen gave Leicester four benefactions only and Hatton eight. No-one would ever entirely supplant Leicester in her affection, but Hatton's newness as an adorer and the vehemence of his passion made a strong appeal to her feelings, and for some years the relationship between them was one of the kind that was Elizabeth's nearest approach to sexual passion, in which Francis Osborne described her as "apter to raise flames than to quench them".[1]

In 1571 a man named Mather was had up for saying that "Mr. Hatton had more recourse to Her Majesty in her Privy Chamber than reason would suffer if she were so virtuous and well-inclined as some noiseth her", while next year Archbishop Parker wrote in extreme distress to Burleigh of a man who had been examined before the Mayor of Dover for speaking against the Queen, "uttering most shameful words against her, as that the Earl of Leicester and Mr. Hatton should be such to her, as the matter is so horrible", the Mayor would not write down the words, "but would have uttered them in speech to your Lordship if ye had been at leisure".

Hatton had encroached upon Leicester's preserves and in 1572 he himself became alarmed by the success of a rival, who, though not a sharer of the intimate relationship that Hatton enjoyed, dazzled the Queen and absorbed the attention of her leisure moments. Edward de Vere, 17th Earl of Oxford, was a young man of high birth, arresting presence and exceptionally disagreeable temper. A pathological selfishness did not deprive him of attraction, and though very poor, he attained for a short time the peak of fashionable celebrity; spoiled and ruthless as he was, the Maids of Honour were wild about him. His father had died nine years before, and since twelve years old, Oxford had been a royal ward, brought up in Burleigh's house. In 1571 the young man proposed for Burleigh's favourite daughter, Ann. The girl was fifteen years old, and as she was not a beauty, surprise as well as bitterness was felt by her contemporaries. The Cecils were not highly born but Burleigh's position made the match an eligible one; though Oxford was not the son-in-law he would have chosen, the connection brought distinction, and as Ann Cecil was of course in love with the young man, her father put a good face on it. He wrote almost pathetically to one of his friends about the prospective bridegroom: "There is much more in him of understanding than any stranger would think." The marriage

[1] Osborne, *Historical Memoirs*.

was celebrated in Westminster Abbey and the Queen herself was present.

The youthful Countess of Oxford was not likely to shine at court, nor did her husband intend she should. Lord Shrewsbury's son, Gilbert Talbot, described to his father Lord Oxford's brilliance as a centre of attraction: "The Queen's Majesty delighteth more in his personage and his dancing and valiantness than any other." Lady Burleigh, as a mother-in-law, said Talbot, was angry at Oxford's amusing the Queen while his wife was left at home, but Burleigh "merely winked at these love matters", and refused to interfere.[1] Another who felt injured by them was Hatton; and as his feelings contained some genuine affection he was in considerable danger of making a nuisance of himself. His friend Edward Dyer warned him that this was not the way to go to work. Once, the Queen had been prepared to submit to a certain degree of masterful behaviour; while she was interested in his passion, she had allowed its natural expression; but the game was one requiring great subtlety and skill, and to overcall his hand would be fatal. "In the beginning," wrote Dyer, "she did bear with rugged dealing of yours, until she had what she fancied, yet now, after satiety and fulness, it will rather hurt than help you." Hatton had the sense to be guided, though he sometimes wrote, if he did not speak, his mind with the anger of a man in love. "Madame, in striving to withstand your violent course of evil opinion towards me"—he would, he wrote, have her to know that he was neither unthankful, covetous nor ambitious: nothing of the sort. But as regards the more intimate relationship, he returned to his strain of desperate but humble longing. In 1573 he was ill; it was decided that he must try the cure at Spa, and Elizabeth sent him off under the care of a court physician, Dr. Julio. Hatton, whose disinclination to go may have been partly owing to the sense that he was leaving the field to Oxford, worked himself into a frenzy. On the journey and after his arrival at Spa he wrote to the Queen describing the wreck to which love and suffering had reduced him: "Scarcely will you know your own, so much hath this disease dashed me." The torments of absence, he declared, were unbearable: "I love yourself, I cannot lack you." Never would he leave her again, on any consideration. "Bear with me, my most dear, sweet lady; passion overcometh me. I can write no more. Love me, for I love you."

He returned in October, and at some time he renewed his plea to be allowed the final privilege of a lover. In an undated letter,

[1] Ward, *The Earl of Oxford*.

Elizabeth replied with serious and calm remonstrance. It had once been put to her, she said, in a game of Question and Answer, Should anything be denied to a friend? The proper answer was no. But who is a friend? "Friend leaves he to be, that doth demand more than the giver's grant with reason's leave may yield. And if so, then my friend no more—my foe." But if a true friend be found, then, "I bid myself farewell: I am but his."[1]

The distinction was quite clear in her own mind, that to be un-chaste meant to commit the sexual act; to display her naked beauty to the gaze of an adoring man did not deserve this term. The distinction explained her solemn declaration that "nothing wrong" had ever passed between herself and Leicester, and the gravity of her reply to Hatton, in a situation where most women would feel that it did not lie in their mouths to reproach the man who tried to possess them. Though the rumour of such doings caused the English Queen to be abused as a monster of unchastity by Cardinal Allen and his colleagues, the usage of the time was not altogether on the Cardinal's side. Diane de Poitiers, Madame de Valentinois, the all-powerful mistress of Henri III, was painted by court painters, naked at her dressing-table, and sitting in her bath, naked to the waist. Most striking of these portraits was the great canvas by Clouet, which celebrates the fact, among others, that Madame de Valentinois was governess to the royal children. Madame de Valentinois, jewelled but naked, occupies the centre of the picture as Pharaoh's daughter. A nurse presents to her the infant Moses, in real life the Duc d'Alençon. In the background the baby's mother is shown, a retiring and somewhat pensive figure. His mother was in fact the Queen of France, the young and then down-trodden Catherine de Medici.

The adoration of the unobtainable may have been the form of love-making that suited Hatton best, for he never married. His private letters, coupled with the story of his dancing, are, however, as an estimate of his general qualities, most misleading. His utterances in Parliament, the speech he made at the trial of the Queen of Scots, proceed from another sort of man altogether. The discrepancy is bridged by the traditional account of how he appeared to the people who knew him. Lloyd said: "An honest man he was, but reserved," and explained Hatton's final promotion to the Woolsack, by virtues that were quiet but not insignificant. "The little the wary man did was so just and discreet, and the little he said, so prudent and weighty, that he was chosen to keep the Queen's conscience,

[1] Nicholas, *Sir Christopher Hatton.*

as her Chancellor." His character in that office was "not with the applause of a great lawyer to split causes, yet with the conscience and comfort of a just man to do equity". His life-long attachment to Elizabeth showed similar qualities: it was kind, comforting and true. He is painted, holding a cameo of her, worn on a long chain round his neck.

One man of great abilities and complete devotion to the state seemed, unlike the rest, to have no personal liking for the Queen. Francis Walsingham was a fervent Protestant by creed, but he had the fanatical strain which would have made him, in other circumstances, an adviser more sympathetic to Mary Tudor than to her sister. Walsingham's utterances and those of Elizabeth, on various occasions, explain their irreconcilable differences of opinion on religious matters. Patriotic as he was, Walsingham felt that, in the last resort, creed was more important than nationality; Elizabeth wanted the English Catholics let alone, provided they conformed to what she thought the necessary minimum of state observance. When Lethington had been in London in 1561 the Queen, discussing the English succession with him, had said that the claims of the various pretenders were like the doctrine of the Sacraments: "some think one thing, some another, and only God can say whose judgment is best." Her tolerance, however, gained her no favour with the Catholics, and none with Walsingham. The latter summed up the position as between Protestants and Catholics with the simple statement: "Christ and Belial may hardly agree." The Queen's intention was to turn and evade and deceive every power with whom she treated, Protestant Netherlanders as well as Catholic Spanish and French, if by doing so she might bring her small nation of less than four million people through recurring crises without the ruinous expense of war. But just as the Catholics looked upon Europe as divided, not into nations, but into Catholic and non-Catholic states, so did Walsingham. He wanted to see Protestant Germany and Protestant Scotland, Protestant rebels in France and the Low Countries, all united with England in a league against the Catholic powers. The warlike implications of such a course aroused the Queen's alarm; but Walsingham said: "what juster cause can a Prince that maketh profession of the Gospel have, to enter into wars, than when he seeth confederacies made for rooting out of the Gospel and religion he professeth?"

His bigotry had been hardened by his experiences. He had been English Ambassador in Paris during the Massacre of St. Bartholomew, and he was beyond the reach of arguments for toleration and expediency.

With religious conviction carried to a fanatical pitch, Walsingham combined what seemed to be the elements of an altogether different personality. In 1572 the Queen made Burleigh Lord Treasurer; as such he was responsible for public finance, and Walsingham succeeded him as Secretary of State for all departments. They worked in the closest co-operation and their spheres overlapped; Burleigh himself ran a widespread system of secret intelligence, but Walsingham became the Grand Master of espionage. "He was," said Camden, "a most subtle searcher of secrets, nothing being contrived anywhere that he knew not by intelligence." It was his motto: "Intelligence is never too dear." The acuteness, the patience, the amazing memory, would suggest an unemotional temperament. Walsingham combined them with a burning zeal.

He was "a watchful servant over the safety of his mistress",[1] but he was not the more congenial to her for that, for it meant his attempting, with unrelenting, steady pressure, to force her hand: he had early made up his mind that the safety of the Protestant religion, the country and the Queen, demanded the death of Mary Queen of Scots.

No lack of sympathy between them, however, prevented the Queen from absorbing Walsingham's services to an extent that left him almost in despair for his health, fortune and private concerns. In 1572 Sir Thomas Smith wrote assuring him he had tried to get him recalled from Paris. "At the signing of her Majesty's letters to you this morning I said: Madam, My Lord Ambassador looks now to have some word from your Majesty respecting his return; it would comfort him very much. 'Well,' said the Queen, 'he shall come.' 'Yea,' quoth I, 'but the poor gentleman is almost dispirited.' . . . 'Well,' said the Queen, 'you may write to him that he shall come home shortly.' . . . I thanked her Majesty and came my ways, for she hasted to go a-walking with her ladies because it was a frost." But a negotiation was going forward at Paris that the Queen was unwilling to leave in the hands of anybody else. Hoping to work upon her, Smith told her that he had put it to Lord Burleigh that it would be a good thing to have Walsingham back. ' "Beshrew you!" said she.' But, Smith said, Walsingham could instruct the outgoing Ambassador, Lord Worcester, and he could also advise the Earl of Desmond who was just going to Ireland. There was nothing in all that, the

---

[1] Naunton, *Fragmenta Regalia.*

Queen said. When Walsingham got back, he would first take physic in London and then go straight off to Tongs, where the Lord Treasurer, it appeared, wanted his colleague to have a long rest. The amount of rest some people felt themselves to require seemed to her very extraordinary. "Madame," said Smith, "I will send him word again this night what your Majesty doth say, and then I think he will not be hasty to come, though I wish he were here."

Then the Queen and Smith settled to serious business. She told him to let Burleigh know that she had had an appeal from the Huguenots whom the French King was besieging in La Rochelle, to send them some gunpowder. One of the first manufactures in which Elizabeth had interested herself was that of gunpowder; it was now made in Essex. The Huguenots wanted a consignment sent to La Rochelle: they said it could be arranged to look as if driven into their harbour by the weather. The idea was attractive but the Queen scarcely knew how it was to be managed, because she had just been very gravely requested by the French Ambassador not to send the rebels any help, but such an opportunity was hardly to be resisted. Smith wrote to Burleigh: "Her Majesty prays you to think of it, and devise how it may be done, for she thinks it necessary."[1]

[1] Digges, *Compleat Ambassador.*

XV

"*HERE IS MY hand, my dear lover England!*" The spring of love drew its source from the knowledge that the Queen's policies were in the interests of economic prosperity. Bishop Jewel, in his *Answer to the Excommunication*, had made a significant comment on the state of the Commonwealth: "Thanks be to God, never was it better in worldly peace, in health of body, in abundance of victuals." Manufacture cannot thrive without peace; the English had peace themselves and offered a refuge to hundreds of skilled workers from France and the Netherlands, who practised in English towns, creating employment for English people. There was humming prosperity in the felt, thread, lace and silk-weaving industries, in parchment and paper-making, among engravers, glass-makers and makers of steel instruments. Alva had nearly ruined Antwerp as a seat of exchange, and Sir Thomas Gresham decided to set up one in London, for in that city merchants had nowhere to meet, and either congregated in Lombard Street, where they dislocated the traffic, or retired to the crowds and disturbance in the nave of St. Paul's. He built an exchange on Cornhill, of three wings enclosing a courtyard, the upper storey consisting of three rows of shops supported on pillars, while below, the pillared walks replaced St. Paul's nave; the centre wing was crowned with a tower. Gresham asked the Queen to open it, and he gave some shop-keepers a year's lease free, to have the shops filled with goods and lit up with candles on the evening of her visit. On January 23, 1571, the Queen came in state, glimmering through the murky air, and brought the French Ambassador with her. They dined with Gresham in the City and then rode to Cornhill. The citizens who, because of outbreaks of the plague, had not seen her in their streets for two years, now saw the Queen there for the first time since the Pope's Bull had appeared in Paul's Churchyard, absolving them from their allegiance to her and laying a curse on all who should obey her. They had had scant notice of her coming, but they had so thrown themselves into their preparations that Fénélon, looking at the hanging and garlanding of the streets, was told that they looked as they had at her Coronation. The Exchange met them with a brilliant spectacle, its upper storeys filled with a show of rich things illumined with scintillating wax-lights. The Queen and her train of ladies and gentlemen examined every part of it; she congratulated Gresham and said the place should henceforth be called the Royal Exchange. A herald announced her will, and then the trumpeters sounded. At eight o'clock she began her homeward procession. The Queen's retinue was lighted by its own torch-bearers, but the citizens were determined to have a good view of her and they had lined the streets with torches of their own. Beneath the darkness of the sky the Queen passed in a glow of light, and at the sight and sound of their welcome she could not restrain her exultation: she said to Fénélon that it did her heart good to see herself so much beloved and desired of her subjects.

But none of these implications made their way to the troubled, uncertain mind of the Duke of Norfolk. To remove him from the neighbourhood of the plague, he had been released from the Tower and was living in his town house under nominal supervision. Before he left the Tower he had signed a paper reaffirming his oath of loyalty to Queen Elizabeth and swearing to have no further dealings with the Queen of Scots; but at the same time he had sent a copy of the document to the Bishop of Ross, explaining that he had felt obliged to sign it and that his signature did not mean anything.

Catherine de Medici and the young Charles IX had just put a temporary stop to religious war by the Peace of St. Germain, and they were now anxious to get the Prince Henri, Duke of Anjou, off the scene, for as a dissolute and cross-grained youth, in the pocket of the Guise family, they foresaw that his presence would cause them endless trouble. They were therefore prepared to consider the plan now proposed by the Guises: that Anjou should marry the Queen of Scots. This suggestion, bringing back all the peril of the French re-entering Scotland and using it as a base for a Catholic invasion of England in Mary's interest, was acutely alarming, to Elizabeth herself, the government, and everyone in England, of whatever denomination, who shrank from invasion and civil war. To meet this desperate situation, Elizabeth began the first of those extraordinary stratagems against the House of Valois, glittering, exotic, horrible, that made her a target for ridicule and abuse, and achieved exactly and precisely the end she had in view. She hinted that she herself might be brought to consider Anjou as a husband.

The possibility even of such a marriage alliance caused the Queen Mother and the King to abandon all interest in Mary Queen of Scots. Elizabeth, having admitted the matter for discussion, now began the delaying tactics that were the essential feature of the negotiation; she said to Fénélon she feared the discrepancy in age was too great for happiness, for she was thirty-seven while the Duke was barely twenty. Fénélon assured her that the Duke's manliness and her own unimpaired youth made nonsense of such fears.

Elizabeth was very much in earnest in wishing to be thought in earnest, and the Ambassador found no lack of seriousness in her advisers. Cecil supported the match because he hoped it would give Elizabeth a child at last, and Walsingham because he envisaged an Anglo-French alliance that would defend the Protestant Netherlands against Spain. The scheme appeared, also, to have an unexpected supporter: Leicester was now an ally of Walsingham's. Gone were the days when he had offered himself to Spain, for support in his marriage to Elizabeth. The Puritan faction looked to him as if it were the coming one, and the Earl found himself much drawn towards them.

Walsingham was sent to Paris to open the marriage negotiations. They could not proceed fast because the object of entertaining them at all was to spin them out as long as possible. Walsingham did not know this; if he had, he would not have undertaken the commission; and he told the Queen in his letters that she should make up her mind quickly, or the situation would become very dangerous. If Anjou did not marry her, he would marry the Queen of Scots; his mother and brother were determined to get him out of France somehow.

The Queen Mother was avidly eager for the English match— "Such a kingdom for one of my children!" she exclaimed to Fénélon —but Anjou himself was being awkward to a degree. "Obstinate, papistical and restive like a mule," was Sir Thomas Smith's description, in a confidential letter where diplomacy gave way to frankness. The English Queen was thirty-seven, elegant, and in the eyes of contemporaries youthful, but she was seventeen years older than the young man, and in 1569 she had developed an ulcer on her shin. As she would not give it the proper rest but went on, riding and dancing, it sometimes ached so much that she had to lie up with it. The Guises had told Anjou that if he wanted the English throne, he had better marry Mary Stuart and take it by force of arms, rather than marry an old woman with a sore leg who was no better than she should be. This Anjou repeated word for word to his distracted parent. On the point as to whether Elizabeth were worthy in morals and reputation to enter the chaste circle of the Valois, Catherine de

Medici anxiously consulted Fénélon. His reply, not diplomatic but giving straightforward information to his government, sheds a light on the Queen's official appearance in her own country. There were a sort of men, Fénélon said, who could not forgive the great qualities of their betters; those who were in a position to know, spoke of the English Queen in a way very different from these. "In her own court, she is very greatly honoured . . . all ranks of her subjects fear and revere her, and she rules them with full authority, which I conceive could scarcely proceed from a person of ill-fame and where there was a want of virtue."

Reassurance on this matter, or the splendour of the match itself, now seemed to be overcoming Anjou's disinclination to it. Walsingham wrote in March that the French court were anxious to go on with the match, provided they could be sure the Queen was sincere; they could not run the risk that a Prince of the blood should be made to look a fool. This attempt to take a short cut through the negotiations was naturally painful to Elizabeth's feelings. She instructed Walsingham that he must beg the Queen Mother "not to be overanxious as desiring so precise an answer until the matter may be further treated of". And since the Queen-Mother had showed some misgiving, Walsingham was to assure her, that Lord Leicester was "ready to allow of any marriage we shall like".[1]

By April, Anjou had been brought round to acquiesce in the serious offer of his hand; he even seemed interested in the prospect himself; but the terms that accompanied the offer were ludicrous. They included a demand that he should be King and joint-ruler of England, that he should be crowned, be given £60,000 a year for life, and rule the country for his children if the Queen pre-deceased him.

While the Privy Council were digesting these terms, the Queen, to whom they were of no importancesince she never meant to make the marriage, had thrown herself into the lighter side of the proceedings with every appearance of eagerness and interest. She had received a eulogistic account of Anjou's person, to which she listened with responsive approval; but the Prince's own description of herself had come to her ears and it was not forgotten. She demanded pertinaciously of Fénélon whether Anjou, in turn, had received any reliable description of her? Whether anyone had spoken to him of her foot? Of her arm? "And of other parts," added Fénélon, "which she did not mention."

[1] Hume, The Courtships of Queen Elizabeth.

The discussions went on, until they seemed to have come to a stop on the question of the Prince's having liberty to go to mass in public. The French could hardly waive this point, nor the English allow it. The obstruction would have acted as a welcome brake on the proceedings, but for the fact of a *rapprochement* between the King of Spain and the Queen Mother, which turned it into a situation suddenly menacing to the English. Elizabeth instructed Walsingham to bring the proceedings forward again on any terms, and he replied that English stock was so low at the moment he must wait a better opportunity. The tide had turned suddenly and was running against the English Queen: and then, all at once, there was no more need to distract French attention from Mary Queen of Scots. So far from there being any danger of her marrying Anjou, it became a question of whether the Scottish Queen would live to marry anybody.

De Spes had thought the negotiations so far forward that Elizabeth's marriage with Anjou was a settled thing. The prospect of the Anglo-French alliance was most alarming to Spanish interests, but so imminent did it seem that de Spes wrote: "The only remedy is that with which Ridolfi is charged."

Roberto Ridolfi, a Florentine banker, whose optimism was based on a hopeless inability to understand the temper of the English nation, had evolved a plan to seize the Queen and Council, liberate Mary Stuart and place her on the English throne and restore the Catholic religion. Through the Bishop of Ross he brought Norfolk into touch with Mary once more, and Mary, far distant as she was, rekindled in his mind the fatal enthusiasm for her cause.

In the four major plots in which she was concerned during her eighteen years' imprisonment, the crucial question in each case was whether she had plotted or connived at the murder of Elizabeth. Her own story was that she never had. She had, naturally, and as she always said she would, used every means to gain her own freedom, but her plans, she swore most solemnly, had never included the murder of the English Queen. She had sworn, too, that she never intended the murder of her husband, who was now festering in his shroud.

Ridolfi had received through Ross a paper of detailed instructions agreed on by Mary and Norfolk; these empowered him to ask the Duke of Alva for guns, ammunition, armour and money, and 10,000 men, of whom 4,000, it was suggested, might make a diversion in Ireland. The instructions contained a clause that the most important part of Ridolfi's mission he would convey by word of mouth only.

Ridolfi went to Brussels, where the much-tried Alva heard him with mounting annoyance and dismay. Alva was holding his position in the Netherlands only with difficulty, and the suggestion that he should send away 10,000 of his men took no account of what was to happen behind their backs. Ridolfi went on his way towards Madrid and Alva sent express to the Spanish Ambassador at the Papal Court, urging him to give the Pope a realistic account of the difficulties inherent in the scheme; otherwise, he feared that the Pope's would be yet another voice, assuring him at a great distance from the scene of action that with the forces at his command, the conquest of England might readily be undertaken. He then wrote to Philip: he said that to wage a serious war in England would be out of the question, and this was what invasion would mean—so long as Elizabeth were alive. "But," he wrote, "if the Queen of England should die, either a natural or any other death"—then he would feel justified in lending troops for a rapid operation to put Mary Stuart on the vacant throne.

Ridolfi arrived in Madrid and presented his written credentials. As he then stated that Elizabeth was to be murdered, it is assumed that this was the subject of the instructions that were too compromising to write down. Later in the day, the Council of State debated his mission. The invasion of England and the assassination of its Queen were discussed as two parts of the same operation.

The most tepid member of the Council was the King himself. His heavy commitments against the Moors in the south east of Spain, the Turks in the Mediterranean and the revolting Netherland provinces, as well as his natural dislike of rash enterprises, made Philip fully agree with Alva that nothing expensive should be done for the plotters until they had done something for themselves. Let them seize the Council and put the Queen to death; then they should have help to maintain their position.[1]

Ridolfi had failed to get help abroad; he now plunged the conspirators in ruin at home. He wrote full and compromising reports of his interviews with Alva to the Queen of Scots, Norfolk, the Bishop of Ross and de Spes, and sent them in cipher to England by his agent Bailly. Burleigh's watch on the ports was so close that Bailly was arrested at Dover. He was taken to the Tower and tortured on the rack, and the information wrung from him led to the arrest

[1] Mignet, *Mary Queen of Scots.*

of the Bishop of Ross. The latter, however, haughtily refused to answer questions; he said he was answerable for his actions to no one but the Queen of Scots. He was therefore put in charge of the Bishop of Ely, who kept him under house-arrest in his palace at Holborn.

The Regent Murray had been assassinated in January 1570, and Mary Stuart, who had command of her French dowry, had bestowed a pension on the murderer of her half-brother. He had been succeeded by the Earl of Mar, who claimed the headship of the country in the name of the six-year-old King James, and was now fighting those who wished to wrest it from him in the name of Mary, whose abdication at Lochleven they ignored, as she ignored it herself. The French government, notwithstanding their conciliatory approaches to Elizabeth, were secretly sending money to the Queen of Scots' party, just as Elizabeth was supporting the Huguenots in La Rochelle. Fénélon had procured 2,000 crowns for Mary to send to her Scots supporters, and Norfolk undertook to send it by his servants to Lord Herries. The Duke's secretaries, Higford and Barker, gave the money to his steward Banister. The bags fell into the hands of Burleigh, and with the money was found a letter in cipher to the Queen of Scots' supporters which disclosed the main shape of the conspiracy.

Elizabeth had no reluctance towards the use of torture for getting information of vital importance. Her instructions were cold-blooded though not vindictive. She wrote to Sir Thomas Smith and to Dr. Wilson, Master of the Court of Requests, who were responsible for interrogating Higford and Barker: "If they shall not seem to you to confess plainly their knowledge, then we warrant you to cause them both or either of them to be brought to the rack and first to move them with fear thereof to deal plainly in their answers." If they refused this chance to save themselves, "then you shall cause them to be put to the rack and to find the taste thereof till they shall deal more plainly or until you shall think fit".

At sight of the rack, Banister and Higford told all they knew. Barker dared the torture, but his resolution failed under it and he revealed an unsuspected hiding-place in Howard House, among the tiles of the roof. Here were found a complete collection of the papers connected with Ridolfi's mission, and nineteen letters to Norfolk from the Queen of Scots and the Bishop of Ross. The latter was now examined by members of the Privy Council, and at first he repeated his refusal, as an ambassador, to submit to interrogation; but

Burleigh had taken the opinion of eleven lawyers, who told him that no immunity could be claimed by anyone for acts of treason against the Crown. Ross, they said, by joining a conspiracy against the Queen had forfeited an ambassador's privileges. Still he refused to answer the Council's questions.

Burleigh was not a man of great presence, and his manner was mild rather than otherwise, but he was able to speak in a way that carried absolute conviction. He told Ross that if he would not answer the questions put to him where he was, they should be put to him on the rack.

The speed, the loquacity and above all the nature of Ross's communications almost overwhelmed Dr. Wilson, who was charged with taking them down. Ross poured out an account of the dealings between Mary and Norfolk from the time of the enquiry at York till Ridolfi's departure for the Continent. In a state bordering on hysteria, the cause of which was but too clear, he went on to say that "the Queen, his mistress, was not fit for any husband . . . she poisoned her husband, the French King, as he credibly understood, she consented to the murder of her late husband, the Lord Darnley. Thirdly, she matched with the murderer and brought him to the field to be murdered. The Duke," he added, "should not have had the best days with her."

"Lord, what people are these!" wrote Wilson in his report. "What a Queen and what an Ambassador!"[1] But the man who used the instrument of deadly fear should have been able to discriminate in its effects. None the less, more than enough of solid evidence had been produced to convict the Duke of Norfolk.

Elizabeth was determined that the people should hear for themselves that Norfolk had asked for 10,000 Spaniards to be sent into England to cow them. The Lord Mayor and Aldermen were summoned to the Court of Star Chamber. There they were shown the documents found in Howard House, and they were asked to relate the matter fully to the citizens in the Guildhall. The Duke was to be tried in Westminster Hall on January 14, but before this event one of minor importance was disposed of; in December, a letter of complaint about de Spes had been sent to Madrid: "Why this unmeet and ungrateful personage is not revoked, or no meeter sent, we know not." In January he was told to leave the country at once.

The state trial of the sixteenth century was little more than a public

[1] Murdin.

justification of a verdict that had already been reached. Norfolk was pronounced guilty of high treason and condemned to death. He returned to the Tower to write letters of passionate repentance to the Queen that he had dealt with her enemies, but denying that he had ever intended harm to her. He wished sorely that he had never concerned himself with the Queen of Scots, saying: "Nothing that anybody goeth about for her, nor that she doth for herself, prospereth." Too late he cursed the hour that he had heard the sea-maid's music.

His life was inevitably forfeit. The jury of his peers demanded it, Burleigh demanded it, the majority of the Privy Council demanded it, the House of Commons demanded it. Only Elizabeth wavered. When she had heard of Norfolk's complicity in the Northern Rebellion, she had sworn that if the law would not provide for his death, she would have his head off by her own authority. Yet now that the law had decreed it, and all that was needed was her signature on a warrant to the sheriffs of London, she was paralysed. Hysterical subjects, it is said, suffer particularly from their memories, and are to an unusual degree dominated by their past; to be obliged to set in motion the machinery of axe and block, which had an awful significance for herself, produced a nervous resistance that was going to need very careful handling. Burleigh recognized the difficulty, and the name he put to it was a just one, though it did not explain the whole problem. "The Queen's Majesty," he wrote to Walsingham, "hath always been a merciful lady and by mercy she hath taken more harm than by justice, and yet she thinks she is more beloved in doing herself harm."

The warrant for the execution was drawn for Monday, February 8. "I cannot write," Burleigh continued, "what is the inward stay of the Duke of Norfolk's death; but suddenly on Sunday late in the night, the Queen's Majesty sent for me and entered into a great misliking that the Duke should die the next day; and she would have a new warrant made that night for the sheriffs to forbear until they should hear further. God's will be fulfilled and aid Her Majesty to do herself good."

Elizabeth's distress of mind culminated in a violent attack of nervous indigestion, of which the "heavy and vehement pains", which might well have been caused by poison, drove the Council nearly frantic with anxiety. Burleigh and Leicester, all differences suspended, sat up with her for three nights running. The attack subsided, and with the doctors' permission, she came out into the

Presence Chamber and spoke to Fénélon. She told him that for five days the pains had so "straitened her breath and clutched her heart", she thought she was going to die. The attack had been ascribed to some fish she had eaten; the Queen herself did not agree; she said she ate fish often without ill effects. She was inclined to think it was owing to the fact that having felt much better of late, she had given up the doctors' routine of purging and bleeding which they had said was necessary to keep her in health.

The warrant was drawn a second time, for execution on April 9; but again the Queen shrank. After midnight on the 8th, she wrote a note to Burleigh, saying the sheriff must be told the execution was postponed. "If they will need a warrant, let this suffice, all written with my own hand. Your most loving sovereign, Elizabeth R." The note was put away among Burleigh's papers, endorsed: "The Q. Majy: with her own hand for staying of the execution of the D.N. Received at 2 in the morning."

In May, Parliament was to re-assemble, and then, not only would the Duke of Norfolk's fate be discussed but that of the Queen of Scots also. Tempers were rising. As regards the immediate danger of a Franco-Scottish alliance, however, Elizabeth's entertainment of the Duke of Anjou had done its work. Anjou had finally declared that he could not consider marrying the Queen of a country that would not permit him full, public exercise of the Catholic religion, and his mother was already enquiring of the English envoys whether Queen Elizabeth could "fantasy" her younger son, her idol, the Duke of Alençon? But behind these airy speculations, a most solid gain had been secured. Burleigh and Walsingham had worked out with the French Government the Treaty of Blois, which was signed on April 19. It laid down that if either country were invaded, "under any pretence or cause, none excepted", the other should send 6,000 men to its assistance. Both countries agreed not to interfere in Scotland, but it should be lawful for the English Queen to attack any Scots who were supporting English rebels in Scotland. Furthermore, a marriage was promised between the King's sister Margaret and the Protestant Henry of Navarre. In the whole course of the treaty, Mary Stuart was not mentioned once. The diplomatic triumph was complete.

The Queen had still to face what was for her a personal crisis. Parliament assembled in a mood of implacable determination. It was not only Norfolk's execution they wanted: the sinister statement was made, "This error has crept into the heads of a number: that there is a

person in this land whom no law can touch." But treason was
privileged in no one; and they asserted that the Queen of Scots was
guilty of treason. She had declared herself Queen of England during
the lifetime of the reigning Queen, she had seduced the Duke of
Norfolk from his allegiance, she had encouraged rebellion in the
north, she had sent money to Northumberland and Westmorland
after their defeat; she had conspired with Ridolfi to bring in foreign
soldiers to overthrow the government. She had been warned before;
now, "the axe must give the next warning," said one speaker. The
House devised two bills: one to execute Mary Stuart for high treason,
the other to say she was incapable of succession to the English throne.
The first of these Elizabeth rejected out of hand; the second she
promised to consider.

The disappointment caused by her reply was bitter and heart-
rending. They thought the Queen culpably careless of her own
safety and they did not separate her safety from theirs. "I would to
God," said one Member, "that her Majesty had beheld the fatherly
eyes which we yesterday saw shed salt tears for her Majesty, upon
report of this message."[1]

Burleigh told Walsingham that both Houses were determined on
the only sensible course—"but in the highest person, such slowness
... such stay in resolution ... I am so overthrown in heart, as I have
no spark, almost, of good spirits left in me to nourish health in my
body". The gout to which he was a martyr from early middle life
was so acute in this time of anxiety and grief that he described himself
as "forced to be carried into the Parliament house and into her
Majesty's presence".

The Queen stood rigid against the attainder of Mary Stuart; she
did not discuss the matter. To the Council she exclaimed: "Can I put
to death the bird that, to escape the pursuit of the hawk, has fled to
my feet for protection? Honour and conscience forbid!" The
Council saw that the matter was, for the time being, beyond them;
but since the Queen was immovable on this point, she could not hold
out for the other. The warrant for Norfolk's execution was finally
signed for June 2. Since she came to the throne, Elizabeth had
ordered no execution by beheading. After fourteen years of disuse,
the scaffold on Tower Hill was falling to pieces, and it was necessary
to put up another. The Duke's letters to his children, his letters to the
Queen, his perfect dignity and courage at his death, made his end
moving in the extreme, and it could at least be said that no sovereign

[1] Neale, *Elizabeth and her Parliaments*, I.

had ever put a subject to death after more leniency or with greater unwillingness.

Mary had received the news of his death with passionate weeping and was for days on end disfigured by her tears. She herself had been saved by the sole effort of Elizabeth, but had the discussion of her fate been postponed for another three months, it is doubtful whether anything could have saved her.

XVI

CATHERINE DE MEDICI, who had encouraged the Huguenot party as a counter-poise to the Guises, had then found them threatening her influence with the King. The plan to exterminate the heads of the party under pretence of treason on their part, while hundreds of Huguenots were in Paris for the wedding of the King of Navarre with the Princess Margaret, succeeded with a completeness that took even the perpetrators aback. The frenzied hatred of the Parisians for the Protestants burst out into scenes of Satanic cruelty. So fierce was the conviction that anything was right which was done to put down enemies of the Catholic Church, that Zuniga, the Spanish Ambassador at Paris, wrote to Madrid: "While I write, they are casting them out naked and dragging them through the streets, pillaging their houses and sparing not a babe. Blessed be God, who has converted the Princes of France to His purpose. May He inspire their hearts to go on as they have begun!" The Pope had a medal struck to commemorate the event.

That the massacre spread from Paris to other cities made the English believe at first that it was the work of a revival of the Catholic League for the Suppression of Heresy formed some years before, and now revived to overthrow the Treaty of Blois. The accounts by refugees crowding into English ports increased the national panic. The national fury was turned upon the Queen of Scots, the niece of the Guises, who had only just failed to bring Alva's troops into the country, so that Protestants in England might share the fate of those across the Channel.

The Queen was on progress in August, and had spent a charming time at Warwick Castle, where Leicester's brother Warwick, Leicester himself, and her dear friend Lady Warwick had entertained her in a house-party in which the whole town of Warwick had seemed to share. The Recorder, Mr. Aglionby, was shaking in his shoes at the prospect of making his speech before this watchful and formidable lady, but when he had acquitted himself, the Queen said: "Come hither, little Recorder. They told me you would be afraid to look upon me or to speak boldly. But you were not so much afraid of me as I was of you!" And the beautiful long-fingered hand was given him to kiss.

The Queen who delighted in jewels and in the coloured glass windows of King's College, was fond also of displays of fireworks. The Warwicks had arranged an enormous, a dazzling exhibition over the Avon, so that the coloured lights were reflected in the water. It was augmented by cannon from the Tower which Lord Warwick, who was Master of the Ordinance, had brought down from London at his own expense. Unfortunately a fire was started at one end of the town bridge and an old couple's house was burned down. Next morning the courtiers took up a subscription for them. After these stirring events, in the middle of which the Queen left her train at Warwick, and rode over quietly to spend two days with Leicester at Kenilworth before returning to finish the public visit at Warwick, the progress resumed its course and the Queen came again, this time, officially, to Kenilworth.[1]

She was out riding when despatches were brought to her; she read them on horseback, and learned the first news of the Massacre of St. Bartholomew. She returned to the castle at once, and Fénélon, who was one of the guests, was not allowed to speak to her. Four days later, when the Court had come to Woodstock, he was summoned to an audience.

The unhappy Ambassador passed through ante-chambers where all the courtiers stood silent, staring at the ground. In a silence, he said, like that of the grave, he approached the Presence Chamber; there, in a semi-circle, were standing the Queen, the chief ladies of her court and the Privy Councillors. All of them were dressed in black.

The Queen, with a sad, stern face, advanced a few steps to meet him. She withdrew with him to a window and Fénélon, whose heart was not in the business, attempted to say that a conspiracy had been discovered against the French King and justice had demanded the most severe reprisals. No enmity, he declared, was entertained against the Protestant Powers. The Queen asked whether justice had demanded the murder of so many women and their children? She feared, she said, that those who had led the French King to abandon his natural subjects would lead him also to abandon his alliance with a foreign Queen. She withdrew on a note of reserved but calm civility and left Fénélon to the severe reproaches of the Councillors. Burleigh opened the attack by saying that the massacre was the greatest crime since the Crucifixion.

The appalling gravity of Fénélon's reception had the effectiveness of a *coup de théâtre*; but the genuineness of Elizabeth's abhorrence of

---

[1] Dugdale, *Warwick and Warwick Castle.*

this conduct in a ruler was shown convincingly in private. One of her secretaries, preparing a despatch for the French Court, wrote in a complimentary reference to two Queens, both so experienced in the arts of government. When Elizabeth read over the draft, she had these words taken out. She said that she used arts of government very different from the Queen Mother's.

Meanwhile the fright and horror caused by the massacre had added formidable strength to the pressure exerted on Elizabeth to have Mary put to death. The Queen's refusal to sanction her execution, or even to remove her from the succession, incurred disappointment, distrust and anger. Burleigh wrote to Walsingham: "I cannot write patiently—all that we have laboured for and had with full consent brought to fashion, I mean a law to make the Scottish Queen unable and unworthy of succession to the crown, was by her Majesty neither assented to nor rejected but deferred. . . ."

But Elizabeth's objection was to the English Parliament's decreeing Mary's death: not to the death itself. Mary's co-adjutors, Philip and Alva, had discussed the desirability of Elizabeth's death "by natural or by any other means", and Elizabeth pondered the desirability of Mary's death, not be assassination but by judicial process of the Scots themselves. This process she had once interfered to stop: since then, the head of the English nobility had transferred his allegiance to the Scottish Queen, the first and only rebellion of the reign had broken out in her behalf, and she had been active in a conspiracy to murder Elizabeth and bring a foreign army into England. The English Queen not only regretted the step she had taken: she began to wonder if it might be retraced.

On November 23, 1572, Sir Henry Killigrew was summoned to a private audience, at which no one was present except Burleigh, Leicester and the Queen herself. He was told to proceed to Scotland and talk to the Regent Mar in such a manner that Mar should renew the suggestion the Scots had made already, that Mary should be given up to them for execution. Killigrew was to agree, but with the stipulation that the prisoner's head should be off within four hours. The mission must be undertaken in the most absolute secrecy; the Queen herself told Killigrew that if anything of it transpired, he must be prepared to answer for it with his life, and Killigrew accepted the mission on these terms. He found Mar very willing in the matter but demanding too high a price for his co-operation; he wanted, among other concessions, the presence of 3,000 English soldiers to safeguard the execution, and that Elizabeth should thereafter pay to the Scots the annual sum she was spending on Mary's upkeep. Burleigh was indignant; Killigrew, he felt, should not have allowed such terms even to be proposed to him. At almost the same moment news arrived of Mar's death. The plan was now out of the question, and Burleigh could only hope that the Queen would consent to a more direct method. He wrote to Leicester, who was with her at Windsor: "God send her Majesty strength of spirit to preserve God's cause, her own life and the lives of millions of good subjects."

The Queen, who got up early and sometimes gave audiences at 8 a.m., used to lie down in the evening before the festivities or the labours of the night. Leicester replied to Burleigh that his letter had come at 6 o'clock, but could not be taken immediately to her Majesty "for she was at her wonted repose". Before the arrival of the letter, the possibility that Mary might, even at that hour, have met her death, had brought Elizabeth into a hysterical condition. Leicester knew this would get about and wrote to tell Walsingham the facts. It had not been raving hysteria: only a few fits, none of which lasted more than a quarter of an hour. Leicester was perhaps the best person to manage these ailments, but he himself confessed that when it came to influencing Elizabeth in political matters, Burleigh stood in a relationship with her that was not shared by anybody. He replied to Burleigh's letter on the failure of the Scots scheme, agreeing that severe pressure must now be put upon the Queen and admitting that no one but Burleigh could do it. "I think your Lordship as the case stands shall do her Majesty and your country more service in one hour" (than anyone else could do) "this seven years. Therefore I can but wish you here."[1]

Leicester, once his connection with Norfolk was severed, seemed to enter a new phase: responsible and industrious, the friend of Walsingham, the trusted colleague of Burleigh, the support and comfort of the Queen. His letters were those of a man of sense and a gentleman. Had modern means of communication been at their disposal, we should have known less about the people of the time, for they would have written fewer letters to each other, and they themselves would have known much more about each other than was often the case. Leicester, living in a relationship of affection and close intimacy with Elizabeth, acutely observant as she was, found it possible to conceal completely from her a most important part of his existence. The royal palaces out of London that lay in a string along the Thames—Greenwich, Richmond, Hampton Court, Windsor—

[1] Digges, *Compleat Ambassador*.

were reached either by rowing on the river, or at the pace of a ridden horse, or a horse-drawn coach. Journeyings to and from them and the nobles' London houses on the Strand or their country seats, Burleigh's at Theobalds, Leicester's at Wanstead, could go no faster than horses or oarsmen could move, and were impeded by heavy roads, bad weather and the coming-down of darkness. Wherever the Queen was, the roads to London were kept open for despatches; but once he had left the great house—a citadel in itself—the traveller who had gone to the other side of the county was as much cut off from its inmates, for the time being, as if he had crossed the sea. If gossip and rumour (which always seemed to outrun normal communication) did not supply a commentary on his doings, those from whom he parted could know little of them except what he chose to reveal.

Leicester, said Osborne,[1] had seen "from the continued high-beating of her heart" that Elizabeth was not going to submit herself to a foreign husband, and had therefore "hoped to have her for himself". But this prospect, though not entirely abandoned, was indefinitely receding, and he had found that, without marriage, he could rely on her affection to keep him in prosperity and power. The Queen was not his mistress in the final sense of the word, and if she had been, she would have been nothing like enough to satisfy him. Leicester had the reputation of a lecher who would expend fantastic sums to gratify himself. The Queen may well have known something of this and disregarded it; she was worldly and no fool; what she would not be likely to forgive was his making a second marriage. That she had refused him numberless times herself deprived her of the right to any logical objection; but no one would pin any faith to the powers of logic in such a situation.

In 1571, Leicester had been one of a house-party that entertained the Queen in Rutland, where, among the guests, was young Lady Sheffield. This girl, née Douglas Howard, and her sister Frances, were the daughters of Lord William Howard, the Queen's great-uncle and her early protector. Douglas Sheffield was "a star in the court for beauty and richness of apparel", and Leicester, suddenly and violently enamoured, found her "an easy purchase". The party broke up, and when Douglas had returned to her husband's house the intrigue was discovered by her sister-in-law, who picked up and read a letter of Leicester's which Douglas had dropped upon the staircase. The former told her brother, who "parted beds" with his wife that night, and went up to London, meaning to arrange a separation.

[1] *Historical Memoirs.*

Before he could thus publicly compromise Lord Leicester, he died, very suddenly. The narrator[1] of the affair had no hesitation in saying that Leicester poisoned him.

On Lord Sheffield's death, Leicester plighted his troth secretly to the widow at a house in Cannon Row. He took no immediate steps legally to complete the marriage, and the young Lady Sheffield was in a miserable position: in the eye of the world, a member of Leicester's circle, but not able to claim her right to his attention. The situation, since all the parties were at Court together, could not be altogether hidden from the Queen, though Leicester did his best to distract her attention from it. In May 1572, Gilbert Talbot wrote to his father, Lord Shrewsbury: "My Lord of Leicester is very much with her Majesty and she shows him the same great good affection she was wont; of late he has endeavoured to please her more than heretofore. There are two sisters now in the Court, that are very far in love with him, so they long have been—my Lady Sheffield and Frances Howard; they, striving who shall love him best, are at great wars with each other, and the Queen thinketh not well of them and not the better of him. For this reason there are spies set over him."

In 1573, four days before the birth of his son, Leicester at last went through a form of marriage with the mother, privately, at Esher; the only witness being his confidential physician Dr. Julio. The utmost caution was necessary, and he fell out with his bride because, in the privacy of her own rooms, she had herself waited on with the ceremony due to a countess.

[1] Gervase Holles, *The Holles Family*.

XVII

IN 1573 THE Queen finished paying off the debts to the City of London left by Henry VIII and Edward VI: a prosaic thing enough, scarcely interesting except to the people to whom the money had been owing, but it forms a revealing background to something repeated with astonishment by the Venetian Ambassador twelve years later. He said the French envoy M. de Lansac had told him that he had often seen the Queen, on her way through the City, "receive such blessings from the people as though she had been another Messiah".

The sparing and the saving, done as the Queen did it, *con amore*, could not be confined only to its proper sphere: the habit showed itself when dealing with men who deserved the utmost generosity. A small royal property, Newhall, Burleigh thought might very well be given to Sussex, who wanted it. The Queen said she would like to give it to him: but then, once a thing had been given, it was gone. Situated as she was, she had to think carefully before she committed herself on these matters. Burleigh kept Sussex in touch with the progress of his interests, and in March 1574, he related a conversation he had had with the Queen. "She answered that she thought it best you should have it, but therewith she mixed speeches also after her accustomed manner, what a notable house it was, and with what charges her father had built it." Burleigh had felt obliged to interpose here and say that so far from its being a notable house, Henry VIII had abandoned it because he did not think it fit for himself to live in. "Then she wore a new doubt, whereof I never heard, whether she should not have a rent for the park?" Burleigh told her straight out that this was utterly unreasonable. He pressed her for a decision but "she would give no resolved answer, yea or nay". But in May she gave Sussex Beaulieu, and in December, Boreham, Walkfare, Old-hall and its dependencies.[1] In the same March as that in which Burleigh could not bring her to a decision about Newhall, Sir Thomas Smith complained to the Treasurer of his own troubles: "It maketh me weary of my life . . . I can neither get the other letter signed nor the letter already signed permitted to be sent away, but

[1] Wood, *Athenae Cantabrigiensis*.

day by day and hour by hour deferred, till 'anon, soon and to-morrow'."

This autumn, Lady Lennox asked permission to go to Scotland to see her grandson, the eight-year-old King James. She had been brought very low by misfortune, for after her son's murder, her husband, who had succeeded the murdered Murray as Regent, was himself murdered in 1571. She had, however, a younger son remaining, Lord Charles Stuart, another body whose veins held a tincture of the royal blood. Nothing, it seemed, could cure Lady Lennox of intriguing for the English crown. At a house-party she met the Countess of Shrewsbury who, at the beginning of her husband's appointment, had been told that she was not to have unofficial conversation with the Queen of Scots, but had now established herself as Queen Mary's familiar and confidante. As a result of the meeting at the house-party, Lady Lennox changed her plans. She did not go up to Scotland, but instead she accepted an invitation from Lady Shrewsbury for herself and Lord Charles Stuart to go to Rufford, another of the Shrewsburys' country seats. Here Lady Shrewsbury brought an unmarried daughter by her second husband, the gentle, docile Elizabeth Cavendish.

At Rufford the roads were impassable under October rains, and Lady Lennox, saying that she was affected by the damp, thought it wise to remain in her own room. Her hostess naturally spent a great deal of time with her, and while the two mothers were shut away, it so fell out that Charles Stuart took a great fancy to Elizabeth Cavendish, "and entangled himself so that he could have none other". The marriage of the young people was quickly arranged, and there was born of it that child of misfortune, the Lady Arabella Stuart. Lady Shrewsbury boasted loudly that her grandchild was in succession to the throne of England. She was, and in the succeeding reign she died in the Tower, as a consequence. Meanwhile Lady Lennox and Lady Shrewsbury were both sentenced to a term of imprisonment for having arranged the marriage of a youth of the royal blood without the permission of the Crown.

Burleigh had trouble enough with the marriage in his own family. Ann Cecil's envious friends were not the only ones surprised when the Earl of Oxford proposed for her; Burleigh himself had said: "I could not well imagine what to think, considering I never meant to seek it, nor hoped of it." But shortly after the wedding, one motive at least of the bridegroom's disclosed itself. The Earl of Oxford was first cousin to the Duke of Norfolk, and when the Duke had been sentenced to death in January 1572, Oxford relied on his father-in-law to save him. In view of the Queen's unwillingness to sign the death warrant, it was clear that had Burleigh wished, he could have obtained a pardon; but of all the men convinced of the necessity for Norfolk's death, he was the most unshakeable. Oxford was capable of generous feeling, but he had a vicious temper. His marriage was only a few months old, but in return for Burleigh's refusal to save his cousin, he swore "that he would ruin the Lord Treasurer's daughter".

The tempest subsided and Lord and Lady Oxford appeared to be living together in harmony. The Earl thoroughly disliked his mother-in-law, and this was the period at which Lady Burleigh, austere in manner herself and fond of her daughter, resented Oxford's flirtation with the Queen. Oxford was twenty-two and Elizabeth thirty-nine, and had they met in society on equal terms, no doubt he would have neither shown nor felt any attraction towards her, but they were not upon equal terms; her interest acted as a burning-glass, kindling ambition: to win it was the aim of every young man who had the chance of coming near her. For the time being, Oxford enjoyed his success and cared nothing for his mother-in-law.

In the New Year of 1575 he went to Italy, and in March Burleigh wrote telling him that his wife was pregnant. Oxford's first reply was that this news made him a happy man; but his determination "to ruin the Lord Treasurer's daughter" now recoiled on his own head. He had, it seemed, once told his cousin, Lord Henry Howard, that if his wife were pregnant it would be by some other man. Howard hated Burleigh as a supplanter of the old nobility, and when the Countess of Oxford was known to be with child, he began to repeat what her husband had said to him.

The Queen, to whom Dr. Masters announced the news, was sympathetically delighted at the prospect of Burleigh's first grandchild; she began by enquiring "tenderly" about Lady Oxford's health. When Masters replied that she was pregnant, the Queen, he said, "rose, or rather sprang up from the cushion, and said these words: 'Indeed it is a matter that concerns my Lord's joy chiefly, yet I protest to God, that next to them that have interest in it, there is nobody that can be more joyous of it than I am'."[1]

But the general knowledge of the pregnancy, combined with the tattle of Lord Henry Howard, meant that Oxford was now talked of as a cuckold. Though he had only himself to thank, he was in-

[1] Ward, *Earl of Oxford.*

furiated, and he was one of those who, like Hamlet, are so impressed with the importance of their own sufferings, they are completely indifferent to the pain they themselves give to other people. It was hopeless to persuade him, reason with him or appeal to his compassion on ordinary grounds. He did not return to England till after the child's birth and then he told Lord Burleigh he did not propose to see his wife "till he was satisfied on some points".

Burleigh could get the measure of most people, but to understand a temperament so bitter and preposterous was beyond him. He had not the slightest idea what Oxford was talking about, and as the Earl's behaviour was not only breaking his wife's heart but also making shipwreck of her social position, Burleigh wrote a long letter to the Queen, giving the facts as they were understood by Lady Oxford's family. He described his daughter as "Your Majesty's most devoted young servant, as one that is toward Your Majesty in dutiful love and fears, yea, in fervent admiration", and he declared he had never seen the smallest reason to suspect her of misconduct; her behaviour had always been that of a devoted wife and a single-hearted young lover. He wondered whether the source of this inexplicable behaviour might lie in his having refused a demand of the needy Oxford for a large sum of ready money; but he had already done a great deal in that direction; he adduced: "my care to get him money when his bankers had none . . . my dealing with his creditors to stay their clamours".

Oxford came back from his travels with some novelties in the way of scented clothing: sweet-bags, a scented leather jerkin and some scented gloves. He gave the gloves to the Queen, who was so delighted with their scent she called it my Lord of Oxford's perfume. She was as ready as ever to be amiable, interested and responsive, but she told him he was not behaving properly to his wife; and when he found out that Burleigh had been discussing his affairs with her, behind his back, Oxford was exacerbated to the point of frenzy. To a simple request from his father-in-law, that he would at least state what reason he supposed himself to have for casting off his wife, Oxford wrote in reply: "I will not blazon or publish it until it please me. And last of all, I mean not to weary my life any more with such troubles and molestations as I have endured, nor will I, to please your Lordship only, discontent myself." He added with surprising candour: "Always I have, and I will still, prefer mine own content before others'."[1]

[1] Ward, *Earl of Oxford*.

The little Elizabeth Vere was brought up in the household of her grandparents. Burleigh was an adoring grandfather. Fuller said of him: "If he could get his table set round with his young, little children, he was then in his kingdom," and indeed his affections were called upon.

Oxford, who at length entered into a sort of intermittent reconciliation with his tormented young Grizelda, had in all four children by her, whom Burleigh had to bring up. As he said: "If their father were of that good nature to be grateful," he himself would have felt the burden less. The power of the sixteenth-century husband over the wife was so great that even such a father-in-law as Lord Burleigh was helpless. Nothing could redress the balance except the wife's being the stronger personality of the two. The gentle and loving Ann Oxford was a victim beyond human aid, and his favourite child was the Achilles' heel in her father's great career. There, where he had garnered up his heart, ill luck found him out.

XVIII

CATHERINE DE MEDICI had an avid desire to see the English crown
on the head of one of her children; but the extravagant courtesy of
her relations with Elizabeth did not prevent her from indulging in a
hideous grinning in what she imagined to be the privacy of her family
circle. Charles IX had died, haunted by nightmares of St. Bartholomew, and Anjou succeeded his brother as Henri III, in 1574. Lord
North was English Ambassador at Paris, and he informed his Court
that among the festivities of the accession, Catherine de Medici had
held one in her private apartments; she had dressed up two repulsive-
ly ugly female dwarfs, and with her maids, egged them on to mimic
what they supposed to be the manners of the Queen of England.
Fénélon, to whom the Queen poured out all this with angry excitement, assured her in dismay that it must all be a misunderstanding:
the Queen Mother was the acme of good-breeding, and a devoted
admirer of the Queen of England, of her beauty, her virtue. The
dwarfs were, in fact, exceptionally pretty ones, and he would lay his
life, the whole story had its basis in the fact that Lord North's French
was so wretched, he understood barely half of anything he heard. The
Queen had no wish to sever diplomatic relations; having vented her
passion, she allowed herself to be mollified, or forced herself to appear
so. Bohun says that she detested dwarfs, and if she did, the story of
Catherine de Medici's doings would arouse a frenzied loathing. If,
however, she felt a detestation of dwarfs in general, she made one
exception, for she had a female dwarf of her own, Mrs. Tomasin; the
little creature appears in the large picture at Penshurst of the Queen
dancing with Lord Leicester, and Dr. Dee in his diary noted that one
of his visiters was "the Queen's dwarf, Mrs. Tomasin".

Dee was living in a house at Mortlake, and in March 1575 Elizabeth
paid him a visit, not in any secret fashion, but, as he said in his *Compendious Relation*, "accompanied by her most honourable Privy
Council and other her lords and nobility". The party arrived at an
unfortunate moment, for Dee's wife was only dead four hours.
Hearing this, the Queen would not come in, but asked Dee to bring
out and show her the magic glass of which she had heard much.
Some say this speculum was made of polished coal and some that it

was volcanic glass. It was acquired by Horace Walpole and dis-appeared after the sale of his effects at Strawberry Hill. Dee said it was brought to him by an angel, which, to anyone interested in occult phenomena, sounds like an "apport". He fetched it out, and: "Her Majesty, being taken down from her horse by the Earl of Leicester, Master of the Horse, at the church wall of Mortlake, did see some of the properties of that magic glass to her Majesty's great contentment and delight."

The episode, it is suggested, may be found, transmuted and en-shrined in *The Faerie Queen*: "*Such was the glassie globe that Merlin made*," into which Britomart, an image of Elizabeth, peers, to see the man she is to marry.

Whatever the crystal showed that gave the Queen contentment and delight, the future, so perilous and so obscure, had at least one splendid gratification in store. The coming summer was that of the great entertainment at Kenilworth. Whether Leicester's secret marriage had made him anxious to give some flourishing demonstration of his devotion to the Queen, at all events this historic house-party for Elizabeth was held for eighteen days in July, on the summer progress of 1575. It was an exhibition, on epic scale, of Leicester's importance, his taste, his wealth, his adoration. He and Elizabeth were now forty-two, and while the Queen, slender and active, was to retain a degree of youth for several years, Leicester was in the last phase of his superb handsomeness, before he turned red-faced, bald and too fat for even such height as his to carry off.

His preparations had been enormous, and if self-interest and treachery were the motive of this act of homage, at least the con-ception and all its details could not have been more in accordance with devoted love.

The Earl had met the Queen and her train seven miles away at Long Ichen, where he feasted her under a tent so vast that when dismantled it required seven carts to carry it away. It was a brilliant July: "this gift did Jupiter confer upon her Highness, to have fair and reasonable weather at command." Hunting by the way, which meant shooting deer with a bow and arrow from horseback, Leicester brought her to the park gates of Kenilworth at 8 in the evening of July 9. The castle, which the Queen had given him ten years before, had then consisted of three sides of a square: the towering oblong known as Caesar's tower, with a banqueting-hall called Lancaster's Building at right angles to its further end, and parallel to this, at the nearer end, a much later and lower wing of Tudor architecture, known as Henry

VIII's Lodging. Leicester had completed the square with Leicester's Building, a block nearly as tall as Caesar's Tower with the tiers of lofty mullioned windows in the height of fashion. Inside, the great dwelling was filled with everything the age could attain to, of luxury and magnificence. The year before, Mary Queen of Scots had written to France that Leicester "took great delight in fine furniture" and said to her correspondent, "If you send him some crystal cup . . . or some fine Turkey carpet, it will perhaps . . . make him suspected by his mistress and will assist me." Kenilworth showed his taste in its full lustre. He had hangings of scarlet leather stamped with gilt, and a Turkey carpet of a light-blue ground, fifty feet long. The four-poster beds were most of them hung with scarlet or crimson, embroidered with silver and gold, but there was one of which the blue curtains were trimmed with gold and silver lace, one covered and furnished with peach-colour fringed with ash-coloured silk, one with green velvet curtains lined with yellow and fringed with gold, one with white tinsel curtains embroidered with purple velvet and copper-gold. The sheets were marked in the corner with a coroneted L worked in blue, the night-stools were upholstered in black quilted velvet, enclosing pewter pans. The grander bedrooms had superb looking-glasses and chairs covered to match the beds.

The brilliance of glass added its magic. The pantry contained rows of glass dishes for cream, and the great rooms were lit by glass candle-sticks. One pair was especially magnificent, of blue glass decorated with gilt. The chess table was made of squares of crystal and precious stones framed in ebony; the pieces were crystal, half mounted in silver and half in gold.[1]

The Queen's household were lodged in Warwick, where special arrangements had to be made for delivering her letters "which came very thick", and twenty horses at a time were in daily use for transport. She herself, with her ladies, was to be in the entire care of Leicester, the object of his devoted attention and ceremonious adoration. Thirty distinguished guests had been invited to meet her, including Leicester's brother-in-law and sister, Sir Henry and Lady Mary Sidney, and their son Philip, and with their servants and the household servants, the castle was like a small township, put down in acres of gently-falling green parkland, studded with great trees. Beyond Lancaster's Building, the windows looked on to the countryside across a wide ornamental water. On the nearer side, another stretch of water lay like a moat against the curtain wall. It was over the

[1] H.M.C. De Lisle and Dudley.

bridge that spanned it that the Queen and her splendid entourage were conducted into the castle. As Elizabeth gained the bridge, an island sparkling with lights floated towards it, bearing a nereid in silk robes, who in a boy's high voice, told her: "I am the Lady of this pleasant lake," and assured her: "The Lake, the Lodge, the Lord, are yours for to command." The Queen smiled and said: "We had thought the lake had been ours, and do you call it yours, now? Well, we will herein commune more with you hereafter."

Robert Laneham, door-keeper of the Council-Chamber, was a humble member of the party, and he described the fine doings with enthusiasm and amazement.

A salute of guns greeted the Queen's entry into the inner court, and when she was led to her chamber, the clock on Caesar's tower was stopped. The two dials, facing south and east, had sky-blue faces with figures of gold and "glittered conspicuous a great way off, showing the hours to town and country". But while the Queen remained, time was to stand still. The twilight of a summer's day came on at last, and with darkness the castle in its fields and groves became a fairy palace: "so glittering by glass a'night by continual brightness of candle, fire and torchlight, transparent through the lightsome windows, as it were the Egyptian Pharaoh's, relucent unto all the Alexandrian coast".

The next day was Sunday. The Queen and Court went to church in the morning; in the afternoon the lords and ladies danced in the garden and in the evening there was a tremendous display of fireworks: "with blaze of burning darts flying to and fro, beams of stars coruscant, streams and hail of fiery sparks, lightenings a'water and a'land, flight and shot of thunderbolts, all with such continuance, tempest and vehemence, that the heavens thundered, the waters surged, the castle shook, and made me," said Laneham, "hardy as I am, very vengeably afeared."

Monday was so hot, the Queen stayed indoors till five o'clock, when she went out to hunt the hart. As her troop was returning in the evening, Sylvanus, a wild man of the woods, met them and ran beside the Queen's horse, uttering reams of congratulatory verse. A close arbour stood in the way, and at the Queen's approach the bushes shook, sweet airs sounded, and Deep Desire stepped out of a holly-bush, expressing Lord Leicester's profound but respectful anguish. At the close of these utterances, Sylvanus in a final act of homage broke the sapling he carried and cast it away. Unhappily one half came down almost on the head of the Queen's horse, which gave a frenzied plunge. Several gentlemen rushed for its bridle, but before they could lay hand on it the Queen had reined in the terrified beast and called out, "No hurt, no hurt!" "Which words," said Laneham, "I promise you, we were all glad to hear, and took them to be the best part of the play."

On Tuesday evening the Queen, attended, went on foot over the bridge and into the tree-sprinkled meadows called the Chase. When she came back a barge was on the pool, filled with musicians playing and singing, and she stood on the bridge, listening in the evening light.

The pensive pleasures were variegated with some of extraordinary violence. On Thursday was held a ferocious bear-baiting. A crew of ban dogs were let loose on thirteen bears in the inner court, "where there was plucking and tugging, scratching and biting, and such an expense of blood and leather between them as a month's licking I ween will not recover". In the evening, after this hideous savagery, for two hours guns discharged and fireworks were sent up of the strangest kind, "compelled by cunning to fly to and fro and to mount very high in the air, and also to burn unquenchable in the waters beneath". While the ear and eye were excited by loud noise and shooting lights, an Italian tumbler went through a rapid performance of such amazing writhings and contortions, and all with such ease, it seemed that he must be boneless like a lamprey or have a lute-string for a spine.

During the next two days the heat abated and continuous showers refreshed the countryside. The castle had its indoor attractions, one of which was a great aviary filled with both familiar and exotic birds. The mesh was stretched between columns whose capitals were painted with a *trompe d'œil* of rubies, diamonds, emeralds and sapphires of enormous size, in gold settings.

Sunday was glorious again and the Queen went to church as before. The afternoon was spent in watching country sports and part of a performance by the men of Coventry of a local play called *The Slaughter of the Danes at Hock Tide*. The more stately part of the evening's programme did not allow time for the performance to finish, but the Queen would not disappoint the men of Coventry. She said their play was so good, she must see the whole of it next Tuesday, and she gave them two of the bucks that had been shot and five marks. That evening there was "a most delicious and ambrosial banquet of 300 dishes", but "her Majesty ate smally or nothing". The ceremonial part was therefor soon over, and the feast was left to the rest of the company, who fell on the dishes, and "all was disorderly wasted and coarsely consumed".

On one of the days when the Queen was out hunting, Laneham was allowed in to take a thorough good look at the garden. It lay east of Caesar's Tower, with the Swan Tower at the far end; in the midst of the lawn and flower-beds stood a magnificent fountain, "of rich and hard white marble", in which two naked figures back to back held up a bowl; from this jets of water rose and fell into a hexagonal basin, where was maintained two feet "of the fresh-falling water". Laneham's inspection was on one of the hot days, and he exclaimed at the delightfulness of "walking aloft, on sweet, shadowed terrace, in heat of summer to feel the pleasant whisking wind above, and delectable cooolness of fountain springs beneath; to taste delicious strawberries, even from their stalks".

As the heat had returned after the rain, the Queen went out in the cool of the early evening, and on her return from one expedition at twilight, a water-pageant greeted her as she rode on to the bridge. While strains of music sounded on the mere, the Lady of the Lake advanced on her floating island, scintillating with lights. A mermaid drew a tail eighteen feet long through the waves beside her, and perched on the bank of a gigantic dolphin, Arion prepared to address the awe-inspiring figure whose horse was reined to a standstill above his head. Some lines, indeed, he did bring out, but the occasion was too much for him; his memory failed, and pulling off his mask in exasperation, he shouted that "he was none of Arion, not he, but honest Harry Goldingham". The Queen was in fits of laughter and said afterwards that this had been the best part of the show.

The tremendous festival at Kenilworth was not a single event after which everyone retired to recuperate; it was merely the highlight of the summer progress. At its close, the Queen was escorted by Leicester on a round of visits to other country houses, while a fine summer made travelling through deep country pleasant.

Turbeville's *Art of Hunting*, published in this year, gives a line-drawing of the Queen taking a picnic luncheon in a wood. She sits upon a small bank in a dress with stiff bodice, high neck, long tight sleeves and spreading skirts and wears a small-brimmed hat with a plume at one side. Two ladies stand behind her; gentlemen are busying themselves about her, and in the foreground, where a table-cloth is spread on the ground, there is a hamper full of cold game, plates of rolls and pitchers of wine.

The itinerary led Leicester to a house of particular interest to himself. This was Chartley in Staffordshire, the house of Lord Essex, who, absent in Ireland on his duties as Earl Marshal, left his wife Lettice to entertain the Queen her cousin. The house party at Chartley was afterwards celebrated as the occasion when Philip Sidney, coming from Kenilworth in his uncle Leicester's train, first saw the Countess of Essex's daughter, the thirteen-year-old Penelope Devereux:

> And yet could not, by rising morn foresee
> How fair a day was near. Oh, punished eyes!

Lettice Devereux's daughter inherited her mother's beauty and magnetism and her mother's inability to estimate their relative Queen Elizabeth: black cat, black kit. Since this inability was strikingly shown in after years by Lettice's son Robert, the future Earl of Essex, now a boy of nine, it might be described as a family failing.

Elizabeth had once liked her cousin Lettice; but the nervous wear and tear, the ceaseless strain of her existence, acting on a temperament that, though capable of self-control, was highly strung, meant that the women with whom the Queen remained on terms of intimacy were those who had a personal affection for her, reinforced by forbearance, sympathy and comprehension. The Countess of Warwick was one, the Queen's cousin Kate Carey, now Lady Howard of Effingham, was another, the Swedish Helena von Snakenburg, the second Marchioness of Northampton, was a third, and yet another was the black-eyed Lady Norris, the Queen's "dear Crow". Lettice Devereux had neither the attributes nor the wish to join such a band; she had not the sense to understand Elizabeth's genius, what she was doing or why she deserved patience and magnanimity in her immediate circle. To Lettice, Elizabeth was merely her cousin, to whom Fate had given a position of superiority and splendour; domineering and disagreeable but really to be despised because she was not the equal of Lettice in voluptuous attractions. The Queen's lover had long ago shown himself susceptible to these attractions, and he was returning to his early passion now. It was true that he already had a wife, or a lady who had been led to believe that she was his wife, and that the Countess of Essex still had a husband; these were academic objections, but the presence of the watchful Queen was one of a more practical kind. The situation was delightful, but it required extreme discretion. Lettice was by instinct as possessive and demanding as her cousin, but against her will she was forced to subdue these qualities.

The Earl of Essex died in Ireland the next year, and Leicester, who was already credited with the death of his own wife and of Douglas Sheffield's husband, was rumoured to have procured the Earl's death by poison. The accusation was not well substantiated, but it was inevitable. Just before his death, Essex had offered Penelope in marriage to Philip Sidney, for he admired and loved the young man, but Sidney had regarded the matter as one of family politics, and when it was dropped he did not mind one way or the other. It was only when the friends of Essex's family, charging themselves with his children, married off Penelope to Lord Rich, that Sidney discovered a devouring passion for her and looked back in amazement at his tardy senses:

> Not at first sight nor with a dribbed shot
> Love gave the wound which while I breathe will bleed.[1]

The fact that though she was unhappy with Lord Rich, Penelope refused, albeit gently, to gratify Sidney's passion, this and his poetry have between them cast a halo over this bold beauty with a high colour, black eyes and yellow hair. Her subsequent behaviour, however, suggests that her only reason for refusing Sidney was the very good one that she did not want him.

Unlike Oxford, who was attractive to those of his own age and looked upon by his elders with a mixture of admiration and disapproval, Sidney was the darling of those older than himself. Burleigh had written of him while still at Oxford, as "the darling Philip", Leicester wrote to Archbishop Parker of "my boy, Philip Sidney". From earliest childhood he had made a remarkable impression by his charm, his gravity, his sense. "I knew him," said Fulke Greville, "from a child, and I never knew him other than a man." The wonderful sequence of poems, *Astrophel and Stella*, in which he recorded his hopeless passion, shows all those mental qualities the poet possesses besides lyricism; but in his daily life, there was, perhaps, a slight sense of moral superiority which, it is easy to see, would at once exasperate the Earl of Oxford.

There was another cause of hostility between the young men; they adopted that of their patrons. Oxford, with a sense and good feeling conspicuously absent in many of his relationships, had attached himself to the Earl of Sussex; Sidney was devoted to the Earl of Leicester, the magnificent uncle who was so very kind to him. The standing quarrel between Leicester and Sussex made it inevitable that Sidney and Oxford should be ready to fall out; Oxford, finding Sidney in

[1] Sidney, *Astrophel and Stella*.

possession of a tennis court, ordered him off as he wanted to play himself, and Sidney refused to go; Oxford called him a puppy, and Sidney sent him a challenge to a duel.

News affecting a favourite was brought at once to the Queen; she forbade any duel and gave Sidney a talking-to. She pointed out that noblemen as such were entitled to respect and that anyone who wanted to live at Court must remember this. Sidney replied, courteously but straightforwardly, that the rights of men came before the rights of noblemen, and he quoted the example of King Henry VIII, who had supported the rights of commoners against the aristocracy. Elizabeth liked boys to speak up for themselves; having given her reproof, she said no more. Though Oxford was at the meridian of favour, Sidney came out of the scrape without any damage; but Oxford's temper was not improved.

Elizabeth's fondness for young people and for children was one of her charms; she loved to see them about her, as she loved to see the flowers and fruits grown on her kingdom's soil. There ran counter to this instinct a vein of jealousy: but where this was not touched, she was full of sympathy and encouragement; instead of, like many people, disliking them for being young, she liked them for that reason.

John and Isabella Harington, the young couple who had been shut up with her in the Tower, had a son, John, to whom the Queen had stood godmother. He was now fifteen. Most of his recollections of her were of a date when he was a man and she an old woman, and though he loved her, they gain their exceptional value from his clear-sighted view of her eccentricities and weaknesses as well as her grandeur; but one recollection he had of this year 1576. The Parliament had again brought forward an urgent request that she should marry, and in the speech with which she closed the session, the Queen had said what, in effect, she had always said, that she did not want to marry but that she would do so if and when the safety of the state required it. The occasion was one of mutual expressions of affection and praise. The Lord Keeper Bacon made a speech returning the Queen's thanks for the subsidy that had been voted, and then began to exhort and advise the Members about the getting of it in; but the figure in crimson velvet robes, sitting in the canopied chair, stopped him and summoned him for a word. Bacon then returned to his place and told the House that the Queen "thought it needless to exhort men so willingly and lovingly disposed". She had rather run the risk of losing some of the money, than allow them to think "by long exhorting and persuading", that she had not every confidence in them.

The Queen herself made a speech in which the enthusiasm which the House had shown for her was returned on her part. The satisfaction with her efforts that they had expressed, had amazed and moved her. "Still," she said, "I find that assured zeal among my faithful subjects to my special comfort which was first declared, to my great encouragement. Haps it oft," she asked, "that Princes' acts are conceived in so good part? . . . No, no, my Lords. How great my fortune is in this respect, I were ingrate if I should not acknowledge." To the question of her marriage, she said: "If I were a milkmaid with a pail on my arm, whereby my private person might be little set by, I would not forsake that poor and single state to match with a monarch. . . . Yet for your behalf, there is no way so difficult that may touch my private person, which I will not well content myself to take." But, she added: "let good heed be taken that, in reaching too far after future good, you peril not the present and begin to quarrel and fall by dispute together by the ears, before it is decided who shall wear my crown." The warning was mildly given, and the farewell was made on the most cordial note: "And this, as one that yieldeth you more thanks than my tongue can utter, I commend you unto the assured protection of the Almighty who will preserve you safe, I trust, in all felicity."[1]

A copy of this speech was sent to young Harington with a covering letter from the Queen, which said: "Boy Jack, I have made a clerk write fair my poor words for thine use, as it cannot be such striplings have entrance into the Parliament House as yet . . . so shalt thou hereafter, perchance, find some good fruits thereof, when thy godmother is out of remembrance; and I do this because thy father was ready to serve and love us in trouble and thrall."[2]

Though her refusal to take a husband had produced the usual dismay in Parliament, a marriage negotiation was now well under way between the Queen and the French Court. Catherine de Medici had offered Elizabeth the hand of her younger son Alençon after the signing of the Treaty of Blois, and the English Queen had declared herself much honoured by the proposal. When Anjou became King of France, Alençon's attitude was so hostile and mischievous that the King and the Queen Mother were eager to get him out of France. The Prince was twenty-one, and though undersized and very ugly, he was lively and responsive. It was said that the impression he made

[1] Neale, *Elizabeth and her Parliaments*, I.   [2] Harington, *Nugae Antiquae*.

in conversation was so good, it misled the hearer as to his real capacity. Unlike his brother, who was entirely Catholic in sympathy and had privately disdained the notion of marrying Elizabeth, Alençon, who was in part a supporter of the Huguenots, appeared to entertain no such feelings. The King would probably have sons who would exclude Alençon from the French throne, and a marriage with the Queen of England would be, for him, exceptionally brilliant. The discrepancy of their ages was formidable, twenty-one years in fact, but Elizabeth's reputation in all but those fanatical circles where she was regarded as the arch-fiend and credited with every moral and physical repulsiveness, was now very high. Her achievement in keeping her realm free from foreign conflict and civil war, with its result of thriving prosperity, formed the economic basis of her high repute, while her intellect, elegance and grandeur surrounded it with a blaze of personal distinction.

Alençon, from the start of the negotiations, had worked himself into a state of emotional as well as political eagerness for the match; in 1572 Walsingham had written from Paris to Burleigh, "Touching the affection towards her Majesty, many ways I am given to understand that his affection is unfeigned and great." As for Elizabeth, the ceaseless fluctuations of the political weather-glass were faithfully reflected in her attitude towards the match. At one moment she said she feared she was too old to retain the affections of so young a husband; at another she was making pointed enquiries into the degree of disfigurement Alençon had suffered from smallpox; but Alençon himself showed no wavering. His agent Maisonfleur gained the Queen's confidence, so far at least as conversation went, and he was allowed to tell her of his master's ardours. He wrote Alençon letters in which Alençon was Don Lucidor, Elizabeth, Madame L'Isle, and the Queen Mother, Madame La Serpente. In these letters the matter was treated in the idiom, at least, of emotional sincerity. Maisonfleur, who wanted his master to come to England and propose like a private gentlemen, could not tell him that Elizabeth had said the one word they wanted to hear from her: but she had said, "Let him come," and Maisonfleur had read her meaning in her eyes: or so he thought; or so, at least he said.[1]

Alençon, weak and incompetent, was now nonetheless amazingly *affairé*. In the complicated situation in the Netherlands, the resistance to Spanish tyranny was divided; for the Catholic states who wanted a degree of freedom did not want to join a Protestant movement of

[1] H.M.C. Hatfield.

revolt; the Flemings therefore made advances to Alencon to accept their sovereignty, and the possibility of his being able to accept and maintain this position was disturbing to Spain, France and England alike. Philip, by means of the Duke of Parma, was about to launch the concentrated attack on the Netherlands called "The Spanish Fury"; Catherine and Henri III foresaw that Alençon's doings might involve them in a war with Spain, and Elizabeth was alarmed at the idea of a strong French influence in the Netherlands, in which France should command the whole coastline opposite to the English shore of the Channel. This situation to which every burning issue, religious, political, commercial, contributed its own range of interlocking considerations, formed a puzzle of vast complexity in which the values of the pieces were perpetually changing and in which failure to find the solution meant, for the country, ruin, and for the Queen and Burleigh, death. The constant presence of extreme danger and the ceaseless weight of care had become the background of Elizabeth's daily life, and though habit and extraordinary powers of mind had enabled her to behave with apparent indifference to it, the oppression and the fear corroded her nerves perpetually: at moments, she was capable of suspecting the loyalty even of Burleigh. At the end of 1575 Lord Shrewsbury had suggested to Burleigh a marriage between his son Edward Talbot and Elizabeth Cecil. Burleigh's refusal was based on the fear that the Queen would mislike so close an alliance between himself and the keeper of the Queen of Scots. Shrewsbury's Derbyshire estates included the spa at Buxton, where he had built a lodginghouse for those who came to take the waters, and when a little while before Burleigh had paid a visit to the spa for the sake of his gout, because Buxton was in the neighbourhood of Chatsworth where Mary was then established, there had darted into the Queen's brain the hideous possibility that Burleigh had gone into Derbyshire for a secret reason. When he came back, Burleigh told Shrewsbury, the Queen gave him "very sharp reproofs" and directly accused him of favouring the Queen of Scots; as he said: "and that in so earnest a sort, I never looked for". It was too much, particularly as he was at the same time accused by other people of being a rancorous enemy and persecutor of the injured and innocent Scots Queen. He wished young Edward Talbot well, but as to a family alliance, that, he feared, was impossible in the circumstances.

The mistrusts, the outbursts of nervous exasperation or flaming anger, were difficult to stomach, but they had no bearing on the real opinion which Elizabeth had of Burleigh, and which he and his colleagues knew that she had. As he had written to Walsingham four years ago: "Lord God be thanked, her blasts be not as the storms of other Princes, though they be shrewd sometimes to those she loveth best." Sussex, as the Queen's Lord Chamberlain, sometimes sent the messages to summon Privy Councillors wherever the Queen might be. In the crucial year of 1576, one of his notes went to Burleigh: "Her Majesty has received intelligence from beyond the seas, which she means (at once) to impart to his Lordship, and to confer with him thereon. Her pleasure is therefore that his Lordship should repair to her as soon as he conveniently may." And again, "Her Majesty spoke of him and of his sound and deep judgment and council, using these words, that no Prince in Europe had such a counsellor as she had of him."[1]

[1] H.M.C. Hatfield.

XIX

By THE TIME she was turned forty, Elizabeth's nervous irritability had become pronounced: it was known that it sometimes drove her to abandon argument in favour of a clip on the ear. Such episodes of course lost nothing in the telling. In January 1576 Mary Shelton, a young lady of the Privy Chamber, married Mr. Scudamore without the Queen's consent. This was a breach of etiquette and one bound particularly to exasperate Elizabeth. Another lady of the Privy Chamber, Eleanor Bridges, who wrote gossiping letters to the young Earl of Rutland on his travels, told him: "The Queen has used Mary Shelton very ill for her marriage; she hath dealt liberal both in blows and words. . . . No one ever bought her husband more dearly."[1] So said the girl's companion. Eight years later, when the story reached Mary Queen of Scots through the Countess of Shrewsbury, it ran, the Queen broke Mary Scudamore's finger and then gave out that the injury was caused by a falling candlestick. The Queen's reputation for flying out was founded on fact, but she had some characteristics that everyone found endearing. Provided they avoided the few points she was known not to tolerate—and secret or stolen matches were one of these—she was cordial and sympathetic to well-behaved young people and sometimes remarkably tolerant to those who behaved badly. It was not only her distinguished servants to whom she gave her loyalty: with her humble ones it was the same. Osborne, by no means her panegyrist, said that she did, it was true, demand exacting standards of physical appearance in her household retainers, and had been known to refuse employment to a good-looking man because he had lost a tooth, but that "she was never known to desert any for age or other infirmity after they were once enrolled in her service"; she either kept them on or discharged them "with good pensions". No one who worked in close association with her was without grounds for criticism or even serious complaint; but the over-riding effect she produced was one that inspired a personal enthusiasm. Nicholas White advised Burleigh that visitors should not have unlimited access to Mary Stuart at Tutbury, for he spoke of the effect on himself of seeing Elizabeth.

[1] H.M.C. Rutland.

"Mine own affection by seeing the Queen's Majesty our sovereign is doubled."

In the New Year 1578 the ulcer on the Queen's leg healed. Like every other symptom of Elizabeth's, this was a matter of international interest. In January the Papal Nuncio at Paris wrote to the Cardinal of Como that he "was told" that the Queen's doctors thought her life in danger because the ulcer on her leg had dried up; they had considered that the discharge from the ulcer had compensated for her having so few monthly periods, and expected the worst effects to follow from its cease. Correspondents had other things to say about her of more positive accuracy. The Nuncio in Spain, in 1577, ascribed the failure of the plans to rescue the Queen of Scotland and place her on the English throne to the vigilance of "The pretended Queen of England", who, he said, "keeps a bright look-out on all sides"; while the Nuncio in Flanders observed: "The Queen of England, I know not how, penetrates everything." The allegorical portrait of Elizabeth at Hatfield, with her hand resting on a rainbow, shows her wrapped in a russet satin robe embroidered all over with eyes and ears.

The watchfulness was maintained at intense concentration by Burleigh, Walsingham and Elizabeth herself. Walsingham was mobile—he had been in France several years, he went to the Netherlands—and Burleigh was the personal administrator of a wide and thorough intelligence service at home; Elizabeth neither went abroad nor did the actual work of collecting and sifting information, but she received the gist of the work of the other two, and though she sometimes submitted to Burleigh's judgment when her own was against it, she never gave her assent to anything without fully going into it herself, to the annoyance of Walsingham, who wished that, "as other Princes did", Her Majesty would leave certain matters "to those best capable of understanding them".[1]

The Queen, however, regarded herself as a working member of the government. She sometimes, it was true, descended to some minor aspect of the foreign scene. In 1577, she saw a portrait of the Marchioness of Havrecht, wearing a white linen partlet, a yoke with a turned-down collar attached. "The Queen in seeing her picture did marvellous delight in the manner of her wearing of her linen in such sort", and instructions were sent to the English embassy in Flanders to get for Her Majesty a set of similar partlets and to send them over in a special box.[2]

[1] Neale, *Queen Elizabeth*. [2] C.S.P. Foreign, 1577.

The situation in the Netherlands, *à propos* the movements of Alençon, was not only intricate but ceaselessly changing. Alençon's determination to enter the arena at once intensified the importance of
every aspect for both Spain and England. Burleigh's minute on this
position of affairs, dated June 2, 1578, shows his conviction that
England was always menaced by a potential attack of the concerted
forces of Catholic Europe. He notes the great expense the Queen
"presently sustaineth to defend her estate against a navy set out by the
Pope and succoured by the Kings of Spain, France and Portugal
whereby her Majesty shall be forced to be at great charges and so
more unable to give them aid". On the other hand, it was vitally
necessary to consider, with the States, the dangers likely to ensue
from their receiving French aid: "that the French will not be content
to be at charges with their people and money but they will attempt
to become Lords of the country". This was the consideration that
weighed most with the English. A complete Spanish victory in the
Netherlands would menace England, but the Spanish base was far off.
If France, just across the Channel, could add the Netherlands to itself,
the danger to England would be frightful. "Matters to be explored,"
wrote Burleigh. "To what end Monsieur's offers do tend, whether to
abuse the States or aid them, and how likely it is that he shall not become absolute Lord;" and, of great importance, "whether the French
King meaneth to further his brother's purposes".[1] The tradition of the
French royal house was that the King's brother should act an independent part and frequently one hostile to the Crown. Alençon had
already proved himself a *mauvais sujet*. Catherine and Henri III had
shown themselves glad that he should have occupation outside France;
but for Alençon to operate in the Netherlands in firm alliance with
his family would be a menace to the English government. Their aim
was to encourage him to enter the Netherlands independently of
France; they wished at the same time to send as much English help
into the States as would prevent French preponderance there, without
provoking Spain to retaliate. The instrument for this extremely delicate work was to be the entertaining of marriage negotiations between Alençon and Elizabeth.

No question of the Queen's marriage could come up without
bringing Leicester immediately to mind. He and Elizabeth no longer
gave scandal by carrying on with the indiscreet eagerness of young
lovers, but their relationship was recognized as one of deep intimacy.
Leicester's marriage with Douglas Sheffield, or what Lady Sheffield

[1] H.M.C. Hatfield.

had taken to be a marriage, remained a secret, though the child was thriving and lived to claim his father's earldom. The Queen, whose overstrung nerves required management, was apt to treat Burleigh, Sussex and Leicester, all three, with the abandonment of self-control' of a patient in the hands of an experienced physician, but whereas her relationship with the first two was one of affection without even the idiom of romance, with Leicester it was romantic always, whether in love-making or quarrelling. In 1578, the very year of the negotiations with Alençon, the Queen gave Leicester a violin with her arms and his engraved on the silver finger-board,[1] and in May she came to Wanstead, "The White House". The visit was a comparatively quiet one, but it was adorned by a masque, "The Lady of the May", which Philip Sidney had written for his uncle's house-party. "Her most excellent Majesty walking in Wanstead gardens, as she passed into the grove"—the masquers came upon her. The intimate, domestic note of the writing gives one of those sudden, close views of startling reality: of the masquing figure, the boy in his disguising female clothes, the pale Queen resplendent in jewels against the soft greenery of trees and grass. The boy's treble voice sounded: "Do not think, sweet and gallant Lady, that I debase myself thus much unto you because of your gay apparel . . . Nor because a certain gentleman hereby seeks to do you all the honour he can in his house . . . I would look for reverence at your hands if I did not see something in your face that made me yield to you"—what was it? The listener is on the verge of illumination; but the speech, for the time being, ends in meaningless compliment: "the beautifullest lady these woods have ever received". But Sidney gave one convincing glimpse of the Queen, of the glittering creature, eloquent and sharp-witted, in the verse he made and spoke kneeling when she gave him a lock of her hair:

> Like sparkling gems her virtue draws the sight,
> And in her conduct she is always bright.
> When she imparts her thoughts, her words have force
> And sense and wisdom flow in sweet discourse.[2]

A picture at Welbeck Abbey of Elizabeth at this period shows her standing in the garden of Wanstead; one of Leicester's oriental carpets is spread on the grass, and the Queen is standing on it with the Sword of State laid at her feet and her little dog sitting beside it. She

[1] Exhibition of the Royal House of Tudor, Catalogue.
[2] Fox Bourne, *Philip Sidney*.

wears a white dress, suitable to May, embroidered with sprays of flowers and leaves in natural colours. In spite of the painter's properties—a hanging with the royal arms behind the Queen, and the great sword at her feet—there is an air of naturalness, of summer out of doors, in the picture. Elizabeth's face is moving; it is frail-looking, of transparent pallor and the expression is gentle, almost tranquil, as if she were in the house of a friend.

The nearness of Wanstead to London and its rural solitude, in the midst of which was found every luxury and comfort and all those attentions from Leicester that romantic friendship could suggest, made it a retreat both convenient and very charming to the Queen: some of the Privy Council meetings at which the Alençon match was most heatedly discussed were held at Wanstead during her visits.

Walsingham, accompanied by Lord Cobham, went over to Flanders to investigate the position of Alençon *vis-à-vis* the States. The difficulty of deciding what part the Queen should take and how much she should pay was faithfully relayed by Burleigh to his sympathizing colleague. The Queen's preoccupation with money was never laid aside for a moment. Burleigh wrote: "When she perceived that the States required more money, I will not write how greatly she misliked thereof. I did as much as I could to mitigate the offence though it fell sharply in speech upon myself." Walsingham, who was handling the negotiations with devoted energy and had thought it essential to the main purpose that the loan the Queen had made to the States should not be called in, as she herself was asking that it should, wrote to Hatton: "It is an intolerable grief to me to receive so hard measure at her Majesty's hands as if I were some notorious offender . . . the greatest fault we may be charged withal is that we have had more regard to her Majesty's honour and safety than to her treasure." But as the Queen saw it, honour and safety could be secured only on a solid basis of treasure. Burleigh bore the trial more patiently than Walsingham, but for all his coolness and lucidity of mind he was not insensitive to the Queen's frantic language. It was a burden that had to be borne. He said: "We all most dutifully bear with her offence not despairing but that, however she mislikes things at one time, at another she will abate her sharpness, especially when she is persuaded that we all mean truly for her safety, although sometimes she will not so understand."[1]

Leicester, Camden said, "saw further into the mind of Queen Elizabeth than any other", and several years before when negotiations

[1] Foreign Calendar, July 1578.

for her marriage with the Archduke Charles had been on foot, he had told some members of the Council that he would not press his own suit to the Queen to the injury of these negotiations; but that very great care must be used in the way his attitude was represented. If Elizabeth thought that he withdrew his own claim because he was indifferent about it, she would never forgive the slight. She was ready now to bring to bear on this problem all the intellectual ability she possessed, all the patience, all the industry, and all the devotion of which she was capable, but she demanded the drug that put her into a state of euphoria. Leicester sent word to Walsingham: "Avoid her Majesty's suspicion that you doubt of Monsieur's love to her", or that Walsingham himself had not devotion to further her marriage. "Though I promise you," he added, "I think she has little enough herself to it." He could write no more then. "Much haste. Her Majesty ready to horseback."

Walsingham reported that Alençon was treating with the States independently of the French King, and this was the information needed to send the negotiations forward. The Queen threw her glittering bait and the tug on the line was immediate. The Duke's agent, de Bocqueville, said that "his master was determined to marry the Queen or the Netherlands", and Elizabeth set herself to play the fish.

De Bocqueville and his suite were received by her while she was on progress at Long Melford. She was bent on displaying her Court to them in all possible splendour, but this was not easily done away from home. A certain amount of gold plate to be used at meals was carried in the sovereign's train, though not of course anything like as much as was used in a palace. When the Frenchmen were dining with her, the Queen, like some deceitful creature in a fairy-tale, attempted to conjure up an illusion of grandeur. She demanded of the Lord Chamberlain why there was so little gold plate in evidence.

Sussex was by nature incapable of playing these games. He answered that he had been on progress with Henry VIII himself, and had never seen so much plate carried as there was here. The Queen flew into a passion and gave him the lie, exclaiming, the more that was done for people like him, the worse they grew. She called upon Lord North for his opinion, and Lord North said he agreed with her. After dinner, Sussex gave North a piece of his mind, whereupon Leicester interposed, and said that this was hardly the way to speak to a nobleman.

Shortly afterwards dancing was arranged for the amusement of the French guests, and as the Queen greatly admired Oxford's dancing, she sent him a message asking him to take part, that the French might see how well the English could perform. The young man declined to dance. The Queen's request was brought a second time; this time Oxford not only repeated his refusal but gave his reason for it. Burning with resentment on Sussex's behalf, he added words to the effect that he would see himself further before he did anything to please the French. Elizabeth, who often showed surprising leniency towards the bad manners of young people, said no more on the matter.

How little her asperity to Sussex represented their actual relationship, he showed by the tone of his letter to her about the Alençon match, written ten days after her public and unjust rating. The letter was one of those written by courtiers to the sovereign or to each other when actually under the same roof: the extent of the palace, the number of the inmates, the lack of privacy and of leisure sometimes making a letter as necessary as if miles sundered the correspondents. Sussex detailed the various arguments for and against the match of which he himself was in favour, and he wrote a straightforward and beautifully sympathetic passage upon her personal feelings. The obstacles to the match from this point of view were, he said, "your own mislike to marriage which might breed a discontented life hereafter", and "the difficulty of the choice of a person that might in all respects content your mind". "These considerations," he said, "receive not the counsel of others but must be decided by yourself. Whereby you be to follow only the counsel of your own heart, whereunto all men must leave you. For it is the judgment of your own heart that may make it ill to you, which no man can say . . . but to be quite good of itself, if your heart like it." [1]

The end of the summer progress led to Norwich, and here was displayed the element for which the Queen schemed and struggled day in, day out. The festivities of Norwich were charming, but its spectacles were a great deal more: they were a demonstration of growing economic power.

On the morning after the Queen's arrival "a very excellent boy dressed as Mercury in a sky-blue doublet with a short cloak of cloth of gold", flew through the city on a car painted with clouds and birds, drawn at a gallop by horses who had wings fastened to them. Alighting beneath the window of the Queen's bed-chamber in the Bishop's palace, he made his speech of welcome, and the Queen was seen smiling "at the boldness of the boy".

What most took the Queen's attention was a bank covered with

[1] Nicholas, *Sir Christopher Hatton.*

turf, on which "eight small women-children" were weaving yarn, and eight more knitting stockings, while a small boy recited verses, explaining in commonplace language facts of the utmost economic importance:

> We bought before the things that now we sell,
> These slender imps, their work does pass the waves.
> God's peace and thine we hold, and prosper well.
> Of every mouth the hands the charges saves.

Elizabeth's interest was keenly aroused. She went up to the little girls and examined the yarn and the knitting, thereby affording the children a wonderful opportunity to examine her. She left, giving the town her thanks for so welcome a sight.[1] It was to promote such interests as this that the elaborate deceptions of the Alençon match were even now being evolved.

While Elizabeth was appearing to consider a marriage, Leicester made one. Two years before, in 1576, when the Earl of Essex had died in Ireland, of what was described as a flux, Leicester had been through a secret marriage ceremony with Essex's widow. As a preliminary to these proceedings he had offered Douglas Sheffield £700 a year to let him hear no more of her, and when she refused the suggestion with angry dismay, Leicester attained his object and saved his money by explaining to her that their marriage had been invalid and she was not his wife. This left him free to contract a marriage, or at least a connection, with Lettice Devereux, which was at first kept profoundly secret. But Lettice's father was Sir Francis Knollys, a man of considerable experience of the world and a Puritan. Knollys heard of his daughter's stolen match, and he had also, by this time, heard of Leicester's doings with the miserable Douglas Sheffield. He told Leicester in uncompromising terms that whatever might have gone before, a marriage must be performed, at which he, Knollys, must be present, with witnesses chosen by himself. He carried all before him. The second ceremony was performed at Wanstead on September 20, in the presence of Sir Francis Knollys, the Earl of Warwick, the Earl of Lincoln and Lord North. Secrecy was enjoined on all the parties, but it was impossible to keep dark what was now known to so many. Yet still the Queen did not hear what had happened. Her ordered and ceremonial existence, with its claims and cares, its distractions and its intense preoccupations, stood like a screen between her and the doings at Wanstead. Leicester was at Court when she expected him

[1] Nichols, *Progresses.*

to be, and the Countess of Leicester continued to call herself the Countess of Essex.

In October the Queen had attacks of toothache, and her plight distressed the men who were fond of her. Heneage wrote to Hatton: "Loving her more than my life, I can pray for her health more than my own. I am in little quiet when I hear that anything impeacheth it." Sussex exclaimed: "God shortly give her perfect health, for with her good estate we all breathe and live, and without her we all stifle and perish."

It was true that Elizabeth in her own person represented security to every Englishman who wanted freedom from foreign invasion and from civil war, so that he could go on with the concerns of daily life; her corporeal existence was his only guarantee of these conditions. Her body was a kind of Palladium, but the strong material inducement to preserve her life and keep her in health was reinforced by an affectionate care of her. Her ailments were anxiously reported and discussed: anything that produced stomach pains and vomiting causing of course a particular apprehension until it was over and a natural cause assigned to it, and these symptoms were fairly frequent. Elizabeth ate simple food and knew what suited her; her digestion could not stand liberties, as it showed when she was given some heavy porridge for breakfast. Hatton had written to Burleigh: "Her Majesty since your going hence, hath been troubled with much disease in her stomach. The cause thereof as both herself thinketh and we all do judge, was the taking in the morning, yesterday, a confection of barley sodden with water and sugar and made exceeding thick with bread. . . . This breakfast lost her both her supper and dinner, and surely the better half of her sleep, but God be thanked, I hope now the worst is passed."[1]

The toothache the Queen had had since October, came in December to a raging climax that kept her without sleep for forty-eight hours. Elizabeth was forty-five, but she had never had a tooth pulled out, and combined with unwillingness to lose one was a shrinking from the operation itself. A meeting of the Privy Council was convened to deal with this emergency, at which the ministers listened to the opinion of a tooth-drawer called Fenatus. He told them it was possible to dress the tooth with a preparation of fennygreek that would make it fall out of itself, but in that case, great care had to be taken to protect the teeth on either side. What he recommended was immediate extraction by the ordinary method.

[1] Nicholas, *Sir Christopher Hatton.*

The Council, having heard him, decided upon extraction to a man, and a body of them, taking a surgeon with them, waited on the exhausted Queen. They had the advantage that among their number was Elizabeth's life-long admirer John Aylmer, now Bishop of London. Aylmer had had charge of Lady Jane Grey when she was four years old, and had gained an experience in crises of this nature which his colleagues had not had an opportunity to acquire. The Council's view was repeated to the Queen, and before she could open her lips to protest, Dr. Aylmer said to her that he had not many teeth left in his head, but such as he had were entirely at her service. The surgeon should now pull one of them out, and she would see that it was no such great matter. The surgeon then drew one of the Bishop's teeth, and the Queen consented to have her own taken out.[1]

In yet another instance, Elizabeth's resolution had failed her and she had been brought through a difficulty by the protective authority of men. To her intimate circle, her fearfulness perhaps endeared her as much as her heroic qualities. It made men regard her, not as an Amazon who was their superior, but as a precious being to be guarded with their lives. To the nation at large it was her high spirit that distinguished her. For twenty years now, the story of her dangers, her devotion to her task, and her success, had been before their eyes. In the New Year, after her exhibition of cowardice over tooth-drawing, Roger North dedicated to her his translation of Plutarch's Lives of the Greek and Roman heroes. He asked leave to do so, though, he said ". . . this be no book for your Majesty's self, who are meeter to be the chief story than a student therein, and can better understand it in Greek than any man make it in English".

Alençon's envoy and confidential friend, Jehan de Simier, arrived in London on January 5, and according to the Spanish Ambassador, Don Bernardino de Mendoza, a consultation of the Queen's doctors was held a few days before, to decide if she could expect to bear a child. The doctors, said Mendoza, "foresaw no difficulty". The Ambassador's words do not sound like those of doctors discussing the prospect of a first confinement after forty-five, but at least the gist of his report appears to confirm that the Queen was not considered physically incapable of child-bearing, and this was the second official medical opinion given during the reign which said that she could expect children. This important matter being settled, the Queen received Simier and his suite; and now opened the last, and the most dazzling of

[1] Strype, *Aylmer.*

the interludes of Elizabeth's favourite pastime. It had everything to make it brilliant, except the person of the wooer, and this, for the time being, was out of sight. The Queen was incomparably more important as a match than she had been in earlier courtships, and yet she still preserved an unusual measure of youth and looks for a woman of her years. "Her skin," said Bohun, "was pure white, and her beauty lasted to her middle age." Tense, spirited, coiled to strike, hers was not the type of femininity men lose their heads over, but she had the looks, the decoration, the wits, to sustain her part in a highly wrought and long-drawn-out negotiation, which was based on the stern realities of power-politics and economic survival, and conducted in the idiom of artificial romance.

Elizabeth had enjoyed a good deal of amorous skirmishing, diplomatic courting and private goings-on, but the game had for the most part been played rather harder and more stylishly by her than by the opponents. Now she was in the hands of a master. The French are considered to make love better than anybody else, and Simier was admitted by the French themselves to possess "*une connaissance exquise des gaietés d'amour*". But his charm, his gallantry, his attentiveness would hardly have achieved their success if he had not felt some genuine admiration; the French value for *esprit* made her, in a purely amatory sense, perhaps more congenial to a Frenchman than to another. Henri III as a young prince had scornfully rejected the notion that he should be married to the Queen of England; now that he was King of France, he spoke about her in a very different manner. He questioned Sir Amyas Poulet as to whether the Queen went on progress by coach or horseback, and said he had heard she rode uncommonly well. So much, to the English Ambassador, might have been policy; but he warned Simier himself that he would have to do with *la plus fine femme du monde*. Simier agreed. His task was to carry on a courtship by proxy for a dubious and grotesque young man and by this means to effect a complicated political manoeuvre; but the method gave him a chance to see at close quarters a most remarkable woman, and the opportunity was not thrown away on him. His response, in one kind, was genuine: he told the French King that her wit was admirable; and the eagerness with which he expressed his own admiration and assured her of his master's, the liveliness and ardour of his behaviour, the amusement, the elegance of his courting, played on the surface of the Queen's susceptible emotions with consummate skill. She revelled in French homage, radiant, adorable, revivifying. Mendoza "was told" that Leicester and Hatton were "growing much annoyed". They saw themselves, in this particular branch of accomplishment, for the time being quite overshadowed. The French Ambassador, Mauvissière, reported the effects of Simier's gallantry to the French Court: "*Elle est plus belle, plus gaillarde, qu'il y a quinze ans,*" and he added: "Not a woman or a physician who knows her, who does not hold that there is no lady in the realm more fit for bearing children than she is."

Yes, the enjoyment was ravishing: but contrary to appearances, it was not all-engrossing. There was a spectacle of more absorbing interest still: a terrestrial globe, on which could be traced the vast possessions of Spain, the size of France with its extensive coastline, the Netherlands territory, complete conquest of which would give either Spain or France the undisputed mastery of Europe, and the smallness of England and Wales which made one kingdom, with an inimical Ireland in the west and to the north a Scotland which at any moment might become inimical.

The French match was scanned with the utmost narrowness by the Council, whether for or against it. As Sussex had written to Walsingham: "The case will be hard with the Queen and with England if ever the French possess or the Spaniards tyrannize in the Low Countries," and again: "Whoever shall think by device to divide her good from the good of the realm, and her ill from the ill of the realm, shall in the end deceive both." Sussex had always wanted to see Elizabeth married and a mother, and as he had already told her, he was in favour of this match, provided she could put up with the duc d'Alençon. Burleigh appeared also to be in favour of it but he was more doubtful than Sussex of its coming off. He had said apropos de Bocqueville, that were he himself the Ambassador, he would not encourage his master to take an optimistic view of the negotiations. Hatton did not disapprove of the match, though he made it clear that should it take place, his personal sufferings would be dreadful. He said to Sir Thomas Heneage that he, from personal choice, loved the Queen "no less than he, who by greatness of a kingly birth and fortune it most fit to have her".

The one wholeheartedly against the affair was, not unnaturally, Leicester. The economic motive of his objection was unmistakable, but it is possible too that he was smarting from a sense of repudiated ownership. In huffing resentment, he put it about that Simier had caused Elizabeth to fall in love with Alençon by using "drinks and unlawful arts."[1] Simier had at once recognized the chief enemy

[1] Camden.

mission. He had been urgent, both with Alençon to come to England and with Elizabeth to promote his coming. He knew that the conditions Alençon was demanding—to be crowned immediately after marriage, to be associated with the Queen in power, to have public exercise of the Catholic religion and a life-long pension—would all be hardly digested by the Government, while the people's view of the match was one of perfect abhorrence; but to overcome all this, in the last resort only one thing was necessary: the Queen's signature on the marriage treaty; and Simier's experience of the last few months had caused him, astute as he was, to believe that her emotions could be raised to the pitch at which she would irrevocably commit herself. He wanted Alençon to come at once and strike while the iron was hot; then, in June, he learned that Leicester had been with the Queen, persuading her that out of regard to public dislike she should refuse Alençon a passport.

The secret of Leicester's marriage with Lettice Devereux was of the kind that Simier could have been relied on to detect, even had it been better kept than it was. As things stood, the information gave him a weapon of extreme effectiveness. He urged the Queen to understand that Leicester, in spite of the incalculable benefits he had received from her, was neither a faithful councillor nor a loyal friend. He was attempting to prevent her marriage—and by what right? He was married himself, and Simier related the facts of the secret wedding.

Elizabeth's rage was shattering. That she had repeatedly refused to marry Leicester herself was, as anyone would foresee, a straw against the torrential force of wounded affection, betrayed confidence, jealousy and anger. The court was at Greenwich, and she ordered Leicester's immediate arrest. In Greenwich Park there stood a tower that had been built by Henry VIII and called by him the Tower Mireflore, or Tower of the Wondrous Flower, because it had then given a lodging to Ann Boleyn. To this ill-omened place Leicester was sent to be out of the Queen's sight; she declared that he should be committed to the Tower of London.

Again, a man saved her. As Lord Chamberlain, Sussex was in attendance at Greenwich; honest, chivalrous and brave, he had been Elizabeth's good angel from the hour he knelt to her and promised that he would take her letter to her sister. He despised, disliked and distrusted Leicester, he had sometimes quarrelled with him to the Queen's very face, and most men in his position, if they had refrained from exciting her vindictiveness, would at least have remained passive

while it took its course; but Sussex stepped in to save her from herself. It was true that she had the power of arbitrary arrest, that she
could send Leicester to the Tower although he had committed no
legal offence; but Sussex told her that she must not do it. The damage
to herself from such an act must be avoided at all costs. Camden says
that "being of right noble mind and inbred generosity", Sussex
reasoned with her and reminded her "that none ought to be troubled
for a lawful marriage", it had "always been accounted honourable".
Under this strong-minded and sympathetic influence, the tempest
spent itself harmlessly. The odious Lettice was given to understand
that she must not show her face, that was only to be expected, but
Leicester was released from the Mireflore and allowed to go quietly
to Wanstead. Here he played the card he had found so successful once
before. The decks were cleared of the Countess, and Leicester became
ill, very ill indeed; Mendoza who had heard nothing of the terrible
éclaircissement, wrote that the Earl was at a house of his five miles out
of London, where the Queen had been to see him, and where "she
remained two days because he feigned illness. She afterwards returned secretly to London."

Elizabeth had much sympathy for illness: she visited her friends in
their sick beds with anxious goodwill, and she was afraid of losing
ones she loved by death.

The terrific force of her fury against Leicester had spent itself; in
the weakness of exhaustion her mind was open to gentle influences,
and the alarm of hearing that he was ill in bed overcame the last of her
anger. The two days she spent secretly at Wanstead gave Leicester
the time, the opportunity he needed, and by throwing in the whole of
his resources and summoning to his aid the experience of their past
lives since eight years old, with everything it had taught him about
her selfish passion and her unselfish loyalty, he managed to repair the
injury and bridge the gulf.

Meanwhile a passport had been sent to Alençon, not in the teeth of
Leicester's opposition only but in that of wide public disapproval.
The notion of a French match, unpopular as a foreign alliance in any
case, was now seen in the perspective of the massacre of St. Bartholomew. An unnerving incident occurred when a member of the
Queen's guard fired upon Simier and it was said the man had been
suborned by Leicester to do it. A few weeks later a really startling
happening suggested another attack upon Simier or, even worse, that
popular detestation of the French match was venting itself in an
attack upon the Queen, though it turned out no such thing. The matter

was made into a popular ballad: "*A new Ballad declaring the dangerous shooting of a gun at Court.*"

On the evening of July 17, the Queen, with Simier, Hatton and the Earl of Lincoln, was coming back from London to Greenwich in the royal barge. The Queen was reading, and she told the oarsmen to row up and down a little before bringing the party to shore:

> *But all the while upon the Thames, in sculler's boat unknown,*
> *A wretched fellow got a gun that none was of his own,*
> *But shot a bullet two or three at random all about,*
> *And gave no great regard to see what time the Queen went out.*

Meaning no harm, this chuckle-headed individual discharged a bullet that passed within six feet of the Queen and wounded an oarsman in both arms. The man shrieked, blood poured from his wounds, and in the horror of the moment the Queen showed more coolness than anyone else. She sprang towards the victim, throwing her scarf to bind him up and called to him to be of good cheer, she would take care of him. What particularly pleased the ballad-writer was that she showed no fear in front of the French Ambassador:

> *What courage in her noble Grace in peril did appear,*
> *Before the French ambassador's face in such a sudden fear.*

It being a cardinal point with the English that they must lick the French whatever they did, the writer cannot contain his exultation, but makes the point a second time:

> *Nor made she any fearful show to seem to be dismayed,*
> *Nor seemed to the ambassador of anything afraid.*

The lines show the popular indignation at the murderous idiocy that had nearly killed the Queen:

> *The bullet came so near her Grace, within six feet at least,*
> *Was never such a cursed case by such a wilful beast.*

And they express the reason that lay behind the terror of such a chance:

> *. . . if that mishap had happened on her Grace,*
> *The stay of true religion, how parlous were the case,*
> *Which might have turned to bloody war, of strange and foreign foes,*
> *Alas, how had we been acurst, our comfort so to lose!*[1]

[1] Harleian Miscellany.

The wilful beast was found to be a serving-man called Thomas Appletree; his master, on hearing of Appletree's exploit, expressed himself with brevity and weight: he said he wished that neither Appletree nor himself had ever been born. Appletree was tried at Windsor and, inconceivable as it sounded, it transpired that in fact he was guilty not of treason but only of maddening stupidity. The penalty, however, for creating a dangerous disturbance in the sovereign's presence was death, and Appletree was sentenced to be hanged in the courtyard of Windsor Castle. He was brought to the scaffold in floods of tears, declaring that he had deserved death and wished for nothing else, but the Queen sent a reprieve to the gallows foot, which was received with enthusiastic cheers by the crowd, who a few minutes before had been hardly restrained from attacking the prisoner. She completed the effect of her generosity by getting his master to take him back.

That Simier might, however, be exposed to no risk of attack in his comings and goings, he was given apartments at Greenwich in what was called the Pavilion, an annexe to the Palace surrounded by gardens. Alençon's visit was now discussed everywhere, but it was supposed to be secret and as the Countess of Derby and one of the Russell ladies persisted in talking about it in a manner that annoyed the Queen, they were shut up in their own apartments and not let out till the visit was over.

The strange thing was that when Alençon arrived he proved fully able to sustain his rôle. Elizabeth's unusually high value for good looks had made people suppose that his appearance would undo him, for he was not only puny and much pitted from smallpox: he had a nose so large it amounted to deformity. But prejudice was overcome by a Prince who was ardent, civilized and a good talker; and if a young man of twenty could be found anywhere to make love convincingly to a woman who had talent, strangeness, elegance but not youth, he might, over-sophisticated and perverse, be found in the House of Valois.

The Duke arrived on the morning of August 16, so very early that Simier was not out of bed.[1] Travel-stained as he was, Alençon was all for starting to make love at once, and he ordered Simier to lead him to the Queen immediately. Simier told him she could not be broken in upon at this hour of the morning: Alençon himself must first rest and be refreshed. The Ambassador saw his master into bed, and then wrote a letter to be taken to the Queen. In it he said: "At

[1] Hume, *Courtships of Queen Elizabeth*.

last I persuaded him to take some rest and soon got him between the sheets and I wish to God you were with him there as he could then with greater ease convey his thoughts to you."

The courtship was now carried on at first hand and the lovers appeared perfectly delighted with each other. Elizabeth had the inveterate English habit of giving nick-names: Burleigh was her "Spirit", the dark-browed Walsingham the "Moor", Hatton the "Mutton" or "Bell-wether", Leicester's name was "Eyes", and he and Hatton sometimes shared the pseudonym, Leicester signing his letters by two circles with a dot in each, for Eyes, and Hatton by two triangles for "Lids". Simier had already received the name of Monkey, and signed himself "votre pauvre Singe", and Alençon was at once christened "Grenouille". The ancient Romans had used the frog, cold and volatile though it was, as a charm for lovers, betokening mutual ardour and constancy.

All the while Alençon's presence was supposed to be unknown, but it would not have amused the Queen had it been really so. Mendoza had said before the Duke's arrival that she was anxious everyone should know that his suit was inspired by romantic enthusiasm for herself, and it was the public spectacle of his homage that she enjoyed most. At a court ball on August 23, Alençon was posted behind the arras; the Queen danced, and in the pauses of the dance, she made gestures towards him as he craned out of his hiding-place, which those present pretended not to see. A crisis in his own affairs in France put an abrupt stop to these gay doings; the news that his friend Bussy d'Ambois had been killed in a duel caused Alençon to dash away on August 27; he went by coach to Dover and wrote such passionate letters on the way, Mauvissière said they were enough to set fire to water. It was plain that the lover's absence was not to mean: out of sight, out of mind. Elizabeth talked of her departed suitor continually, of his accomplishments and masculine graces, and wore upon her hand the superb diamond that Catherine de Medici had chosen from her store as a betrothal ring.

The political situation which had given rise to the negotiations had now become acutely threatening. The religious war in France, which had so effectively acted as a brake on any hostile intentions of the French, was temporarily ended by the treaty of Nerac, and Spain was about to annex Portugal on the death of its childless king. With France whole and disengaged, and Spain acquiring a substantial increase in territory and resources, alliance with a Prince who, though bringing French friendship to England, would act in the Netherlands

against Spain but independently of France, was of extreme importance. The game that Elizabeth found exquisitely enjoyable had always been based on very serious political considerations; now the
considerations were of vital importance. To the success of the negotiations, it was essential that the Queen should be believed to be in
earnest: not that she had actually made up her mind to marry
Alençon but that she was seriously considering the possibility and
that French co-operation would bring about the desired result. It was
amusing, it was delightful, it was stimulating to a degree, but behind
the pretence was stark, threatening reality. The Pope had absolved
her subjects from their allegiance to her: the King of Spain in open
council had discussed her assassination as a prelude to the liberation
and enthronement of the Queen of Scots: the wavering fortunes of
the Netherland States might founder altogether beneath the Spanish
power, and then the Spanish army would move across from the Low
Countries to the shores of England. Should fortune favour France
rather than Spain, then the French would fulfil their long-cherished
design of moving into Scotland, and streaming southwards, join with
disaffected Catholics in rescuing and exalting the Queen of Scots.
The clue leading through this labyrinth to a position of temporary
safety was the holding out to Alençon of the possibility of becoming
King of England. So necessary was it that the game should be played
exactly as the Queen directed that for mere incautious gossiping,
Lady Derby and her friend had been shut up and not released till
Alençon had gone; and then, no sooner had the Duke left the shore,
than John Stubbs, a high-minded, warm-hearted, zealous Puritan,
published a pamphlet which he called "*A Gaping Gulphe wherein England is like to be swallowed*". The gulf was the French marriage.

The English dislike of foreign rule, which had shown itself strongly
on the marriage of Mary Tudor, was now indissolubly connected
with a fear of Catholic persecution. The idea of a French Catholic
husband for the Queen roused an abhorrence which, in the Puritans,
reached almost to frenzy. Stubbs' objections to the match were based
both on fear and detestation of the Catholics and loathing of the
French. The interesting feature of his pamphlet is the warm, protective love it shows for the Queen. He saw in the proposed alliance
"the very foundation of our commonwealth dangerously digged at
by the French, and our dear Queen Elizabeth (I shake to speak it) led
blindfold as a poor lamb to the slaughter". The project was perilous
to her in every way. Let the physicians say honestly "how exceedingly dangerous they find it by their learning for her Majesty to have

her first child at these years, yea, how fearful the expectation of death is to mother and child; I fear to say what will be their answer". The match was hateful to her people: could it be to the Queen's own satisfaction, considering her "constant dislike and indisposed mind towards marriage, from the flower of her youth", and that Monsieur, to state the case mildly, was no paragon. Even if the Queen genuinely liked him, it would still be the duty of loving subjects to warn her off him. If anyone did not think so, then that person was to learn "of every parent or other whatsoever that hath a loving care of their daughter or dear friend". Everything was against this suitor; his very youth was a sign of his ill-intent, for not one young man in a hundred but has dishonest motives in marrying a woman so much older than himself; as for his person, let the Queen look at it, that was all Stubbs asked. Let her "view it and surview it", and in doing so, "fetch her heart up to her eyes and carry her eyes down to her heart". The Valois stock was afflicted with infamous disease, "God's punishment on flesh and bones", and Stubbs concluded, it amounted to impiety for the Queen, "the head of the land, to join in any manner with that person over whom the inevitable plagues of the most true Lord do hang". He besought Heaven to grant her "honourable, healthful, joyful, peaceful, and long sovereignty, without any superior over-ruling commander, especially French, namely Monsieur".

The pamphlet was in every line an expression of loyalty and love but its appearance was inopportune to the last degree. By stating that Alençon could hardly be seriously considered as a suitor, and that if he were, he ought not to be, it cracked open to the peering day that elaborate erection behind which the Queen was manipulating a diplomatic course of extreme complexity. This offence was unforgivable and it was combined with another.

Elizabeth's marriage negotiations had been of great diplomatic value all through the reign: with Philip, with Charles of Sweden, with the Archduke Charles, with Charles IX, with Anjou, and now they were of the highest importance with Alençon. But she was forty-five. This instrument would not be within her hold much longer, for though a foreigner would be willing to marry the Queen of England without prospect of children, the English Parliament would never sanction such a match except in hope of heirs. Such negotiations could not be carried on once the Queen was obviously past the age of child-bearing, and then, not only would the political weapon be useless, but the pleasure and excitement that were so dear to her would be finished also. Stubbs' words were kindness itself but they had the ruthless realism of family conversation. The Queen was everything to her subjects, she was the treasure of their lives, but she was too old to risk childbirth, and marriage with a woman of her age was so much against a young man's natural inclination, that his motives for proposing it must be disreputable. Elizabeth but a few weeks before had had the shock of finding that Leicester was married to her cousin; now Stubbs had put it in print for all to read, that the graceful and passionate love-making she had received from Alençon not only was a sham, but could not, in the very nature of the case, be anything else.

This serious attempt at interference with her diplomacy, edged as it was with a sexual insult, put Elizabeth almost beside herself. Stubbs, the publisher and the printer were put on trial in October on a charge of seditious libel. In this month there were daily council Meetings discussing and re-discussing the marriage from all points of view. The councillors were divided. On the dangers of childbirth, Sir Ralph Sadler said bluntly: "Few old maids escape." In the minutes of one meeting, drawn up for Burleigh, the passage occurs:

Q. The doubt that her Majesty may not have children or that she may be endangered in childbirth:
A. This is only in God's will, whereof no person can make any certain judgment; but if God shall move her heart to marriage, then, hope is that she may prosper therein.

The Council concluded their deliberations for the time being with the resolution that whatever the Queen decided to do, they would support her decision, and if she wished to release herself from any commitments, they would extricate her, taking all blame upon themselves. They waited on the Queen to tell her this and she heard them with angry agitation. She said that though her mind was by no means made up, she had expected that they would all urge her to marry and produce an heir to the line of Henry VIII.[1] The searing recollection of Stubbs' words made a painful background to the fact that whereas once her councillors had driven her with her back to the wall, in their urging her to marry and conceive, now they debated that prospect with grave anxiety, with doubt and misgiving. It was a saying of her own, "Green wounds scarce abide the toucher's hand", and meeting with reserve and concern where she had once encountered strong eagerness, she burst into tears. Why was she only, she demanded, to

[1] Murdin.

be denied marriage and children? The councillors left her without giving the reply.

Meanwhile, the court had exonerated the printer of the pamphlet, but Stubbs and the publisher had been found guilty of seditious libel, and a penalty was imposed on them which had been devised in Mary Tudor's reign to punish the libellers of her and Philip; it was that the convicted man should have his right hand cut off. This savage and odious sentence caused a great deal of public disapproval, from sympathy with Stubbs and his arguments, but Elizabeth, who had said she wished Stubbs might be hanged, was fiercely determined on it. She had generously pardoned the man whose idiocy had nearly killed her, but she had no mercy on a loyal, warm-hearted subject who said she was too old to marry and could not exert any genuine attraction over a man as young as her French suitor.

Camden was among the spectators on Westminster Palace Green, when the men's right hands were cut off by the executioner with a butcher's cleaver. The bleeding was stopped by searing the stump with a hot iron. Elizabeth was the more disgraced because when her sentence had been carried out, Stubbs pulled off his hat with his left hand and cried: "God save the Queen!" before he fell down in a dead faint. The crowd were ominously silent.

XX

On new year's day 1580 the Earl of Leicester gave the Queen fifteen large and thirty-six smaller gold buttons; his marriage notwithstanding, they were engraved with his arms and decorated with diamonds and rubies arranged in true-love-knots.[1]

While his uncle did his best by these charming improprieties to undermine Alençon's influence, Philip Sidney went more directly to work. Sidney, as a boy of eighteen, had been in Walsingham's household in Paris during the massacre of St. Bartholomew, and like Stubbs, he did not separate the religious from the political issue; his personal abhorrence of the match was inevitable. He had besides another reason for condemning it. The great and good Earl of Leicester was against the French marriage, and therefore his relations must do their best to support his policy. Sidney resolved to put the matter to the Queen in a strong light, and he wrote her a letter, explaining to her that the French match would not do. "A Frenchman and a Papist, a son of the Jezebel of our age!" The English abhorred the very notion of such an alliance, and it would cause them to withdraw from her the affection which, Sidney could assure her, they had entertained for her up till now.

Henri III had described Elizabeth as "la plus fine femme du monde", but Sidney, though he had once praised her intelligence in verse, seemed hardly to share the French King's opinion of it. He reminded her that she had always said she would never marry from personal inclination and he pointed out to her with solemn kindness that if she were to contract a marriage that was both disagreeable to her and disastrous for the realm, "it were a dear purchase of repentance". Then the young man who was so ready to instruct and guide the sharpest woman in the world, disappeared, and for an unforgettable moment his place was taken by the poet. "Nothing can it add unto you but the bliss of children, which I confess were a most unspeakable comfort." But, Sidney continued, a marriage with Alençon was not the only means of getting children. The advantages of marrying him were no greater than those attached to marrying anybody else, and the disadvantages were exceptional, having regard to "his person and

[1] Nichols, *Progresses*.

condition". And this brought Sidney to another point. A marriage with such a man would give credence to those scandalous stories about the Queen that Sidney himself, he said, always regarded as blasphemy. "No, no, excellent Lady, do not raze out the impression you have made in such a multitude of hearts."

In writing to the Queen in such a strain Sidney may have shown a lack of some qualities, but courage was not among them. There was no fear of his meeting with a penalty such as Stubbs had suffered, for Stubbs' remonstrance was not only much more offensive in itself, it had been printed, while Sidney's was confined to a private letter. But it was plain speaking on a topic on which the Queen did not invite plain speaking except in conference with the Privy Council. It was not surprising that during this year Sidney left the court and spent much time at Wilton with his sister the young Countess of Pembroke. Here, while she sat in the room with him, he wrote his chivalric romance, *Arcadia*, handing the sheets to her as he finished them.

Alençon began the New Year with a show of extreme generosity and understanding. He wrote to tell the Queen how much he regretted the punishment of Stubbs, for whom he would have interceded had he known of the matter in time. As for Lord Leicester's resistance to the match, the Earl had acted, as he thought, in the Queen's interest; how then could Alençon blame him? No! Alençon looked forward to finding in him a brother. This letter, besides the beauty of its sentiment, had a considerable intrinsic value, for in the wax of the seal a large emerald was embedded. Alençon may have discovered that the Queen was particularly fond of emeralds; with pearls, diamonds and rubies, they were the stones most often given to her in ornaments. "The emerald, so precious and green of hue, it showeth the faces of the beholders to be green," said Sir John Ferne.[1] One of Hatton's presents had been "a flower of gold containing a great emerald, fully garnished with diamonds and rubies, and three pearls pendant, one bigger than the rest".

A love-letter with a jewel stuck in the seal carried with it an importance that was altogether greater than its explicit contents. The French alliance, with its implications of policy in the Netherlands, was becoming increasingly necessary. The Spanish attack upon England was slow-maturing, but Burleigh could see its intention developing as a man in the small light of his camp-fire sees the heads of wolves, appearing and withdrawing and showing themselves each

[1] *The Blazon of Gentrie.*

time a little nearer. Supporting the King of Spain was the Papacy with some material force and enormous moral influence; in the Netherlands was an enclave of disaffected English and a Spanish army whose troops were supposed to be the finest and most terrible in Europe. In England itself were numbers of Catholics who were thought to be quiescent only because they were looking forward to the accession of Mary Stuart, and who were, therefore, though as it turned out, unjustly, assumed to be a lurking danger. Finally there were, in close neighbourhood, Scotland and Ireland, both of which countries were regarded as suitable bases for a Catholic invasion of England. Philip had got as far as Ireland already. In 1579 the Pope had sent Dr. Sanders to Ireland as Papal Nuncio, and in 1580 a detachment of Italian soldiers led by a Spanish general, Recalde, landed in Smerwick Bay.

By March, Elizabeth was greatly agitated; in an audience she told Mendoza that if the King of Spain did not refrain from meddling in Ireland, she would "let out" in Flanders. Mendoza, who felt that the tide was flowing in his master's favour, replied, first that the Spaniards were doing nothing in Ireland, and secondly that if King Philip were driven to act against her, he would do it with so heavy a hand that she would have no time to breathe where she was, let alone to do anything in Flanders. Philip commended his Ambassador. "You have acted prudently," he wrote. "It will do no harm for her to be alarmed at our fleet, and you are doing well in fostering this fear."

The project of the French marriage was, ostensibly, as firmly held as ever. In June a strange letter was written to Alençon from one of his confidential London agents. It said: "She wants nothing in the world so much as you; there is no one in the world she would rather have near her," if only, said the writer, "il se pouvait faire sans enfants." In spite of what the doctors had said, "il semble que par la disposition de son corps, elle aye peur de mourir".[1] It was perhaps this rumour, well founded or not, that was the origin of Brantôme's saying that Elizabeth had a very narrow passage.

Whatever the difficulties of political courtship, romantic friendships made the happiness of private life. In September Hatton went up to Northamptonshire, where he had built Kirby, and disbanded his household because of an outbreak of smallpox. As the infection seemed rife, he sent Sir Thomas Heneage a ring to give the Queen; he had been told it contained a preventive and he wanted her to wear it round her neck "betwixt the sweet dugs, the chaste nest of most

[1] British Museum Cotton Galba E vi, fol. 15.

pure constancy". To the Queen herself he wrote ten days later: "Your words are sweet, your heart is full of rare and royal faith; the writings of your fair hand do raise in me joy unspeakable."[1]

At the end of this month, September 1580, there occurred one of the great events in the history of the world. Drake, whose companion Winter had separated from him eighteen months before and who had been given up for lost, brought the *Golden Hind* into Plymouth after a voyage of three years in which he had sailed round the world. The story of genius and heroism, which reads like legend rather than fact, seemed as wonderful then as it does now, and amazes this century as it did his own. The effect of his achievement on national confidence and public imagination was indescribable. The exquisite "Drake Cup", the bowl and cover two halves of a gold terrestrial globe, shows the desire to symbolize his achievement, and so, too, does the portrait of him wearing a doublet decorated with medallions formed by the world enclosed in a ring. Beedome's lines to him are written on the pre-Galilean fallacy that the sun travelled round the earth, but their splendid image has a visual aspect of truth:

> *If men were silent, stars would make thee known,*
> *Phoebus forgets not his companion.*

The political significance of Drake's exploit was however much narrower and of an urgent topical nature. The *Golden Hind*'s hold was crammed with silver, amounting in value to $1\frac{1}{2}$ million ducats in money of the time, and with jewels whose value could scarcely be computed; this was loot from Spanish ships taken in the Pacific, whose vast emptiness the Spaniards had till then had entirely to themselves, and Mendoza demanded its return to the King of Spain.

No one with a personal knowledge of the Queen could have supposed that she would return it unless at the point of the sword. She herself had been among the investors in Drake's enterprise, and if the loot were retained they stood to gain 100% on their outlay. Then, too, the splendour of Drake's success was a national asset: to allow the nation's enemy—undeclared but known—to take his spoils away from him would have been completely against the national feeling. The personal profits of the investors and the uproarious enthusiasm of the people both demanded that the riches should be kept hold of; and there was another reason for denying their return to the Spaniards. Henry VIII would no doubt have kept such money because he wanted to spend it, but Henry VII

[1] Nicholas, *Sir Christopher Hatton.*

would have kept it for a more important reason, and his grand-daughter did as he would have done. The shares were paid out to the investors and to Drake himself, and the Queen's commissioners were told that in making their inventory, they were not to treat Drake with pettifogging exactitude. The Captain was to be allowed to make his own dispositions. When all arrangements had been concluded, the great sum of bullion remaining was brought up to London and stowed away in the Tower.

Mendoza tried repeatedly to gain an audience of the Queen but he was told that her Majesty was at present looking into the question of Spanish interference in Ireland and would speak to him when she had been able to gain some insight into that situation. The infuriated Ambassador was a little comforted by the action of Burleigh and Sussex. Drake had offered the former ten bars of gold and the latter a service of gold plate, but they had declined the presents, saying, according to Mendoza, that they did not feel they could accept things which had been stolen. Drake meanwhile had given a commission to some London jewellers for a present which he had no fear would be refused. From a quantity of diamonds and five enormous emeralds, of which two were round and three long-shaped and nearly the length of a little finger, the jewellers fashioned a crown, and the Queen wore it on New Year's Day, 1581.[1]

At the French Embassy, de la Mothe Fénélon had been replaced by Mauvissière, and the latter reported, in January, an awkward and sinister quarrel between the young men at Court. Lord Oxford had suddenly accused Lord Henry Howard, Charles Arundel and Francis Southwell, not only of being secretly reconciled to the Roman Church but of being in treasonable correspondence. The Queen, said Mauvissière, was distressed because she was fond of all the young men, and as to their Catholicism she would have said nothing provided they kept to the observance required by law. "The Queen said to me, I knew quite well her favourable attitude towards Catholics who did not place their conscience in antagonism to the state." It was thought necessary to imprison and examine all of them, including Oxford himself, and of the charge of treason, Howard, Arundel and Southwell managed to clear themselves; but Lord Henry Howard was not a person to be offended with impunity. In his examination, he made a point of showing how the relationship between Oxford and his former friend had become one of open

[1] C.S.P. Spanish, 1581.

enmity. He declared that Oxford had "railed at Francis Southwell for commending the Queen's singing at Hampton Court and protesting by the Blood of God that she had the worst voice and did everything with the worst grace that ever woman did, and that he was never nonplussed but when he came to speak of her". And Howard went on to speak of Oxford's "daily railing" at the Queen, and of his falling out with them all for taking her part and speaking in defence of her. Who could say how much of it was true: whether Oxford said so, or if he had, how much of it was his genuine opinion? That such things should be repeated by young men was the penalty exacted from Elizabeth by the cult of her charm and desirability. Whoever had been originally to blame, there was no doubt as to who was the principal victim of Oxford's reverses. "My lord," wrote his young wife. "In what misery I may account myself to be, that neither can see any end thereof nor yet any hope to diminish it. . . . Good my lord, I beseech you in the name of that God that knoweth all my thoughts and love toward you; let me know the truth of your meaning toward me, and upon what cause you are moved to continue me in this misery."[1] For the unfortunate wife there was nothing to care for but private happiness; for the Queen, private happiness, however important, was a part only, of a great whole. She was constantly taken out of herself, her faculties absorbed in an engrossing preoccupation.

"What is this about Scotland? Did I order anything of this sort to be done?" cried her Majesty, on February 27, to Walsingham. A body of Scots had raided Carlisle, and Lord Hunsdon, the Governor of Berwick, had organized a counter-raid, in which 200 English had been killed. Walsingham supported Hunsdon, and he did not think the loss a very great matter. The Queen could not agree: all losses mattered to her and the principle of unauthorized reprisals was a most dangerous one. "You Puritan!" she exclaimed. "You will never be content till you drive me into a war on all sides and bring the King of Spain on to me." This approaching menace required ceaseless defensive action, and the Alençon marriage, which was now firmly desired by Henri III and the Queen Mother as well as by Alençon himself, was brought forward by the French with every show of willingness to meet the English Queen's demands so far as this might be done. In April an embassy was to be sent from France to conclude the marriage treaty, and to house the festivities a banqueting pavilion was hurriedly built in the riverside garden of Whitehall. The struc-

[1] Ward, *Earl of Oxford.*

ture was of canvas, painted on the outside to look like stone, with 292 glass windows let into its fragile walls. The roof was painted with clouds, stars, suns and sun's rays and the Queen's arms garnished with gold. From it hung wreaths of holly, ivy and rue and baskets of pomegranates, oranges, cucumbers and grapes, the fruit all spangled with gold.[1]

While the pavilion was building, the Queen, on April 14, went to Deptford, where the *Golden Hind* had been laid up, and dined on board with Drake, on such a banquet as had not been seen, it was said, since the days of Henry VIII. She was attended by Alençon's confidential agent, Marchaumont, and as she entered the ship, her purple-and-gold garter came untied and trailed after her. Marchaumont besought and insisted that the Queen should give it him to send to his master. Elizabeth said he could not have it for the time being as she had nothing else to keep up her stocking, and she made no ado about tying it again in front of him. She gave it to him when they got back to Westminster.

Meanwhile, after the banquet, the Queen prepared to knight Drake. The Spanish demands for action against him were common hearing, and as he approached to kneel at her feet, she told him gaily she had a sword ready to cut off his head. She commanded Marchaumont to give the accolade, and as he did so, France was joined with England in honouring the man who had dealt such injuries to Spain.

Drake had a present ready for the Queen to mark this occasion, and it was appropriately topical. Elizabeth already possessed among her ornaments "a little flower of gold with a frog thereon, and therein Mounseer his phisnomye", and Drake now gave her, besides a large silver casket, a frog made all of diamonds.[2] Nevertheless, or so Mendoza heard, before the commissioners arrived at the end of April, the Queen summoned Burleigh, Sussex, Leicester and Walsingham and told them that for some time past she had felt great repugnance at the prospect of the marriage. She was a woman of middle age, and the ardent desire of so young a man as Alençon to marry her must give rise to grave considerations. The horror of giving herself and the intense pleasure of being desired, and known to be desired, were united to play their part over the council table in a negotiation based upon international politics, finance, armies and navies, trade routes and the configurations of the terrestrial globe.

At the end of April the French commissioners arrived, attended by 500 followers. The Queen, in a dress of gold tissue, wearing

[1] Holinshed, *Chronicles of England*.　　　　[2] C.S.P. Spanish, 1581.

ornaments of diamonds and rubies, greeted the embassy in the great pavilion. The crowd was dense, the heat oppressive, but the large and splendid reception appeared to confirm that the marriage would take place. The commissioners, after three days of banqueting, intimated that they would be glad to open their negotiation. They were summoned to Cecil House in the Strand, where Lord Burleigh received them with much courtesy.[1] Then, to the astonishment and dismay of the French, the first of the Queen's delaying tactics was displayed. From notes prepared by Burleigh, Walsingham made a speech, to the effect that for the last eighteen months the mere rumour of this Catholic marriage for the English Queen had heartened Catholic aggression. The Pope had launched Jesuit missionaries into the kingdom and subsidized an invasion of Ireland; as to Alençon himself, he had entered into a treaty with the Flemish behind the Queen's back. The Queen had written to the Prince about this matter, and Walsingham said the matter must halt until she received his reply. The commissioners were astounded and indignant. They said that now that the Queen, by allowing Drake's depredations, had offended the King of Spain beyond repair, she needed the alliance with the Valois. The Queen's ministers replied with stately reproof that her Majesty had no *need* of the alliance: the proposed marriage was one of affection only. They suggested that in the meantime a political treaty should be framed between France and England.

To such extraordinary statements the French had but one reply. They had come to make a marriage-treaty, they had no authority to make one of any other kind. So far as they were concerned, it was that or nothing.

Meanwhile the Queen sent Alençon a letter, asking him to come to her, and coyping his own graceful usage, she stuck a diamond into the wax of the seal. Alençon could not come immediately, for he had undertaken to raise the siege of Cambrai, which was being beleaguered by Parma; but he declared that he would fly to England the moment he could and sent his fine clothes on in advance.

Catherine de Medici, who feared that Alençon's activities against the terrific Spanish general would end by plunging France into war against Spain, besought him to retire, and the King his brother forbade further enlistment of Frenchmen in Alençon's army. Alençon saw that any assistance could be had only from England, and determined to leave the field for a lightning visit to procure it from the English Queen. Elizabeth received word that he was coming, and

[1] Hume, *Courtships of Queen Elizabeth.*

her own attitude to the commissioners, which had been one of eager courtesy, underwent an alteration: she struck out from the proposed terms of the treaty the clause which granted Alençon the right to free exercise of his religion in England.

The sudden arrival of Alençon on June 2 exasperated the commissioners. They themselves were treating on behalf of the French King, and they felt that the unauthorized appearance of the bridegroom to treat over their heads could only darken counsel. Alençon remained, incognito, for two days, and during that time he cut the ground from under their feet. Elizabeth learned from him that the French King was forcibly disbanding his brother's levies. Alençon, therefore, was now dependent on English money to keep him in the field, and henceforth his actions in the Netherlands would be in the interests of England, not of France. So far as the position could be held, it was a triumph.[1]

But the success barely gave time to draw breath. The position in Scotland had become very threatening. The young James, now fifteen years old, precocious, conceited, neurotic, had suffered keenly from an upbringing by severe Scots Puritans; and when a connection of the Lennox Stuarts, Esmé Stuart, Count d'Aubigny, was sent from France by the Guises to obtain a footing in the Court of Scotland, the treacherous but charming young man made a complete conquest of his awkward, strange cousin. The only point on which Esmé Stuart met defeat was in attempting to convert James to Catholicism. Instead of accomplishing this, he was obliged to give out that the young King's theological genius had converted him to Protestantism. D'Aubigny's inaugural coup was astonishingly successful. With the young King completely under his influence, he struck down the Anglophil Regent, Morton. He caused Morton to be arrested in the middle of a Council Meeting, and charged with complicity in the murder of Darnley. Morton confessed to having with others foreknown the deed, and said that nothing had been done to prevent it because it was known that the Queen of Scots desired it.

Honest but forbidding he had never gained James' affection, and the latter lured him willingly to his death, treating him the day before his arrest with revolting deception, calling Morton his "father". The news of this behaviour aroused Elizabeth's disgust. Morton's condemnation and execution were a serious calamity, for they meant the eclipse of the English party in Scotland, but James' behaviour showed a viciousness of which Elizabeth herself had no taint. She

[1] Hume, *op. cit.*

was exacting and inconsiderate to a degree in her behaviour to her ministers, but they remained her ministers. Unlike other sovereigns, including her own father, she threw over no tried and trusted servant. "That false Scots urchin!" she exclaimed indignantly. James' youth seemed in her eyes to make the matter worse. She said that for "a young Prince" to treat a faithful servant like this was odious.

The Queen of Scots was filled with exultation at Morton's death. She wrote to Philip saying that James was abandoning the heretics who had brought him up and was planning to declare war on England to gain her release. All that was needed to implement the design was a promise of the Spanish King's support. Mary had not seen her son since he was a year old, and she did not understand that the only thing he wanted, so far as she was concerned, was that the abdication she had made at Lochleven and afterwards repudiated should be considered binding, and he himself acknowledged as King of Scotland without dissent.

It now seemed that the Catholic interest was to triumph once more in Scotland, bringing the old threat to England in its train. This gave to the negotiations with Alençon even more urgency and significance. By the end of June it was understood that England would not consent to the marriage without a firm guarantee from Henri III of an Anglo-French alliance against Spain.

The French reply was: perform the marriage, and the alliance you desire will naturally follow. But Elizabeth would have repudiated this, even if she had meant to marry. It is not, in the last resort, marriages which safeguard alliances, but the negotiations which lead up to them. The marriage would not necessarily bind the French King to join her and his brother in an alliance against Spain, but the protracting of the negotiations would prevent him from taking a step that could be construed as an act of hostility towards her. She wrote a letter to Alençon in July, in which, addressing him as "Mon très cher", she explained that she loved him tenderly, but it now seemed that the King of France would only move against Spain in conjunction with England, after their marriage. She had always struggled to keep her realm at peace and this tying of her marriage to a war was something which for her people's sake she could not face. It would deprive her of their love. While matters remained at this pass, she could not see her way to marrying him.

A second expedition manned by Italians and Spaniards had been sent to Smerwick, and the Queen had told Mendoza that if she saw people disturbing her in Ireland, she would find means to disturb them. She evaded his enquiries as to what she meant to do about giving back the property taken by Drake, and for a fortnight she refused to grant him audience. When he was admitted on July 4, the position in the Netherlands, and the fear that she might be drawn into a war with Spain while France retreated from it, had made the Queen a prey to nervous distraction. The Ambassador pressed for action against Drake, and taxed her with her refusal to take any and her declining to receive himself; the Queen told him that she had postponed an interview with him only while she made enquiries about the second act of aggression in Ireland: she had not said that she *would* not see him. She called to Sussex and Walsingham, who were present at a little distance, and asked them to confirm this. Nevertheless Mendoza contradicted it; he had applied for an audience and it had not been granted. "Then," he said, "she screamed out louder than before, saying that I was to blame for everything."

Mendoza's noting of her tones of voice made his reports unusually interesting. On October 20, he received a message that the Queen would see him at Richmond at 2 o'clock. It was then 12, and he took boat immediately, but as he presented himself, they told him he was late.

As a rule, when an Ambassador was given audience, the Queen rose, stepped down from her daïs and advanced several paces, holding out her hand. This time she remained sitting on a couch, and to his respectful greeting replied only that she had had a pain in her hip for several days. "I said," wrote Mendoza, "how sorry I was to see her suffering like this", but he then in plain terms renewed the demand for the restitution of the Spanish treasure. The Queen answered, with what he called "such terrible insolence and evil intent", that Mendoza decided the time had come for a full-scale demonstration. He told her that as she would not listen to words, they must try cannon and see if she could hear those.

There was no screaming now. The Queen answered, "without any passion", but in a careless, impersonal manner "as one would repeat the words of a farce," that if Mendoza spoke to her like that again, she would put him in a place from which he could not speak at all. From her light, cool tone, she realized that the threat was made in deadly earnest.

The Ambassador at once made light of the situation. He said no one could gainsay so beautiful a lady, and he recounted contemptuously that his compliment caused her to smile and soften, "so absurd is she". But he said that before he left her, she had risen, and standing at a window, she had exclaimed under her breath: "Would to God that each had his own and all were content."

The Queen would readily have agreed to a state of each having his own, though it had meant sacrificing the heaps of silver, the gold bars, the diamonds and emeralds brought from the Pacific. She meant to keep the realm that was hers, and to preserve its liberties and its prosperity intact; but the forces of the Papacy, of Spain and of the Guise party in France, all of whom used Mary Stuart as their figurehead, were beginning to close in.

The elements of power-politics and religion were inextricable. The devout Catholics felt that the practice of their religion was incomparably the most important duty in life, but many, perhaps even most of them, were prepared to go on living quietly under a heretical government that allowed them this practice, subject to a formal observance of the state religion. They thought it possible to do this even after the publication of the Bull. As Acton himself observed: "Needless to say, there were still many people who thought it possible to be a Catholic without being also a murderer." But the dividing line between the political and the religious was becoming extremely thin. The body to which devout Catholics owed their first obedience was determined upon the restoration of Catholicism as the state religion of England, and, as an inevitable consequence, the pulling down of Elizabeth and the setting up of Mary Stuart. All over the country there were families owing this obedience to the Roman Church who, in the event of armed invasion, would be called upon to show it. How would they reply?

William Allen, a priest of driving energy and inflexible purpose, had founded a college, established first at Douai and then removed to Rheims, for training carefully selected young men as missionary priests to England. A similar one had been founded by Gregory XIII at Rome. The ostensible object of the missionaries was to save the souls of those Catholics who were lapsing for lack of a priest, and to rescue as many non-Catholics as they could for everlasting life. No one would deny that many of the priests had this object only and were altogether innocent of wishing to stir up political disaffection, but the framework within which these dedicated men acted threw an inevitable suspicion on their political innocence. In December 1580 the Papal Nuncio at Madrid wrote to the Pope on behalf of two English noblemen who wanted to know if assassinating Queen

Elizabeth would be a sin. The Cardinal Secretary Como replied: "Since that guilty woman of England . . . is the cause of such injury to the Catholic faith and loss of so many million souls, there is no doubt that whosoever sends her out of the world with the pious intention of doing God service, not only does not sin, but gains merit, especially having regard to the sentence pronounced against her by Pius V of holy memory."[1] Since the maintenance of the Catholic religion was, to the Catholic Church, of an importance infinitely transcending that of any earthly concern, the Pope's view was perfectly reasonable, but how could the English government be expected to regard it?

It was, however, pointed out to Gregory XIII that the Bull, declaring Elizabeth deposed and commanding the English to withdraw their allegiance from her, made a situation in which the missionaries would be set down by the English as traitors and nothing else. The Pope therefore conceded that while the Bull was still binding on the Queen and on the heretics, Catholics were allowed to continue in their allegiance to her, until a Catholic invasion should release them from her government. This concession allowed the missionaries, when questioned by the government's commissioners, to say truthfully that they regarded Elizabeth as their lawful Queen.

The population of England was something under four million, and the Catholics, it was claimed, comprised nearly half of it. The great majority of them were living in varying degrees of acquiescence under the government regulations. But there they were. There was always the possibility that in case of a foreign invasion they might turn the scale by rising in support of it, and Allen himself declared that they would. It was true that he had left the country in 1565 and not returned to it since, but that did not modify the vehemence and the decision of his pronouncements. The English Catholics as a body never did rise, and no evidence has been produced to show that they ever intended to do so. All that was heard on this head was that in the calculations of conspirators, certain Catholic nobles were put down as able to bring so many thousands of followers with them. The normal part of the population who were Catholic wanted the ministrations of their priests: there was no proof that they were ready to plunge the country into the horrors of invasion, rebellion and civil war. Mendoza, in fact, was obliged regretfully to say that they were not. They held the faith, he said, but not with that burning zeal for

[1] Black, *Age of Elizabeth.*

self-sacrifice which he himself would wish to see. But in 1583, Allen unhesitatingly assured the French and Spanish adherents of Mary Queen of Scots that the English Catholics all over the country would rise the moment a foreign invasion touched the shore.[1] Since Allen himself declared that this was so, were the English government to blame because they acted as if it might be so? After the publication of the Bull in 1571 it had been declared illegal to make converts to the Catholic Church, thus drawing a distinction between converts and those already Catholic; after 1581, when more than one hundred Jesuit missionaries had been sent into England, the Pope's forces had invaded Ireland and Morton had been overthrown by the Guise instrument, the English Parliament declared it felony to "harbour" Jesuits and seminary priests, and fines for evading the statutory monthly attendance at the parish church were raised to £20 a month. This meant that innocent Catholic families who thankfully received a priest to say mass and hear their confessions were by law "maintainers of rebels" and liable if caught to crushing fines, dreadful conditions of imprisonment and possibly to death. The situation was a hateful one, but it was not of Elizabeth's choosing. She could have avoided it only by becoming a Catholic herself. Since this was what Catholics felt she ought to do, she gained no sympathy from militant Catholics, particularly those who lived abroad; but from many Catholics who lived in England, she did receive a degree of loyalty that touched her keenly. "This man is a member of the old religion," she said to Fénélon, when an old man cried, God save her, in the street.

To make clear, to their own satisfaction, the political implications of the Jesuits' crusade, the government framed a question to be put to those priests who were arrested. It was this: in the event of an invasion sponsored by the Pope, to dethrone the Queen, would you fight on the Queen's side? The Catholics called this the Bloody Question and contended that it could not reasonably be asked: the thing had not happened, they could not act as judges between the Pope and the Queen, they did not enter into political questions. But it was clear that one reply and one only would satisfy the government, and that was a straightforward "yes". Any other answer would confirm the suspicion that the priest was a potential if not an active traitor.

It was possible to be entirely sincere in refusing to envisage disobedience to the Pope and yet mean no harm to Elizabeth, but it

[1] Mignet, op. cit.

was a state of mind almost impossible to explain to English Protestants in the 1580's. The Spanish Fury, conducted by Parma, was
raging in the Netherlands, and the tales of what was happening on the
other side of the Channel to cities which opposed the forces of the
Catholic King of Spain were overlaying even the memory of St.
Bartholomew. The fall of Maestricht was but one agony among
many, but every Englishman who heard of its garrison slaughtered
with maniacal cruelty, of the women who had manned its defences
torn to pieces in the streets and of Parma carried triumphantly in a
litter over mutilated corpses and seas of blood, knew that when
Philip had reduced the Netherlands to his will, England's turn would
come next. The English Protestants were savage with panic and they
thought that by hunting down Catholic missionaries and stamping
out their hiding-places, they were helping to save English cities from
the fate of what had once been the rich and peaceful cities of the
Netherlands.

That the English government's persecution of the priests was
political and not religious was not only admitted by Allen: he
thought the worse of them for it. "The question is not about
religion, of which our enemies have not one bit," he wrote, "but
about the stability of the kingdom, about worldly prosperity."
Elizabeth did indeed care about the stability and prosperity of the
kingdom, and it was generally recognized that she had no healthy
instinct for religious persecution. The Puritans condemned this lack
as much as the Catholics. In the parish church of Bury St. Edmunds
there appeared one day, written up under the royal arms: "Because
thou art neither hot nor cold, therefore will I spew thee out of my
mouth."

Among the first of the missionary priests sent to England in 1581
was Edmund Campion, who as a graduate had entertained the
Queen with a paper on the moon and the tides. She had recommended him to Leicester as a protégé and her notice had at first
dazzled him. "The sugared words of the great folks, especially of the
Queen, so enticed him that he knew not which way to turn."[1] His
mind at length made up, he became a Catholic and a student in
Allen's seminary. The early brightness and charm which had struck
the Queen became recognized as part of a rare and extraordinary
character, in which supernatural spiritual strength was mingled with
natural human fears, and sternness of purpose with radiant serenity.
Passed on from house to house in the countryside, where Catholic

[1] Simpson, *Edmund Campion.*

families were longing for his ministrations, he evaded capture for a year and was caught at last in Berkshire. The horrible and degrading effect of persecution on the public mind was shown as he was brought to the Tower through a yelling mob, a placard tied on him saying, "Campion the Seditious Jesuit". He was kept for two days in the abominable dungeon, "Little Ease", but on the night of July 25 he was brought secretly to Leicester House in the Strand. There, in a private room, he saw not only Leicester, but the Queen. Elizabeth asked him if he acknowledged her as his Queen. He answered readily: Yes, as his lawful Queen. Then she asked if he thought the Pope might lawfully depose her? Campion made the fatal evasion. It was not for him, he said, to judge betwixt her Majesty and the Pope. He was asked what he would do if the Pope sent an army to dethrone her? He replied: "I would do as God should give me grace." Still Elizabeth persisted. She explained the position as she saw it and that all she asked was the statutory attendance at the parish church. In Campion's case, he was told, he would be required to attend only once. That once would be enough.

As Campion saw it, the once would be more than enough; it would negative everything he had worked for and for which he had put himself in ghastly peril. He refused, and the Queen could do no more.

Campion was racked in an effort to make him disclose the houses where he had been sheltered, and while still weak from his sufferings, he sustained a dispute in the Tower Chapel with four Protestant divines, to whom, "worn with the rack, his memory destroyed, he answered easily, readily, patiently". The Privy Council, who now regarded all families sheltering a priest as possible conspirators, determined to gain from Campion a list of his hosts, and he was so mercilessly racked that his joints were dislocated. When brought to trial in Westminster Hall he could not hold up his own hand; one of his companions raised it for him, kissing it as he did so. He and five other priests were convicted on the charge that with Dr. Allen and his followers at Rheims and at Rome, they had plotted the dethronement of the Queen. Campion said: "The only thing we have to say is that if our religion do make us traitors we are worthy to be condemned, but otherwise we are as true subjects as ever the Queen had." It was undoubtedly the truth as far as he himself was concerned; but the onlooker who cried out at the scaffold: "In your Catholicism all treason is contained!" held a

ment would be instructed to demand terms which the French King would refuse, thus infuriating his brother.

These particulars were not confided to Leicester and Hatton; Elizabeth merely soothed them and told them she would evade the obligation; they might set their minds at rest. Meanwhile both gentlemen found themselves appointed to sit on the commission for drawing up the marriage articles.

A glimpse, vivid almost as second sight, is given by a correspondent of the Fugger banking house. "On the afternoon of December 7, I saw the Queen out hunting. . . . Alençon was following immediately after. I stood so close to her that I heard her speak. She does not look so old as she is said to be."[1]

And now the unravelling of the web began. Elizabeth, after a wakeful night, sent a message to Alençon that she feared, if she married him, she would not have long to live; she hoped he did not want his love to prove fatal to her. She would be his friend, always, even more than if she had married him. Alençon was thunderstruck. He tore off the ring and pitched it on the ground, cursing the inconstancy of women and islanders.

At this inappropriate moment the envoy arrived from Henri III, bearing his congratulations; and so earnest was the French King to complete the matter, that every stipulation made by the English Council was agreed to, one after another—until the Queen said she must have Calais back again. This preposterous demand was taken as an insult, and Leicester, really alarmed, suggested raising £200,000 and sending Alençon back to the Netherlands with it. Elizabeth, oblivious, it seemed, of what was plain to everybody else, that the French in their indignation were on the verge of severing diplomatic relations, absolutely scouted the idea of giving away so much good money. She said if Alençon thought fit to forget her in exchange for her money, she would neither marry him nor give him any money, and he might do the best he could.

Though she had made up her mind to it, the actual process of dislodging the Frog Prince proved unexpectedly difficult. He declared that sooner than leave the Queen without marrying her, he would rather they both perished. Elizabeth exclaimed that he must not threaten a poor old woman in her own kingdom. She begged him not to use such terrible language. The young man, who had been pitiably tried, cried out: "No, no, Madame, you mistake. I meant no hurt to your blessed person. I meant only that I would sooner be

[1] Fugger News Letter.

cut in pieces than not marry you and so be laughed at by the world," and he burst into tears. The Queen gave him her handkerchief.[1]

At last, in return for substantial promises of money, and on the understanding that he should come back in six weeks and marry her, Alençon consented to depart. But it was the end of December: a great on-shore gale sprang up and blew continuously, and the climax of leave-taking spun out into a long and agitating anti-climax. The Queen sent for Sussex; while the winter winds raged, she told something of her secret to the man whose chivalry had protected and comforted her for thirty years. She hated the idea of marriage more every day, she said: she had reasons against it that she would not divulge to a twin soul, if she had one.

That such words were brought to Mendoza was due not only to his exceptional ability as an organizer of spies, but to the sixteenth-century fashion of living in public. In great houses one large room opened into another, and only at the end of the suite, in a small room a few yards square with one window and a small hearth, was it possible to hold a completely private conversation. Elsewhere, ushers and ladies and gentlemen-in-waiting were always within sight, if not within ear-shot. One great lady or another slept in the Queen's bed-chamber, and her servants as well as the Queen's added to the numbers who had the entrée to the royal presence, while beyond the rooms the Queen was occupying, there were fifty Gentlemen Pensioners on duty. With so many people to work upon, a great deal could be picked up, but Mendoza's system was remarkably clever; it moved from point to point up to the Queen's very bedside, and back again to the Spanish embassy.

The gales which prevented Alençon from leaving the shore blew the French commissioners across the Channel in a trice. Henri III's secretary, Pinart, arrived in mid-January. His errand was a simple one. It was to say that if the English Queen persisted in her present course, she would drive his master to seek alliance with the King of Spain.

At this threat, the nearest approach to mortal peril her diplomacy had yet encountered, the Queen passed an entirely sleepless night. Lady Stafford, the Mistress of the Robes, who was in waiting, was in nearly the same plight, for Elizabeth kept waking her up. In the morning the Queen was feverish and stayed in bed. After dinner she sent for Sussex to her bedside and told him she supposed she must sacrifice herself—she must marry Alençon. Sussex begged her not to

[1] Hume, op. cit.

discuss the matter with him any more; let her only tell him her decision when she had made it.

But Burleigh took a different course. After some members of the Council had visited the Queen, he stayed behind for a private interview. He told her that in face of the Franco-Spanish threat, Alençon must be gratified either by the marriage or by a large quantity of money. Both alternatives were distressing, but one or the other must be adopted immediately.

Once the necessity of it was admitted, the choice itself presented no difficulty. £30,000 was made over to Alençon, with bills for £20,000 more, and a squadron prepared to take him to Flushing, where the Netherlanders were offering to make him Duke of Brabant. The Earl of Leicester was to sail with him, and the Queen herself accompanied him as far as Canterbury. She besought him, in moving terms, to take the greatest care of himself. Nothing could exceed the sensibility, the elegance and the absurdity of her leave-taking. But while the party was at Rochester, an expedition was made to show Alençon the dockyards at Chatham. They presented a spectacle that took the Frenchmen's breath away. The masts of completed ships shaded the quays like groves, while in the yards vessels were building upon new and improved designs of which the world was presently to see the advantage. With enthusiastic courtesy the French exclaimed: Well might nations call Queen Elizabeth the Queen of the Sea![1] The Queen assured Alençon that these ships should do him service if he needed it, but she was pleased with the opportunity to show the sight to foreigners. Harrison's *Description of England*, published this very year, said how proud and delighted the Queen was with the English ships, since "for strength, assurance, nimbleness and swiftness of sailing, there are no vessels in the world to be compared with ours . . . by this means . . . are . . . sundry foreign enemies put back, which would otherwise invade us".

Alençon embarked at the end of February. He wrote letters to Elizabeth full of desolation at leaving her, and she exclaimed she would give a million pounds to have her frog swimming in the Thames again.

The success of the negotiation, which for the last three years had been of extreme importance to English foreign policy, had been due to Elizabeth's being able to convince Alençon of a genuine, if metaphysical passion, and in doing so she had generated in herself a weird, cold brightness, a simulacrum of emotion, in which she wrote,

[1] Nichols, *Progresses*.

astonishingly, some verses on a model of Petrarch's—"On Monsieur's Departure":

> *I am, and am not, freeze, and yet I burn,*
> *Since from myself, my other self I turn.*

Twelve years later the theme of Alençon's courtship was given a different interpretation. In *A Midsummer Night's Dream*, Oberon says he watched Cupid's fiery arrow quenched in moonlight,

> *And the imperial votaress pass on,*
> *In maiden meditation, fancy free.*

XXII

THE QUEEN OF SCOTS appeared to be living with her Court the life of a private gentlewoman at one or other of Lord Shrewsbury's country seats. Actually, since she had freedom of communication with France and Scotland and with the French and Spanish Ambassadors in London, and had moreover the whole of her French dowry at her own disposal because Elizabeth paid Shrewsbury for her maintenance, Mary was ceaselessly engaged with political intelligence and intrigue. In 1582 she was revived with hope of an invasion of England on her behalf planned by her uncle the Duke of Guise and promoted in Scotland by D'Aubigny. There had been talk of an Association of herself and James in the Scottish Crown. James wanted no such Association with his mother in Scotland, but if the Guises saw their way to getting the English Crown for her, with reversion to himself, James would not stand in their light.

The invasion was discussed at the house of de Tassis, the Spanish Ambassador in Paris, between de Tassis, the Bishop of Glasgow, the Duke of Guise and Dr. Allen. It was to be paid for by the Spanish King but launched in the Pope's name, that the French might not be jealous of Spanish influence, and Dr. Allen assured his colleagues that thousands of Catholics would rise all over the country to welcome the invaders.[1]

D'Aubigny kept Mary in close touch with the conspiracy and she wrote, heartily approving of it, but saying: "It is not my intention in any way to allow it to be proved that the said negotiations were carried on under my name."

Walsingham caused the Scots to be warned of the imminent Association of James with his mother, and their fears, at once aroused, were increased to panic by the arrival of a present of horses for James from his great-uncle Guise; for the man who brought them was Guise's master-stabler, Signor Paul, who had planned the organization of St. Bartholomew. By a sudden coup, James was kidnapped while hunting with the Earl of Gowrie, and D'Aubigny, after an attempt on Edinburgh, saw that the game was up and bolted back to France, where he died a short time afterwards.

[1] Mignet, *op. cit.*

Invasion from Scotland was now out of the question and Guise decided on a direct attack at different points on the south shores of England. Spain was expected to make a diversion in Ireland and release 4,000 soldiers from Flanders, and Guise and his brother Mayenne were to land in Rye harbour, when, Allen assured them, a general insurrection of Catholics would at once break out. It had occurred to the Duke, if not to Dr. Allen, that some English Catholics might not altogether relish the prospect of Spanish soldiers swarming over their country, so a message was sent, assuring them that the soldiers were coming only to establish the Catholic religion and to restore the English Crown to the Queen of Scots, "to whom that Crown of right belongs". If the soldiers declined to go away after that, then Guise would help the English to turn them out. This assurance, it was felt, should satisfy anybody. The plans went on and were known of course to Mendoza, who by no means encouraged his already hesitating and reluctant master. Mendoza's spy system was first-rate, but so was Walsingham's, and when so many people already knew of the conspiracy, the only chance of success was to bring it quickly into effect. Guise hoped that Philip would make it possible for the invasion to sail in September 1583.

That June Elizabeth had a terrible loss. Sussex died. His aid as a councillor could not compare with Burleigh's, and she felt nothing for him to compare with what she felt for Leicester; but the quality of his loyalty was like no one else's. He died expressing it. Hatton was beside him, and Sussex knew that Hatton and Leicester were colleagues. He said: "Beware of the gipsy. He will betray you. You do not know the beast as well as I do."

Leicester was, indeed, deep in plans. He had approached Lady Shrewsbury to suggest a marriage between the fated Arabella Stuart and his son by his wife Lettice, the child who was to die at six years old, whose tiny suit of armour is in Warwick Castle; but it was within the verge of possibility that Arabella Stuart might one day be Queen of England, and her redoubtable grandmother was in no hurry to afford yet another speculation to the house of Dudley. Leicester had another plan. His wife had presented him with a second stepdaughter besides the famous Penelope Rich; he and Lettice thought this girl might be married to the young King of Scotland. This came to Elizabeth's ears, and to disapproval of a scheme so unsuitable in itself was added a passion of anger against the presumption of the Countess. Elizabeth exclaimed that she would sooner see

James stripped of his crown than married to that she-wolf's cub.[1] The matter was discreetly dropped.

Leicester, who had Mauvissière to dine at his house, and introduced him to his wife (of whom, Mauvissière said, he appeared extremely fond), told the Ambassador sadly that he had now lost his favour with the Queen. But the storms of the relationship showed only how enduring it was; by September it was said: "My Lord of Leicester groweth in great favour with her Majesty."

A comet appeared over London, and the general fear was that it boded the death of some great person. Elizabeth was at Richmond when it was seen in all its baleful beauty, and the ominous supposition, unspoken, was felt by those around her. She braved it, "with a courage answering to the greatness of her state". She ordered the window to be opened on the sinister light, and walked towards it, saying: "Jacta est alea"—the dice are thrown.[2]

The probability of attempts upon her life had been recognized since the Bull of 1571. The Pope had sanctioned her murder, provided it were undertaken in a proper spirit, it had been discussed in open council at Madrid, and now it formed a necessary feature of the Enterprise. Guise and Mayenne had at first considered having her assassinated without waiting for the invasion, but somehow the design fell through. Philip's comment was: "If they had done it, it would have been no harm, though they should have made provision of certain things before-hand."[3]

This extreme caution of the Spanish King's in fact assured the failure of the Enterprise before it started. Walsingham got wind of the conspiracy, and the capture of Francis Throckmorton, a nephew of Elizabeth's old minister, placed a mass of incriminating documents in the Council's hands. Throckmorton twice courageously withstood the agonies of the rack. The third time his resistance collapsed, and he revealed some extremely alarming information: the plans for the landing of Guise and his brother, the names of the Catholics who were expected to support him, the connivance of Mendoza and finally that the Queen of Scots was conversant with the whole. When he had finished his confession the pitiable man rose from a seat beside the rack and exclaimed: "Now I have betrayed her who was dearest to me in this world." Now, he said, he wanted nothing but death.

The publication of the conspiracy aroused the fiercest passion in

[1] C.S.P. Spanish.   [2] Malcolm, *Manners and Customs of London.*
[3] *Letters and Memorials of Cardinal Allen.*

large numbers of the people, both of fury against the Queen of Scots and of love and protection for the English Queen. On December 19 Mauvissière described to Henri III how he had ridden with Elizabeth from Hampton Court to London. The Queen was riding a splendid horse and she and the Ambassador were at some distance from the retinue. The roads were in their winter state but people knelt down in the mud as she passed, calling out blessings on her and wishing that her enemies and theirs might be punished. After one such demonstration, the Queen said to him, she perceived that not *everyone* wished her dead.

But the dangers of Mary Stuart and the Catholic powers, that had loomed from the day of Elizabeth's accession, were massing, towering, darkening like the clouds of a high-piled thunder-loft, and in spite of the people's love, there was treachery at home. Throckmorton's was less unnerving than Norfolk's had been, but it was more serious because the invasion it had tried to bring about had been far nearer success than Ridolfi's attempt. The wonderful portrait of the Queen painted by Zuccari in 1583 marks the period when the long-drawn-out, glittering delusion of the Alençon match was over and the great crisis was ushering in. Elizabeth is sitting in the foreground of a colonnade, in which some of the Gentlemen Pensioners are visible. The light of the scene is behind her; her dress is plain black with a striking absence of ornament, her very jewels a rope of black pearls and a narrow girdle of gold and agate stones, and a white lawn mantle is thrown round her. In her left hand is a small sieve, the emblem of a Vestal Virgin. Her face, with its delicate oval and aquiline nose, speaks intellect and strength of mind to an extraordinary degree, but an air of misery tinges the whole expression. On the black marble pillar to her right are the words, in Italian: "Weary I rest and having rested still am weary." At her left is a terrestrial globe, its blue-green ocean dotted with ships, and on its rim the words: "I see all, and much is missing."

The opening of the final act before the storm was the dismissal of Mendoza. The Privy Council received him, and as he did not speak English readily, Walsingham addressed him in Italian on behalf of the rest. Mendoza was told that he had abused his diplomatic privileges; therefore it was Her Majesty's pleasure that he should leave the kingdom within fifteen days. Mendoza declared that he must first inform his master of her decision: whereupon the whole Council rose to their feet and told him that he must depart without waiting. Mendoza said that as he had not been able to please the

Queen as a minister of peace, he would hope to satisfy her in war. In his despatches he wrote: "The insolence of these people so exasperates me, I desire to live only to be revenged on them."

The Queen of Scots was the centre of this aspect of European politics, and also of the family situation of Lord Shrewsbury. The great Earl had been chosen for her guardian not only for his enormous possessions, his castles and manors and his influence in his own neighbourhood, but for his character; he had sufficient breadth to be sympathetic to Mary while being inflexibly loyal to Elizabeth. The flaw was in his wife. Bess of Hardwick was much liked by people so long as she was on their side. Elizabeth had said she would always be glad to see Lady Shrewsbury at Court, and in one of his early letters, Shrewsbury had written: "My sweetheart, I give God thanks daily . . . that He hath sent you me in my old years to comfort me withal." When his long trial was over, he was to thank the Queen for having delivered him from two devils, the Queen of Scots and his wife. The domestic situation was made difficult by the grasping and shrewish temper of the wife and the properties she had inherited from previous husbands, which absorbed money and attention that her present husband thought due to himself, and it received additional complication from the fact that the Earl's children, Gilbert Talbot and Grace Talbot, had been married to the Countess's children, Henry Cavendish and Mary Cavendish. Lady Shrewsbury had once been on very intimate terms with the illustrious prisoner: they had naturally taken great pleasure in each other's society. But when the Countess became the grandmother of a potential heiress to the English throne, her feelings towards the presumptive heiress underwent an alteration. An indiscreet intimacy was followed by a vindictive quarrel, and as the Countess' feud with her husband was now raging, she and her sons William and Charles Cavendish put it about that the Queen of Scots was the Earl's mistress and had borne him a child. The Recorder of London, Sir William Fleetwood, had before him an Islington innkeeper who had been telling his clients he knew where the baby had been christened.

Mary had a long-pent-up torrent of anger and hatred to discharge; with deft economy, she wrote a letter to Elizabeth, detailing repulsive slanders against her and citing Lady Shrewsbury as the source of the information. The latter had told her, she said, that Elizabeth had lain with a man to whom she had promised marriage, she had lain with Alençon and with Simier, and to Simier she had betrayed the secrets of her councillors. She had so much embarrassed Hatton by the love she showed him, he had been obliged to leave the Court. She swallowed such ludicrous flattery, her ladies dared not look at each other for fear of laughing; in her ungovernable ferocity, she had broken the finger of one and hacked another with a knife; she was not made like other women and no marriage with her could be consummated, and as the ulcer on her leg had dried up at the same time that her monthly periods ceased, Lady Shrewsbury had said that the Queen had not long to live anyway. Mary concluded by saying that she had many more things "in reserve", and would tell them to Elizabeth if a meeting could be arranged between them.[1]

The passage about Hatton suffered from Lady Shrewsbury's not having had a sight of his letters to the Queen, while the statement that Elizabeth had betrayed state secrets to Simier, showed that neither lady had the artist's gift of knowing where to stop. As the letter was found with Lord Burleigh's papers, it was assumed that with masculine discretion he kept it from Elizabeth's hands.

The accusation against the Queen of Scots and Lord Shrewsbury was however brought to the Queen's ears by the Earl himself, with a demand for retribution against his wife. Elizabeth had levied an enormous toll on Shrewsbury for the past fifteen years, on his time, patience, loyalty, and on his money also, for when the subsidy paid for Mary's upkeep did not meet her expenses, Shrewsbury bore the loss. The Queen did her best to give this tried and faithful servant satisfaction. The Countess and her two sons were summoned before the Privy Council, and there they all admitted having repeated the slander, but only because they had heard it from other people; they said they themselves had never believed it. The Queen said she hoped a reconciliation between husband and wife might now come about, but the Shrewsburys had so many and such varied causes of mutual recrimination, they had quarrelled themselves to a standstill. Well, said the Queen, would Shrewsbury accept her efforts at mediation? Should she herself look into the matters under dispute and give the opinion of a disinterested third party? A grateful acceptance was returned and the family papers were made available to the Queen's advisers. Deeds were scrutinized, settlements, expenses, contributions: £1,000 worth of Lady Shrewsbury's own linen, it seemed, had gone to sundry of the Earl's houses "to serve his turn", to say nothing of thirty mattresses and twenty quilts supplied every year. The inventories of household stuff were examined, down to a very porringer which the Countess had taken away while the Earl kept

[1] Murdin.

hold of the lid. Rents, assurances of lands, agreements with tenants, all were sorted out and methodically arranged that a comprehensive picture of the position might be gained. Then the Queen invoked Walsingham's assistance, and between them they drew up a suggested scheme by which the Countess was to receive £300 a year housekeeping money plus expenses for fuel and to have the wages paid for five servants. A furnished house was to be put at her disposal in Derbyshire and she was to be free to go to her own properties of Hardwick and Chatsworth, and free to come back to her husband's house. This was regarded as an interim measure pending a reconciliation. "If she shall do her best to recover his former good opinion and love, then it is to be hoped that continual cohabitation shall follow, which her Majesty greatly desires."[1]

The Shrewsburys accepted the Queen's suggestions, but nothing could bring them together again. The Queen of Scots had meanwhile been transferred to the keeping of Sir Ralph Sadler, a less sympathetic guardian.

The assassination of William of Orange in July 1584 sharpened the fears of the loyal and devoted numbers of the English, for it showed how easily Elizabeth might be murdered. She impatiently refused the suggestion of an armed bodyguard; the idea of being cut off from free communication with the populace made her say she would sooner be dead than "in custody".[2] The passion of protectiveness she aroused was for a courageous woman, frail and precious. This is the image of her given in that extraordinary publication of 1584, an anonymous attack on the great favourite, called *Leicester's Commonwealth*. This pungent, racy piece of journalism gives a sensational picture of Leicester as a master-criminal, with his tribe of poisoners, bawds and abortionists, his Italian ointments and aphrodisiacs, the bottle at his bed's head worth £10 the pint, "his good fortune in seeing them dead who, for any cause, he would not have to live", the list of his victims beginning with his wife and ending with the Earl of Sussex; but its chief interest lies in the relative positions, which, in a work of immense popular appeal, are ascribed to Elizabeth and Leicester, in which the Queen, fragile and angelic, is the prey of a licentious ruffian. It accused Leicester of preventing the Queen's marriages by his "preoccupation of her Majesty's person" and his impudence: "giving out everywhere that he (forsooth!) was assured to her Majesty and that all other princes must give over their suits for him";

[1] Rawson, *Bess of Hardwick*.   [2] Bacon, *Apothequies*.

of his oppressing the Queen by his exorbitant demands: "Her Majesty had no rest permitted to her until she had yielded and granted the same"; and of threatening the security of the state, "with a Queen of no great good health or robustious and strong constitution". His disappointment over the marriage he had failed of, it was said, "stirreth him daily to revenge", and it was all too plain what her Majesty might expect "if by offending him she should once fall within the compass of his furious paws". This work gained a brilliant success, so much so that the Privy Council addressed a minute about it to Justices of the Peace, "as though her Majesty should want either goodwill, ability or courage (if she knew these enormities were true) to call any subject of hers whatsoever to render sharp account of them". The book's details contained exaggerations amounting to burlesque, but its wild-fire success showed that the outlines of the two central figures were, not necessarily true to life, but what the public accepted as true.

The impression of the Queen as frail and irritable is borne out by Walsingham's instructions to Stafford at Paris this October. He told Stafford when writing despatches for the Queen's eye, to give the gist only of what was said by the King and the Queen-mother, "for that she cannot now away with any long discourses in letters". But, he added, "let *me* know all".

The German traveller Von Wedel, who visited England at this time, saw the Queen at a Christmas dinner, in mourning for the Prince of Orange and for Alençon, whom disease had brought to a premature end the previous May. The Queen wore black velvet, sumptuously embroidered in silver and pearls, and "a silver shawl of mesh, diaphanous like a tissue of gossamer, hung down to the hem of her skirt".[1]

Ever-increasing prosperity had brought a degree of luxury that exasperated the moralists. The *Anatomy of Abuses* of 1585 deplored women's use of scent, "whereof the smell may be perceived not only all over the place where they be present, but also a stone's cast off, the bed wherein they have laid their delicate bodies, the places where they have sat". Their stockings "of fine yarn as it is possible to have", were of such colours, green, red, white, russet, tawny, as could hardly be worn without grave suspicion of impropriety. Their shoes were as bad, some black velvet, some white, some green, some yellow. Their ruffs too were abominably eye-catching, trimmed with gold, or silver or lace, "speckled and sparkled here and there with the sun, the moon, the stars".

[1] Klarwill, *Queen Elizabeth and some Foreigners.*

The Court was the centre of these temptations to lust of the eye. The Queen loved rich and precious objects. In Hampton Court palace there was a cabinet called Paradise; it was indeed like the mystic's vision of heaven, for it was all colour, transparency and light. Its walls were panelled with gold and silver; the chair of state stood under a canopy studded with pearls and precious stones, among which large diamonds, sapphires and rubies shone out "like the sun among stars". On one wall hung a crimson cloth, the royal arms emblazoned on it, in their centre a table diamond of enormous size and lustre. This small brilliant room contained a musical instrument of fairy-like strangeness; except for its strings, it was made entirely of glass.[1]

The reach of the river in front of Whitehall Palace was covered with swans, and in the palace garden were thirty-four columns, each surmounted by the effigy of a heraldic beast. In this palace was the great tilt-yard; stands for spectators surrounded three sides of it, but the fourth was looked down upon by the windows of a long room in the Palace. The art of jousting had developed from the murderous struggle of the Middle Ages to a contest of skill, requiring high training in man and horse. A loud fanfare of trumpets ushered in a spectacle of dream-like strangeness. The knights and their followers rode into the lists, "some dressed like savages, some like natives of Ireland with hair streaming like a woman's down to the girdle, some had crescent moons on their heads, some with horses caparisoned like elephants, some driving their carriages drawn by people most oddly attired".

On feast days, but only then, the Queen dined in public, and Wedel saw her in the great hall at Greenwich. She sat at a table alone, and after she had sat down, five countesses took their seats at another table. The visitor saw in attendance Lord Leicester, Lord Howard of Effingham, who had succeeded Sussex as Lord Chamberlain, Lord Hertford and Sir Christopher Hatton. He described them as "handsome old gentlemen". The Queen barely stayed till the second course was brought. The countesses, who had watched for her to move, rose just before she did and curtseyed deeply twice. The Queen turned her back to the hall while two bishops said grace; then a gold basin and a towel were brought her, and she took off a ring which she handed to the Lord Chamberlain. When she had washed her hands, she put it on again.

A stately dance was performed by ladies "slender and beautiful

[1] Heutzner, *Travels in England;* Platter, *Travels in England.*

but no longer very young". This was followed by an extremely lively one by young men, who took off their cloaks and swords, and danced with the young ladies. While this was going on, the Queen held conversations, summoning young and old, and talking continuously. When she had finished, she waved her hand to the assembled company, and withdrew to her chamber.[1]

Klarwill, *op. cit.*

XXIII

THE EVIDENCE AGAINST Mary Stuart discovered through Throckmorton was not pressed against her; but the Privy Council, who had always foreseen what would happen to them if Elizabeth were murdered, had been infuriated by it and they drew up what they called a Bond of Association by which they bound themselves, in event of the Queen's murder, to pursue to death, not only the persons who were guilty of the act, but the person in whose interests it had been done. Signatures were invited, and a mass of documents bearing signatures and seals were shown to the Queen at Hampton Court.

A Parliament full of alarm and determination was opened in October 1584. The Queen, in her crimson robes, rode to the ceremony in a coach drawn by six grey horses, their manes and tails dyed orange; they were bridled with pearls, and diamonds hung upon their foreheads.[1]

The principal business was the matter of the Queen's safety. The Houses adopted the Privy Council's Bond of Association, but the Queen herself insisted on some modifications of it. She sent word by Sir Christopher Hatton that a claimant on whose behalf treason was undertaken must not be summarily put to death, but be tried before a committee of councillors, bishops and judges. Parliament wanted to make the heir to such a claimant also forfeit his right to the succession, but the Queen demurred. If the Protestant James were to be excluded, the basis of her negotiations with Scotland would be lost. The matter finally stood that in the event of rebellion or assassination of the Queen, any claimant who, before a commission, could be proved to have had foreknowledge of the act, should be put to death.

The second Bill before the Houses ordered all Jesuits and seminary priests, and all those who had entered the Catholic priesthood since 1559, to leave the realm within forty days. It was first declared treason to shelter or maintain them; this was afterwards reduced to felony.

At the Christmas recess, the Queen sent the House of Commons her thanks for their care of her, which she declared to be greater than

[1] Wright, *Queen Elizabeth and her Times;* Klarwill, *op. cit.*

she deserved. And when the Members' thanks were returned for her gracious message, the Queen sent again: "most hearty and loving thanks unto this whole House, yea, redoubling to them their thanks, to ten thousand, thousand fold". Hatton told the House he had a prayer in his pocket, written by a godly man for the Queen's preservation. He asked if he should read it aloud. This he did, sentence by sentence, the House repeating it after him on their knees. These doings might be interpreted in many lights, but at least they showed in what temper Parliament would decide the fate of anyone who contemplated the murder of Elizabeth.[1]

While the Bill for exiling Jesuits was under discussion one man only had spoken against it, electrifying the House with anger and astonishment. This was Parry, a man of the most varied and contradictory antecedents, who had been a protégé of the Jesuits, a spy of Walsingham's, who had gained admittance to the Queen to tell her that the Catholics were plotting her murder (at which, he said: "I find her very calm") and then retired to plot it himself with a disaffected Catholic called Neville. He had such a talent for convincing people, that he had been elected M.P. for Queenborough. He was betrayed to the government by his fellow-plotter, and the statements made at his trial, at which he was sentenced to be hanged and quartered, showed that Elizabeth was in acute danger of assassination. The opinion was now generally held that no rebellion or invasion could succeed so long as she was alive. Let her be safely dead, and every Catholic in the land would then, inevitably, acclaim Mary Stuart. But while Elizabeth still lived—that was an altogether different matter. The motive for a single act, requiring but one person to perform it, was overwhelming, and Parry's statements showed that the deed should have been easy. The Queen's accessibility was notorious. He and Neville had discussed riding up one on each side of her coach and discharging pistols at her head. Then, it was well known that she was fond of walking in St. James' Park, accompanied by ladies, with but few gentlemen. One fine day a little determination would settle the matter. Or so it seemed until it came to the point. Parry said that on the occasion when he himself came nearest to doing it, he was daunted because she reminded him of Henry VIII.

So far, her preservation appeared miraculous, and the Queen herself ascribed it to the protection of God. The Puritans, in the person of Walsingham, feared that her religious convictions were

---

[1] Neale, *Elizabeth and her Parliaments*, I

faint, and Dr. Allen said she had no religion at all. Indeed, plain commonsense was the most obvious feature of her religious attitude. The Anglican Church in this year was under criticism for the number of unsuitable and incompetent clergymen the bishops had appointed.

" 'Well,' quoth her Majesty, 'burden them that have offended.' The Bishop of Rochester said there were 13,000 parishes in England. It was not possible to find a learned preacher for each of them. 'Jesus!' quoth the Queen. '13,000 is not to be looked for. . . . My meaning is not that you should make choice of learned preachers only, for they are not to be found, but of honest, sober and wise men and such as can read the Scriptures and the Homilies well unto the people.' "[1]

But she felt the value of intercessary prayer. The Lady Magdalen Dacre, who had been Mary Tudor's lady-in-waiting, had retired from her sister's Court, but although a Catholic, she prayed earnestly for Elizabeth; and Lady Scudamore wrote to her saying: "The Queen commissions me to signify to your Ladyship that she is persuaded she fareth much the better for your prayers and therefore desireth you ever hereafter to be mindful of her in your prayers."[2]

Scrofula, the King's Evil, had been supposed, from the time of Edward the Confessor, to be curable by the sovereign's touch. The latest discoveries of the power of hypnosis to cure eczema suggest that scrofula, a tubercular affection of the skin, may also have been amenable to strong suggestion, and that the cures claimed for "touching" may have been in fact due to it. Elizabeth was eager to exert, if she might, a power that proved the sacrosanct nature of royalty, and her chaplain Tooker described the intensity of emotion with which she prayed to transmit the healing touch: "How often have I seen her most Serene Majesty, prostrate on her knees, body and soul rapt in prayer . . . how often have I seen her with her exquisite hands, whiter than whitest snow, boldly and without disgust, pressing their sores and ulcers, and handling them to health . . . how often have I seen her worn with fatigue, as whe n in one single day, she healed eight and thirty persons of the struma." Tooker claimed that "most" of the patients regained health.[3] But sometimes Elizabeth did not find the inspiration, and then she said so. At Gloucester, when the numbers of pitiable creatures thronged about her, she exclaimed: "Would, would that I could give you help and succour.

[1] MSS. Dometic, quoted by Froude.   [2] Smith, *Life of the Viscountess Montagu.*
[3] Crawfurd, *The King's Evil.*

God, God is the best and greatest physician of all—you must pray to Him."[1]

Of the collection of prayers written by herself, the fact that some are written in Latin, Greek, Italian and French may recall the translation exercises set by Ascham, but the English ones show a poignant, unforced earnestness: "Thou has set me on high, my flesh is frail and weak. If I therefore at any time forget Thee, touch my heart, O Lord, that I may again remember thee."[2]

It is with thrilling recollection that we follow in the Prayer Book the prayers for "our most gracious Sovereign Lady Queen Elizabeth", that were read in the Queen's hearing every Sunday.

[1] Dictionary of Literary Anecdote.
[2] Chamberlin, *Private Character of Queen Elizabeth*.

XXIV

THE PRINCE OF ORANGE had already asked the English Queen to
accept the sovereignty of Holland, Zeeland and Utrecht, and she
had refused it. When the murder of Orange and Alençon's death
occurred in the same year, the States renewed the offer and Elizabeth refused it again. This was, perhaps, one of the most original
acts performed by an English monarch. To accept would mean that
England was inescapably committed to open war with Spain, but
most English sovereigns would have thought the gamble too tempting to refuse. Elizabeth did not even consider it. She did not, in
foreign policy, make many declarations that were absolutely sincere,
but this was one she did make. She promised armed assistance in
exchange for holding the ports of Flushing, Brill and Rammikens,
but the sovereignty of the Provinces, bringing with it an invitation
to a full-scale Spanish war, she would not have in any circumstances.
An English force was to be sent and some English noble of the first
distinction, who was prepared to spend a great deal of his own money
on the enterprise, must be chosen to lead it. Lord Leicester fulfilled
both these requirements, and though he was not a general, capable
officers would be with him, and Burleigh and Walsingham both considered that he had sufficient ability and experience to manage the
administrative side of the task.

The necessity of helping the Netherlanders to hold the Spaniards
in check so that they might be kept out of England was obvious, but
the risk of Spanish reprisals, and the expense, caused Elizabeth so
much misgiving and uncertainty that she had worn down Walsingham to a state of grim endurance before she had made up her mind
to it. At the very last moment, he received a letter from Leicester
saying that the Queen had been so low in her mind that evening "by
reason of her oft-disease taking her of late, and this night worst of
all", that she had "used very pitiful words" to him, he said, "of her
fear that she shall not live, and would not have me from her".
Walsingham might imagine how this had affected him; he had comforted her as well as he could and reminded her of how forward his
preparations were. He admitted that he, too, was worn down by her
varying purpose, "weary of life and all". However, he was at last

embarked with his train, taking Philip Sidney with him, and arrived at Flushing in January 1586.

Hardly had he done so, when the States, thinking that a titular head would make easier the complicated task of unifying their separate, conflicting forces, and determined somehow to force the Queen of England to throw the whole weight of her alliance into their scale, offered the position which she had refused to Leicester. Inconceivable as it would appear that a man who understood Elizabeth's position, and had had a warning of this very possibility before he left, should have accepted the offer, there was one thing yet more impossible: that the son of Northumberland should refuse it. Leicester was created Governor-General of the United Provinces, and the letter in which he announced the fact to Elizabeth, with an explanation of his motives, did not reach her until she had already learned the fact itself.

She had been ailing, languishing, scarcely able to relinquish him when he left, but this news restored her to all her powers. She wrote a letter which she despatched by Sir Thomas Heneage: "How contemptuously we conceive ourselves to have been used by you, you shall by the bearer understand. . . . We could never have imagined . . . that a man raised up by ourself, and extraordinarily favoured by us above any other subject of this land, would in so contemptuous a sort have broken our commandment." The description of the ceremonial festivities that had marked Leicester's inauguration had reached her, and with her unerring instinct for the effective, she announced that on the very spot where he had received the office, there, in the eyes of all, he must resign it. But Heneage, as well as others in the Netherlands and at home, could see that however ill-judged Leicester's acceptance might have been, such a public humiliation would be disastrous. He advised a temporizing course, and this drew him one of the Queen's letters for himself:

"Jesus! What availeth wit when it fails the owner at greatest need? Do that you are bidden and leave your considerations to your own affairs: for in some things you had clear commandment, which you did not, and in others, none, and did . . . I am assured of your dutiful thought but I am utterly at squares with this childish dealing."[1]

Her anger was fanned by Lady Leicester's doings. The latter resented strongly being forced to keep in the background; here, she thought, was a superb opportunity to assert and display herself, and the Queen, already justly angry with Leicester, heard that his wife

---

[1] Harrison, *Letters of Queen Elizabeth*.

was about to join him in the Netherlands "with such a train of ladies and gentlewomen, and such rich coaches, litters and side-saddles as her Majesty had none such, and that there should be a court of ladies as should far pass her Majesty's court here".[1]

This project was decisively quashed; but Burleigh and Walsingham made the strongest protests against Elizabeth's order to cancel the Governor-Generalship. They were in entire agreement with her as to the striking effect her plan would produce; and Burleigh said the results would be so catastrophic that if she persisted in it, he must resign from the government. This powerful remonstrance and touching letters from Leicester, full of contrition and remorse, saying all he now hoped for was to be employed in the Queen's stables, "to rub her horses' heels", and above all the fact that his behaviour had not had the dire results which might have been expected from it, led the Queen at last to concede that he might retain his honours. The passion of anger against him was succeeded, as always, by a relenting tenderness. No one could have supposed, from her letter of the following July, that such a cause of unkindness had arisen six months before:

"Rob: I am afraid you will suppose by my wandering writing a midsummer moon hath taken large possession of my brains this month but you must needs take things as they come in my head...."[2]

Money had been sent with him, £20,000 to pay the soldiers' wages, but the usual peculation among the paymasters was rife and the men were on the verge of starving: "It frets me not a little that the poor soldiers that hourly venture life, should want their due, that well deserve rather reward. Look in whom the fault be proved, let them smart therefor . . . though you know my old wont, that love not to discharge from office without desert, God forbid . . . now will I end, that do imagine I talk still with you and therefor loath to say farewell, OO. [Here she drew the sign of Eyes, Leicester's nickname] . . . with my millions and legions of thanks for all your pains and cares.

"As you know—Ever the Same. E. R."

The campaign was a hopeless maze of administrative difficulties, and its only decided action was Leicester's attempt to take Zutphen, in which Philip Sidney was wounded in the thigh and carried off the field, with immortal words on his lips. His wife, Walsingham's beautiful daughter, came out to nurse him, but he died of blood-poisoning three weeks later. The shock and the woe felt at the

[1] Sidney Papers.   [2] Harrison, *op. cit*.

untimely death of a hero and a poet echoes still in memorial verse. The present year, however, was to bring a crisis that overshadowed every other happening.

The Queen of Scots had been in close communication with Elizabeth's enemies for the past seventeen years; she had encouraged all their plans for invasion of England and used her money to pay their agents. From her point of view she was eminently justified in doing so, but the disclosures of Throckmorton determined the English government that she must not be allowed to do it any longer. She was removed to Tutbury Castle once more, this time under the guardianship of Sir Amyas Paulet, loyal, puritanical, and so efficient, that when told by the Privy Council that he must prevent Mary or any of her servants from communicating with the outside world except through him, all private communication to and from the prisoner was completely checked.

But in 1586 Walsingham was extremely anxious to have an insight into Philip's intentions towards England, for these must guide English policy in the Netherlands, and it was inconvenient that the Queen of Scots should be *incommunicado*. Walsingham therefore got Elizabeth's consent to an arrangement, but he confided it to none of the Council, not even to Burleigh. Mary and her household were removed to Chartley (their baggage, books and apparel requiring the transport of 80 carts, to Paulet's annoyance and disgust), and there Mary was betrayed by Walsingham's spy, Giffard, into resuming her secret correspondence through a medium Walsingham had devised. Her letters were sent out in a beer-barrel, and the answers sent in to her in the same way. The brewer was in her pay but also in Walsingham's, and every letter that went to or from Chartley was deciphered by Walsingham's expert, Phillips, and then forwarded to its destination. Walsingham, having set up this elaborate machinery, now watched Mary's intrigues developing. He wanted to know if a Spanish invasion was toward, and he waited for something of consequence to come into his net. Elizabeth waited too.

Mary had been established at Chartley in December 1585, and from that hour, Elizabeth had been in expectation of some deadly peril. She had once promised Cecil she "would not fail to keep taciturnity" in anything that required it, and she kept it now, but the tax on her nerves showed itself in a series of unmistakable signs.

In February it was reported at the French Court that the English Queen had fainted and remained unconscious for two hours. In

March, Mendoza received another report from England. Greenwich Palace stood very close to the margin of the Thames, where it makes its serpentine course through the downs: so close that those on board ship making for the Thames estuary could see people at the Palace windows. A Scots shipmaster, firing a salute as he passed them, was summoned in to an audience with the Queen. He had just come from Spain and he told her of the naval preparations he had seen there, of 27 galleons at Lisbon, "not ships, but floating fortresses". Some told him these were destined for Rochelle, some for Flanders and some that they were for England. Walsingham was with the Queen; she said three or four words to him at a distance the seaman could not catch; then he saw her take her slipper and fling it in Walsingham's face.

The crisis was not long delayed. In May there appeared under Walsingham's eye the last and most formidable of the plots for the Queen's assassination. It had originated with Ballard, a Jesuit, and was concerted with Morgan, the Queen of Scots' agent in Paris who managed the payments to her of her dowry. It was discussed there with Mendoza, who told Philip it was the most hopeful of the plots yet undertaken because it was based on the murder of Elizabeth, without which it was now assumed that nothing of the sort could be expected to succeed. Morgan had drawn into it the rich young Catholic, Antony Babington, who had long cherished a romantic devotion to the Queen of Scots; and Morgan, Ballard, Babington and Mary herself were all duped by Giffard, the renegade Catholic spy, a sinister youth with an abnormal look of innocence. Babington had chosen six of what he called "noble gentlemen", all in positions about the Court, who were only waiting the appropriate moment to shoot or stab Elizabeth, and in June, Morgan wrote to Mary's secretary Curle, saying: "There be many means in hand to remove the beast that troubles all the world."[1]

Every word was noted by Walsingham before it reached Chartley: and in the last week in June, Mendoza's agent reported a strange thing of Queen Elizabeth. She was going to Chapel, in full magnificence, when suddenly she was "overcome by a shock of fear". The pang was so severe, she could not recover herself, but at once returned to her apartments, "greatly to the wonder of those present".

Mary meanwhile had heard that England and Scotland had signed a treaty, in which she herself was not once mentioned. In her rage

[1] Mignet, *op. cit.*

and indignation she determined that her heretical son must never become King of England, and she informed Mendoza that she was bequeathing the English crown to the King of Spain.

She might, however, first wear it herself. A letter to her from Babington of July 12 outlined, in an almost final form, the plans for her release and for her ascending the throne. A harbour must be chosen for the landing of the Spanish troops Parma was expected to send, Babington himself would undertake to rescue her from her gaolers, and then he mentioned the third, essential point: "the usurping competitor" must be "despatched". Six noble gentlemen, he said, were ready to undertake "that tragical execution".

Elizabeth sometimes gave the impression that she was insensible to fear, but she was not; she was terrified now, but she held on. In many respects she treated Walsingham badly, but in the supreme effort of his career, she supported him at the imminent risk of her life. Babington and some of the conspirators could be seized on the strength of the letter: but the letter had not yet been answered. On the answer to the letter would depend the greatest catch of all. As Phillips wrote to Walsingham: "We attend her very heart at the next." Mary's reply was written on July 19, a long, detailed, capable comment on the plans for her rescue, cautioning and encouraging, telling Babington to find out from Mendoza just when the Spanish help might be expected. Then, she wrote: "When all is ready, the six gentlemen must be set to work, and you will provide that on their design being accomplished, I may be myself rescued from this place." This letter contained almost everything Walsingham wanted, but before he sent it on, he forged a postscript which was added to the cipher, asking for the names of the six gentlemen.[1]

Babington was not at Lichfield, where he was expected to receive the letter, and the latter was eleven days in reaching him. During this time the Queen came very close to death. The six had been chosen because they had means of coming into her presence, and could, as Ballard had said, stab or shoot her as she sat on her daïs, or went to chapel, or walked in the garden, for it was well known that she went about unguarded. Babington, in the height of elation, had had a picture painted of himself and his six accomplices; someone, possibly Giffard, had got possession of the picture long enough to show it to the Queen and, it seemed, only just in time. She was walking in Richmond Park with her ladies and a few gentlemen, of

[1] Conyers Read, *Mr. Secretary Walsingham and the Policy of Queen Elizabeth.*

whom Hatton was one, when, on the outskirts of the group, she saw Barnwell, an Irishman whose portrait was among the six. She gave him a long, penetrating stare, and as he slunk away, he heard her say to Sir Christopher Hatton, "Am I not well guarded today, with no man near me who wears a sword at his side?" Barnwell repeated this in his trial, and Hatton, who was one of the commissioners, told him grimly that had anyone else recognized him he would not have got away as he did.

Walsingham began the rounding up of the conspirators by arresting Ballard in August, on the ostensible ground that he was a disguised seminary priest; the rest took fright and fled, precipitating their arrest. Fourteen in all were taken up, as concerned with the proposed murder of the Queen, but these arrests were less important than the final bringing home to the Queen of Scots of being an accessory to the deed. Under pretence of a hunting expedition she was conducted from Chartley to Sir Walter Aston's park at Tixall; here she was arrested in the Queen's name and detained while her rooms at Chartley were searched, and her papers, her letters from the Catholics abroad, the lists of those whom she relied upon to support her at home, and the keys to sixty different ciphers were collected, sealed and sent to London. The list of the English nobles who had tendered their allegiance to Mary as their future sovereign was shown to Elizabeth. She read the names and then burnt the list, remarking: "Video taceoque"—"I see, and I say nothing."

The trials of Ballard, Babington and their twelve confederates resulted inevitably in the verdict of hanging and quartering, the sentence for treason. The horrors of semi-strangulation and of being split open alive for the heart and intestines to be wrenched out were regarded, like those of being burned to death, as awful but in the accepted order of things. The severity of the sentence depended on whether the victim were, as it enjoined, cut down alive or allowed to remain hanging till he was dead so that the butcher's work was performed on a corpse.

Elizabeth had endured the submerged menace of assassination for fourteen years, since Ridolfi's attempt had failed. The anger she had felt at the Rising in the North was renewed, and in fiercer form, for her reign had conferred more benefits on the country in the meantime and the ingratitude was blacker, while mounting rage against Mary Stuart's attempts to unseat her, and the severe fright of knowing herself exposed to hourly risk of murder during the last four months, risks which the confessions of the conspirators revealed to have been even greater than she knew, had lashed her into a state of savage fury. She exclaimed to Burleigh she thought that hanging and quartering was not terrible enough; something worse should be thought of, that the populace might see and take a lesson from the just vengeance on traitors. Burleigh wrote telling Hatton what she had said, and giving his own reply. First, he explained to her that to alter the penalty would be illegal; and secondly, there was no need to find anything worse, "if the executioner took care to protract the extremity of their pains in the sight of the multitude". The victims were despatched in batches of seven on succeeding days, Babington among the first. On him and his fellows the sentence was exactly carried out; but before the second day's work, Elizabeth had undergone a revulsion of feeling. "The Queen," said Camden, "hated the first day's cruelty when she heard it," and the second batch of victims were allowed to hang till they were dead.

The hundreds of letters removed from Chartley were deciphered, every translation being signed by Burleigh, Walsingham, Shrewsbury, Cobham and Knollys. The contents showed that Mary had been in correspondence over every plan to invade England or stir up domestic rebellion, over the last eighteen years; but only in Ridolfi's plot and Throckmorton's plot had it been capable of proof that she knew of the intended murder of Elizabeth and on both these affairs Elizabeth had refused to prosecute her. On the evidence of Babington's letter and Mary's reply, it was not possible to refuse any longer. As long as Mary could be left alone without Elizabeth's being in imminent danger of assassination, Elizabeth, against the advice of her councillors and the wishes of Parliament, would continue to leave her; but for the last six months Elizabeth had been in acute, almost hourly danger from Babington's noble gentlemen, and she wanted this danger removed, and the cause and inspiration of it to cease. The motive was there—the instinct for self-preservation of any living creature, and the next-strongest, the determination to keep her own crown; the evidence was there on which to do it, and the whole-hearted support of the Protestant part of the nation, to encourage her in the doing; but the men nearest to her knew what a struggle was ahead of them, before the thing should be done.

Mary was brought to Fotheringhay Castle in Northamptonshire, to stand her trial, and a commission of thirty-four, consisting of councillors, peers and judges, in accordance with the Act of Association, was convened, and set off, along bad roads in the unfavourable autumn weather. Burleigh and Walsingham were of course the two principal actors; Walsingham's under-secretary, Davison, remained with the Queen, who, whatever just cause for complaint she might give to the Lord Treasurer and the Principal Secretary, did not like being parted from both of them, especially as Leicester was abroad in the final phase of the Netherland campaign. Davison wrote to them on their arrival at Fotheringhay, saying he was especially commanded by her Majesty to tell them both "how greatly she doth long to hear how her Spirit and her Moor do find themselves after so foul and wearisome a journey".[1]

Mary's behaviour at the trial was what it had always been when she was called to account: emotional, dignified, full of self-justification and refusing to give a straight answer to a straight question. She was to be charged with being accessory to the attempted murder of Elizabeth; she herself declared that she was about to die in the cause of her religion, and wrote telling the Duc de Guise not to fear that she would fail in the supreme test.

She began by refusing to attend the trial unless it were understood that she did so, not as a criminal and not as one subject to English jurisdiction. This answer had been foreseen and a letter brought from Elizabeth, which was now given to her. It had been written in a burst of nervous fury: there was none of the elaboration or ambiguity that frequently characterized the Queen's letters; there was not even an opening: the letter merely said: "You have in various ways and manners attempted to take my life and to bring my kingdom to destruction by bloodshed. . . . These treasons will be proved to you and all made manifest. It is my will that you answer the nobles and peers of the kingdom as if I were myself present. . . . Act plainly without reserve and you will the sooner be able to obtain favour of me. Elizabeth."[2]

Actually, nothing was going to prevent Mary from appearing before the commissioners; it was an opportunity of a sort for which she had longed ever since she came into England; she had frequently demanded to be heard by Parliament. She felt her powers called for some such occasion, and as a display of personal courage, energy and virtuosity her performance over the two days was arresting; the one effect it did not achieve was that of truth. The state trials of the sixteenth century were little more than a public explanation of a verdict which had been already decided on, but the evidence against Mary was brought out and her method of dealing with it was to make

---

[1] Nicolas, *Life of Davison*.   [2] Mignet, *op. cit.*

denials that contradicted themselves, and then to withdraw to the position that it was impious for ordinary mortals to challenge the word of a Queen. The confessions of Ballard, Savage and Babington were produced, and the depositions of her secretaries who had written her reply to Babington from a minute dictated by her and ciphered it in her presence. She declared she knew nothing of Babington, she had never spoken to him, never heard from him, never written to him. When it was proved to her that she and Babington had been in correspondence for two years, she said she had written some letters to him but not the incriminating one.[1] If her secretaries said she had, they lied, and she demanded to be believed "on the word of a Princess". She admitted that she had used every means she could to bring about her own rescue, but every piece of evidence connecting her with the plan of the Queen's assassination she met with a flat repudiation. Everyone else was lying, it seemed; she only had the right to be believed. She did not speak to the point but she spoke with flaming eloquence. She accused Burleigh of being her adversary. He replied: "I am the adversary of the adversaries of Queen Elizabeth."

After two days' hearing, Elizabeth, from whom Fotheringhay was separated by many slow leagues, ordered the commission to return and finish their process in the Court of Star Chamber. The verdict was a foregone conclusion; it pronounced the Queen of Scots guilty of being privy to conspiracy and of "imagining and compassing her Majesty's death".

At the end of October, Parliament reopened, but in view of the business to be discussed, the Queen was not present. A petition from both Houses "that just condemnation should be followed by just execution" was carried by a deputation to the Queen at Richmond. Sitting in her canopied chair, she made them a speech, vivid, familiar, confidential, on her past difficulties, her present shrinking from what they had come to urge:

"I protest . . . for mine own life, I would not touch her. Neither hath my care been so much bent how to prolong mine as how to preserve both, which I am right sorry is made so hard, yea, so impossible . . . I have not used over-sudden resolutions in matters that have touched me full near: you will say that with me, I think." Their care, their anxiety to preserve her, touched her deeply; she would try to be worthy of such subjects. "And as for your petition, your judgment I condemn not . . . but pray you to accept my

[1] Camden, *Annals.*

thankfulness, excuse my doubtfulness, and take in good part my answer—answerless."

But this would not do, and Burleigh now had all his faculties addressed to the last and hardest stage of the task. The Queen remained at Richmond and he came and went, lamenting the expense of time in journeying: "I am come home after daylight." At last he got her to consent that the sentence should be drawn up, should be engrossed, should be published. On December 4 the publication was greeted with wild enthusiasm; bells pealed, bonfires blazed, psalms were sung "in every street and lane in the City".[1] The death-warrant had been engrossed at the same time: a mere clerkly matter, that received no publicity; but until the Queen's signature had been written on it, the sentence could not be carried out.

The French Court had sent an ambassador, Belièvre, to protest against cutting off the head of a crowned Queen and a sister-in-law of French kings, and this formal remonstrance was based on a sound political consideration; since Mary had bequeathed the English Crown to Philip, at her death Philip would consider himself King of England and might come to take possession of his property. Elizabeth on the throne, and Mary a prisoner, appealed to the French as a preferable alternative. James, who now learned that his mother had left the English Crown away from him and had advised his being sent to Spain to be re-educated as a Catholic, was in a state of strong resentment. But the Scots' national pride was outraged at the idea of the Queen they had themselves rejected being put to death by the English, and under pressure of a temporary revival of feeling for her, James said his honour required that he should demand his mother's life. Let her, he said, be shut up in solitary confinement "in some firm manse"; her life was his only stipulation.

The diplomatic situation with France and Scotland required handling but it was not the real obstacle to the execution. On December 19 Mary had written a long letter to Elizabeth. It omitted any mention of the charge on which she had been convicted, merely saying that she had been unjustly condemned by those who had no jurisdiction over her, and that she had "a constant resolution to suffer death for upholding the obedience and authority of the apostolical Roman church". Perverse ingenuity could go no further, but the rest of the letter was a series of requests for her servants, the treatment her body should receive after death, and for her burial. It harrowed Elizabeth; she wept as she read it and Leicester reported to Walsingham

[1] Neale, *Elizabeth and her Parliaments*, II.

in some alarm: "There is a letter from the Scottish Queen, that hath wrought tears, but I trust shall do no further herein: albeit, the delay is too dangerous."

The delay was lengthening; a letter from Court to the Earl of Rutland said: "Her Majesty keepeth herself more privately than she was wont",[1] and in this privacy she sometimes sat speechless, and sometimes sighed and murmured to herself, "Strike, or be stricken, strike, or be stricken."[2]

By January the mounting impatience had found expression in an outbreak of false alarms. It was said the Queen of Scots had broken out of prison, that the City of London had been set on fire, that a Spanish army had landed at Milford Haven. The Court was at Greenwich, and on February 1, the Lord Admiral, Lord Howard of Effingham, came to the Queen. His father had been her great-uncle and protector, Lord William Howard, his wife was Kate Carey, one of her favourite cousins; from this privileged position Lord Howard spoke with severe plainness. The people would not tolerate much more of this suspense, he said; the public temper was becoming dangerous.

The Queen listened to him, as she had once listened to his father. She would sign the warrant, she said: let Davison bring it.

For six weeks Davison had been agog to hear these words, but at the actual moment they were uttered he was out walking in Greenwich Park. A summons brought him hurriedly indoors. He collected the papers he had by him for the Queen's signature, the warrant among them, and sent in his name by Mrs. Brooks, the lady-in-waiting. The Queen had him shown in at once.

Elizabeth said, the morning was so fine, had he been out? When Davison said he had, she asked if Lord Howard had told him to bring the warrant for the Queen of Scots' execution? Yes, said Davison. Elizabeth took it, read it through, then called for pen and ink and signed it. This done, she dropped it on the floor beside her. She asked him if he were not sorry to see it signed. Sorry for the necessity, Davison answered. The Queen smiled; then she asked what else he had brought her and signed the remaining documents. Davison stooped to take up the long-hoped-for prize, and the Queen told him to carry it to the Lord Chancellor for sealing but to get this done as secretly as might be; on his way, she said, he had better call in at Walsingham's house; the latter was ill, and the news, said the Queen with weird gaiety, would go near to kill him outright.

[1] H.M.C. Rutland.   [2] Camden.

Then in all seriousness she told Davison she had delayed so long, that people might not think her eager to put the Queen of Scots to death. Davison was bowing himself out, but Elizabeth had not finished. By the Bond of Association, its members had bound themselves "to prosecute to the death" anyone found guilty of attempting the Queen's life, and Elizabeth thought that of so much spontaneous zeal —they had been obliged to bring the signatures to Hampton Court in a trunk—a little might surely be found to do her a real service in the matter. It was not a question of whether Mary Stuart were to live or die: her death was decided. It was a question of *how* she was to die. Elizabeth had twice before said in Davison's presence that she felt some way should be found of relieving her of the hateful burden of dooming her rival to death. Called back on the threshold, he now heard himself asked whether Sir Amyas Paulet and his fellow commissioner Sir Drue Drury could not take the business upon themselves. The Queen commanded that he and Walsingham should write to Fotheringhay and sound them on the matter.

Davison assured her it would be a waste of time; nevertheless she would have it done.

Davison went off to Walsingham and told him the morning's doings, then he carried the warrant to the Chancellor to be passed under the Great Seal. On his return with it, he found Walsingham had written the letter to Sir Amyas Paulet. The reply was prompt and in the terms that had been foreseen. Paulet said his goods and his life were at her Majesty's disposal, but he would not "make so foul shipwreck of his conscience as to shed blood without law or warrant", and Sir Drue Drury agreed with him.

Next day the Queen asked Davison if the warrant had passed the Seal. He replied that it had. The Queen, it was clear, was not pleased with the answer. "What needeth that haste?" she said.

Her instructions the day before had not been, it was true, to get the warrant sealed "at once", but that had been their implication. Davison began to feel the creepings of alarm. As soon as he could get away he went to Hatton, and said he wanted the support of the Privy Council. Hatton agreed that he should have it and went with him to Burleigh. The Lord Treasurer heard everything that Davison had to say; then he summoned the other available members of the Privy Council: Walsingham, Leicester, Howard, Hunsdon, Knollys, Cobham and Derby. Burleigh said the Queen had done her part in signing the warrant: she was asking to be spared the painfulness to herself of the final move; he said that in his view they should now act for her. The ten decided that their numbers gave them sufficient protection. The warrant was directed to the Earls of Shrewsbury and Kent who were in the neighbourhood of Fotheringhay. Burleigh wrote letters to each of them and the Council's secretary, Beale, was sent to deliver these and to show the warrant.

Next morning, February 5, Burleigh was with the Queen when she called in Davison. Smiling, she told him she had dreamed the night before that the Queen of Scots was executed, and this had put her into such a passion with him, she could have done she knew not what. Davison made a slight reply but then asked her earnestly if she meant the warrant to be executed. "Yes, by God," she answered, she did mean it, but she thought it should have been managed so that the whole responsibility did not fall upon herself. This was the crucial moment. Neither Burleigh nor Davison said to her that the warrant was already on its way to Northamptonshire. Davison declared afterwards that every word the Queen had uttered made him believe she knew it.[1]

On February 8, in the great hall of Fotheringhay, the awful deed was carried out. The power of Mary's personality over the minds of those who saw her was maintained to the last hour. The official reporter described her as "tall, round-shouldered, corpulent, her face fat and broad"; but spellbound gazers were there who declared, her beauty was such, all men were astonished at it. The Stuarts did not know how to reign, but they knew how to die. Mary's behaviour at the block was worthy of the traditions of martyrdom, and in the dreadful act of cutting off her head, those whom she had attempted to betray and kill were in the instant transformed into sacrilegious criminals.

Elizabeth knew that it would be so. To put to death by judicial sentence a crowned Queen was something that appalled the world. The death in itself was nothing in comparison with the sentence. Henri III said it would have been better to have poisoned Mary or smothered her with a pillow, and Elizabeth had tried to procure the death by some such means. She had not been allowed to do so, and her councillors, Parliament and the Protestants of the nation had insisted on the Queen of Scots' execution as a common criminal. From childhood, Elizabeth had assented to and upheld the sacrosanct nature of royalty. To be forced now to act as if she did not believe in it was to be made alien from her very self. But though the rational objections were most powerful, behind them was the fearful power of

[1] Nicolas, *Life of Davison.*

the irrational: cutting off the head of a Queen, a cousin, a woman, called up the spectre that had dominated her existence.

The prospect was intolerable—but it was inescapable. Her long, delicate-fingered, jewelled hand had drawn the elaborate signature, and she had let it go from her with a sarcastic word, an eerie smile, and no hint that the ordeal was threatening to unseat her reason.

Shrewsbury's son set off from Fotheringhay to announce the deed, rode all night and arrived at Greenwich on the morning of February 9. The Queen was just going out to ride, and did not see him. When she came back, bells were ringing all over London, a pealing that lasted twenty-four hours. The news could not be kept back. Elizabeth received it calmly, then, in her own rooms, burst into a passion of weeping such as she had never given way to in her life.[1] The following day she sent for Hatton, and told him that Davison had betrayed her. The day after that, a Saturday, she summoned the councillors, and raged furiously at them all, especially Burleigh and Davison. She declared that she had signed the warrant but had told Davison to keep it in his hands. She had not meant to have it executed then, perhaps never: they had stolen a march on her, they had wickedly encroached on her power, and made her an object of hatred and calumny to the world.

So much might perhaps have been expected, and the treatment of Davison followed a pattern that conformed to the expectation. He was tried in the Court of Star Chamber for having abused the Queen's confidence, where, with weeping, he begged the commissioners not to ask him to say too much, and was committed to the Tower, deprived of his office and ordered to pay a fine of 10,000 marks. His conditions of imprisonment were exceptionally favourable, he was released a year later, his fine was remitted and though he was not reinstated, his salary was paid to him for the rest of his life. Had this been all, it would have borne out the view that the Queen had used him in an elaborate deception for gaining her ends while appearing to reject the means. But this was not all.

Burleigh had been banished from the Queen's presence for two months, but he did not need to be at Court to understand what was going on. To his utter dismay he heard that the Queen had gained the opinion, as he said, "I know not how", that by an exercise of her prerogative, she could, without trial, have Davison hanged.

Burleigh was not only forbidden to come to her; he could not have done so, for he was laid up by a fall from his horse; and in his

[1] MSS. Scotland, quoted by Froude.

state of helpless isolation, he heard that Elizabeth was seeking confirmation of this wild and shocking idea from the judges of the Queen's Bench. With unerring instinct she had laid her finger on the one who was going to agree with her. Mr. Justice Anderson, Burleigh heard, had told her that her prerogative was absolute, and the Queen was saying that Mr. Justice Anderson had given his opinion in her favour and that now she intended to hear what the other judges had to say. Burleigh was almost aghast. He wrote in cipher to an unnamed correspondent, urging him to warn the judges secretly to be very careful how they replied. He said: "I would be loth to live, to see a woman of such wisdom as she is, to be wrongly advised, for fear or other infirmity . . . with an opinion gotten from the judges that her prerogative is above her law."[1]

The Queen's attempt came to nothing, but it showed that at one point her proceedings against Davison were no mere feint to conciliate the Scots and the French. She was acting on the conviction that Davison had betrayed her. Any review of the facts made such a conviction impossible: but an explanation of her attitude is supplied by the clinical description of hysteria. Hysterical phenomena, it is said, are the outcome of emotional distress, and of faulty reaction to situations of exceptionally exacting or distressing character. The patient either falls ill—or, disowns the memory of these situations.

Burleigh's letters until he was recalled to his proper sphere were couched in terms of conventional abasement, but they were still the writings of a man of sense, who had been deeply wounded. "To utter anything like a counsellor, as I was wont to do, I find myself debarred by your Majesty's displeasure." He could only, as one who loved her, "pray Almighty God to deliver your person, as He hath hitherto done, rather by miracle than ordinary means".

Her young cousin Robert Carey said: "I never saw her fetch a sigh, but when the Queen of Scots was beheaded."

A song was sung set by Byrd to a strange and frightening air:

> The noble famous Queen
> Who lost her head of late
> Doth show that kings as well as clowns
> Are bound to Fortune's fate,
> And that no earthly Prince
> Can so secure his crown
> But Fortune with her whirling wheel
> Hath power to pull them down.

[1] Neale, *Elizabeth and her Parliaments*, II.

XXV

Rejoice unto the Lord with mirth
Which us, from foreign fears
Preserved hath in quiet state
These eight and twenty years!

THE WORDS, IN Byrd's setting, poured out the thankfulness of those whom the Lord had kept in peace "through His handmaid Elizabeth". But the next year, in 1587, it was plain that the Spanish invasion was coming at last.

Philip had not moved while Mary Stuart was alive and an expensive and perilous enterprise would result merely in putting the English crown on somebody else's head. But now the crown was his own, he thought. Mary had bequeathed it to him and genealogists had traced out for him a hereditary claim through John of Gaunt. He meant to take possession of England and give it to one of his daughters.

Mary's execution had brought the great menace over the horizon, but it had done something else. An invasion to put the Queen of Scots on the throne would have had the sympathy, at least, of the English Catholics; an invasion to make England into a Spanish province was not going to meet with sympathy from the English of any denomination.

Nevertheless Dr. Allen assured Philip that every honest Englishman longed to see a Spanish banner hoisted on the Tower,[1] and Philip himself believed that the English Catholics were only waiting to welcome him. His mind was fixed upon what was to take place on English ground. The Armada that was being assembled carried tiers of guns, but it was built primarily for the transport of troops with their horses and stores. The ships were to sail up the Channel to the Flemish coast and convoy Parma and his 17,000 troops in their barges across to the Thames estuary. The fighting would be done on land; the expedition was to be, essentially, not naval but military.

Its setting out was delayed for a year because in April 1587 Drake made a lightning raid, burning the shipping in the harbours of Cadiz and Corunna. The bulk of the Spanish navy was lying in the mouth of

[1] MSS. Simancas, quoted by Froude.

the Tagus, but Drake was stopped in his design of burning these also by a pinnace which brought him a message from the Queen. She was still trying to make a treaty with Parma in the Netherlands. Drake came home disappointed but bringing with him the vast and richly loaded *San Philip*, one of the largest of the treasure-ships ever to fall into English hands.

In spite of Walsingham's efforts to convince her that the task was hopeless and a waste of valuable time, Elizabeth, alone, kept the stubborn hope that war might be avoided by negotiation; the government meanwhile prepared as for a certainty. Plans to contend with a landing army were made, for barricading roads and destroying bridges, and a chain of beacons was set up whose lights would summon the contingents of the militia to their posts.

The City of London, when called upon for their contribution to defence, asked how many men and ships they were expected to provide. The Council told them, 5,000 men and fifteen ships. The aldermen asked for two days to consider, and then announced that they would provide 10,000 men and thirty ships. Lord Howard of Effingham, the Lord High Admiral, Drake the Vice-Admiral and Hawkins, Treasurer and Comptroller of the Navy, were all satisfied with the sea-worthy condition of the Queen's ships, thirty-four in number. Plymouth harbour was crowded and Hawkins had had four of the largest vessels riding in the Sound during "an extreme and continual storm" and they had felt it "no more than if they had ridden at Chatham". Howard wrote to Burleigh: "I do thank God that they be in the state that they be in; there is never a one of them knows what a leak means." Dr. Allen did not share the Lord Admiral's opinion; he told Philip the English Navy was so riddled with dry rot, not four ships in it were seaworthy.

Allen, who had been made a Cardinal, now addressed *An Admonition to the Nobility and People of England*. They must support the invasion, he told them, for it was a crusade to restore the Catholic religion, and to rid them of Queen Elizabeth, that monster of impiety and unchastity, who, he said, "cannot be tolerated without the eternal infamy of our whole country, the whole world deriding our effeminate dastardy, that have suffered such a creature almost thirty years together to reign over our bodies and souls". The explanation of these astonishing remarks was to be found at the foot of the *Admonition*: "From my lodging in the Palace of St. Peter, Rome." Allen's view of the English Queen, like his opinion of the English fleet, had been formed at a distance.

Elizabeth's unfounded optimism over the prospects of a peace treaty with Parma had a result that Walsingham and the naval commanders found both dangerous and infuriating. She had allowed the whole naval strength to be made ready in December, but only for six weeks, by which time she hoped to have concluded a peace. She had had no experience of a full-scale war and of the methods it demanded, but her experience of the incompetence and the flagrant peculation during the campaign in the Netherlands had so alarmed and angered her that she determined not to see the like again. Instead of giving plenary powers to Howard and Hawkins, as she might safely have done, she kept the administration of supplies in her own hands. She demanded explanations of every charge and she would only allow crews to be taken on and stores bought in for very short periods at a time. No one appeared to understand or really to care for the shocking outpourings of the Netherlands campaign, where she had found the Crown's treasury bleeding to death for lack of capable and honest supervision. She could not make them see the dangers of letting money drain away at so terrifying a rate; nor could Howard and Hawkins make her see the dangers of keeping her ships without their full complement of men, munitions and stores. "Sparing and war have no affinity together," said Howard. Such words only increased her agonized resistance, and in the end the English sailors did their work on short rations and fell back on powder captured from the enemy.

The land forces were divided into an army of 30,000 under Lord Hunsdon based on Windsor, whose task was to defend the Queen, and 16,000 who were to prevent an attack on London. These were to be encamped at Tilbury under Leicester.

Mid-July of 1588 was fraught with storms, its nights were moonlight. On July 19 at 3 p.m. watchers on the Lizard saw, at last, the great nightmare, rising above the horizon's rim and creeping over the sea towards them. "The Spanish Armada," said Camden, "built high like towers and castles, rallied into the form of a crescent whose horns were at least seven miles distant, coming slowly on, and though under full sail, yet as the winds laboured and the ocean sighed under the burden of it." The Spaniards anchored at nightfall outside Plymouth, and when the moon rose at 2 in the morning they saw that the English ships had come out behind them. The first engagement showed the amazing speed and power to turn of the low-built English ships; the Spaniards said they had never seen ships so handled or that flew so fast. When Lord Howard's flag-ship was rammed and brought to a standstill, surrounded by galleons who expected to make her their prey, the flag-ship's boats towed her head round and she then sailed out of their reach at such a pace, "though the swiftest ships in the Armada pursued her they seemed by comparison to be at anchor". Three engagements on the 23rd, 24th and 27th inflicted heavy damage on the Spanish Fleet, but by July 28 they had struggled up the Channel and were anchored in Calais roads not far from where Parma expected to embark. On the night of the 28th they were dislodged by fire-ships sent among them on a favouring wind, and the next day when they reassembled the fearful battle was fought off Gravelines. Sixty English were killed, but the slaughter of the close-packed Spanish soldiers under a fire they could not avoid or return was ghastly; as one ship heeled over, blood was seen pouring from its lee scuppers. The ships fled up the east coast of England and the pursuing English ships passed the bodies of the mules and horses the Spaniards had thrown into the sea. They made for the north of Scotland and on to the west coast of Ireland. Storms, wrecks and savage inhabitants continued the chain of their disasters and sufferings, and of 30,000 men embarked for England, less than 10,000 returned to Spain.

The news, however, of their spectacular destruction was delayed, and England was waiting for the landing of Parma's troops. Elizabeth had said that she intended to come down to the coast, but Leicester in a letter of great good sense replied: "I cannot, most dear Queen, consent to that." But, he said, her courage and resolution would be a heartening sight for the troops, and he thought that if he took Mr. Rich's house for her, a mile from Tilbury, that would be reasonably safe and from there she might visit the camp. "So far, but no further, can I consent to adventure your person."

Elizabeth had made Leicester Lieutenant General of the forces and she accepted his decision. She came with her train to Tilbury on August 8, bringing with her a beautiful horse, white with dappled grey hindquarters, that had been given to her by Burleigh's son Robert Cecil. On the 10th she was dining with Leicester in his tent when a post arrived. Its intelligence was in fact false but it was highly alarming; it announced that Parma had embarked all his forces and was even then crossing the Channel. The troops were warned of imminent action and Elizabeth said she would review them.

Allen had declared in his *Admonition* that the invasion was directed not against the nation but against the Queen, and it was now urged on her that she should not appear in the middle of an army without ample bodyguard, or a single shot might accomplish the purpose for which the whole invasion was designed. But Elizabeth knew that the effect she had in mind would be destroyed by any such accompaniment. A steel corselet was found for her to wear and a helmet with white plumes was given to a page to carry. Bareheaded, the Queen mounted the white horse. The Earl of Ormonde carried the sword of state before her, Leicester walked at the horse's bridle and the page with the helmet came behind. At a considerable distance the ladies and footmen followed. The Queen rode through the lines to a piece of rising ground; there she dismounted and walked up and down the ranks, sometimes, said Camden, "like a woman, and anon with the countenance and pace of a soldier". She and the army believed that the terrible forces were within a few hours of the English coast. "Her presence and her words," Camden said, "fortified the courage of the captains and soldiers beyond all belief." Her message for them was written down and read out by the officers. It said that she had come to live or die amongst them: "I know I have the body of a weak feeble woman but I have the heart and stomach of a king, and a king of England too, and think foul scorn that Parma or Spain or any prince in Europe should dare to invade the borders of my realm." The men who heard it told each other that they would die for her.

The news came in at last of the tremendous victory and of the enemy's flight into the North Sea; but the burst of rejoicing and relief did not cause the Queen a moment's relaxation from care. The expenses, she declared, must be stopped instantly: she allowed no margin to carry over from a state of war to a return to peace. Howard, Hawkins and Drake were faced with an epidemic of dysentery among their crews, who were carried on shore to die in the streets of Margate for lack of anywhere to receive them, and rather than spend time explaining to the Queen what was needed, they supplied wine, arrowroot and other comforts for the sick out of their own money.

Walsingham was told by one of his agents: "Nothing so much displeased the King of Spain as the loyalty of the Catholics to their Queen during the late enterprise." The most striking evidence of this loyalty was found in the English fleet itself, for Lord Howard of Effingham was a Catholic; but another sign was seen in an altogether unexpected place. When the news of the English victory was heard in the Jesuit College at Rome, some of the young English students burst out cheering.[1]

Leicester had been competent to discharge the duties of Lieutenant General at Tilbury; his care and affection for Elizabeth had been

[1] Meadows, *Elizabethan Quintet.*

thoroughly proved, and the sense of having emerged with him from a mortal crisis had renewed all her old tenderness. She proposed to create him Lieutenant General of England and Ireland. This newly-invented appointment would carry with it such enormous powers that even left to herself, Elizabeth might, in the end, never have ratified it. As it was it met with strong resistance. Hatton had been made Lord Chancellor the previous year, and the Lord Chancellor and the Lord Treasurer both besought the Queen not to place such powers in the hands of a subject.

Leicester was consumed with anger and bitterness, but to a bystander the great Earl appeared to enjoy almost kingly powers already. An agent reported to Mendoza that in the period of festivities and tournaments after the victory, he had seen Leicester going from Wanstead to St. James, riding alone in his coach, accompanied as if he were a king by his household and a troop of light horse. "The last time I saw him," said the agent, "was at the Earl of Essex's review, at a window with the Queen."

It was said, in these brief, halcyon weeks, that Leicester dined with the Queen, a thing hitherto unheard of.[1] He was suffering from a low fever, caught perhaps on the Essex marshes; Elizabeth also was ailing; they discussed each other's symptoms and Elizabeth recommended him a specific. At the end of August he decided to try Buxton waters; on his journey, via Kenilworth, he put up at Ricote, where Elizabeth had stopped on her way to imprisonment at Woodstock and where she and Leicester had afterwards been entertained in delightful house-parties by Sir Henry and Lady Norris. From here he wrote to Elizabeth "to know how my gracious lady doth"; he himself was much better for her medicine, which, he said, had done him more good "than any other thing that hath been given me". It was signed "from your old lodging at Ricote, this Thursday morning ready to take my journey".

He came as far as Cornbury, and there his sickness, which the times could neither diagnose nor cure, overcame him, and on September 4 he died, in the fifty-fifth year of his age. He had made his will, in the form of a letter addressed to his wife, and by it he left Elizabeth a pendant of a great diamond set in emeralds, on a rope of 600 "fair white pearls".[2]

It was Elizabeth's habit to withdraw into herself in grief, and she did so now; but the loss was so severe, her reaction to it was alarming. She shut herself up, and allowed no one to come in for so long, that at

[1] C.S.P. Spanish, 1588.   [2] Nichols, *Progresses*.

last Burleigh took control; he ordered the door to be broken open.[1]

When Henzner visited Whitehall Palace he said that in the Queen's bed-chamber, beside her bed, was a casket, ornamented all over with pearls, in which she put the earrings and bracelets she was wearing, and "other things of especial value". After her death, there was found in this casket Leicester's letter from Ricote, and on the outside of it, written in Elizabeth's hand: "His last letter."

The Queen collected herself. The grimness of her loss did not alter her nature or throw any fictitious colouring over matters of plain fact. The Earl had died considerably indebted to the Treasury and she ordered his goods to be distrained on for the repayment of the sum. The dead could feel this no injury or unkindness, and if it were disagreeable to the widow, that could not be helped. In any case, Elizabeth's grief was not shared by the Countess. Before Leicester's death, the latter had tormented him by jealousy of Sir Charles Blount, whom she now married without wasting time over formal mourning.

The tremendous act of national thanksgiving for deliverance was performed on November 24, in a state procession from Somerset House to a service at St. Paul's. A Spanish agent had noted at the beginning of the month: "The Queen is much aged and spent and very melancholy. Her intimates say this is caused by the death of the Earl of Leicester." He preferred to think "It was the fear she underwent and the burden she has on her". But for one day the great surge of national emotion carried all before it. The procession was headed by palace officials, aldermen and judges; the Lancaster, York, Somerset and Richmond Heralds introduced the Dukes, Marquesses, Earls and Viscounts; behind these began the supremely exciting part of the spectacle: the Lord Treasurer of England, the Lord Chancellor of England, the Archbishops, the French Ambassador, the Mayor of London, then the Sword of State, the Serjeants-at-Arms, the Gentlemen Pensioners, and then "Her Majesty in her coach". This was a chariot, open on all sides, and the canopy was a gilded crown.

Drawn up Fleet Street and Ludgate Hill, the Queen arrived at the west door of the Cathedral. When she stepped inside she knelt in the aisle and prayed silently. Then the procession re-formed and she was led to her seat in the choir, the Litany chanted before her.[2]

The danger had receded; it was respite, for the time being. The national mind was charged with vigour and confidence; the poets

[1] C.S.P. Spanish, 1588.   [2] Nichols, *Progresses.*

echoed it, and the sea itself was viewed as joining in the nation's triumph:

"*And every billow bounds as if to quench the stars.*"

On New Year's Day, Hatton's present to the Queen of the Sea was a superb necklace of golden scallop-shells, gemmed with pearls, diamonds and rubies.[1]

[1] Nichols, *Progresses.*

XXVI

ONE DECEMBER EVENING after the victory, it being "about five
and very dark", a young man near the Strand heard the cry: "If you
will see the Queen you must come quickly." He ran with the crowd
into the courtyard of Somerset House and there they waited more
than an hour in a blaze of torchlight. At last the Queen came out in
great state, and at their shouts, said Goodman, "she turned to us and
said: 'God bless you all, my good people.' And as they cried once
again: 'God save your Majesty!', the Queen said: 'Ye may well have
a greater Prince but ye shall never have a more loving Prince'." The
rite between the people and herself was performed. "And so the
Queen and the crowd there, looked upon one another a while, her
Majesty departed." The crowd dispersed, and "All the way long,"
Goodman said, "they did nothing but talk of what a great Queen she
was and how they would die for her."[1]

But the defeat was not a final release from peril: it was a victory in
one more round. The joy, the triumph, the relief, had done nothing
for the Queen's nerves and temper. In the month of the public thanksgiving Burleigh wrote to Walsingham: "All irresolutions and lacks
are thrown upon us two in all her speeches to everybody. The wrong
is intolerable." It was, but it was ephemeral; it did not alter the
estimate, the affection of a lifetime. Burleigh left his considered
opinion on record: "She was so expert in the knowledge of her realm
and estate as no counsellor she had could tell her what she knew not
before"; and "when her counsellors had said all they could say, she
would then frame out a wise counsel beyond them".

The spectacular event, the climax of so many years, seemed to break
up a long-standing order and to inaugurate widespread changes. The
dramatis personae were altering. Walsingham was to die in 1590,
Hatton in 1591, and though Burleigh himself, "the Atlas of the
Commonwealth", supported his vast load till 1598, men who had
made their mark before 1588 now assumed the positions of those who
had brought Elizabeth so far, although the newer generation never
replaced the old.

The early 1580's had seen the emergence of the new group. Oxford,

[1] Goodman, *Court of James I.*

after an audience at Greenwich in which many bitter things had been said, was at last and altogether reconciled to the Queen, and the matter was helped on by Walter Ralegh. This dark, arrogant, brilliant man, so versatile that Fuller did not know whether to catalogue him as "statesman, seaman, soldier, learned writer or what you will", had served in Ireland under Lord Grey de Wilton, and being sent over with despatches, gained the attention of the Privy Council by explaining to them the incompetence of his senior officers. The opening he took was characteristic and so was its success. "He had gotten the ear of the Queen in a trice, who loved to hear his reasons to her demands." Elizabeth was struck by his virility, his charm and his acute intelligence; they formed the combination she found irresistible. In the esoteric circle of Royal nick-names, Ralegh was Water. Hatton, jealous as ever, sent the Queen by Heneage a gold bodkin and a gold charm made like a little bucket, with a letter saying he knew she would need the latter—Water was sure to be near her. The Queen tried to stick the bodkin in her hair but she was on horseback, so she gave the whole packet back to Heneage to hold for her till they came to a standstill. Then she sent Hatton a message, saying she had so well-bounded her banks, Water should never overflow them, and as he knew she was a shepherd, he might know how dear her Sheep was to her.

It was soon Ralegh's turn to be jealous, not, like Hatton, from wounded affection, but with the furious, egotistical jealousy of a greedy, ambitious man who finds another sharing his advantages. Leicester had seen that the engrossing attraction Elizabeth felt for the young man as a cavalier could not be weakened by himself or Hatton, beloved and valued as they were; but his stepson, the twenty-year-old Robert Devereux, who had been Earl of Essex since he was nine years old, would be a formidable rival to Ralegh. So it proved. Elizabeth, who had known him since he was a child, now found him presented to her as a courtier. The youth entirely charmed her. He was tall, powerful, with a stooping gait, a striding walk and carrying his head thrust forward. With his mother's auburn hair and black eyes he had inherited her vanity and her powerful egotism, but with these went the honesty that had been his father's. "He always carried on his brow either love or hatred and did not understand concealment"; he was "a great resenter", and though he was Leicester's protégé, he was "no good pupil to my Lord of Leicester, who was wont to put all his passion in his pocket".[1]

[1] Lloyd, *State Worthies*.

It was a character to attract, enchant, absorb, until its flaws and weaknesses, its violent, irrational bad temper had torn down the structure of an intercourse and laid it to waste.

When Essex's influence began, he was twenty-one and Elizabeth was fifty-four, but any affection that she felt for an attractive man was romantic affection and no response gratified her unless it were in the romantic idiom. To have the entrée that countless other men would have given anything to gain, to have the intimate companionship of this legendary being of such talent, singularity and grandeur, and to find her generous, high-spirited and endlessly kind to himself, all produced in the imaginative young man a heady attraction, and at first the charm was mutual. In the summer of 1587, it was said: "When she is abroad, nobody near her but my Lord of Essex, and at night my Lord is at cards or one game or another with her, that he cometh not to his own lodging till the birds sing in the morning."[1]

When the figures changed, the mood changed also. The tone among the men of Elizabeth's last circle was one of clamorous self-assertion, varied by a passionate sense of ill-usage, amounting to stark tragedy, if their material ambitions were postponed or thwarted. This was notably so in Ralegh and Essex, and more discreetly expressed it was found in the third faction, the two sons of the late Lord Keeper, Antony and Francis Bacon. One was exceedingly able and the other a genius, but their uncle by marriage, Lord Burleigh, did not advance them. The Lord Treasurer wanted to keep all his benefits for his son Robert Cecil, clever, dearly loved of his father and a hunchback. The latter was eminently prudent and well-behaved; the rest eyed the Queen like famished hounds and snarled if she gave something to anybody else.

"When will you cease to be a beggar, Ralegh?" she once exclaimed. "When your Majesty ceases to be a benefactor," was the cheerful, shameless answer. The powerful courtiers who were patrons often, it was true, wanted favours for their dependants. Essex as a small boy had spent many years in Burleigh's house; he disliked the Lord Treasurer, and as he wanted the defeat of the Armada to be followed by a vigorous policy of aggression against Spain and Burleigh still supported one of pacific caution, Essex was able to regard the old man with contempt. The clever young Bacons attracted his attention; the astonishing ability of Francis drew out his admiration, their ill-usage at their uncle's hands aroused his Quixotism. He became their

[1] Bagot, *Memorials*.

patron and determined that the Queen should be made to do something for them.

The new men looked upon advancement as their right. The Queen was a generation older than themselves, they had not shared her dangers, her difficulties were hearsay to them. They were interested in her position rather than in her; and yet at times the two blended, and spontaneous, lyrical homage was given;

When she came in like starlight, thick with jewels.

Elizabeth's fame in Europe in the years after 1588, her exaltation, as to some supernatural sphere, her radiant splendour, her virginity, fitted her for the cult that developed in her later years, symbolizing her as Diana, as Cynthia, goddess of chastity and moonlight. Three years before Leicester's death, Oxford's secretary Lyly had produced the court play *Endymion*, which, in the legend of the adoring shepherd and the Moon, shadowed forth the loves of Leicester and the Queen, and the vacillations of Elizabeth's temperament were defended as the Moon's attributes: "O fair Cynthia, why do other men term thee inconstant? . . . There is nothing more admirable in the sea than ebbing and flowing, and shall the moon from whom the sea taketh this virtue, be accounted fickle for increasing and decreasing?"

Ralegh, in Ireland, had become Spenser's patron and friend, and from the Queen's nickname "Water" came strange poetic echoes. Spenser celebrated him as the Shepherd of the Sea in bondage to his mistress Cynthia, and when three years later Ralegh had been committed to the Tower, he wrote the long and poignant lament, "The Lady of the Sea, being the Ocean's love to Cynthia"; while George Chapman's Hymn to Cynthia from *The Shadow of Night*, in all the melancholy brightness of moonlight and the strangeness of a dream, shows Elizabeth at once as a political power in Europe and as the Queen of Night:

> *Then set thy crystal and imperial throne*
> *Girt in thy chaste and never-loosening zone*
> *'Gainst Europe's sun directly opposite*
> *And give him darkness that doth threat thy light.*

The Queen in her later years, by chance or having this role in mind, wore a great deal of white and silver. "All in white, sitting alone in her splendid coach, she looked like a goddess," said a foreign visitor.[1] The French Ambassador de Maisse noticed that her dresses were

---

[1] Klarwill, *Queen Elizabeth and some Foreigners.*

usually silver and white; cloth of silver slippers were in her wardrobe lists, and in 1589 LadyWalsingham's New Year gift was a little cloth of silver muff, fastened with seed-pearl buttons and lined with carnation plush. The charming fashion of jewellery mounted in white enamel belongs to these years, and in 1589, the Swedish Marchioness of Northampton gave the Queen white enamelled bracelets set with pearl daisies whose centres were rubies.

But the moon—radiant, remote, serene—was a symbol only in a far-fetched sense. The heat and burden of the day had never lessened, and having been borne for so long, they had produced an effect of hardened endurance. Burleigh said: "She knew all estates and dispositions of all Princes and parties,"[1] and now the dispositions were as complicated and dangerous as ever. In 1589 Henri III was assassinated, the Huguenot Henry of Navarre became Henri IV of France, and, immediately, the secret League between the Guises and Philip of Spain came into open force to prevent a Protestant from holding the French throne. Elizabeth at once concluded an alliance with Henri IV, and 4,000 English troops were sent to his assistance. The situation rapidly became extremely menacing; the Spaniards entered Brittany and it was understood that they would use it as a naval base from which to launch a second invasion of England. The Spanish threat was back again, nearer than before.

When Leicester died, the young Jesuit Robert Southwell had written: "I think now the Queen is freed from her slavery to this man she will adopt a milder policy towards us,"[2] and had she been left to herself Elizabeth would have fulfilled his hopes. But the Jesuits, unlike the English Catholics, were identified with Spain. Their order wished to see England forcibly re-converted by a Spanish invasion, and in 1594 Father Parsons produced a work in which he declared the English Crown should go to Philip's daughter, the Infanta Isabella. With a Spanish army based on Brittany and the Jesuits saying that the Infanta should have the English Crown, the inevitable result was an increase of severity against recusants and missionary priests.

The principle of hostility to the Jesuits was understandable but it was constantly operated, in all the horrors of breaking in and searching by pursuivants, the ensuing tortures and the final agonies of a traitor's death, against quiet and innocent Catholic families and priests whose sanctity and courage came from a supernatural source.

The unspeakable Richard Topcliffe and his victim Robert South-

[1] Nares, *Memoirs of Lord Burleigh.*   [2] Devlin, *Robert Southwell.*

well epitomized the worst elements of the one side in conflict with the best of the other. The whole process of hunting down priests and examining them under torture was quite outside the domain of the law courts; the pursuivants had no legal office and were merely appointed by the Privy Council. Before Southwell was caught he had written his *Supplication* to the Queen, which however was not published till some years after his death, telling her, for he said that she did not know, of the sufferings of recusants in Bridewell in the power of vicious and cruel jailers, and of the treatment of those priests from whom information was wanted about their harbourers: as a release from torture, their deaths, he said, were welcome to them, "even though as full of pangs as hanging, drawing and embowelling quick can make them". "Some are hanged by the hands 8 or 9 or 12 hours together, till not only their wits but even their senses fail them . . . some have been watched and kept without sleep till they were past the use of reason and then examined when they could scarcely give account of their own names . . . What insufferable agonies we have been put to on the rack, it is not possible to express, the feeling so far exceedeth speech."

The upholders of Protestantism and of Catholicism were as horrified by the tortures of their fellows as they were silent about those inflicted by themselves on their enemies. The agonies endured in the dungeons of the Spanish Inquisition, and methods of judicial execution in France in which the vile torments were prolonged over days, indicate the climate of the time and explain, though they do not excuse, the savage cruelty of the English government in the last decade of Elizabeth. The Queen had never objected to the use of torture and she did not object to it now; but a Nemesis was preparing for her in the encouragement she gave to Topcliffe. This man spoke with a brusque and hearty loyalty and with a caricature of the courtier's personal devotion, and he undertook to extract by torture the information that would make the Jesuits harmless. He boasted that he could inflict tortures worse than those of the Tower rack, and the Council allowed him to torture prisoners in his own house in Westminster. It was here that he inflicted the hanging by the hands or "torture against the wall" on Robert Southwell. At his subsequent trial for treason, Southwell made a simple declaration of Topcliffe's doings, and when the latter attempted a blustering defence, the Lord Chief Justice told him to hold his tongue. Southwell's declaration that he had come, not for the murdering of bodies but for the saving of souls, could not preserve him from the sentence of a traitor's death, but at his execution, a noble, who was thought to have been Lord Mountjoy, ordered the hangman to let him die before he was cut down.

The delight in physical cruelty shown by Topcliffe, combined with lewdness, appears to have been the result of a state of mind near to insanity. Acting as *agent provocateur* to another Jesuit, Father Pormort, he told Pormort that he had been allowed to put his hand into the Queen's bosom and that he had seen her above the knee. Pormort repeated this on trial, and Topcliffe's career of service to the state was tapered off.

That such a man should have been used by the Council and personally employed by the Queen was deplorable; but though time had not mitigated Elizabeth's hardness, neither had it worn out her wish to tolerate, even with a Spanish army on the opposite coast and Father Parsons publishing the claims of the Infanta. In the sickening struggle she rounded on the Council at last in anger and despair, and told them that if they wanted to convert Catholics to Protestantism, let them do it by the example of their lives, "for I", she cried, "will persecute no more as I have done".[1]

[1] C.S.P. Domestic, 1601.

XXVII

In 1593 ELIZABETH was sixty. The thirty-five years of the reign, so hard, so dangerous, so successful, had scarcely altered, they had intensified her character. The confidence of hard-won but great success had imparted a stability, her health had improved, her minor ailments were less frequent, and she no longer gave way to hysterical collapse. But her nervous irritability had become a standing condition; a vast experience of this harsh world had imparted a roughness to her impatience. Her high voice was now described as "loud and shrill";[1] she once spat on a courtier who had disgusted her, she slapped the Maids of Honour when they annoyed her beyond bearing.

But the wonderful qualities of her intellect were unabated also; she still found absorbing interest in presenting herself in clothes and jewels as a magical incarnation of sovereignty, and the assurance of the people's love was the deepest emotional satisfaction of her existence.

Her nose had slightly thickened, her eyes become sunken, and as she had lost several teeth on the left side of her mouth it was difficult for foreigners to catch her words when she spoke fast, but the impression she made in her last decade was one of astonishing energy for her years. She was erect and active as ever and though her face was wrinkled her skin preserved its flawless white. The wigs she wore were a darker red than her own hair and made by her silk-woman Dorothy Spekarde. In 1602 the latter was paid for "6 heads of hair, 12 yards of hair curl and 100 devices made of hair".[2]

Elizabeth had never had much appetite; she now ate less than ever; she mixed her wine with water for fear of its "clouding her faculties" and, in Bohun's words, she "was not subject to love of sleep". Her routine was a strenuous one. Often she was at work before daylight with her secretaries. All Orders in Council, all measures relating to public affairs were read over to her and she made notes on them, either in her own hand or dictating her comments to secretaries. If anything left her undecided she summoned the available councillors, made them discuss the point with each other and then formed her own opinion. Burleigh in a memorandum he made for Robert Cecil's

[1] Continuation of Stowe's Chronicle.
[2] Rye, *England as Seen by Foreigners*.

guidance warned him not to override the Queen's judgment. It could be done, but most would be gained by allowing her to make up her own mind. When she had done so, the value of her opinion would be unique.[1]

The Queen's frugal habits and hard work were thrown into contrast by her undying passion for visual splendour. Persian and Indian carpets spread their strange, unaccustomed beauties in her palaces, the counterpanes of her beds were of gold or silver cloth lined with ermine. Thomas Platter, admiring a box "all of glass, of great artistry" as he was shown round Greenwich, was told that her Majesty delighted in "strange and lovely curios".

The national vigour and self-confidence, rising to its peak, expressed itself in a proliferation of ornament and a flamboyancy of dress such as had never been conceived. Men's and women's clothes, and the latter especially, achieved an air of visionary strangeness by combining grotesque exaggeration with the utmost delicacy of tint. The female bodice was elongated till its point reached the fork, the skirt of wide circumference was hung on a plate-like frame encircling the hips, the sleeves swelled and rose nearly to the ears, and in addition to the small ruff a transparent muslin one stood like a nimbus behind the head. In the Ditchley portrait of 1592 Elizabeth's huge white silk dress is studded all over with aiglets of black onyx, coral and pearl; she stands on a map of England in white shoes, she wears three ropes of milky, translucent pearls and the fan she holds is tied to her waist by a coral-coloured ribbon. Her face is wasted like the waning moon's with eyes that look as if they never slept.

Her personal fastidiousness had not declined. In 1599 over £700 was paid for "fine linen for her Majesty's own person" and the fame of her toilet preparations had been carried by English merchants to the Middle East. The mother of the Turkish Sultan sent the English Queen a set of oriental robes, a ruby necklace and a diamond wreath, asking in return for some of the famous English woollen cloth and some of the Queen's "distilled waters for the face and scented oil for the hands".[2]

Elizabeth's sensitiveness to disagreeable smells was as keen as ever, and Robert Cecil, who did not want her to know the extent of his communication with James, was one day much beholden to it. He was riding with the Queen in her coach at Greenwich when the horn of the post from Scotland was heard on the green, and to the Secretary's dismay the Queen put her head out of the coach window and

[1] Rowse, *Queen Elizabeth and her Subjects.*
[2] Strickland, *Queen Elizabeth.*

said she would take the letters there and then. Obliged to think fast, Cecil said to her, should not the letters be opened and aired before she touched them, as they came out of a filthy budget and he knew how much she hated "all ill smells". She agreed that this would be best and the Secretary kept tight hold of the mail.

John Harington's liveliness amused his godmother but it sometimes got him into trouble. In 1597 he produced in three parts a satire on the times in the form of a discussion of the nastiness and indecorum of the privies in great houses. He called it *A Metamorphosis of Ajax*, punning on the word jakes. The Queen suffered from a primitive sanitary system as much as anyone but she objected to these disgusting inconveniences being commented on with humorous gusto. Besides it was said that one of Harington's veiled allusions attacked the Earl of Leicester. In such a context this was intolerable. She told him to go away and stay away—but then her mind reverted to something in his pages. In a welter of horrid descriptions and indelicate jokes he had introduced a plan with diagrams for a water-closet; by this means he said a privy could be kept sweet all the year. It was worth trying. The Queen had his device installed at Richmond and it was found to work. The delightful improvement "pacified her", Harington said, and she sent him "thanks for his invention". He returned cock-a-hoop and in no time at all a Latin epigram was going the rounds, addressed to the Maids of Honour on "their perfumed privy at Richmond". The Maids of Honour were girls in their teens whose influential relatives had gained for them this coveted post, in which they were expected to marry eligibly. The tradition of Elizabeth's morbid and spiteful jealousy towards other women's marriages rests on some instances which have indelibly coloured the whole picture. She was irritated by the spectacle of ardent courtship of another woman and if she were interested in a man she disliked him to get married, she had been offended when Essex married Walsingham's daughter, the widowed Lady Sidney: but she was responsible for the girls to their families, and any sovereign is expected to object to fornication among the Maids of Honour. Ralegh, Southampton and Pembroke were all imprisoned, not for marrying but for getting Maids of Honour with child. Ralegh and Southampton married the young women but Pembroke, while admitting paternity, repudiated Mary Fitton with brutal insolence.

> For if with one, with thousands thou'lt turn whore,
> Break ice in one place and it cracks the more.

His lordship's own verses explained the unfitness of such a lady to be Countess of Pembroke. It was the task of the Queen's Privy Council to explain it to the girl's father.

There were matches and weddings to which the Queen was charmingly kind; she promised to come to the wedding of Lord Burleigh's grand-daughter Elizabeth Vere with Lord Derby and said she would hope to see Burleigh among the dancers. Lame, old and near to death, Burleigh said he would "dance with his heart" to see the Queen do so much honour to her maid "for the old man's sake".

Henri IV had checkmated the League by declaring himself a Catholic, but this had not got the Spaniards out of France; they were now waging war to gain the French crown for Philip's daughter in right of her mother Elizabeth de Valois. The English supported the French King with men and money and when the Spanish guns at the capture of Calais could be heard at Greenwich, Elizabeth finally authorized the departure of the expedition to attack Spanish bases. The Cadiz expedition of 1596 was a brilliant success of which the chief honours went to Essex for his courage, initiative and his splendid chivalry. An expedition the following year to the Azores was a failure but the English alliance was of the utmost importance to Henri IV, and a series of distinguished Ambassadors kept him in close touch with the English Court. In December 1597 de Maisse was accredited to St. James' and his journal gives a vivid, arresting view of Elizabeth at the age of sixty-four.

He saw her first in a large chamber where a great fire was burning. She wore a dark red wig decorated with jewels and though her face looked old and her neck was wrinkled, her bosom was delicate and white and her figure still beautiful in its proportions. She wore a white taffeta gown lined with scarlet, ornamented with pearls and rubies. She was most gracious and very talkative. She complained of the heat of the fire and had it damped down, and she was perpetually twisting and untwisting the long hanging ends of her red-lined sleeves. De Maisse gazed intently at that face "où le génie, les soucis et les passions avaient laissé leur traces". The Queen's conversation when she got upon men and affairs held him spellbound, but on one occasion she startled him. At a private audience on December 15 he found her standing by a window in an Italian gown of black and gold; under it was a dress of white damask and under this a lawn chemise. These garments fastened in front and she held their edges in her hands, often as she spoke turning them back so that, he said, he could see her belly "even to the navel."[1] Her intellect was otherwise functioning with its usual acuteness and she held a conversation with him of two hours or more.

"*Be thou so chaste as ice, as pure as snow, thou shalt not escape calumny*", and this sort of lunatic impropriety, the nemesis of an unchecked propensity in the past, could not fail to breed calumnies of the gravest kind and most exaggerated degree.

De Maisse however showed a remarkable tolerance and sense of proportion in the face of this experience. The impression the Queen's conversation made on him was so profound it counted for more than her aberration. His verdict was: "She is a very great Princess who knows everything."

Such was the view of an experienced Ambassador but it was not shared by the Devereux family. Essex in 1597 was thirty-one, and for ten years his rise in the sphere of Court had been steady. On Leicester's death he was given the appointment, the first Leicester had ever received from Elizabeth and which he had never relinquished, that of Master of the Horse. He had had the military career open to a nobleman, he had fought under Leicester in the Low Countries, he had commanded the English contingent sent to help Henri IV. He was a Privy Councillor at twenty-seven, and though the value of his advice, like the value of his generalship, was uncertain, it was sense that he lacked rather than ability. He could not banish the Queen's other favourites but it was plain that her fondness for him was greater than she had shown for any other man, and the thirty-three years' difference in their ages was an advantage that gave him almost unlimited power over a woman who loved him; so at least it seemed to every onlooker except one—but that one was Francis Bacon.

It is often difficult for the young to assess the generation immediately behind them. Essex had been at first dazzled and grateful but all that he really understood of Elizabeth was that she had a passionate affection for himself and that he could sometimes by a mixture of vehemence and sulking persuade her to do something she did not want to do. This made him boast of "doing the Queen good against her will".

His tendency to underrate her was fatally encouraged by his mother, who was still not allowed to come to Court, and by his favourite sister Penelope. The latter had reacted with spirit against the tiresomeness of being married to Lord Rich and had formed a publicly accepted liaison with the discreet and elegant Lord Mount-

[1] Harrison, *Journal of De Maisse.*

joy. She had borne Rich seven children and was in process of bearing Mountjoy five more, but her radiance and ebullience were undimmed. She had been the adored of the celebrated Sidney, she was a beauty, a toast, the sister of the incomparable Essex. Her self-confidence was natural but, as it turned out, it was unfortunate. Burleigh's spies knew that she was corresponding with a member of the Douglas family at the Scots Court. The correspondence was carried on under assumed names, Penelope herself was Rialta, James was Victor, even Lord Rich was pressed into service here and figured as Ricardo, while Essex was "the Weary Knight". "Writing for her brother", the spy reported, she described him as "always exceeding weary and longing for the change".[1]

Since it was said that Essex could not dissemble it may be that his sister did him an injustice, and that some at least of what he professed for Elizabeth he actually felt and that when he wrote: "It is not in your power, great Queen as you are, to make me love you less", the words owed something of their ring to an echo of genuine emotion. At all events when he wrote: "Since I was first so happy as to know what love meant, I was never one day nor hour free from hope and jealousy",[2] this much at least was true: his jealousy of anyone who shared the Queen's favour was devouring. He was a close friend of Mountjoy, but he had begun by violently insulting the latter when the Queen gave him one of the queens out of a set of gold chessmen, for distinguishing himself in the tilt-yard. "Now I perceive every fool must have a favour!" Essex snarled. He told Elizabeth that he "disdained Ralegh's competition in love", and when she made Lord Cobham Warden of the Cinque Ports, Essex in his own words told the Council: "that I had just cause to hate Lord Cobham for his villainous dealing and abusing of me . . . that in him is no worth; if therefore her Majesty would grace him with honour I may have right cause to think myself little regarded by her".

Lord Howard of Effingham, who had been commander-in-chief against the Armada, was created Earl of Nottingham in 1597; but the patent, besides the Armada service, mentioned the Cadiz action. Essex was furious that anyone should be mentioned in this connection except himself; besides, whoever held the post of Lord Admiral took precedence of all his peers; therefore Howard as Earl of Nottingham would now take precedence of the Earl of Essex. This was death and damnation and Essex did his level best to force the Queen to rescind

[1] Spedding, *Life and Times of Francis Bacon.*
[2] Devereux, *Lives and Letters of the Devereux.*

the honour. He did not succeed but his explosions of fury over these two creations showed his influence to an ominous extent. After Cobham's appointment the Queen soothed his feelings by making him Master of the Ordinance; after the bestowal of Nottingham's peerage she made him Earl Marshal of England.

From his intolerable temper may be divined how great was the charm that outweighed it. In spite of his overbearing nature—the Queen said "he had it from the mother's side"[1]—he could assume an enchanting courtesy and gentleness. His passionate egotism was matched by an impetuous generosity to those he favoured. The contrast entered into his physical make-up; despite his vigour and vehemence he was subject to mysterious collapses when he was too weak to rise from his bed. His appearance, too, with youth and height and auburn hair, was the more striking for a hint of melancholy. In the great tournament of 1591, when the other knights appeared in white and sky-blue, green and silver, gold and orange-tawny, Essex rode into the lists on a coal-black horse, armed in black, shaded with black plumage

> That from his armour borrowed such a light
> As boughs of yew receive from shady stream.[2]

In 1596, after the triumph of Cadiz, Essex was in the height of the firmament, but Bacon, who had attached his own hopes to the fortunes of his splendid young patron, saw with alarm a state of things that seemed to everyone else supremely enviable. In a letter of extraordinary penetration he begged Essex to realize how the Queen must view him: "a man of a nature not to be ruled, that hath the advantage of my affection and knoweth it"; Essex should do his best to allay the misgiving she was bound to feel at his domineering ways and above all at the people's enthusiasm for him. He should accept civilian honours only, deprecate popularity and study to please her in every way he could. So far as this meant dissimulation Essex could not do it, and he saw no need to do it.

When in some dispute he had forced his will on the old woman he would ask Bacon triumphantly which method of dealing with her was the right one, Bacon's or his? Bacon was very far from being reassured. He saw though he could make no one else see the desperate perils ahead in such a course. He began to withdraw from his close attendance on Essex. So, to a strain of melancholy music in the night, the god Hercules whom he loved withdrew from Marc Antony.

[1] Spedding, *op. cit.*   [2] Peele, *Polyhymnia.*

Bacon was not alone in an estimate of Elizabeth's abilities that should have made Essex pause. When Henri IV sent over as his Ambassador the future Duc de Sully, Elizabeth said that she would give him her view of the European situation with reference to the House of Austria. She began her explanation, which built up in stroke after stroke a conspectus of the vast and complicated scene so masterly, so brilliant that Sully gazed upon her with rapt astonishment. Meeting his tranced stare the Queen paused, thinking he had lost her drift. The Ambassador quickly recovered himself and assured her that his silence was caused by admiration. Elizabeth resumed the thread, and proceeded to take him through the details of one of the little-known side issues which contributed to the great whole. On the evidence of this conversation alone, Sully was convinced, he said, "that this great Queen merited the whole of that great reputation she had throughout Europe".[1] This was the being whom Essex thought he could manage for her own good.

His policy was naturally a martial one and when Henri IV made a separate peace with Spain in 1598 and it became a question of whether England should do the same or continue to wage war on Spain in Spanish waters, Essex was determined to carry the latter policy. The Council meeting at which he was loudly urging his views was the one at which Lord Burleigh made almost his last public appearance. As the young man insisted in violent terms on action that went contrary to everything the old man had worked for during forty laborious years, Burleigh drew out his prayer book and laid it before Essex, pointing to the last verse of the 55th psalm: "Blood-thirsty and deceitful men shall not live out half their days." The gesture was to become a blood-chilling recollection.

Meanwhile affairs in Ireland demanded immediate handling. The Earl of Tyrone, who would have been friendly to the English Crown, had been driven into hostility by the misgovernment of succeeding Deputies, and relying on Spanish aid he began a war of resistance in the northern province of Ulster. The Queen proposed to send out Essex's uncle Sir William Knollys as Deputy to deal with this critical situation. Essex was unwilling to lose his uncle's support in the balance of Court factions and wanted her to send Sir George Carew, whose absence would be a disadvantage to the Cecils. It was June, the Court was at Greenwich and the matter which had been under continuous debate was brought up again at a small conclave consisting only of the Queen, Robert Cecil, Nottingham, Essex and the Clerk to the

[1] Sully, *Mémoires*.

Council. Essex repeated his desire that Carew should go to Ireland and the Queen, having at last positively made up her mind, said that Knollys was going. Essex saw he had lost the trick; anger and frustration possessed him; in vindictive contempt he turned his back on her. At this unheard-of insolence the Queen flew at him, smacked his head and told him to go and be hanged.[1]

The action by which Essex had provoked the cuff was extraordinary; his reaction to the cuff itself was almost unbelievable. Shouting that this was an outrage he would not have endured from Henry VIII, Essex the Earl Marshal, whose duty it was to prevent any disturbance in the presence of the sovereign, clapped his hand to his sword and only the rushing forward of Lord Nottingham stopped him from drawing it. He dashed from the room and out of the palace and made his way at once to Wanstead.

What his fate would have been had he offered to draw his sword on Henry VIII, even Essex might have fathomed without difficulty. He met with no reprisals from Elizabeth, but the utter silence with which she received his conduct, however he may have taken it, did not reassure his well-wishers. The Lord Keeper Egerton wrote advising him in the strongest terms to apologize to the Queen. Essex could see no ground for apology: "When the vilest of all indignities are done unto me, doth religion enforce me to sue? . . . Cannot Princes err?" He had inherited Wanstead from his step-father and the great house on the river shore below Fleet Street that had once been Leicester House was now Essex House. The buildings, the gardens, the properties of the Earl who had "seen farther into the mind of Queen Elizabeth than any other", surrounded Essex, but their associations gave his unteachable spirit no guidance. Among his books was one called *The Royal Oracle of Fate*, a fortune-telling device of a design used to-day. Many of the questions are those to which answers are still sought: "What description of person shall be the enquirer's husband?" "Shall the horse win the race?" but some suggest the more dangerous background of the time: "Is an absent person alive or dead?" "If one in prison at this time shall be delivered?" and some bore a particular reference to problems of Essex's own: "Shall the enquirer obtain favour of King, Prince or Lord?" "Of two fighters, which shall prevail?"[2]

For five weeks even Essex was not the first object of the Queen's thoughts. Burleigh was dying. Elizabeth prayed for him daily, sent every day to enquire for him and frequently visited him herself.

[1] Camden, *Annals.*   [2] Raphael, *The Familiar Astrologer.*

When the patient's food was brought and she saw that his gouty hands could not lift the spoon, she fed him. Charmed and deeply touched, Burleigh's mind went back to the only issue on which, in the long run, Elizabeth had ever disappointed him. He told his son of the Queen's attentions and said though she would not be a mother, she showed herself a most careful nurse. He died at the end of August, and for months the Privy Council did their best not to mention him at Council meetings when the Queen was present: his name made her turn her face away and weep. Two years later Robert Sidney saw with pity that she still had fits of crying over the loss. The death could not but make a profound impression of awe upon everyone. At the state funeral, in his place among the mourners Essex was seen, looking shocked with grief.

XXVIII

ONCE IT HAD been seen that the Queen would scarcely allow Essex out of her sight; now when people spoke to her about him she listened willingly, eagerly even, but she made no move to end the estrangement and Essex saw that if he wanted to return to Court he must make the move himself. He carried the matter still in the tone of the injured party "...When I think how I have preferred your beauty above all things . . . I wonder at myself what cause there could be to make me absent myself one day from you. . . . I was never proud till your Majesty sought to make me too base . . . since my destiny is no better, my despair shall be, as my love was, without repentance." But it was said that "he relented much and sought by diverse means to recover his hold".

In October he was at Court again and the Irish question, still unsettled, was now of acute urgency. In Armagh, Tyrone had inflicted the heaviest defeat the English forces had ever experienced in Ireland and at the news of his victory rebellion had broken out all over the country. The Queen still proposed to send out Sir William Knollys but now she had an alternative; with her astonishing gift for detecting ability before it had proved itself, she had singled out Mountjoy as a soldier who could handle this difficult situation; but Essex overbore both these suggestions on the ground that Knollys and Mountjoy had not the necessary vigour and initiative, and when the command was finally conferred upon himself, he spoke of it at first as a personal triumph. The Queen and Council, fully alive to the necessity, gave him a far larger army and more supplies than had been allowed for any Irish expedition before, and when he demanded even more than this, his further demands were met also.

But almost at once, and long before his forces were embarked, Essex was regarding his appointment with self-pitying bitterness. He had felt he owed it to himself to allow no one else to take it, but he foresaw that once he was over the Irish Sea, his enemies in Council would undermine him. The choice of him as Lord Lieutenant, though not the Queen's own, was ostensibly a sound one; Bacon said he was the best general of the day, he had the prestige necessary for the office and he was popular with the army. He departed on a tide of popular enthusiasm, the crowd following him for four miles as he rode out of London, but from the outset he bore himself in an injured and almost hostile manner to the Queen and Council.

He disembarked at Dublin on April 15 and from that hour he completely disregarded his instructions. He had been told to proceed north immediately and attack Tyrone with the full weight of the forces that had been given him for the task. Instead of this he agreed with the Irish Council that later in the year would be a better time, and he spent the next two months in marching over Leinster and Munster, putting down minor insurrections and receiving acclamations from the Anglo-Irish. The Queen, who was increasingly bewildered and annoyed by what she heard of his tactics, said she appeared to be paying him £1,000 a day to go on progresses. When she learned, with difficulty, for Essex did not keep her punctually informed of his doings, that three months after his landing his army of over 16,000 had been reduced to 4,000, that in direct disobedience to her order he had made Southampton his Master of the Horse and that, in spite of additional resources sent at his demand, he still had not marched against Tyrone, she wrote him a series of letters, not indeed abusive but making a bitingly accurate criticism of his incompetence, his disobedience and the stark failure in which they had resulted. The legend of a young man pursued by a shamefully infatuated old woman is exploded for anyone who reads them. They are not couched in the language of infatuation. On July 19, the Queen wrote, after receiving one of his communications:

"Yet have you in this despatch given us small light either when or in what order you intend particularly to proceed to the northern action." So far, nothing had been gained, "if you compare the time that is run on and the excessive charges with the effects of anything wrought by this voyage". What had been the results of his three months' reconnoitring? "You have now learned, upon our expenses, by knowledge of the country, that those things are true which we have heretofore told you, if you would have believed us." In reply to the Queen's command that he should cancel Southampton's appointment, Essex had declared that if he did, his officers would be so indignant, he would scarcely keep them together. With the scenes of Tilbury Camp behind her, Elizabeth said: "We cannot as yet be persuaded but that love of our service and the duty which they owe us have been as strong motives to these travails as any affection to the Earl of Southampton, or any other."[1]

[1] Harrison, *Letters of Queen Elizabeth*.

The results of his mismanagement did not inspire Essex either to admission or apology. "What talk I of victory or success? Is it not known that from England I receive only soul's wounds?" he wrote to the exasperated Queen. To Lord Egerton he wrote: "What can you expect from an accursed country but unfortunate news?" Goaded by letters from the Queen, pointing out his mistakes with unfeeling lucidity, he at last announced that he was going to march with his depleted forces into Ulster. The Queen replied: "You have, even to this hour, possessed us with expectation that you would proceed as we have directed you, but your actions always show the contrary though carried in such sort as we were sure to have no time to countermand them." She recapitulated the provision she had made of men, money and supplies, his persistent refusal to put them to the use for which they were intended and his making further demands, to which he attached the authority of the Irish Council:

"There followed from you and the Council a new demand of 2,000 men to which if we would assent you would speedily undertake what we had so often commanded. When that was granted and your going onward promised by diverse letters, we received by this bearer new fresh advertisement, that all you can do is to go to the frontiers and that you have provided only 20 days' victuals. In which kind of proceeding," the Queen went on, working to a crescendo, "we must deal plain with you and that Council, that it were more proper for them to leave troubling themselves with instructing us by what rules our power and their obedience are limited," and to think over the calamitous results of their interference. Since neither the spring, nor the summer, nor the autumn, nor the winter had been considered a suitable time to march against Tyrone, "then surely we must conclude that none of the four quarters of the year will be in season for you".[1]

When at last Essex and his dwindled forces came face to face with Tyrone, effective action was no longer possible. On September 14 the commanders held a parley on horseback, Essex on the river bank, Tyrone in the water up to his horses' girths. The conversation lasted half-an-hour and there were no witnesses to it. The upshot was that Tyrone agreed to a truce of six weeks, terminable at a fortnight's notice, and issued to Essex a set of conditions, which when they were finally produced amounted, as has been said, to Home Rule for Ireland. These conditions Tyrone said Essex must carry in his head; they must not be written down for fear the Spaniards should get at them.

[1] Harrison, op. cit. .

Essex had lost 12,000 men and spent £300,000, and this climax of his endeavours left the Queen aghast. She did not, she emphasized, suspect him of treason, but she denounced his incompetence in the strongest terms, she forbade him to guarantee Tyrone a pardon and she demanded to hear at once what arrangements he was making with his garrisons. Her letter did not reach its destination.

Before he left England Essex had extracted from her a promise that he might return when he saw fit; when she saw affairs plunging to disaster Elizabeth had cancelled this permission and ordered him to stay where he was and carry out his duties. But Essex could now divine, if he had not actually heard, what his enemies were saying about his dealings with the rebel. He decided to ignore the Queen's command and come back to play what he thought was his strongest card, the old woman's absorbing fondness for himself. He had considered bringing the remains of the army with him, "4,000 choice men", to stand behind him while he made his points to the Council. He was dissuaded from this desperate step; he brought 200 men only, and with them and six officers he crossed to England, arriving in London very early in the morning of September 28. The Queen was at Nonesuch, ten miles south of the Thames. Everything was now staked on her personal affection and on his gaining access to her in time to tell his own story first. He and his six friends crossed the river by ferry, landing at Lambeth, and there they seized some horses that were waiting for their riders on the bank. The wild ride began and ahead of them on the Nonesuch road they descried Lord Grey de Wilton, whom Essex declared was his enemy. Sir Thomas Gerard overtook Lord Grey and asked if he would allow the Earl of Essex to ride on before him. Lord Grey said no, he had business with Mr. Secretary Cecil. Sir Christopher St. Laurence offered to kill Lord Grey there and then and the Secretary when they got to Nonesuch. Essex declined these offers but they showed the mood of determination in which the party was arriving.[1]

Grey was already with Cecil when Essex entered the palace and there was not an instant to lose. It was now ten o'clock. He had ridden so hard that his very face was covered with splashes of mud but he rushed upstairs to the Presence Chamber, through it to the Privy Chamber and, finding that empty too, pushed his way into the Queen's bed-chamber. Elizabeth, surrounded by her waiting-women, was sitting at her dressing-table, her grey hair "about her ears". Essex fell on his knees, seized her hands and covered them with kisses.

[1] Spedding, op. cit.

Elizabeth did not know he was in England until he was kneeling at her feet; taken by surprise, at the disadvantage of not being dressed and not knowing whether he had come with an army at his back or who there might be outside her bedroom door, in this annihilating moment she kept her head. Essex indeed thought he had succeeded. When presently he went to wash and dress he was heard to say "he thanked God that though he had suffered much trouble and storms abroad, he had found a sweet calm at home". The Queen, fully dressed and in possession of herself, received him after dinner. Her manner was now reserved. She said he must explain himself to the Lords of the Council. A meeting of the Privy Council was convened and a preliminary examination of Essex on his doings was opened that afternoon. By eleven at night the Earl had been ordered to keep to his own room. Next day he was committed to the custody of Lord Egerton and lodged in York House, the great house that stood next to Essex House on the Strand.

It was understood that Essex was not to be charged with treason; the difficulties presented by the Irish and their terrain, a run of misfortune and the fact that the post had required administrative capacities which he did not possess, in the long run were accepted as explanations of his failure; but its overwhelming nature in a man supposedly able and receiving unlimited support from the Crown demanded very serious enquiry, particularly as it had been incurred while he was doing exactly the opposite of what he had been told to do.

In the past when Essex had jarred with Elizabeth, it had been as a rule because she was annoyed by some matter in his private life; she had resented his marriage and had disapproved violently of his carrying-on with four of her Maids of Honour. The very quarrels had served to enhance his power; he had been in the superior position of a young man contending with the jealousy of an old woman. He was now facing the formidable anger of a clever, exacting, arbitrary ruler whose costly enterprise had been thrown away by a policy that directly disobeyed her injunctions. Essex however did not acknowledge even a mistake, let alone a fault. His present situation he ascribed to the machinations of his enemies, of Cecil, Ralegh, Cobham, Grey and their supporters, but his chief danger he recognized in the fact that Elizabeth refused to see him. Before, he had been the one who withdrew; it seemed scarcely possible that their rôles could be reversed; but here he was, a prisoner in York House debarred from access to her, and no matter what the kind or the degree of his feeling for her, in worldly considerations the withdrawal of her favour meant an arctic night.

The fierceness of his agitation and dismay brought on one of his attacks; he was declared to be almost at death's door and illness made its usual appeal to Elizabeth's feelings. With tears in her eyes she sent him a message that he should "comfort himself" and that she would come to see him "if it were consistent with her honour". Lady Essex, just out of childbed and dressed all in black, had come to Court imploring to be allowed to visit her husband. She had been refused, but now permission was granted and the young wife was at York House by seven every morning and stayed till six at night.

But the Queen's relenting mood was checked. The citizens heard of Essex's illness and prayers were offered for him in all the churches in London. On "the very white walls" of Whitehall itself, abuse of Cecil was scrawled and an even more sinister sign appeared of the position the Earl occupied in the public mind. A Latin history was published of the first year of the Reign of Henry IV—the king who had landed with an army in Wales and gained the crown by the murder of his cousin Richard II. Twice in the Devereux line, females had married with the Plantagenets; there was a family connection however distant between her and the man who had tried to draw his sword on her. The associations with Henry IV were sinister. She opened the book and found that it was dedicated to the Earl of Essex. Such a demonstration added force to rumour. It was naturally asked what Essex had really been doing in Ireland; some said he had meant by compounding with Tyrone to make himself king of the island, and after that—who knew?

The Queen was a prey to doubts and fears on a subject that affected her more deeply and bitterly than the agitations of sexual passion; but she made a courageous effort and to onlookers she seemed astonishingly calm. Harington had been with the army in Ireland, and when he came to pay his respects on his return, the Queen had given him a furious rating that sent him off, he said, as if the Irish rebels were at his heels; but shortly afterwards she sent for him and having frankly discussed his conduct she accepted his apologies and dismissed him graciously. He said: "Until I come to heaven I shall never come before a statelier judge again."[1] The Queen was not only self-possessed but cheerful. There was dancing at Court every evening and Elizabeth still enjoyed her favourite pastime. Lord Sempil said that someone looking through a window had seen the Queen dancing the

[1] Harington, *Nugae Antiquae*.

Spanish Panic, all alone except for Lady Warwick and a man who was playing the pipe and tabor. Platter, waiting for a sight of her in the Presence Chamber, saw her come in "alone and without escort, very straight and erect still, in white satin covered with pearls and diamonds, a humming bird on her head".

The Christmas was one of unusually brilliant festivity and its events displayed the Queen in the full exercise of her admired, beloved attributes. On St. Stephen's Night the ravishing comedy of *Twelfth Night* was played before a dazzling audience that centred round the Queen and her guest the Count Palatine. The Count sat between the Queen and Lord Grey and the Queen helped Lord Grey to translate the players' language to him.

This exquisite entertainment was contrasted by a bull-baiting at which "a great bull brake loose from the stake" and ran amok in a crowd of 300 spectators. At the sight the Queen screamed: "Jesus! Save my people! Jesus, save my people!" and in all the hideous tumult no one was hurt;[1] while in *Cynthia's Revels*, acted by the Children of Queen Elizabeth's Chapel, the loveliest of lyrics enskied her:

> Earth, let not thine envious shade
> Dare itself to interpose.
> Cynthia's shining orb was made
> Heaven to clear when day did close.
> Bless us then with wishèd sight
> Goddess excellently bright.

The indifference with which the Queen appeared to bear the absence of Essex was the despair of his party. His mother and sister were next door to him in Essex House, from whose windows they could see him in the garden of York House walking with his wife. At the height of his influence Essex had succeeded on one occasion in persuading the Queen to receive his mother, but after this once abhorrence had reasserted itself and Lettice Blount had not been allowed to come again. Penelope Rich however had the entrée and she thought that a letter from herself to the Queen, pointing out to the latter where she was wrong in her conduct to Penelope's brother, would now be in season. The Queen's avid fondness for gallantry was a by-word and where her view of her own attractions was concerned she was a vain and foolish old woman; but it was a mistake to think that she was nothing else or that she could not recognize impertinence when she met it. Lady Rich's letter opened with a parody of the style

[1] Hotson, *The First Night of Twelfth Night*.

in which letters to the Queen were often couched, speaking of having her own eyes "blessed by your Majesty's beauties" and complaining that the Earl should be sequestered—as though "his love, his life, his services to your beauties and the state had deserved no absolution after so hard prisonment". Essex, the letter said, was being sacrificed to "those combined enemies that labour on false grounds to build his ruin . . . only to glut themselves in their own private revenges". The Queen would not know this, but "I have reason to apprehend", said Lady Rich, that if the Queen did not "check the course of their unbridled hate", and grant Essex a personal interview, they would "disable him from ever serving again his sacred goddess". The men of whose fortunes Lady Rich said, "I fear they will grow more dangerously high", and whom she stigmatized as "evil instruments with officious cunning and poison in their hearts" included members of the Privy Council and the Queen's chief adviser, Robert Cecil. Her indiscretion did not stop short with naming them in these terms. So elated was she by her own composition that she showed it round among her friends, and some enterprising huckster getting hold of it, the letter was printed and sold in the streets.

The Queen's reply was prompt. She conveyed by Robert Cecil her opinion of the "stomach and presumption" of Lady Rich and ordered her to keep to her own house until further notice. After a severe talking-to by the Privy Council, the ingenious letter-writer "expressed sorrow for her Majesty's displeasure and her great desire to recover her Majesty's favour". It was understood that by that time "she had written to her Majesty in another sort".

In May, Essex was sent back to Essex House, but still as a prisoner. He had got over his illness but he was in torments of frustration and bitterness.

"Your Majesty" he wrote, "that hath mercy for all the world but me . . . your Majesty, I say hath now in the eighth month of my close imprisonment, as if you thought mine infirmities, beggary and infamy too little punishment, rejected my letters and refused to hear of me, which to traitors you never did." But the Queen preserved her unnerving silence. In June he was heard before a special commission sitting in York House. He was charged with disobedience to the Queen's commands and with grave misuse of her commission in his treatment of the rebel. His sister's letter was declared "insolent, saucy and malapert, an aggravation of offence". He was suspended from all office and ordered to remain a prisoner in his own house till the Queen's pleasure was known.

The Queen meanwhile was at Greenwich; it was told Sir Robert Sidney, "she uses to walk much in the park, and takes great walks out of the park and round about the park", and that though all the time the fate of Essex was in suspense, she appeared to think of nothing but fixing the date of her maid Ann Russell's wedding to Lord Herbert. Since Elizabeth had consented to be present it was left to her to appoint the wedding day. At the wedding feast however she showed that during her great walks about the park, Essex had not been absent from her mind. Eight Maids of Honour, dressed in cloth of silver with mantles of carnation taffeta, danced a masque. At its close their leader approached the Queen and begged her to dance with them. It was Mary Fitton, brilliant on the edge of her eclipse. Elizabeth graciously asked her what quality she represented. The girl said: "Affection, Madam." The moment was stamped with a historic significance. " 'Affection!' said the Queen. 'Affection's false!' Nevertheless her Majesty arose and danced."[1]

In August, Essex was released; he might go where he would, but still he was not to come to Court. The long, public humiliation of the Queen's neglect was driving him frantic. "Till I may appear in your gracious presence time itself is a perpetual night and the whole world a sepulchre unto your Majesty's humblest vassal." Though Elizabeth had been generous to him, he was heavily in debt. At Michaelmas the chief source of his income, a monopoly-tax on sweet wines, was due to expire. It was of the greatest financial importance to him that the Queen should renew it, and under other aspects of greater importance still. When the time came for renewing the grant, Elizabeth said: "An unruly beast must be stopped of his provender", and she returned it to the Crown.

Essex was beside himself. Harington, who saw him at this time, said: "He shifteth from sorrow and repentance to rebellion and rage as well proveth him devoid of good reason or of right mind. . . . His speeches of the Queen become no man that hath *meus sana in corpore sano*."

Essex was now keeping open house for his sympathizers and his utterances were no longer private. One day in impotent rage he exclaimed, "that the Queen's conditions were as crooked as her carcase", and the words were repeated to Elizabeth. It was Ralegh's opinion that if Essex had not said them, he need not have died. This view is contradicted by words of Elizabeth's own, but it shows the impression made by the insult on those who heard it.

[1] Sidney Papers.

Essex had never shown either understanding of his shortcomings or genuine repentance, or any reason at all why the Queen should restore him to favour, and his conduct now proved that her judgment was sound in refusing to trust him. Mountjoy had been appointed Lord Deputy in his place and had sent on Essex's behalf a messenger to James, telling him that Cecil and his friends opposed the Scots King's succession in favour of the Infanta's. James' accession, it seemed, depended on the mediation of Essex. If James would send a body of troops to London to demand the reinstatement of Essex and the proclamation of his own right to the Crown, Mountjoy would send the English army over from Ireland to ensure effective pressure on the Queen. But when Mountjoy arrived in Ireland in February 1600 he vindicated the Queen's judgment. The smooth, dapper nobleman who took such care of himself with hot drinks and afternoon naps and wrapped himself up to an extent thought perfectly extraordinary in so young a man, proved a tireless, patient, brilliant organizer, an administrator of outstanding ability as well as a first-rate soldier in the field. Elizabeth had told him she knew he would settle Tyrone and bring her to her grave in peace, and Mountjoy received Tyrone's submission a few days before her death. By the time Essex sent to demand a renewal of his co-operation Mountjoy had relinquished any interest in treason.

But to Essex no other alternative commended itself. The galling sense of defeat where he had once enjoyed absolute supremacy was destroying his balance; he developed a persecution mania in which he actually believed that Cecil and Ralegh, deep in a conspiracy with Spain, were planning his murder. Essex House became a magnet for disaffection; the Earl's presence-chamber was thronged with soldiers from Ireland, Puritans who disapproved of the Queen, Catholics who sought toleration and adventurers who wanted opportunity. With Southampton, Sir Christopher Blount and Sir Charles Davers, Essex determined that he must "surprise the court and the Queen's person". This done, Essex with all duty was to tell the Queen she must dismiss his enemies; he would then put them on trial for their lives and afterwards summon a Parliament "and alter the government". This scheme caused such excitement among the crowds frequenting Essex House, that the Queen became aware of "a general churme and muttering", and on the afternoon of Saturday, February 7, Essex was summoned to the Privy Council. He declared himself too ill to go and it was determined that he and his party must move at once. They discussed whether they should first seize the Tower or surprise the Court and determined on the latter, for Essex thought himself so beloved in the City that it was virtually his already. On Sunday morning the courtyard of Essex House was crammed with between two and three hundred swordsmen, but as ten o'clock struck, Lord Egerton, Sir William Knollys, Lord Worcester and the Lord Chief Justice arrived at the gates demanding admittance. They were shown into the library, but the mob was already out of hand and Essex was borne on by them. He turned the key on the delegation and with 200 men with drawn swords at 'his back came out of his gates into Fleet Street. It was plain that the Court could not be surprised and the plans were hurriedly reversed. Instead of turning to the left towards Whitehall, the crowd turned right up Ludgate Hill. As Essex walked at their head he called out: "For the Queen!" telling the passers-by that his life was sought, that the realm was sold to the Infanta, and calling them to take up arms and follow him.

The government had already warned the citizens to arm themselves for fear of trouble, but there was no trouble. "There was not," said Bacon, "in so populous a city where he thought himself held so dear, one man from the chiefest citizen to the meanest artificer or prentice that armed with him." The dreadful silence of the Sunday morning streets reduced his cries to a theatrical absurdity. With sweat pouring from him, "though without any cause of bodily labour, but only by the perplexity and horror of his mind", he came to the house of one of the sheriffs, where he went in and changed his shirt. The sheriff at once left by the back door. Essex decided he must get back to his house. Heralds in the streets were proclaiming him a traitor, there had been a clash between his men and the Queen's on Ludgate Hill and that road was closed to him. He dived down a side street leading to the river, took boat and was rowed up-stream to the water-gate of Essex House. Here he found that his captives had been let out. Penelope in his absence had endeavoured to bring in the Earl of Bedford, whom she had called for in her coach and obliged to leave his house in the middle of a sermon. His Lordship had remained passive until he was set down at Essex House; he had then made the best of his way to Court and proclaimed himself at the Queen's service.

At dusk, Lord Nottingham and Sir Robert Sidney landed at the water-gate and the latter came up the garden, shouting to Essex and Southampton to capitulate. Essex spoke to him from the roof, demanding as a condition of surrender to be allowed an audience of the Queen. The Lord Admiral's reply was to send down-stream to the

Tower for ordinance and kegs of gun-powder. One hour he would grant, to let the ladies Essex and Rich with their shrieking gentlewomen get out of the house, then he would blow it up. The kegs were being landed on the lawn when Essex and Southampton came out, knelt to the Lord Admiral and presented their swords. They were lodged that night in Lambeth Palace and next day taken to the Tower.[1]

[1] Spedding, *op. cit.*; Abbott, *Bacon and Essex.*

XXIX

Essex's attempt at rebellion had been futile—Bacon said of him: "he knew not how to play the malefactor"—nevertheless he had done deliberately the deed for which the legal penalty was death. He and Southampton and five of their associates, including Sir Christopher Blount, were charged with high treason, and on February 19, the two Earls were sentenced to be beheaded.

Essex was thirty-three and his shining career had extinguished itself in utter desolation. He had disregarded Bacon's warning when it might have saved him, but this did not mitigate the pang that Bacon, whom he had admired and befriended with all his heart, should have accepted a brief from the prosecution to appear against him. As he was led through the streets back to the Tower the citizens came about him. "He went with a swift pace, bending his face towards the earth and would not look upon any of them though some of them directly spoke to him."[1]

He fell into a state of mind well known in such circumstances; under the eager, relentless ministrations of his chaplain, he poured out a hysterical confession, declaring himself "the greatest, the vilest, the most unthankful traitor that has ever been in the land". It was reported, to her intense indignation, that he had blamed Lady Rich. "It is known," she exclaimed, "that I have been more like a slave than a sister!" "My sister," he said, "did continually urge me on with telling me how all my friends and followers thought me a coward and that I had lost my valour." His defences were broken down under a flood of remorse but he accepted the prospect of his death with a dignified and moving courage. To many, looking back, it was unbelievable that the Queen should allow the sentence to be carried out. Those who thought so knew her as little as Essex had known her.

Elizabeth reprieved Southampton as a follower of Essex merely; for Essex there could be no reprieve; he had meant to come into her presence with armed men and force her to do his will. The disappointment and the savage humiliation he had inflicted on her might all have been washed away in an impulse of renewed affection, but this offence admitted of no reconciliation, no pardon, no oblivion.

[1] Nichols, *Progresses*.

On the morning of February 25 the Queen was sitting in the Privy Chamber playing the virginals, while several men, among them Oxford and Ralegh, stood about her. Admission was sought for a messenger who, on his knee, announced that sentence on the Earl of Essex had been carried out. A dead silence filled the room. Then the twanging, plangent notes struck the air as the Queen began to play again.[1]

Almost at once, melodramatic versions of the story were evolved, whose false and lurid colouring has never lost its popular appeal. The French Ambassador Beaumont heard Elizabeth's version from her own lips. He could see that she was in deep grief and when she spoke of the matter she was almost in tears but she said: "I had put up with but too much disrespect to my person, but I warned him that he should not touch my sceptre." Beaumont saw that the subject was too much for her composure and yet that she could not leave it, so with gentle tact he turned the conversation to something else. A few days later the topic revived itself. Henri IV had found the Duc de Biron engaged in treason and had ordered his execution. In discussing this news, the Queen spoke again of Essex, with tears in her eyes. "In such cases there is no middle course," she said; "we must lay aside clemency and adopt extreme measures." The King of France must have shrunk from putting to death a man he so much loved and honoured, she knew only too well what those feelings were. "Yet," she said, "when the welfare of my state was concerned, I dared not indulge my own inclinations." She had found the satisfaction of doing the right thing, however painful. The King of France would find the same.[2]

Grief however had not conquered the deep, bitter anger aroused by Essex's assault upon majesty; that he meant to use his Plantagenet blood as an excuse actually to lay his hand on the Crown had not been brought against him at his trial, but the rumour of it was prevalent, for he had sent to assure James that it was untrue. It had never been driven from Elizabeth's mind. The old antiquarian Lambarde had collected and transcribed the records kept in the Tower and presented a copy to the Queen, who, with her historical bent and her interest in her forebears, declared that she had never had a gift that pleased her more. She gave Lambarde an audience at Greenwich, where she said to him: "You intended to present this book to me by the Countess of Warwick but I will none of that, for if any subject of mine do me a service I will thankfully accept it at his hands." She ran over the pre-

[1] Nannton, *Fragmenta Regalia*.   [2] Von Raumer.

face and asked Lambarde the meaning of various technical terms. At the section devoted to the reign of Richard II she stopped suddenly and exclaimed: "I am Richard II. Know you not that?" The old man said: "Such a wicked imagination was determined and attempted by a most unkind gentleman." The Queen admired a device of "my good grandfather Henry VII, sparing to dissipate his lands and treasure". Then, reverting to Richard II, she asked Lambarde if he had ever seen a portrait of that king. Only the well-known ones, he said. Elizabeth told him that Lord Lumley, a lover of antiquities, had found a portrait of Richard II nailed on the wall in a basement room and had asked her to put it in the royal collection; she said: "I will command Thomas Knevett, the Keeper of my house and gallery at Westminster, to show it[1] thee." When she was called away to prayers, she said: "Farewell, honest Lambarde," and left the room taking the book with her.

The response to life was vivid as ever, but the scene itself was changing. Admiration, gratitude, affection, she had them all, but her very success had resulted in bringing a new England into being and the new was not the old. In her last years, Elizabeth, weary and worn down, had to face situations she had never known before. Essex's attempt at a rebellion supported by Scots and Irish forces might have proved exceedingly formidable; it had collapsed in ignominy because the ordinary Englishman would not contemplate rebelling against the Queen. Nevertheless Essex had enjoyed some of that magical popularity which up till then had been exerted only by Elizabeth herself, and in the mourning for his death—the popular ballad declared "Sweet England's Pride is gone!"—the Queen's own grief was troubled by a still darker and colder shadow. The times too had overpowered her great skill as an economist. In the last ten years she had not been able to keep pace with the inflationary tendencies of expanding prosperity. Aid to the French and Dutch had swallowed her painfully accumulated reserves; Mountjoy had the Irish position well in hand but it required an increasing flow of money, for the Spaniards were about to launch another attempt at invasion from the Irish base. In her last years the Queen had to sell Crown lands and her jewels. In 1601 a Parliament was summoned, for the need of a large subsidy was urgent.

The Houses were perfectly willing to grant it but they took the opportunity to complain strongly of the Queen's rewarding her servants by allowing them to tax articles of general use. "Is not bread

[1] Possibly the one now in Westminster Abbey.

there?" a member had exclaimed on hearing the new list of products subject to the monopoly tax.

Elizabeth was indeed old; at the opening of the session her robes of velvet and ermine had proved too heavy for her; on the steps of the throne she had staggered and was only saved from falling by the peer who stood nearest catching her in his arms; but her regnal instincts were not impaired. She told Robert Cecil she had not known how the monopolies were abused; the matter must be set right, and he announced to the House of Commons that the offensive taxes were being removed forthwith: salt, brandy, starch were among the articles to be freed, and the restrictions were removed on the growing of woad, with the proviso, that as the vegetable had a nauseating smell, her Majesty hoped that people would not grow it near any of the palaces.[1]

When a deputation waited on her at Whitehall at 3 in the afternoon of November 30, to tender the thanks of the Houses for this prompt and most substantial concession, the Queen made in reply one of the most celebrated speeches of her life. She told them, "Though God hath raised me high, yet this I count the glory of my Crown that I have reigned with your loves." "I do not," she said, "so much rejoice that God hath made me to be a Queen as to be a Queen over so thankful a people." In the simplest words she expressed the guiding motive of her existence: "I have cause to wish nothing more than to content the subject; and that is a duty which I owe." As she drew to a close, she said: "It is my desire to live nor reign no longer than my life and reign shall be for your good." The shade hovered but it withdrew in the last cordial, ceremonious gesture: "And I pray you, Mr. Comptroller, Mr. Secretary and you of my Council that before these gentlemen go into their counties, you will bring them all to kiss my hand."

"We loved her," Harington said, "for she said she did love us." The mutual love was inexhaustible, but it was mingled now with treasons, independencies, new-fangledness. The situation she had driven off for forty-three years could be driven off no longer; hope and expectation were directed to the heir, not to her any longer. Behind the distractions, the richness, the labours of hour-to-hour existence there was a vast darkness. Leicester was dead, Hatton was dead, Burleigh was dead, and the last death of all was still an open wound. In 1602 Harington heard that there were times when the Queen sat alone in the dark, lamenting the fate of Essex.

The energy of genius did not forsake her, it nearly wore her out.

[1] Neale, *Elizabeth and her Parliaments*, II.

She rode still though it made her very weary; she refused help in stepping into the royal barge, stumbled and bruised her shin. She paid a visit to Sir Robert Sidney and his wife, who had exerted themselves to the utmost to make the occasion a success. Fanfares saluted the Queen's arrival and departure, dances were performed, the family had put on their richest clothes, the children made speeches "very graciously received" by the glittering old lady whose velvet train was carried by four gentlewomen. But she called for a stick to help herself up the staircase; "she was wearied in walking about the house and said she would come another day".

For the first time she became forgetful, and her autocratic temper made these lapses difficult to explain to her, for "who dares say, your Majesty hath forgotten?" But the infirmities of age brought no numbing of her feelings. The Coronation-ring she had worn for forty-three years had now grown into her finger and they had to file it off. The nature of the act oppressed her with horror and desolation.

Though she was weary and despondent and those about her were looking to the rising sun, in the nation at large the great treasury she had amassed of confidence, gratitude and love was valid still.

> *Naked the fields are, bloomless are the briars*
> *Yet we a summer have,*
> *Who in our clime kindleth these living fires*
> *Which blooms can on the briars save . . .*
>
> *Winter, though everywhere*
> *Hath no abiding here.*
> *On brooks and briars she doth reign alone,*
> *The sun which lights our world is Always One.*[1]

Winter it was. In January 1603 the Queen had a bad cold. Dr. Dee, whose adventures had carried him to Poland and to regions of the mind of uncharted distance, had emerged from his vicissitudes and told her to beware of Whitehall. Elizabeth decided to go to Richmond, the warmest of the palaces, and the Court removed there on January 14, "being a filthy rainy and windy day".[2]

She was sixty-nine and the doctors said she might live for several years; they now considered her, after all her ailing, to have "a sound and perfect constitution". But it soon became clear that she was not going to do so. By the end of February she was declining fast. It was put about that grief for Essex had deprived her of the wish to live, but

[1] Edmund Bolton, 1600.   [2] Camden, *Annals.*

as potent a reason was perhaps a perfect sense of timing. She had told the Houses she did not wish to live and reign after her life and reign could do them good. "She grew worse," said her cousin Robert Carey, "because she would be so." She refused all medicine, and when the Archbishop of Canterbury and Cecil urged her to try some, she replied impatiently that she knew her own constitution better than they did.

The death at the end of February of the Countess of Nottingham —who had been Kate Carey, one of her favourite cousins—prostrated the Queen with weeping. She asked Beaumont to excuse her for a day or two, she could give no audiences. When Robert Carey was admitted to see her, he kissed her hand and said something of being glad to see her better. She took his hand and wrung it hard and said, "No, Robin, I am not well," and she sighed and sighed as he had never heard her do except when the Queen of Scots was beheaded.[1]

Her symptoms increased, of fever, restlessness, sleeplessness, perpetual thirst and phlegm in the throat. When she was too much exhausted to walk about she sat on the floor-cushions and once there she would not move. Cecil said, "Madame, to content the people you must go to bed." The Queen gave a smile of indescribable scorn. "Little man, little man," she said, "the word *must* is not to be used to princes. If your father had lived ye durst not have said so much."

The Lord Admiral, widowed as he was, came to see if he might persuade her. While he was with her he got her to take a little broth and he reminded her of how courageous she had always been, but the response was missing. "I am tied with a chain of iron about my neck," she said, "I am tied, I am tied, and the case is altered with me."

She remained silent for hours at a time and when one of the doctors ventured to ask "how she spent her time in so much silence: 'I meditate,' quoth she." For the last two days, Beaumont was told, she had had her finger almost always in her mouth, her eyes open and fixed upon the ground; in this awful trance she remained for four days on end, eating nothing and sitting upright on her cushions, except when she slept for an hour or so, and wasting visibly. At the end of the fourth day she was so faint they were able to carry her to bed. Here she revived a little, and asked for some meat broth. An abscess burst in her throat and she felt better. The Privy Councillors said they must speak with her; though every arrangement was made for the accession of James, opposition from rival claimants was possible and Cecil wanted Elizabeth's own word in support of the Scots King's claim.

[1] Carey, *Memoirs of Himself.*

She asked for something to rinse her throat and as it was still very sore they begged her, as they stood about her bed, only to sign with her hand if she agreed with their proposals. When they asked her if James should succeed her on the English throne she made the sign that everyone expected.

Presently she asked for the Archbishop of Canterbury, and at six in the evening Whitgift was brought to her bedside; when the Archbishop entered the bed-chamber Robert Carey came in too and knelt at a distance. Many people were in the room, and as the Archbishop uttered prayers the bystanders gave the responses. The Queen made no sound, but when, after half-an-hour, Whitgift blessed her and rose from his knees, she made a sign and Lady Scrope, who was her cousin Philadelphia Carey, interpreted it and asked the Archbishop to go on praying. He did so for another half-hour; his knees were weary and he attempted to rise, but again the Queen gestured with her hand. He prayed again, uttering exclamations of his own, fervently imploring mercy for her until at last she sank into unconsciousness.

Everyone now left the bed-chamber except the ladies who were attending the Queen. The palace was silent and a hush deeper than the tranquillity of night possessed the river, the fields and London itself. Father Weston, a Catholic priest at that time in the Tower, said that during the few days when the Queen lay dying "a strange silence descended on the whole city . . . not a bell rang out, not a bugle sounded." Midnight came and then it was March 24, the Feast of the Assumption of the Blessed Virgin. At a quarter-to-three the watchers again approached the great bed.

Elizabeth was lying with her head on her right arm. Her warfare was accomplished.

When the grief and lamentation of a national mourning had subsided and the cares and interests of a new era had begun, Camden's words enshrined the opinion of his own and of succeeding centuries:

"She was a Queen who hath so long and with so great wisdom governed her kingdoms, as (to use the words of her Successor who in sincerity confessed as much) the like hath not been read or heard of, either in our own time or since the days of the Roman Emperor Augustus".

BIBLIOGRAPHY

H.M.C. Historical Manuscripts Commission
C.S.P. Calendar of State Papers

Abbott, E. A., *Bacon and Essex*, 1877.
Allen, Cardinal, *Letters and Memorials*.
Aubrey, John, *Brief Lives*.
Archeologia, 1937.
Auerbach, Erna, *Tudor Portraits*, 1954.
Bacon, Sir Francis, *Felicity of Queen Elizabeth*.
  Apophthegmes.
Bagot, William, *Memorials*.
Baker, Richard, *Chronicles of the Kings of England*.
Ballard, George, *Memoirs of Learned Ladies*.
Barlow, William, *Answer to a Catholic Englishman*.
Beesly, E. S., *Queen Elizabeth*, 1895.
Besant, Walter, *Tudor London*.
Biographical Dictionary, 1820.
Birch, Thomas, *Memoirs of the Reign of Queen Elizabeth*.
Black, J. B., *The Reign of Elizabeth*, 1936.
Bohun, Edmund, *Queen Elizabeth*.
Bradford, C. A., *Blanche Parry*, 1935.
Brantôme, Pierre de, *Famous Women*.
Brice, Thomas, *Register of the Martyrs* (Tudor Tracts, 1903).
Cabala, III.
Camden, William, *Annals of Elizabeth*.
Carey, Sir Robert, *Memoirs of Himself*.
Chamberlin, F. C., *The Private Character of Queen Elizabeth*, 1922.
Clifford, H., *Life of Jane Dormer*, 1887.
Collins, A. J., *Jewels and Plate of Elizabeth I*, 1955.
Crawfurd, R., *The King's Evil*, 1911.
Creighton, Mandell, *Queen Elizabeth*, 1896.
Cunningham, P., ed., *Extracts from the Revels' Accounts*, 1842.
D'Aubeuf, *Messieurs de Noailles en Angleterre*.
De Castelnau, Michel, *Memoires*.
De la Ferrière, Artaud, *Projets de Mariage de la Reine Elisabeth*, 1882.
De la Mothe Fénélon, *Correspondance Diplomatique*.
Devereux, W. B., *Lives and Letters of the Devereux, Earls of Essex*.
Devlin, Christopher, *Robert Southwell*, 1956.
Dictionary of Literary Anecdote.
Dictionary of National Biography.
Digges, Dudley, *Compleat Ambassador*.
Dugdale, William, *Warwick and Warwick Castle*.

Ellis, Henry, *Letters Illustrative of English History*.
Evans, Joan, *History of Jewellery*, 1953.
Exhibition of the Royal House of Tudor: Catalogue, 1890.
Falls, Cyril, *Mountjoy, Elizabethan General*, 1955.
Foley, Henry, *Records of the English Provinces*.
Foxe, John, *Imprisonment of the Princess Elizabeth*.
Fox-Bourne, H. R., *Sir Philip Sidney*, 1891.
Froude, J. A., *History of England*, 1870.
Fugger News Letters, 1926.
Fuller, Thomas, *Worthies of England*.
Gascoigne, George, *Princely Pleasures of Kenilworth*.
Giles, J. A., ed., *Letters and Works of Roger Ascham*.
Gonzalez, Tomaso, ed., *Documents from Simancas*.
Goodman, Godfrey, *Court of James I*.
Gotch, John, *Homes of the Cecils*, 1904.
Greville, Fulke, *Life of Sidney*.
Halliwell, J. O., ed., *Diary of Dr. John Dee*.
Harington, Sir John, *Nugae Antiquae*.
Harleian Miscellany.
Harrison, G. B., *Journal of de Maisse*, 1931.
    The Earl of Essex, 1937.
    Letters of Queen Elizabeth, 1935.
Harrison, William, *Description of the Island of Great Britain*.
Haynes, ed., *State Papers*.
Hayward, John, *Observations on the Reign of Elizabeth*.
Henderson, J. F., *Mary Queen of Scots*, 1905.
Hentzner, Paul, *Travels in England*.
Hilliard, Nicholas, *The Art of Limning*.
Holinshed, Raphael, *Chronicles of England*.
Holles, Gervase, *The Holles Family*.
Hotson, Leslie, *Queen Elizabeth's Entertainment at Mitcham*, 1953.
    The First Night of Twelfth Night, 1954.
Howe, Bea, *A Galaxy of Governesses*.
Hume, Martin, *Courtships of Queen Elizabeth*.
    Love-Affairs of Mary Queen of Scots.
James, M. R., *Manuscripts of Dr. John Dee*, 1921.
Jessup, A., *One Generation of a Norfolk House*, 1913.
Johnston, Robert, *Historia Britannicarum*.
Klarwill, V. von, *Queen Elizabeth and some Foreigners*, 1928.
Laneham, Robert, *Entertainment at Kenilworth*.
Lang, Andrew, *The Mystery of Mary Stuart*, 1901.
Leycester's Commonwealth.
Lloyd, David, *State Worthies*.
Loke, W., *Materials for Queen Ann Boleyn*.
Lysons, Daniel, *Environs of London*.
Machyn, Henry, *Diary*.
Madden, Frederick, *Privy Purse Expenses of the Princess Mary*.
Malcolm, James, *Manners and Customs of London*.
Manningham, John, *Diary*.

Meadows, G. D. *Elizabethan Quintet*, 1956.
Melville, Sir James, *Memoirs*.
Mignet, F. A., *Mary Queen of Scots*, 1882.
Mumby, F. A., *The Girlhood of Queen Elizabeth*, 1904.
   Elizabeth and Mary Stuart, 1914.
   The Fall of Mary Stuart, 1921.
Murdin, ed., *State Papers*.
Nares, Edward, *Memoirs of Lord Burleigh*.
Naunton, Robert, *Fragmenta Regalia*.
Neale, Sir John, *Queen Elizabeth*, 1934.
   Elizabeth and her Parliaments, I, II, 1953–1957.
Nichols, John, *Progresses of Queen Elizabeth*.
Nicholas, N. H., *Sir Christopher Hatton*.
   Life of W. Davison.
Osborne, Francis, *Historical Memoirs*.
Peck, Francis, *Desiderata Curiosa*.
Pecle, George, *Polyhymnia*.
Platt, Hugh, *Delights for Ladies*.
Platter, T., *Travels in England*.
Pollen, J. H., *The English Martyrs*, 1905.
Puttenham, George, *The Art of Poetry*.
Rait, R. S., *Royal Palaces of England*, 1911.
Raphael, *The Familiar Astrologer*.
Raumer, Frederick von, *Elizabeth and Mary Stuart*.
Rawson, M. Stepney, *Bess of Hardwick*, 1910.
Read, Conyers, *Mr. Secretary Walsingham and the policy of Queen Elizabeth*,
   1925.
   Mr. Secretary Cecil and Queen Elizabeth, 1955.
Rowse, A. L., *The England of Elizabeth*, 1950.
   The Expansion of Elizabethan England, 1955.
   Queen Elizabeth and her Subjects, 1935.
   An Elizabethan Garland, 1953.
Rye, W. B., *England as seen by Foreigners*, 1865.
Sharpe, Cuthbert, *Memorials of the Rebellion*.
Sidney Papers.
Simpson, R., *Edmund Campion*, 1896.
Singleton, Esther, *The Shakespeare Garden*, 1923.
Smith, H., Clifford, *Jewellery*, 1908.
Smith, R., *Life of the Viscountess Montagu*.
Spedding, James, *Life and Times of Francis Bacon*, 1878.
Speed, John, *History of Great Britain*.
Stow, *Annals of England*.
   Historical Memoranda.
Strickland, Agnes, *Edward VI*.
   Lives of the Tudor and Stuart Princesses, 1888.
   Queen Elizabeth, 1870.
Strype, John, *Collected Works*.
Sully, Duc de, *Mémoires*.
Tytler, P. F., *History of Scotland*.

Vaughan, William, *Directions for Health*.
Ward, B. M., *The Earl of Oxford*, 1928.
Weston, William, *Autobiography*, trans. Philip Caraman.
Wilson, Violet, *Society Women in the time of Shakespeare*, 1924.
Wood, Anthony à, *Athenae Cantabrigiensis*.
Wotton, Sir Henry, *Reliquae Wottonianae*.
Wright, Thomas, *Elizabeth and her Times*.
Younghusband, Sir G. J., *The Jewel-House*.

INDEX